Religious Enthusiasm
in the New World

Religious Enthusiasm
IN THE
New World

HERESY TO REVOLUTION

David S. Lovejoy

HARVARD UNIVERSITY PRESS
Cambridge, Massachusetts
London, England
1985

Library of Congress Cataloging in Publication Data

Lovejoy, David S. (David Sherman), 1919–
Religious enthusiasm in the new world.

Includes index.
1. Dissenters, Religious—United States.
2. Enthusiasm—Religious aspects—Christianity.
3. United States—Church history—Colonial period, ca. 1600–1775.
4. United States—History—Colonial period, ca. 1600–1775.   I. Title.
BR520.L633   1985   280'.4   84-22377
ISBN 0-674-75864-1 (alk. paper)

49,047

For my sister
Elizabeth Chase

Acknowledgments

IT HAS BEEN my pleasure to rub shoulders with a splendid group of helpful people since beginning this study of enthusiasm. Like many books about early America, this one began at the John Carter Brown Library in Providence, Rhode Island, where Librarian Thomas R. Adams, Laurence Hardy, Jeannette Black, and Samuel Hough turned the place inside out for me, finding books and pamphlets, sermons and tracts, when I was a research fellow there a few years ago. A winter and several summers at the Bodleian Library at Oxford compounded my respect for it and my indebtedness to Robert Shackleton, then Librarian, and particularly to Penelope Pearce and Mary Major in the Upper Reading Room, who went out of their way to be helpful and friendly.

Life is always pleasant at the Folger Shakespeare Library in Washington, D.C. An academic year there as a fellow was both intellectually stimulating and socially enjoyable. My thanks go to Director O. B. Hardison, Jr., and to his excellent staff, chiefly Leni Spencer, Suellen Towers, Earl Storm, and Pat Senia. A continued association with the State Historical Society of Wisconsin has made scholarly life in Madison as agreeable as it is rewarding. Former Librarian Peter Draz provided me with comfortable space for research and writing, and Ellen Burke and Sharon Mulak for some time have ably aided me in the search for pertinent materials.

In a number of ways help from the Graduate School of the University of Wisconsin has meant a great deal to me—chiefly research grants and graduate assistants. A mere listing of the latter hardly does justice to their contributions over the past few years. They are Robert Bliss, Jr., John Raimo, Lilith Kunkel, Timothy Dillon, and Arnold Sparr. Particularly helpful at the outset of research was J. William Frost, whose good suggestions and keen eye for out-of-the-way sources were invaluable.

A fellowship from the Institute for Research in the Humanities at the University of Wisconsin afforded me time for writing and a congenial group of scholars as colleagues, including Director Robert Kingdon. Loretta Freiling of the Institute helped in ways too numerous to mention. A Rockefeller Foundation Humanities Fellowship made it possible for me to bring the book to completion. I am grateful to both these institutions for generous financial help at very opportune times. Two grants-in-aid from the American Council of Learned Societies were much appreciated and timely.

Frequent conversations with John F. C. Harrison have heightened my understanding of several complex issues in the religious and social history of Britain and America. A number of colleagues and friends—Richard Sewell, Paul Conkin, Sargent Bush, John Walsh, Charles Carlton, and Jesse Lemisch among them—have shown more than ordinary interest in the subject of this book. Robert Kimbrough alerted me to Thomas Middleton's play *The Famelie of Love*, whose substance fitted nicely into Chapter 2, about English attitudes toward enthusiasm. I am grateful to my friend Alan Hodgkinson of Stonesfield, Oxfordshire, for his translation from Latin of a key passage by Servetus, used in Chapter 1. Another good friend, Attracta Coppins, of County Cork and Oxford, too often graciously listened to me when she should have instructed, given her expertise in the literary context of enthusiasm.

Jane Mesler expertly typed the manuscript, demonstrating an interest beyond the call of duty besides a rare patience. Karen Isenberg's help in a number of details was essential. To both I am heartily grateful.

Bett Lovejoy has continued to make my life worth living as human being and scholar.

A substantial part of Chapter 9 first appeared as the introduction to a collection of sources called *Religious Enthusiasm and the Great Awakening*, ed. David S. Lovejoy (Englewood Cliffs, N.J.: Prentice-Hall, 1969). I thank the publisher for assigning the copyright of this volume to me in September 1975.

A brief survey of some of the ideas described at length in this volume first appeared in an article entitled " 'Desperate Enthusiasm': Early Signs of American Radicalism," published in Margaret Jacob and James Jacob, eds., *The Origins of Anglo-American Radicalism* (London: George Allen and Unwin, 1984), pp. 231–242. I am grateful to Allen and Unwin for permission to reproduce a few paragraphs from this article in the present work.

Contents

What is become of our faith, if a company
of poor Historians can turn us besides our path?

—*William Aspinwall*

Much reading is an oppression of the mind
and extinguishes the natural candle,
which is the reason of so many senseless
scholars in the world.

—*William Penn*

Books are for the scholar's idle times.

—*Ralph Waldo Emerson*

~ Introduction ~

WHAT DID John of Leyden, Anne Hutchinson, William Penn, and George Whitefield have in common? On the face of it they seem unlikely individuals to herd together for any reason, historical or otherwise. They certainly would not have gotten along very well had they lived contemporaneously and their lives touched. To most Englishmen in both realm and colonies, these people's common thread was "enthusiasm," which marked them like race or color. They shared contemptuous dismissal from polite orthodox company because they were enthusiasts. Religion, it seems, like politics, makes strange bedfellows.

What was enthusiasm, and who were the enthusiasts? The meaning of the word has not been consistent. To early Greeks *enthousiasmous* meant actual inspiration from the gods and, therefore, carried positive, even admirable import. From the sixteenth century well into the nineteenth, *enthusiasm* bore usually a pejorative connotation, and Englishmen on both sides of the Atlantic used it to damn religious extremists who stepped across orthodox lines and claimed a close, warm, emotional relationship with God. By enthusiasts I mean a variety of unconventional but religiously devout sectarians who would not, could not, contain their zeal within the organized limits of religious convention. Called enthusiasts by established society, these several brands of Christians cut across numerous sects and practiced a personal experimental religion which hinged, they believed, on direct inspiration. To orthodox Christians, who thought them hopelessly deceived, enthusiasts were both heretical and blasphemous.

This book is a study of the enthusiasts who migrated to the American colonies in the seventeenth and eighteenth centuries and of those who emerged there. Enthusiasm, which tinged much sectarian dissent, was not new to Englishmen or to the colonists who settled America in its first century and later. They and their fathers had been wholly aware beforehand of these outsiders, an awareness which helped to color their attitudes toward them once they themselves had planted communities in the New World. Although in their theology and practice Anglican and Puritan sharply argued differences, they agreed largely in their contempt for enthusiasts, who, they said, presumptuously claimed through spiritual intimacy to be the precious children of God and, therefore, to be immune to everyday constraints which orthodox societies placed on religious and civil affairs.

It is the fashion today to play down the idea of "exceptionalism" in describing colonists' lives and their institutions. This may very well be a good thing, for historians in the past have found it tempting to celebrate the uniqueness and the "Americanness" of life in the New World at the expense of Old World customs, traditions, and influences which were perhaps as strong or stronger in forming a colonial and then an American culture. Still, a number of enthusiasts found in America conditions which encouraged spiritual extremism. Far from the sinful Old, the New World, it seemed, made spiritual truth easier to come by. In many instances it was a radical truth which threatened to turn orthodox society on its ear. Arguments for and against the upheavals and confrontations provoked by enthusiasts were closely related to the colonists' conceptions of the New World.

Enthusiasts were radical in several ways. First, their holy zeal was a return, they believed, to primitive Christianity, a going back to the very heart of religion found in direct inspiration, before it had become cluttered with man-made accretions such as organized churches, the priesthood, ritual, and dogma. Enthusiasm was radical in the original meaning of the word, since it cut through paraphernalia to a fundamental immanence of spirit which was really the root of the matter.

In a modern sense enthusiasts were radical, too, because they turned their backs on religious convention. Owing to their intimacy with the Spirit and what they insisted was holy and true, they believed they were in a position to recast religion, in some instances society itself, and make both consonant with the truths revealed directly to them. Some attempted to do this by example, by demonstrating in their beliefs, their lives, the societies they formed the unquestionable truth behind their inspiration. Others, more aggressive, more presumptuous, resorted to exhortation and proselytizing, sometimes openly, sometimes surreptitiously, and sometimes in defiance of established custom and law. Still others attempted to reshape religion, government, and society by force and rebellion, a few even to reduce them to anarchy. Most enthusiasts provoked strong reactions from conventional believers, who claimed to find in their fanaticism radical schemes which threatened everyday institutions. The usual limitations which society afforded, its customary means of control over belief and behavior, were not effective against a set of presumptions which knew no ordinary earthly restraints but depended on spirit and the imagination and the promptings of the heart. Besides established religions, enthusiasts, it was feared, endangered constituted government, the social structure, traditional economic organization, even intellectual endeavor and sexual morality. Calling them first heretics, then subversives and conspirators, established society sought ways to suppress or banish them.

What did enthusiasts believe which set them apart, and what did they contribute to British colonial society? The inquiry pokes into a number of sects and individuals and their ideas, from followers of Anne Hutchinson to pietistic Moravians, from martyr-bound Quakers to heaven-bent revivalists of the Great Awakening. Enthusiasts were certainly not all of one piece; they embraced a multitude of sins, or so claimed their opponents. Over and above direct dependence upon the Holy Spirit, they held a variety of beliefs which were manifested in a variety of ways. Contrast, for instance, the religious anarchy of Samuel Gorton with the steady piety of the Moravians, or the modesty and reticence of Quaker John Woolman with the spiritual arrogance of the Ranters and French Prophets. Yet, despite differences in religious intensity, social attitudes, and behavior, all were enthusiasts, and all boasted an intimacy with God, who spoke directly to them.

The final chapter is entitled "Enthusiasm and the Cause of Mankind." Events and circumstances in the latter half of the eighteenth century gave rise to political ideas and actions with characteristics which strikingly resembled the extremist tendencies in enthusiasm and were repeatedly recognized as such. They lent a radical strain to the Revolutionary movement, a strain it did not derive from Englishmen's rights or "Whig ideology." By 1776 enthusiasm seemed metamorphosed into politics, and as political enthusiasm it was not subject to ordinary constraints, even sometimes Whig constraints. Like the fanaticism of antinomians and revivalists, political enthusiasm sometimes was irrational and destructive; but, as radical patriots demonstrated, it was frequently positive and constructive, too, and conducive to revolutionary goals.

The word *enthusiasm* no longer bears the pejorative implications attached to it in the seventeenth and eighteenth centuries, for its meaning has become broader, having shed its religious connotation. This does not mean that religious enthusiasm has faded from American society in our own century, or that individuals and sects have ceased to believe in direct inspiration. We have only to look about us today to give the lie to that. If the recently renewed interest in Pentecostalism, revivalism, religious communitarianism, and, perversely, in witchcraft and the occult are today matters of national concern as symptoms of disillusionment with material success and a nuclear ideology, then a study of enthusiasm in the formative period of the nation's history might very well tell us something about these later manifestations and put them in proper historical perspective. "Everywhere," Emerson wrote in 1841, "the history of religion betrays a tendency to enthusiasm." And well he might know, since Transcendentalism, for all its intellectual claims, was but another form of it.

1

The Finger of God:
Religious Conceptions of the New World

W HY DID Englishmen venture to the New World in the early seventeenth century? One of the reasons, preached to us from the
very outset by the adventurers themselves and those who sent them, was
for religion's sake. Probably no historian today would doubt that religion
played a vital role in settling America, but when one offers this even as
partial explanation, one offers a mouthful, more than can really be understood by the words alone. Several fundamental questions still remain
unanswered.

If religion was a legitimate cause of colonization, how did promoters
and colonists conceive of religion's role in America? Were Old World
institutions to be established in the New; that is, were colonists to believe
and organize and worship in America as they had in Europe and con-
template their religious life and churches as mere geographical extensions
of what they were used to? Or did colonists to whom religion was a
primary, or even a secondary cause of migration, anticipate that religion
in America might be different from what they had known at home, that
premises might be different, that it might play a different role, that even
God might look upon colonists in America in a way he did not on those
who remained behind? Were there among those who crossed the Atlantic
Europeans who identified the New World with new religion, maybe a
new relationship to God? Among those who took with them conventional
religious ideas, were there some who found life in the New World conducive to a change in these conventions, both theological and ecclesiastic,
once they had settled? What was the effect of New World experience
upon the religion of colonists? Did it cause them to seek protection and
security in the God and Church of their fathers, or did it encourage them
to ask unconventional questions about God's ways with men and women
on the edge of a new continent thousands of miles distant from what
was familiar and habitual? At this point one might ask what dissenting
sectaries hoped to find or realize in America. Did they identify the New

World with a change in the relationship between God and man, or maybe even among men themselves, over what prevailed at home? There are no conclusive answers to these questions. Colonists settled for a variety of reasons, and for a variety of religious reasons, and one is not always able to lay them bare. Given the nature of seventeenth-century English society, secular and religious interests were not always separable, as one can learn from the Puritan migration to Massachusetts in 1630, and particularly from John Winthrop's attempt to rationalize his acceptance of the governorship of Massachusetts Bay.[1] The same overlapping of causes can be found in the settlement of Virginia several years earlier, as Perry Miller has explained so well.[2] Not only did religious and secular motives intertwine in these years, but purely religious motives were themselves difficult to separate one from another, since they too overlapped or ran closely parallel in early colonists' thinking. The idea of America was different among different Englishmen—positive here, negative there, Edenic to some, and demonic, even diabolic, to others. The idea of America, wrote Howard Mumford Jones, when one traces it back to its origin, is "as conflicting, inconsistent, and difficult to identify as the components of other great episodes in the history of Western man."[3] And so were purely religious ideas about the New World, for they too were "conflicting, inconsistent, and difficult to identify." Still, some kind of sorting out is necessary if we are to understand as clearly as possible religious conceptions of America and the role religion played in the lives of New World settlers, then colonists, and later citizens.

The burden of this inquiry is the sectaries who came to the colonies in the seventeenth and eighteenth centuries, and of these chiefly the enthusiasts among them. But first we ought to look at some of the more general religious conceptions and expectations to which enthusiasm was closely related and without which it would lose much of its meaning and significance.

Utopia and Asylum

To many Europeans, America has always been a kind of utopia. The idea of a New World beyond the sea, where one might shed the past, where life might begin again according to one's dictates, has attracted the idealist and the theorist, even the artist, as something worth depicting, even if few of them ever became actual adventurers. Sir Thomas More, Francis Bacon, and William Shakespeare all toyed with the foundations of society in a New World frame in their writings. Although religion played a role in each of their schemes—slight in Shakespeare's *Tempest*—it was secondary, sometimes minor, and more a by-product of radical social change than an indispensable ingredient.[4] But religion was paramount in the minds of a good many others who ventured abroad and who hoped to shape the New World to their liking.

Asylum and utopia are not the same, although some colonists who sought the first in America carried blueprints for the second in their baggage. The utopians doubtless ventured on their own accord, while those seeking asylum either were pushed out of their homelands or foresaw circumstances which they would eventually find intolerable.

As early as 1535 heretic Michael Servetus, already on the run from Protestants and Catholics alike, wished that he could flee with Jonah into the sea or "into some new island," for which read America, according to Roland Bainton. Servetus took his case of persecution to Christ, who bade him stick it out at home and do his duty. John Calvin, as we know, caught up with him at Geneva, where Servetus was burned at the stake in 1553, all the while "pouring out his ungodly soule amidst most horrible blasphemies in the very fire." But Calvin was opposed only to Servetus and his heresies, not the New World and conversion of the Indians, and it was not very many years later that he was responsible for sending from Geneva some "Eminent Christians and Ministers" to Brazil, *autrement dit Amérique*. They had their work cut out for them, given the Romans' head start, and one of them, Jean de Léry, has left us a splendid account of some of the difficulties, published in la Rochelle in 1578.[5]

Early in Queen Elizabeth's reign her government considered dumping die-hard Catholics on Ireland—not for missionary purposes—followed by testy Presbyterians who had upset her schemes of uniformity. Carrying the intention a step farther, Sir Humphrey Gilbert's plans in 1582 included a Catholic colony on the shores of what later became Rhode Island. Although the Queen's Church would prevail in the new venture, refugees would find toleration there.[6] About the same time a promoter of Nova Scotia sought investment in his expedition by holding out to the "godly Mynded" a "libertie of conscience" (to Protestants) along with the possibility of discovering the Northwest Passage, an unabashed linking of religion and profit.[7] As war with Spain became imminent, Richard Hakluyt proposed more narrow terms for refugees, eliminating altogether Catholics, who, he feared, might prove disloyal to the realm. Protestants, fine, even Puritans and foreigners; he particularly recommended artisans among them, but let each be strong and lusty who "can best handle his Bowe or his harquebush."[8]

French Huguenots were the most likely foreign Protestants to plant English settlements overseas. They needed no pushing, and a contingent attempted a colony in what became the Carolinas as early as the 1550s, as well as in Florida and Brazil. Establishing bases against Spain was partly behind the venture, writes David B. Quinn, but so also was the idea of refuge should Catholic France make life miserable at home. Although the Saint Bartholomew's Day Massacre of 1572 destroyed their leadership, it led to a stubborn determination to make a go of it in France—supported, of course, a few years later by the Edict of Nantes, which afforded toleration. In 1629 Sir Robert Heath, Charles I's Attorney General, aroused some excitement among Huguenots for a settlement called "Carolana," which would have stretched from sea to sea, but it fizzled when Heath lost interest and soon disposed of the huge grant which the King had given him. Only after Louis XIV revoked the Edict of Nantes in 1685 did French Protestants look again to America for asylum, and not many years later Huguenots could be found in every English mainland colony, most thickly in South Carolina.[9] A few years earlier a group of Jansenists, in their search for isolation and a place to avoid persecution, seriously considered leaving France altogether and settling in America but later changed their minds.[10]

Clearly, then, the idea of asylum in the New World was well known but more popular in European minds than in reality. Not until the Pilgrim Fathers settled Plymouth in 1620 did a refugee group succeed in establishing itself as an escape from religious difficulties in Europe. A conception of the New World as asylum endured, however, and as late as 1776 Tom Paine—of all people—speculated that the discovery of America had preceded the Reformation as a deliberate part of God's plan simply "to open a sanctuary to the persecuted in future years, when home should afford neither friendship nor safety."[11] Following the Pilgrims other religious groups sought refuge in the English colonies, and some were enthusiasts, as we shall see.

Escape of Religion

America as asylum was an escape of people who took their unorthodox views with them, and in some cases good riddance. Closely related was the idea that the New World served, too, as an escape *of religion* from a nation where it had become corrupted and choked with sin. In this view successive sanctuaries of true religion emerged, a retreat from sin commencing on the Continent. "The Kingdome of God shall bee taken from you," God warned Europe through the sermons of William Crashaw in 1610, for the greater part of the Continent, he said, was already overrun with Turks or Papists. God would lodge the Kingdom in a "Nation that shall bring foorth the fruits thereof," meaning, of course, England, and Crashaw admonished Englishmen not to fail in their duty.[12] Much less sanguine about England's holiness was Samuel Ward, brother of Nathaniel, who later went to Massachusetts. No wonder the Catholics spit at us, he wrote, and the "quesi-stomaked Brownists" cut themselves off from the Church, given the dearth of devotion and reformation in our religion. "God stands at the doore and knocks . . . his locks are wet with waiting," and before he turns from us "to some other nation more worthy, let us open the doore, that he may come in and sup with us." Ward, a Puritan, charged his flock to hear God's voice and "bee zealous."[13]

George Herbert, Anglican priest and metaphysical poet, carried the charge of corruption farther and then the process of retreat one step more, but a large one. England had sunk so low in its iniquity, its malice, "prodigious lusts," "impudent sinning," and even witchcraft that to Herbert there was only one escape: "Religion stands on tiptoe in our land, / Readie to passe to the American strand." These revealing lines in "The Church Militant" came close to preventing a whole volume of Herbert's poetry from being printed, for such a thought, despite its poetic expression, seemed disloyal, even subversive. Nicholas Ferrar, literary executor in 1632 of Herbert's estate—the poet having died before publication—ran into trouble with the licenser, who was Vice Chancellor of Cambridge University. Ferrar refused to delete the couplet which caused offense; it was the Vice Chancellor who gave in, remarking only that he knew Mr. Herbert was a "divine poet," but he hoped the world would "not take him to be an inspired prophet." Prophet or no, the poet summed up the attitudes of a good many who conceived of the New World as a land to which religion might escape in order to retain its purity against the disastrous decline of the Church of England. George Herbert would save Anglicanism from itself.[14] Dissenting John Winthrop and his people built Congregational Massachusetts on a similar assumption.

At the height of the English Civil War, with the world turned upside down, colonists already coddling the truth in Massachusetts were apprehensive lest the mother country's foundations crumble. "The Heavens, Sea, and dry Land have been shaken," William Hooke told his Taunton congregation; there "hath been both a Church-quake and a State-quake in that Land" which had swallowed up cities and people. But be of good courage, a presumptuous Hooke told his flock, for God is ours; "we trust he is England's." Our greatest comfort above all others, wrote a complacent Salem minister, is "that we have here the true religion" along with "the holy Ordinances of Almightie God," implying that England no longer enjoyed either.[15] Iniquity had come to such straits in the Old World that true Christianity could no longer thrive there. Why not carry the truth to the New World, which was ready to nurture it to fulfillment?

Gospel

How did the prospect of settling the New World fit into Englishmen's overall religious framework? What did anticipation of overseas expansion do *for* religion as seventeenth-century Englishmen understood it? Given the religious intensity of their times, the fact that religion rigidly shaped their conceptions of themselves, their kingdom, and their world, that it helped to make sense out of their role as a people, out of their very history, surely they could not conceive of planting in America as a historic event outside their set of religious ideas. It might, however, be outside the orthodox framework, for God had not finally revealed himself or all of his plans; it was apparent to some that there was "further light" to be shed, more to come which might surprise even his saints. Chiefly upon such a premise did enthusiasts conduct their exercises, as we shall see.

In peopling the New World, God was in charge, of course, as he was of every grand event, as well as keeping an eye upon the sparrow. What is fascinating about Englishmen's attempts to explain God's actions is that no one of them could successfully encompass or fathom the overwhelming sense of divine providence in these events, nor did those who tried reach ultimate agreement about God's purposes and means. The result was a large body of literature whose writers could usually agree only that the glory of God and the spreading of the gospel were fundamental causes behind the discovery and peopling of the New World. They had less success agreeing about why God worked the way he did, and, in allowing Englishmen to migrate to America, which prophecies and promises he was actually fulfilling and how. Religious conceptions of America were based primarily upon England's missionary role in spreading the gospel, but explanations of it were often conflicting, even confusing.

Profit or private gain, or, when nationalized, mercantilism, was fundamental in sending Englishmen westward. But, it was argued, God's plan and colonists' religious mission encompassed profit, subordinated it, and explained it in relationship to more holy motives. Yet promoters and well-wishers could not agree altogether about this either—that is, whether it was justifiable even to consider profit and material well-being while performing God's commission in America. Several years ago Perry Miller made us all very aware that Massachusetts Puritans held no monopoly in interpreting their migration in religious terms, that the settlement in Virginia was equally wrapped in religious justification which described the enterprise as an unfolding of God's plan.[16] While John White, who zealously promoted Massachusetts, could explain that necessity, novelty, or material gain might attract some settlers to New

England, the most sincere and godly people had the "advancement of the *Gospel* for their maine scope."[17] Englishmen who promoted Virginia seemed equally sanguine that religion was a prime mover, and if it were not, it should be. William Crashaw lectured the Virginia Company and adventurers in 1609 with a warning that if the planting of a colony and the King's Church, the converting of Indians, the propagating of the gospel, and enlarging the Kingdom of Christ were not strong enough inducements to carry out their tasks, they ought to stay at home. Private gain, he said, had been the "bane of many excellent exploits." "Let us therefore cast aside all cogitation of profit, let us looke at better things." But after several paragraphs of these searching inquiries into motives, lest one "flye hath corrupted the whole box of oyntment," Crashaw softened his tune and held out considerable hope of less spiritual rewards. If they sought first the propagation of the gospel and conversion of souls, he told the company, God would "undoubtedly make the voiage very profitable to all the *adventurers* and their *posterities* even for matter of this life."[18]

The charge to Virginia Company treasurer Thomas Smyth in 1612 was less lopsided in its assumptions, although more negative in approach. Do not discourage the ordinary settlers in "growing religious," on the one hand, or in "gathering riches," on the other, James I's Virginia Council told Smyth. These were two special bonds, whether "severed or conjoined," which would keep the settlers obedient—one for the sake of conscience, the other for fear of losing their shirts. For, lacking the first, the Council warned Smyth, the settlers would become profane and, without the second, desperate and factious. Religion and profit worked together, and Smyth was to see to it that Virginia offered both—a large order in 1612.[19]

A decade later John Donne, again preaching to a departing contingent of the Virginia Company, described rewards as much less practical. Christ's apostles had sought neither liberty nor abundance in their mission, and neither should prospective colonists. Even when the principal purpose was the "propagation of the glorious Gospell," God did not promise a kingdom, or ease, or abundance in all things; and what he did intend for them he did not promise presently. However, there was "something equivalent at least," and this was the power of the Holy Ghost in them, for they would be his witnesses *"unto the uttermost parts of the Earth."* Donne explained God's stratagems. A variety of attractions had drawn them to the task of settling—examples of other good men, defense against England's enemies, and hope of "future profit"—but each, regardless of its origin, was *vehiculum Spiritus Sancti,* a chariot in which God entered into them. Forget profits, postpone consideration of "temporall gaine" (although in an aside he admitted that profit and religion may well consist together), study the advancement of the gospel of Jesus, and the "Holy Ghost is fallen upon you."[20] Let us hope the adventurers listened well, for this particular contingent was sorely tried upon its arrival in Virginia, where half the colony had been wiped out by war with the Indians only a few months earlier.

John Donne's conception of the New World had not always been as holy and spiritual. As a young lover and lyric poet he had found America symbolic of something very different from the New Jerusalem. The Church, it is clear, was not Donne's first calling, as the lines from Elegy XIX, "To His Mistris Going to Bed," metaphorically attest:

> Licence my roving hands, and let them go,
> Before, behind, between, above, below.
> O my America! my new-found-land,
> My kingdome, safeliest when with one man man'd,
> My Myne of precious stones, My Emperie,
> How blest am I in this discovering thee![21]

George Herbert agreed with a good deal of John Donne's sermonizing—if not his bedtime lyrics—about the relation between profit and the gospel. But he gave his explanation a wry twist which Englishmen would just as soon have forgotten. The flight of religion to America had serious liabilities, according to the poet. God had prepared a way for converting the Indian by letting the white man steal his gold: "For gold and grace did never yet agree, / Religion alwaies sides with povertie." But the Indian was the gainer by the exchange. What the white man left in place of gold was the gospel, while the wealth he sent home led to his nation's ruin: "We are more poore, and they more rich by this." Robert Gordon, in promoting a plantation at Cape Breton in 1625, saw the exchange less cynically—or, given the outcome, maybe more cynically—if still poetically: "As by merchandizing and trade wee buy at them the pearles of the Earth; we ought to communicate unto them the pearles of Heaven." John Cotton, later of Boston, said it even more simply: "As you reape their temporalls, so feede them with your spiritualls."[22]

Despite the popularity of colonization, or planting, in the first half of the seventeenth century, a great deal of effort was spent in attempting to justify it. Most arguments were simple enough and stemmed from the biblical injunction to be fruitful. John White, whose *Planters Plea* ran the gamut of reasons in support of the Puritan move to Massachusetts, regarded God's law of marriage as a trustworthy example. Young people marry, leave their parents' homes, and cleave each to the other, and what are new families but petty colonies? From this he concluded that as long as "there shall be use of marriage, the warrant of deducing Colonies will continue."[23] Christopher Levett, a member of the Council of New England, argued in the 1620s that Englishmen would be guilty of grievous sins against God should they willingly endure poverty in England and suffer so good a country as this "to lye wast[e]," for certainly God had created all for the use of man. John Cotton followed Levett by two years with an example from nature which taught how bees seek new dwellings abroad when their hives become crowded. "So when the hive of the Common-wealth is so full, that Tradesmen cannot live one by another, but eate up one another, in this case it is lawfull to remove." Of such a colony, he wrote, "wee reade in *Acts* 16:12."[24]

But was colonization a direct call from God? This question kept a number of people busy not just before settlement but during and afterwards. Besides, it draws us close to the heart of the problem of religious conceptions of the New World and the role Englishmen believed they played in God's schemes. The simplest analogies again were from the Bible, and Virginians as well as Puritans in Massachusetts found them useful. There was no doubt, according to William Symonds, who preached also to the Virginia Company in 1609, that the God who called Abraham into another country also, by the same hand, called them who sat before him to carry the gospel to America. In promoting a settlement in New Foundland in 1624, Richard Eberne told his readers that they would become the sons and daughters of Abraham and his people, those "famous, godly, and holy patriarchs," whom God had commanded to forsake their kindred and their father's house and "go into that land which He would show them." John Rolfe, not tied to the Bible, called his fellow Virginians "a peculiar people," chosen by the "finger of God" to possess their land. In summing up the religious feeling behind the settling of Virginia, Perry Miller has demonstrated that Virginians answered "a special and supernatural summons," proceeding, as one of them remarked in a presumptuous phrase, "from the extraordinary motion of Gods spirit."[25]

Promoters of New England appeared a little wary of presuming too much upon God in these vital matters. Doubtless no people felt more religiously moved to settle in the American wilderness than these Puritan saints; still, one has the feeling that they thought twice about their explanations, lest they exceed the bounds of religious propriety. New England Puritanism stemmed from orthodox Protestantism and indeed demonstrated an intense religiosity, but it was not enthusiasm, at least not in the bulk of its adherents. As orthodox Protestants, these Puritans believed that God had revealed himself to man once, for all practical circumstances, in the Bible, sometimes confusingly called the "mouth of God." He did not do business with man directly, that is, by direct communication; rather he worked through his revealed Word, which regenerate man could rightly read and apply its teachings to his needs. God could intervene directly, of course, through personal means: visions, revelations, miracles, and such—after all, God could work in any way he chose. But he probably would not, since his will was recorded in the Bible, and the saints' regenerate reason found sufficient guidance there to live pious lives for his glory. Promoters of Puritan New England, no doubt convinced that God was on their side in pushing migrants to America, could not actually describe the drive as a result of a direct call— an opportunity for asylum, yes, escape from disagreeable developments within the King's Church in England, a chance to set up in America what they could not bring the Church to accept at home, yes again. But Puritan settlers came to these conclusions primarily by rational means, not through the flashes of divine revelation that enthusiasts—Anne Hutchinson, for instance—claimed they experienced. What convinced them they were right was that their conduct coincided with what they believed God wanted, based on their interpretation of the Bible and their own inclination—and *inclinaton* was a key word in their understanding the whole business of how God imparted his will to man.

But how did the process work when it came to major questions? To plant or not to plant? How does God advise? John White explained generally the Puritan technique for making decisions, but it was no simple exposition. Who shall inform his conscience, White asked, and by what rule shall his conscience judge? "It is out of peradventure that God must informe the conscience." But how shall men discover what God advises? To be sure, if scanning the Word of God shall give resolution, then it must be followed. Unfortunately many of the Scripture's rules, though in themselves clear, are ambiguous and doubtful in application "because they cannot determine particulars." Then must John White's man resort to "Christian wisdome," assisted first by the counsel and advice of wise and godly friends; second by the observation of the "concurrence of opportunities, *Occasiones sunt Dei nutus* [nudge]"; and third by thoughtful consideration of the "inclination of the heart," of course after earnest and frequent prayer. Any resolution taken after full use of these means, in the presence of God, without prejudice, and with a sincere desire to know the will of God and to obey it "may be taken for the voice of God at present, and ought to direct the practise." Then White gave a homely but worthy application of this technique, almost as an afterthought: "Suppose I would marry a wife, nothing but Christian wisdome so assisted . . . can shew mee which is the woman"; and no doubt "inclination" would play a strong role in the choice.²⁶

Like John White, John Cotton gave due respect to biblical analogies. Only in Bible times, Cotton explained, did God settle land upon his own people through "special appointment" and "by his owne mouth." Since then, God's people had taken land "by promise" while others through providence. Canaan, therefore, was a land of promise. But there were "speciall providences" and "particular cases" which applied over and above general warrants for certain people to transplant themselves. First among these was a man's "inclination" to one course or another, for such an inclination was in the spirit of men, and "God is the Father of spirits." Paul, Cotton explained, discovered a calling to go to Rome by his "ready inclination to that voyage." Therefore, respecting migration to the New World, if a man's heart be inclined to advance the gospel by right judgment, and at the same time to support his family and utilize his talents fruitfully, "or the like good end," then, wrote Cotton, "this inclination is from God." Cotton had more of the poet in him than John White and closed his argument with a figure worthy of the best of them: "As the beames of the Moone darting into the Sea leades it to and fro, so doth a secret inclination darted by God into our hearts leade and bowe (as a byas) our whole course."²⁷

One might well ask where these people drew the line between "secret inclination" and the enthusiasts' personal call or direct sign from God. Puritans, at least most of them, found no confusion here, and defended the one while they dismissed the other with contempt. It was this difference which distinguished the enthusiasm of Anne Hutchinson from the "special providences" and "particular cases" of John Cotton. At her trial in Boston she boldly told the court that she had been directed to Massachusetts by the voice of God in her soul, and that was sufficient to run her off the land. Meanwhile, John White continued his justification of settlement without falling into the trap set for enthusiasts, who believed their relationship with God to be extraordinary.

To John White the opening of a passage to, and the discovery of, the New World was "almost miraculous," a phrase he may have snitched from Alexander Whitaker of Virginia. It would be worse than impiety to imagine that God—"whose Will concurres in the lighting of a Sparrow upon the ground"—had no hand in superintending "one of the most difficult and observeable workes of this age." Furthermore, it would be as great a folly to conceive that God, who made all things, had no other idea in permitting the colonizing of a new hemisphere than the "satisfying of mens greedy appetites, that thirsted after the riches of that new found world"—all acceptable arguments to the orthodox mind but presented backhandedly to avoid any recognition of a divine and explicit call. Colonization to relieve overpopulation or to replenish "wast and voyd Countries" had sufficient warrant from the Bible. But spreading the gospel and converting Indians—this task more immediately "suites with the mind of God," which again avoided the problem of direct communication and linked man's wishes, even conduct, with God's will. Still, White struggled with the question of whether the planting of colonies was an "extraordinarie worke." If so, then it followed necessarily that those who planted must have an extraordinary call. This conclusion, however, he shrank from, for a strong argument lay in its path. Any duty that is commanded by perpetual law, meaning Scripture, cannot be extraordinary. Since colonization was ordered by the Bible, it therefore could not be an "extraordinary duty." After flirting dangerously with the enthusiasts' God, White, beginning with the Bible, syllogistically fell back into the arms of orthodoxy.[28]

Explicit call or not, the results, once colonists had settled, were even greater than anticipated, if not extraordinary. Are there any people in the world, asked William Hooke of Taunton, "who have tasted more of the sweet of God, and Christ, and Ordinances" than we? Where God is, there is no wilderness, Nathaniel Ward added. "Witnesse his large benefice to us here beyond expectation." If not special pleading, Hooke's and Ward's satisfaction exceeded their farthest wishes for the blessings of religion in the New World.[29]

Millennial Prospect

Utopia, asylum, escape of religion, the linking of religion with profit, and recognition of a general duty to expand Christianity all, sometimes singly, sometimes in combination, contributed to how Englishmen conceived of the New World and helped to shape their attitudes toward it. But encompassing all of these and forming a larger framework within which each took on greater meaning and purpose was an implicit millennialism which lent order and direction to the whole business. English Protestantism in the first half of the seventeenth century, whether Anglican or Puritan, incorporated into its world view a strong millennial character which gave the nation a cosmic purpose in the ongoing history of Christendom.[30] To this millennial faith the discovery and settlement of America had added a new and prophetic measure, and several heretofore only vaguely understood fragments of divine will fell into their proper places. Among dissenters in particular the prospect of "further light" upon the meaning of it all was a distinct possibility, for strong within the dissenting tradition was the assurance that God had not yet told all but had reserved "further light" for whom he chose. And where better might the chosen few entertain such a glorious prospect than in a New World, a New Jerusalem, a likely spot for the unfolding of God's promise? Again the Bible afforded the text, and the Revelation, besides prophecies, the very direction. The most popular metaphor for explaining the inexorable and irresistible spread of the gospel since the time of Christ was the progress of the sun, the light, which immemorially moves from east to west. Thomas Bastard, one-time fellow of New College, Oxford, artfully expressed the figure in a series of sermons published in 1615, appropriately called "The Marigold and the Sunne," which established both direction and biblical promise. Wrote Bastard:

> *Thy word is a light* &c. and arising first from them as from his East or Orient, is carried over all the world, and hath given light to us that sate in darknesse . . . *Goe and preach Repentance and remission of sinnes to all Nations, beginning from Jerusalem.* Hence sprang this blessed light first: and then besides his dispersion into other parts of the world, was carried over all Greece, Italy, Germany, Spaine, France, and rose to us also, and is now making day to the Indians and Antipodes; for the world shall not end till hee have finished his course: I meane till (as the Evangelist Saint *Matthew* saith) the Gospell *be preached in all the earth, and be a testimony to all Nations.* And then the end shall come.[31]

Thomas Bastard said it all; others only elaborated the main theme with pertinent illustrations which defined England's unique mission, the role of settlers, and the Indians.

Expansion of the world by discovery had not altered the divine command, only intensified it. The known world in Christ's time, when he sent forth his apostles to preach *"unto the uttermost parts of the earth,"* was indeed of pygmy size to what Englishmen knew it to be in their time. Christ's command, then, was to "a succession of Apostolike men," not just his contemporaries, to publish the gospel among all nations. You who go, and you who send others, John Donne told the Virginia Company, "doe all an *Apostolicall* function." Before the end of the world, before mortals can put on immortality, before the world's creatures can be delivered from the prison of corruption, "before the Martyrs under the Altar shalbe silenc'd," before Christ's Kingdom can be perfected and death, the last enemy, destroyed, before all these can occur, "the Gospell must be preached to those men to whom ye send; to all men." Hasten, then, charged John Donne to the prospective Virginians, quicken this blessed, joyful, "glorious consummation of all, and happie reunion of all bodies to their Soules, by preaching the *Gospell* to those men." Make tobacco, my foot! Virginians were the Lord's chore boys, precipitating the glorious end of the world.[32]

In promoting a colony of Scots at Cape Breton—to be called New Galloway—Robert Gordon insisted that his chief motive was the spreading of the gospel to the heathen people there. His determination rested on a conclusion derived by learned divines that "these are the latter Dayes, wherein we live," recognized from signs in Scripture. Christianizing Indians was but part of what was prophesied. By opening the eyes of the poor ignorant natives to the mysteries of the gospel, Massachusetts colonists would effect that which God had already determined. Who knows, asked John Cotton, whether God had not reared the whole plantation for this end?[33]

The dispersion of people, wrote John White, carried religion to the whole world, so that all quarters of the earth might sound with God's praise. Then Christ would take in all the nations for his inheritance, "according to Gods decree and promise." The great men of the Church, noted for both learning and position, White explained, have believed that God's scheme for the propagation of religion from the beginning "falles in this last age, upon the Westerne parts of the world."[34] It is a fair bet that John White had read *Manuductio to Theologie* (1621) by Bartholomew Keckermann of Danzig, a learned Protestant divine who helped to systemize the arts and sciences into compendia useful to Puritan scholars and Harvard College students among them. In 1624 T. Vickars translated Keckermann's *Manuductio*, in which the author explained that even running second to the Spanish in the New World had its advantages. God released his truths successively, and a little popish light here and there among the Indians only prepared the way for "further truths," which would follow from Protestant efforts by "true and faithful Ministers of the Gospel." Keckermann predicted that "toward the end of the world the true Religion shall be in America" and Christ's prophecies may be fulfilled.[35]

New England Indians, Edward Johnson has told us, were well warned of the great events soon to occur in which they were to play a curious part. Before any settlers arrived, a bright flaming comet appeared to them, "whose motion in the Heavens was from East to West," pointing out to the recipients the "progresse of the glorious Gospell of Christ." And if this were not enough to impress the Indians with the wondrous but paradoxical events soon to roll over them from the East, the next year brought a great plague, drastically dissipating their numbers, and making room for the Plymouth Pilgrims and Winthrop's Puritans, who eventually followed.[36]

William Hooke told his Massachusetts congregation that God from the death of Christ had made way for the conversion of Gentiles, and the progress had been from east to west. Before Christ's coming, said Hooke, the truth, God's worship, and salvation were pent up in the narrow confines of Judea, darkened and obscured by ceremonies and shadows, as was Jerusalem with hills. "But now all should be laid open before all the world, from *East* to *West*."[37] (When Hooke uttered these words, the Puritans of New England had carried the conversion of Gentiles about as far west as Dedham.)

Comets and blazing stars held religious and theological implications for Massachusetts's Samuel Danforth, too. While Edward Johnson asserted that such phenomena were worthy signs, warning the Indians of an impending brush with holiness, Danforth cautioned his readers that a comet they had recently seen was a prodigy for all. And while William Hooke took his cue from the Jerusalem of Christ's time, Danforth spent his efforts explaining the potential new one. God forbid that we should be "wandering stars," erratic and eccentric in our motions, he told his people. Instead, "may we all become fixed Stars in the *new Jerusalem,* which cometh down from God, observing the Heavenly order prescribed by his holy word," irradiated by righteousness, and all in Massachusetts.[38]

To reformed Christians, as Perry Miller has told us, the Devil was no abstraction, and where better might he build his redoubt than in the American wilderness, his Indian imps flourishing close at hand? What more encouragement did Christians need than to know that the Devil was the chief enemy of the whole scheme?[39] How better could good men promote God's will, asked Robert Gordon, than to "cast down the Altars of Devills, and to raise up the Altar of Christ"? The dazzling fire of Christian zeal would never be quenched, wrote Edward Johnson, until it had "burnt up Babilon Root and Branch." And if the colonists of Massachusetts were not mistaken, the "downfall of Antichrist was already at hand." Richard Eburne expanded upon some of Bartholomew Keckermann's earlier themes. God, who characteristically worked by degrees, had permitted the Spanish to soften up the Indians, preparing them for the English brand of Christianity, which was the better, the true. Brutal conquest punished the Indians' atheism and idolatry, wrote John White, after which the Spaniards introduced civility and the gospel of Christ among them. In the same way he had dealt earlier with Englishmen's forefathers after the "bitter desolations" of the Romans and Picts. Others found similar analogies in the early history of Britain. "Even we," wrote Richard Whitbourne, "were once as blinde as [the Indians] in the knowledge and worship of our Creator, and as rude and savage in our lives and manners"—as if to say, and look at us now since God and Christ have taken us in hand. In another passage of *The Planters Plea* John White credited God with permitting the Romans to civilize Britons before introducing his religion, for it could not prevail, he wrote, among a people before they were subdued to the rule of "Nature and Reason."[40]

Richard Hakluyt looked upon the prospect a little differently. He had no quarrel with converting infidels as long as they were not drawn out of Scylla into Charybdis, from one error into another. A more practical benefit he alone saw and thumped for was that teaching the Indians Christian principles would give English ministers something to do, leaving them less time to coin new opinions and get into mischief.[41]

Manifest Destiny

And why particularly had this mission fallen to England? There was little disagreement among most writers on the subject. If Americans today think the idea of manifest destiny was a product of the 1840s and had to do with the Oregon question alone, they ought to look farther back in time. The seventeenth century, given Englishmen's religious conceptions of the New World, is a fruitful place to start. William Crashaw found the "passage into *Virginea*" "so faire, so safe, so secure, so easie, as though God himselfe had built a bridge for men to passe from *England* to *Virginea*." John Rolfe thought Virginians were marked "and chosen by the finger of God" for their worthy task. Supporters of the Virginia Company, John Donne preached, would make "this *Island,* which is but as the Suburbs of the old world, a Bridge, a Gallery to the new." In so doing they should "keepe the wheele in due motion" and join all "to that world that shall never grow old, the Kingdome of heaven." In the very first year of young King Charles I's reign, Robert Gordon found him to be the "selected instrument" to cast the "pearles of Heaven" among the Indians, and John White was certain that England had been "singled out unto that worke."[42] As usual it was left to Edward Johnson to sum it all up. Were not New Englanders the "fore runners of Christs Army" and the "marvelous providences" he was about to explain to his readers "the very Finger of God"?—a popular phrase among Englishmen, as one can see, to describe their doings in America. Had not the Lord sent these colonists to preach in the wilderness and to "proclaime to all Nations, the neere approach of the most wonderful workes that ever the Sonnes of men saw?" Will you not believe, he asked his readers, "that a Nation can be borne in a day?" for certainly here was something very close to it. Moreover, there were still greater things, "further light," in store for God's people.[43] If all colonists who ventured into the American wilderness did not share the holy mission described by those who packed them off, it was not for want of effort on the part of the packers.

There were discordant voices, although doubtless the number was small. The "cool-tempered" Francis Bacon, as Perry Miller called him, was less interested in the will of God in planting Virginia than he was in what the needy settlers there might harvest from the soil, since he hardly found tobacco the answer for the good of all. Francis Bacon asked hard questions about the economic success of colonies.[44] George Herbert clung to the high ground already staked out by those who justified the westward venture as the will of God, but he found the prospect much less encouraging than most. It was the same old world, and religion's escape to America would not solve the problem of the fundamental nature of man, at least not for long: "Yet as the Church shall thither Westward flie, / So Sinne shall trace and dog her instantly." Herbert accepted Thomas Bastard's delightful metaphor of sun and gospel inexorably charging westward, but he forecast some stormy weather along the way, since darkness and sin would chase them both.[45]

But Bacon's and Herbert's voices were small among a chorus of others which sang the praises of colonial ventures as positive evidence of England's spiritual preeminence. For was not the English nation a selected instrument, a holy bridge, the supplier of godly pioneers whose destiny in the New World was already manifest and who could only hasten the glorious Kingdom of Christ so long promised by the prophets of old? This vision was, for the most part, orthodox; it was extreme, in a few instances, to be sure, but it spoke to its times, and it had a good deal to do with settling America. Besides being believed by many, at least at the outset, it clothed more material motives in religious wraps so closely that even the adventurers were hard put to sort them out.

That Englishmen conceived of America in religious terms there is no doubt. No wonder, then, that a handful of enthusiasts, who barely clung to the edge of orthodoxy, if at all, saw opportunity abroad for a radical fulfillment of their religious needs. No wonder, too, given the intense religious meaning of America, that some colonists once settled would be drawn to a freer, less orthodox, and more personal religious expression, for after all it was a New World, and to some a New World meant "further light," even a new birth.

2

Whirligig Spirits:
English Attitudes toward Enthusiasm,
1550–1660

SEVERAL broad strains of enthusiasm existed in the English society from which settlement in America derived. Two of them, Anabaptism and Familism, were sixteenth-century imports from the Continent; the third, Separatism, or Brownism, was home grown. Cutting across all three was a variety of sects besides shades of antinomianism and millennialism which helped to blunt their differences. Yet distinctions were sharper in the minds and hearts of the sectarians themselves than among their opponents who described and attacked them and from whom, unfortunately, flows most of our information. Critics of these supposed heretics tended to lump the lot together, finding that their heresies overlapped and were frequently repeated. The enthusiast was a chameleon, wrote Thomas Scot in 1616, who "nought but ayre doth eat." In England he was a Familist, "at *Amsterdam* a Brownist, further on an Anabaptist." Thomas Edwards, who summed up all his bitter invective against enthusiasts in *Gangraena*, published in 1646, catalogued sixteen heretical sects but claimed that they and most of the people in them were compounded of many, some of all, the heresies. There was no simple Anabaptist or antinomian or even Independent, but an amalgam: "Anabaptisticall, Antinomian, Manifesterian, Libertine, Socinian, Millenary, Independent, Enthusiasticall." "Anabaptistical Familist" was his favorite epithet.[1]

Mistakenly, a number of Anglicans, including James I,[2] saw little reason to exclude Puritans from their lists of sectaries. We know today that most Puritans, believing themselves true descendants of the Protestant Reformation, were as opposed to enthusiasm as were members of the King's Church. Still, several groups of Puritans were very susceptible to the smear of enthusiasm; one of these was the Separatists, and Robert Browne and his progeny were often damned as Anabaptists, or Familists, or whatever for their stubborn independence, unorthodox organization, and strange practices.

Anabaptists

Most Englishmen in the early seventeenth century identified Anabaptism with John of Leyden and the catastrophe at Münster in 1535. This was true despite the fact that a large majority of Anabaptists, who represented a wholly spiritual side of the Reformation, were peaceful, sober dissenters preparing the way for harmless Baptists, calm sectarians, and devout pietists who burgeoned in the latter half of that century and the next. But the Münster of fanatical Anabaptists was hard to forget, and it afforded a convenient club with which to beat any dissent from orthodox Protestantism. Münster meant blind zeal and bloody tyranny, to say nothing of a radical new Zion built on polygamy and common property and other gross delusions. Münster apart, Anabaptists supposedly attacked civilized institutions, since they rejected infant baptism and preached a kind of equalitarianism and pacifism, besides condemning capital punishment and advocating a community of goods, all highly subversive of religion and government.[3] Anabaptists' progeny had become serene Baptists long before the legacy of Münster faded, while Anabaptism endured as historic heresy, no doubt the most notorious confronted by Europeans with long memories for the next two centuries.

Harassment of Protestants in France and Holland led to the migration of a good many refugees to England in the 1550s. Hospitable Englishmen under Elizabeth welcomed the stream, and the newcomers spread out, mostly in the Southeast—Norwich, Colchester, Sandwich, and Canterbury, but also in London, Maidstone, and Southampton—where they settled down peaceably to their callings and were left alone. It was not long, however, before Church and State realized that hospitality might have been tempered with a closer scrutiny, for among the persecuted Continentals were several "Anabaptists also and Sectaries, holding Heretical and ill Opinions," who accepted asylum under pretense of orthodoxy but brought with them a number of disturbing ideas. From this migration, "if not before," wrote John Strype, spread several heretical doctrines which plagued both Church and civil State for some years to come. About the same time the Jesuits mounted a campaign to overthrow England's newly reformed religion by blowing up and inflaming existing divisions within society. One of their ploys was to plant Catholics in the guise of Puritans, who, like Thomas Heith, came armed with a leather pouch full of heresies, teaching the doctrines of David George and John Hus, along with the principles of the *"Anabaptists, Arians, and Enthusiasts."* Heith ended up earless in the pillory and with a slit nose. Such was the fear of enthusiasm during Elizabeth's early years.[4]

Englishmen suppressed the Anabaptists when they got the chance. Whole congregations were seized in 1575 and held for questioning and sometimes punishment. Prelacy was strong enough to hang Henry Barrow, John Penry, and John Greenwood in 1593. These early Separatists and Congregationalists stoutly denied the charge of Anabaptism, but they died convicted of "Brownism, Donatisme, Anabaptistrie, Scisme, Heresie, &c ... after so many yeares kept in miserable close prisons." The government persecuted countless people as Anabaptists when their crime was simple dissent, so strong was the tendency to equate religious differences with enthusiasm and, worst of all, "Anabaptistrie."[5]

Edmund Jessop could call them "this little silly sect" in 1623, but on the eve of the Civil War there was nothing little or silly about Anabaptism, according to archcritics of "the World turned upside down." By this time orthodox Anglicans and Puritans alike were convinced that all "Hell broke loose."[6] Sects of enthusiasts, hitherto kept under wraps, now burst forth almost with impunity, and all that seemed left to confront them was confutation and ridicule—and there was plenty of both. Neither Royalists nor rebels were willing to give over to fanatics, but for a time it was fanaticism they got, and in large doses. The English Civil War intensified the enthusiasts' drive while breaking the back of government control, offering plenty of opportunity for expression of the most exaggerated religious claims.

Thomas Fuller, moderate Anglican and popular preacher, studiously compared Anabaptists to fourth-century Donatists. In *The Holy State* (1642) he described these African schismatics, who had pulled away from Rome over the validity of Bishop Caecilian's consecration, as rigorous purists, presumptuously believing that theirs was the true church, and on this basis practiced rebaptism. To these he likened the Anabaptists, then spreading in England, who drove God's church into their own corner and bragged of their holiness above all others. They rebaptized their saints as adults, scorned unregenerate ministers, and insisted that magistrates were powerless to compel the worship of God. Because learning, they believed, was the cause of many heresies, they condemned it along with eloquence, the bane of good preaching. For proof Fuller unfairly cited long-dead Greenwood and Barrow as Anabaptists, claiming they had tried to persuade Queen Elizabeth to do away with both Oxford and Cambridge. On top of this, Fuller stated, Anabaptists boasted of visions and miracles and strove for martyrdom.[7]

Scholarly Robert Baillie, the Scottish Presbyterian, found Anabaptism to be the mother lode of all the heresies which troubled orthodoxy in the 1640s. It was the true fountain of "Independency, Brownism, Antinomy, Familisme, and most of the other Errours" for which the land mourned. Historically speaking, he was not far from the truth. Denying resurrection after death, heaven and hell, and the day of judgment, Anabaptists allegorized the lot "all into fancies." God was in every creature, which made the saints of this world "fully perfect" and "omniscient as God," even becoming God. Baillie could not leave Münster alone, and he retold the story of John of Leyden's visible kingdom, where he ruled over the saints according to revelations of the spirit. For his account Baillie drew heavily upon Johannes Sleidanus, annalist and historian of the Reformation, whose *Mock-Majesty: or the siege of Münster*, written not long after the event, was translated and republished in London in 1644. Like Sleidanus, Baillie focused on the means by which King John forced his "Teachers" to accept and promulgate his increasingly wild revelations, particularly God's command to practice polygamy according to the Old Testament, "that every man might marry so many wives as he pleased." Baillie spared us, however, the German's vivid description of King John's torture and death and the kingdom's demise, once the siege was broken. To the long list of Anabaptist heresies Baillie added several unsavory practices including faith healing and anointing the sick with oil, both of which kept reemerging from the enthusiasts' bag of tricks, at least among the extremists. Like Thomas Fuller, who had written a few years earlier, he scored the Anabaptists' "bitter invectives" against "humane learning, the arts, sciences, and the universities."[8]

Between Fuller and Baillie we get a pretty good idea of how moderate Anglicans and Puritans alike regarded the sectaries, and the Anabaptists in particular. Granted the religious excesses of the 1640s provoked the orthodox believer into strong reaction, the arguments by Fuller and Baillie summed up British outrage against a long train of abuses which reached a peak when many of the barriers to enthusiasm dissolved in the turmoil of civil war.

Family of Love

Just how the Family of Love differed from Anabaptism was not altogether clear to Britons under Elizabeth and James I, nor is it to historians today. Not only did their doctrines overlap here and there, but neither's were wholly consistent; in fact, both were guilty of contradiction and, in the Familists' case, were frequently accused of denying their principles for the sake of preserving them and themselves when the going got tough. Hendrik Niclaes, a German from Münster, born in 1502, stands out as the father of the Family. But it was an Anabaptist messiah, David George or Joris, a Dutchman, who was the teacher of both Niclaes and King John of Leyden, and so the lines of origin are not as clear as they might be. John Rogers explained "that *David George* was the hatcher of this heresie, and layde the egge, but *H-N* brought foorth the chickens."[9] And it was the prophet Hendrik Niclaes who set himself up in Holland about 1540 in answer to a divine command to establish a new sect. David George receded into the background (he died in 1556), for Niclaes claimed he owed nothing to men's ministry but only to the mouth of God, whose voice he heard. Once free of David George, Niclaes announced himself "a crying-voyce of the holy spirit of Love." Furthermore, he preached that Christ's first coming was only one of several historic breakthroughs in the course of Christianity. It was not the last, however, for the last and the greatest was his own, which left him "Godded with God," "code-ified," and God "homnified" in Hendrik Niclaes.

The Family of Love had a number of Anabaptist traits. Particularly strong was a reliance upon an inward light and motions of the spirit which took precedence over Scripture, but, according to R. A. Knox, it is doubtful that they felt the need to rebaptize their people. Rather, they delayed baptism until their children had reached the age of discretion— which the Anabaptists eventually did too. Familists believed that it was possible for them in their lifetime to attain the innocence of Adam before the Fall—a good example of the root idea of *radical*. Once in this state of perfection there was no need for belief in resurrection of the body after death, promised in the Bible, for it had already occurred, and Familists were the sign.[10]

No wonder Familists confused their orthodox contemporaries. Despite a willingness to get along with anyone and everybody, to live under all kinds of magistrates, attend parish churches, borrow doctrine from a variety of places, Familists at heart were Separatists and elitists and perfectionists, convinced of being God's chosen. They believed, according to H. N.'s teachings—which they equated with Scripture—that there was no salvation outside the Family, and that those who opposed them were already lost. Yet to add to what seems sharp contradiction, there was throughout the flock an overriding spirit of charity, meekness, and love. Accompanying eclecticism, their willingness to forego outward forms, and a tendency to deny their principles when cornered, there was a strong emphasis on the purity and integrity of a deep inward faith, a "Heavenly Knowledge," which sustained them through some pretty rough times in the hundred or more years of their existence.[11]

Christopher Vitell, a Dutch joiner from Delft and a disciple of Niclaes, brought Familism to England, probably in the early 1550s. Vitell wandered through a good deal of eastern England, teaching Familist principles as he traveled. Although he settled in Colchester, his ideas spread about him. The strongest incidence of Familists, who numbered about a thousand, seemed to be in Norfolk and Cambridgeshire. Vitell drew enough attention to himself to be seized and forced to recant his heresy at Paul's Cross in London in 1559, but he continued his lay preaching of the doctrines nevertheless.[12]

By 1575 both Church and State were thoroughly aroused by the spread of the Family of Love. Besides preaching, Vitell busied himself with translating into English Hendrik Niclaes's works, which he sent to Holland for printing, whence they were smuggled back into England and distributed. In 1574–75 about fifteen Familist tracts, mostly by Niclaes, burst upon the scene. The Privy Council, the Bishop of London, and a number of other bishops in several places took up the chase, discovering Familists in Norfolk, Suffolk, Cambridgeshire, Devon, and Exeter, besides a half dozen in the Yeomen of the Guard. Niclaes's writings provoked not only answers and attacks but defense and support. John Rogers, William Wilkinson, and John Knewstub all published major tracts, exposing, they claimed, the danger of "that poysen which dayly floweth frō our Lovely Familie." Englishmen who wished to read about them in the middle 1570s had ample opportunity. No doubt the government began active suppression of the sect as a result of this intense exposure of its ideas and the spread of its people—action which commenced with inquiry by government and bishops and eventually included a Royal Proclamation, charges, arrests, even a purge, continuing sporadically until the Civil War.[13]

Deepest penetration seemed to be in Cambridgeshire—particularly the Isle of Ely and Wisbech—but also Norwich in Norfolk and Bury St. Edmunds in Suffolk. The Isle of Ely enjoyed a unique reputation, one which obtained for several years. Ely means "Eel District," and the Venerable Bede claimed the city got its name owing to the large number of eels the fens afforded. It was difficult terrain, marked by watery land which inhibited agriculture. Cottagers spent a good deal of time fishing and shooting, and when they drove their cattle to higher dry spots, they walked on stilts. In wintertime the Isle of Ely was just about inaccessible, and these limitations upon the lives of the people there, "subject to ague of mind as well as body," affected their point of view about themselves and outsiders. The rest of England came to learn just how stubborn and different they were when attempts were made to drain the fens in the early and later years of the seventeenth century. The upshot was that the Family of Love found easy access among a deprived and susceptible people, and the Isle of Ely, where "dayly those swarmes increase," from Elizabeth's early years was known as a redoubt for notorious fanatics, a reputation that continued for some time.[14]

Following translations of Niclaes's works and the hardy attacks upon his doctrines by Rogers, Wilkinson, and Knewstub, the Privy Council intensified its investigation. Armed with Queen Elizabeth's Proclamation, it directed bishops in likely places to work with ministers and justices of the peace to root out the heresy. A number of suspects whose secret conventicles punctuated the landscape were rounded up. Some denied Familist belief and claimed no revelations but Scripture for their inspiration. Others, like Anne Hutchinson later in New England, defended their meetings out of church as necessary to improve their knowledge of the Bible. Some recanted outright and then hid under the shadow of orthodoxy. A similar number chose prison over forsaking their faith and were packed off to jail.[15]

Interest in the Family faded for a time after Elizabeth's purge of 1580, for probably the sect sought protection underground. James I, confused over the beliefs of the martyrs Barrow, Penry, and Greenwood, lumped the Family with Separatists and Puritans and condemned the lot in 1606, while the Family emerged long enough to petition His Majesty in order to defend themselves. Stephen Denison and John Etherington fought a pamphlet war over Familism in the 1620s, and the latter, who was one of them, spent time in jail for his pains, only later to recant the whole business and expose the sect widely. In the passionate literature against heretics and enthusiasts during the Civil War, the Familists took a beating along with other sectaries, and the Isle of Ely again bore a large share of the attack. "That Isle of Errors and Sectaries," charged Thomas Edwards in *Gangraena,* sported, besides fanatics, "a woman-preacher also," the "Woman of Ely" as she was called, whom we shall hear of again in Massachusetts when Anne Hutchinson commands the stage.[16]

The Restoration dampened enthusiasm, as it did a good many other religious irregularities, except for Quakers and Quakerism, as we shall see. A brave group of Familists surfaced in the 1680s to bless James II for a declaration of indulgence. Curious, James asked them just who they were and how many there were of them. Blandly they replied they were "sort of refin'd Quakers" who read Scripture and preached sermons, small in number, not above three score and "chiefly belonging to the Isle of Ely." The foremost American Puritan, Increase Mather, must have been stung with the indignity of it all when he realized that he had traveled all the way from Massachusetts to London in 1688 only to find himself in a queue with a motley group of Familists and a variety of beaming Catholics in order to thank James II for not persecuting dissenters.[17]

In the early seventeenth century the Family of Love found most of its English children in East Anglia and nearby. This in itself is significant for early American history, since not only was East Anglia the origin of a good many Massachusetts Puritans, but Anne Hutchinson, from nearby

Lincolnshire, and her followers, rightly or wrongly, were frequently labeled Familists. Mistress Hutchinson's accusers in Massachusetts had been well conditioned in their suspicions about them long before they settled in the New World, and they had every reason to be, given the attitude of most Englishmen toward Familists and the general Puritan response to enthusiasm.

Separatists

All enthusiasts were Separatists in one way or another. This was true chiefly because they were radicals who wished to pull away from establishments in order to preserve their purity from corruption—usually to return to what they called the primitive church and its practices. Some tried to accomplish this physically, by meeting in "private conventicles" and avoiding public worship; others separated themselves in spirit only, like many Familists, who often continued to mingle with the people and ministers they distrusted. But they were all reformers at heart, believing their way was the true way which others eventually would recognize. Until such time, they would honor the call to be separate, defending their integrity, sometimes with their lives. But probably not all Separatists were enthusiasts—at least not all English Separatists, who separated physically from the Anglican Church and hoped, at first, to go it alone within the realm.

Martin Luther had pulled in his horns once the Reformation took hold. The "priesthood of all believers" was feisty stuff when one considers that a number of people took it literally and supported the new freedom with the help of Bibles in their own languages. Individual interpretation of Scripture was not what Luther had anticipated, and he fell back upon the written Word as he and other "pundits" agreed upon it in order to avoid further chaos in Christendom. As free spirits such as John of Leyden and the Anabaptists experimented with immediate revelation and other fanatical religious beliefs, official Protestantism on the Continent and in Britain stiffened against their freedom and enthusiasm. Anabaptism went underground after Münster, only to burst out on occasion in a variety of related sects, some of them in England, while a majority of dissenters against the new Anglican establishment there took moderate methods to express their dissent, which was known as early Puritanism. Most of these late sixteenth-century Puritans accepted the state Church with the strong hope of capturing it and improving it, yet they carried on secretly behind the Church's back an independent and radical association which developed religiously and politically first into an underground and then eventually into an open revolutionary threat.

English Separatists were part of this dissenting tradition. Less radical politically than the Puritan Independents, they were more radical in church matters because they attempted to go their separate ways in individual churches based on covenants of believers alone. They encouraged a freer movement of the Holy Spirit than main-stem Puritans enjoyed—a closer, more primitive, less sophisticated relationship with God, which they sought through the sacred truths of the Bible, to be sure, but also through truths which the Holy Spirit helped them discover in experience and within themselves.

English Separatism evolved during many years of religious turmoil. A few years ago it was sufficient to trace the movement back only to the unstable Robert Browne in the late sixteenth century. But to do so was to ignore the evidence of Champlin Burrage, who in 1912 described the tendency to Separatism as early as 1550–51. Recently B. R. White has written more positively of its beginnings in the days of Queen Mary, and I. B. Horst, finding traces of Lollardy in its origins, supports Burrage's early date. Early Separatism was not consistent, and it was not until the time of Robert Browne that it took on some kind of form and developed into a recognizable sect.[18]

Separatism meant precisely what the word implies: "That a true visible Church of Christ, is a company of faithful people, called out by the word of God, and separated from the world, and the false waies thereof, gathered and joyned together in fellowship of the Gospell, by a voluntary profession of the faith and obedience of Christ."[19] Separation usually meant Congregationalism, for Separatists chose their own ministers and elders and did not look beyond them to any authority but God and the Bible. Needless to say, these hardy nonconformists were thorns in the side of the established Church from the outset. Besides, they were Calvinists, setting them off in the eyes of the King's Church, which under James I became increasingly Arminian. But more serious than theology was their stubborn insistence that the Church of England was not only corrupt but wrong and false; it refused to regulate itself or be regulated by what Separatists said was the Word of God. And so scattered groups of "Brownists" left the herd and attempted to carry on by themselves.[20]

It was not an easy thing to do at any time before the Civil War. Barrow, Penry, and Greenwood suffered martyrdom in 1593 for trying. Robert Browne, Francis Johnson, Henry Ainsworth, John Robinson, and Henry Jacob escaped to Holland at different times, some with and some without their flocks. Despite freedom abroad to survive, trouble and schism punctuated their sojourns there. Browne disagreed with his own people and returned to England, eventually accepting again the Church of England, which ordained him. Francis Johnson, who established an independent church in Amsterdam in 1596, had Presbyterian leanings, and his and his elders' use of authority offended some of the congregation, who split off, led by Teacher Henry Ainsworth, to preserve the original scheme of Separatism. Like Browne, Henry Jacob returned to England but remained independent. Meanwhile, John Robinson and his Scrooby group from Nottinghamshire had set up in Amsterdam, where they became uneasy with their fellow Separatists and shortly left that city for Leyden in 1609. The course of English Separatism in Holland was never smooth, and the accumulation of difficulties had a good deal to do with the departure of the Leyden group, or part of it, for New England in 1620.[21]

To be separate, nonconforming, and independent in England meant thoroughgoing dissent, but were Separatists enthusiasts? A number of their critics believed so and painted them in the same vibrant colors of fanaticism they splashed over Anabaptists and Familists. Moreover, some of their practices suggested it. No doubt strong believers in a single established religion found Separatism enthusiastic because it was a succumbing to impulses outside the unity of the national Church, its worship, and discipline. Since the established Church supposedly encompassed the will of God, then Separatists, who hearkened after other voices, other commands, for direction and inspiration, were enthusiasts, and a succession of them followed the lead of Browne, Barrow, Greenwood, and Robinson. There is but one truth, wrote Sir Walter Raleigh in his *History of the World* (1614), and it is now in contempt and attacked by "every contentious and ignorant person cloathing his fancy with *the spirit of God,* and his imagination with *the gift of Revelation.*" And who are to blame for this contention, asked Raleigh, but the Familists, Anabaptists, and Brownists? Although there is "but one Spirit of Truth," wrote Edmund Jessop, "yet there be many spirits of error, and ways of deceit." Let the kingdom guard against them. When liberty of conscience was anathema to authority and an established Church was God's way, Separatism was fanatical and idolatrous, the result of gross error, fraud, imagination, and revelation—in short, it was enthusiasm.[22]

Escape to Holland did nothing to improve the Separatists' reputation in England. Ugly rumors spread back home, and a number of them got into print. Particularly severe in its criticism was Thomas White's *Discoverie of Brownism* (1605), which was a bitter attack on Francis Johnson and his congregation in Amsterdam. Johnson was a notorious Separatist who had been in and out of English jails before hurrying off to Holland, where like-minded Englishmen in exile had called him as their minister in 1596. Bad enough were their blasphemous doctrines, their "errors and abhominations," which smacked of Familism. White concentrated primarily on their sexual immoralities—adultery, incest, sodomy—about which the minister and church did nothing. They need never have separated, White added, "for any Godly societie wil quickly thrust them out from them so practising as they doe."[23] Plymouth's Pilgrims later left Leyden for a variety of reasons, foremost probably the fear of being swallowed up in a worldly European society, but early attacks on Separatists like Thomas White's may have convinced them also that they were still too close to home.

A popular and useful way to define Puritanism, perhaps better to describe it, is to extoll its fine balance between passion and reason, the heart and the head. Puritanism contained strong doses of both, we are told, but one of its accomplishments was the ability to harmonize them and let neither get out of hand. Reckless zeal had a tendency to fanaticism and enthusiasm, while hard-headed reason and intellect deadened religion and led to dryness and mediocrity, against which the Puritans were struggling.[24] Samuel Ward of Ipswich, Suffolk, older brother of Nathaniel Ward, who later ventured to Massachusetts, probably traveled farther in defense of religious emotion than any other Puritan of the period. Had his parishioners not listened carefully, they might have been seduced into enthusiasm, for Ward emphasized zeal as the heart of religion and gave his teachings a warmth and devotion not approached by his contemporaries. Still, so far would he go and no farther, for zeal, that "spiritual heat wrought in the heart of man by the holy Ghost," was "guided by the word, not humours." It was a "good servant but an ill master." It was often wrong-headed, a "smoaky fire," an "ignus fatuus." Mistaken in this way Ward found many Separatists, most of whom were "sicke of self-conceitednesse" and "new-fangleness." Who could not suspect the intensity of a people who condemned all the reformed churches and refused communion with those they knew to be Christians? Theirs was zeal misplaced, "like mettle in a blind horse." And so Samuel Ward of Ipswich distinguished between true Christians and enthusiasts, between good Puritans, who balanced religious fervor with rational understanding, and zealous Separatists, who sorely wanted both "knowledge and discretion." It would grieve a man indeed, wrote Ward, to see them "take such paines, and yet fall into the pit." "Pseudo-puritans," Patricke Scot dubbed them a few years later; they would do well "not to trust every spirit."[25]

Champlin Burrage called Separatism a slow evolution from its beginnings in the 1550s. By the time of the Civil War and Commonwealth periods, however, its growth was surprising, and the final product contained a variety of characteristics contributed not only by Brownists and other Separatist leaders but also by the main body of Puritans and Independents. Burrage also found elements of Anabaptism and Familism and still other sectarian peculiarities which marked these hectic years, all of which made Separatists considerably diverse in the 1640s and 1650s and also more open to attack. Staunch Anglicans lamented the decline of the national Church and blamed the "dissenting Sectaries," of whom, said some, the Brownists were the worst. Their pretended sanctity and dissembled piety contaminated the purity of religion, while in "private conventicles" they delighted in "voluptuous wantonnesse." Ignorance, idolatry, lewdness, and subversion, besides heresy, were the "Anatomy of the Separatists"; they were offensive to God, defiled the flesh, and affronted the government. Robert Baillie might find Anabaptism the true fountain of errors; others traced them to these "factious Brethren," the Separatists, who "Amsterdamnified" the countryside with "Brainlesse opinions" and senseless religions.[26]

Separatists were Puritans and along with them took their place in the mainstream of English dissent in the late sixteenth and early seventeenth centuries. Their act of separation, the peculiar character of differences which grew up around them, and the primitive, even radical, church practices they fell back upon as expressions of their boasted purity— some of which the Leyden Separatists brought to America, as we shall see—marked them in the eyes of their contemporaries as extremists and enthusiasts.

Subversion

According to most Englishmen, enthusiasm was subversive. Dissent itself was somehow disloyal, but dissent characterized by blasphemy and heresy, to say nothing of challenging the state's authority and undermining the structure and principles of society, this was dissent with a vengeance, a clear and present danger. That enthusiasts were blasphemous and heretical there was no doubt. One only had to recall the catastrophe at Münster, the denial of heaven and hell, and the whole practice of rebaptizing by the Anabaptists, or the Familists' equating Hendrik Niclaes with Christ and his writings with gospel. What other conclusion could one draw from a people who tested Scripture by an intense inward light, who relegated the Jesus of Jerusalem to history, relying rather upon the Christ within, and who preached an immunity to sin, a perfectionism which relieved them of the need of law, spiritual or temporal? Moreover, they distorted the millennial dream either by giving it a "local habitation and a name" or by pretending it had already occurred and for them alone. Separatists did not subscribe to all of these outrages, to be sure, but the mere fact that they believed they had been "called out by the word of God" qualified them for heresy and enthusiasm along with it.

Besides blasphemy and heresy, enthusiasts threatened to overthrow the Church itself. Separatism of any kind was disloyal and disruptive of a national Church, while "private conventicles," "teaching in corners," made a shambles of public worship. Faith healing and anointing the sick were unsavory practices, and attempts to resurrect the dead were morbidly blasphemous, besides being a waste of time. The widespread use of untrained preachers flew in the face of an organized clergy; the artisan and working-class status of these preachers was an insult to God, the King, and the established hierarchy, as it was also to the Puritan clergy, which prided itself on the intellectual level of its members. On top of this enthusiasts encouraged women preachers, which the Bible explicitly forbade. To support all of these most enthusiasts advocated the separation of Church and State and freedom of dissent, which, if they were guilty of nothing else, was enough to provoke distrust and contempt from both Anglicans and nonseparating Puritans, who accepted the principle that the state was obligated to enforce the public worship of God, as long as it was in their churches. The sectaries' "plea for liberty," wrote Thomas Edwards, was the Devil's scheme to pull down religion altogether. Enthusiasts ransacked and made abominable theological doctrine and ecclesiastical order. The one they reduced to strange and suspicious interpretations, "turning light into darknesse, truth into falsehood, histories into allegories, and sound religion into fancies of men"; the other they "transvert[ed] . . . to a most deformed shape, or misshapen forme."[27]

Once enthusiasts had undermined the Church, what could prevent them from subverting the state? Opponents were all too willing to see this as the next step and warned against it. Three methods seemed apparent. It might come by way of another Münster, and with "thorowe rapine, violence, and extortion, level both Church and Common wealth, equal with the ground," a possibility which kept the memory of the bloody zeal of the Anabaptists in the forefront. It might come by way of the dreams and schemes of the visionaries through pursuit of a More's Utopia or Plato's Community, peaceable to be sure, but nonetheless subversive. Most likely it would be the result of the wearing away of the state and its functions by way of several subversive practices. Most sectaries harbored antimonarchical principles; they condemned the magistracy, particularly since it enforced public worship; they refused to take oaths or to go to war—all disloyal practices which could only bring the state to its knees. Subject as enthusiasts were to the motions of the spirit, to their fancy and imagination in all things, would not these lead to the overthrow of the commonwealth?[28]

The class structure was not safe either. There is no doubt that most Englishmen regarded sectaries as social radicals. After all, they encouraged artisans and mechanics to breach the ranks of the clergy when their very class and lack of education made them ineligible; they applauded the prattlings of felt makers, cobblers, horse rubbers, and leather sellers. Many refused to recognize distinctions among good subjects, for they preached that all "are equal in degree among themselves: *all Kings* and a Kingdom of Kings." They taught that God was no respecter of persons, and assured their people that "he regards neither fine clothes, nor gold rings, nor stately houses, nor abundance of wealth, nor dignities, and titles of honour, nor any mans birth or calling, indeed he regards nothing among his children but love." What kind of a society could one build on these bases so destructive of the state? Moreover, some of the sectaries preached common ownership of property—"Let no man seeke his owne, But every man anothers wealth" (1 Corinthians 10:24)—and held that a Christian society was characterized by loving and sharing, by which no believer was left to want but shared in the whole. Ephraim Pagitt rang the changes on this appalling principle and claimed that the enthusiasts' fancies were a threat to all classes of society, for they insisted that "the wicked have no property in their estates," and the "meek must inherit the earth." Thomas Edwards recorded in his glossary of enthusiasts' errors that fanatical saints believed the earth was theirs, and they recommended a community of goods wherein they could share the estates of wealthy gentlemen. Pagitt and Edwards wrote in the 1640s when, to a good many, the world did seem turned upside down, but they merely reflected the tendencies which Englishmen believed were not very deeply buried in the radical social principles of Anabaptists and Familists and other enthusiasts of the first half of the century. What the sectaries began, the Levellers and Diggers were bound to finish.[29]

First religion and the Church, then the authority of government and the structure of society—these would fall before the attack of those who lived only from the Spirit or, rather, succumbed to the dictates of their fancies as the will of God. But these were not the extent of society's demise. Sectaries walked roughshod over sexual morality, did they not, and the institutions of marriage and family? Of all the charges leveled against enthusiasts, from Donatists to Methodists, Shakers, and beyond, free love and sexual promiscuity were the most consistent. It was self-evident that those who defied Church and State would naturally tear down sexual barriers, too, and indulge their lusts at will—or so it appeared.

Again the Anabaptists at Münster were the example, and again the English public read of divorce and polygamy in the Kingdom of the Saints under John of Leyden. Not that the exercises of some enthusiasts did not suggest practices which prejudiced minds might easily build upon, because they did. Anabaptists had run naked through the streets of Amsterdam as a chilly reminder of the "naked truth," while later Quakers in both Old and New England stripped entirely and appeared "naked for a sign" to shame contemporaries into acknowledging their own poverty of truth. There were biblical precedents, to be sure, for these holy acts, the enthusiasts argued, but pop-eyed audiences judged otherwise. Unless they might become like little children, the Anabaptists supposedly believed, they could not enter into the Kingdom of Heaven. And so, Englishmen read, in Germany men rode "naked upon sticks and hobby horses, like children in great companies, and women would run naked with them, and then in pure innocency they lay together, and so in the end it proved childrens play indeed."[30]

The accusations of sexual immorality were a part of the larger attack upon enthusiasts, and like others they were linked with charges of antinomianism, which were frequent in the first half of the seventeenth century. Enthusiasts' contempt for the law, whether scriptural, ecclesiastic, constitutional, or moral, hinted strongly of perfectionism and antinomianism. Perfectionism was sinlessness, a belief that conversion and grace led to a permanent rooting out of sin, leaving believers suffused or flushed with a love of God and his creatures which displaced evil within them. But perfectionism could and sometimes did spill over into antinomianism, since some believers argued that freedom from sin placed them above the demands of the law. Antinomianism was not a sect but a condition. Enthusiasm became antinomianism when it led believers to assume that they were filled with Christ to the point where good works made no difference, and they could do no wrong. All enthusiasts were not antinomians, but there was enough evidence around to convince their enemies that the threat to Church and State was owing to the enthusiasts' contemptuous disregard for the accepted rules of society, spiritual and temporal.[31]

Once Anglicans had turned away from Calvin, they, like the Catholics, taught that grace depended on a good life. Calvinist Puritans insisted that good works did not precipitate grace, but grace, arbitrarily given, precipitated good lives, which, in fact, became contributing evidence of salvation—although the law obligated them to lead good lives anyway, saved or not. The antinomian enthusiasts went a step farther—a long one—and based their lives on the assumption that good works had little to do with grace before or after conversion. Chosen by God, brimming with the Holy Spirit, they became wrapped in Christ's righteousness; they were freed of the burden of sin and the law; good works were not required of them, because sainthood was absolute, making good works unnecessary. Since the Spirit within relieved them of the guilt of sin, no sin could drag them down.

Among extreme antinomians freedom *from* sin meant freedom *to* sin, for sin mattered not at all, and the exaggerated forms of enthusiasm sanctioned a rolling in the mud to prove the beauty of true grace and innocence. Strenuous enthusiasts worked this last conclusion around to justify sin as a basis of purity, sin which they were free to indulge in with impunity, for the Spirit relieved them of the consequences. Needless to say, this kind of argument and the conduct which supposedly resulted from it made no sense to Anglican and Puritan, who chalked up the antinomians' abominable excesses ("eccentricities," Ronald Knox has called them) as prime evidence that the grossness of their sins was equal to the magnitude of their spiritual deception.[32] Ranters carried the logic to its extreme in the 1640s and 50s and won for themselves a reputation for wallowing unmatched before or since,[33] except perhaps by the French Prophets of half a century later.

Whether the Family of Love was antinomian there is some question. That Familists based their principles on an intense inward light there is no doubt, and therefore, on many counts, they displayed antinomian tendencies. Their defenders, however, denied that these tendencies led them to be libertines despite what people said about them. Hendrik Niclaes insisted that his spiritual revelations, far from overthrowing the law, fulfilled it in love. Nevertheless, contemporaries lumped the Family with the antinomians and made few distinctions. This was equally true of the Anabaptists, about whom there was less doubt. Münster had set the scene, and so too the stories of their running naked through the streets of Amsterdam. In fact, Robert Baillie regarded Anabaptism as the "True Fountaine" of all the heresies, including antinomianism.[34]

Antinomianism did not necessarily mean licentiousness. The English radical William Walwyn eloquently expressed its less militant and more spiritual side, which must have appealed happily to a variety of enthusiasts and sectaries who felt oppressed by the ecclesiastical authorities and who, like Walwyn, found release through free justification of Christ alone. Announcing his antinomianism, he celebrated the ease and freedom he felt, no longer entangled like others "with those yokes of bondage, unto which Sermons and Doctrines mixt of Law and Gospel do subject distressed consciences." The law was a prison, but the love of Christ offered escape: "I am not a preacher of the law, but of the gospell; nor are you under the law, but under grace: the law was given by *Moses*, whose minister I am not: but grace and truth came by Jesus Christ, whose minister I am: whose exceeding love, hath appeared." If righteousness proceeded from the law, he wrote, Jesus died in vain.

The antinomians' idea of assurance was overwhelming. Nothing, claimed Walwyn, could separate believers from Christ's love already purchased—not impenitence, infidelity, unthankfulness, not even sin. Nothing could annul the bargain, since his sacrifice fully discharged the believers' debts, "past, present, and to come." On this basis, Walwyn argued, believers were free to "shun high places," lofty things and people, and equate themselves with "men of low degree." Again the spiritual reformer had transcended the purely religious dimensions of enthusiasm to a social radicalism which lined him up on the Lord's side to do battle against the evil forces which oppressed mankind. For real Christians, concluded Walwyn, hated tyranny, oppression, cruelty, perjury, and deceit, and, bold as lions, they feared not the "faces of men." Spiritual and political antinomians would do away with that law or that government which tyrannized over the people. But William Walwyn and his radical friends were an embattled minority and remained so; their attempt to add social revolution to civil war was a chaotic failure.[35]

Many Englishmen had difficulty accepting civil war, let alone kicking over the traces of society. Enthusiasts like Walwyn, they said, guided themselves not by the rule, nor did they weigh their actions in the "ballance of the Sanctuary, but onely of their owne head." Certainly God must say of them as he said of Saul, "Rebellion is as the sinne of witchcraft, and stubbornnesse is as iniquity and idolatry," and all because they rejected the Word of the Lord and overthrew the moral law. "Blush you Antinomians, who are taught, and do believe, That being in Christ, you cannot sin; or if you do, God cannot see it." Enthusiasm was not just heretical, unscriptural, and sinful; in the hearts of some it was antinomian and revolutionary.[36]

If antinomians were free of the burdens of sin, they were free, then, the orthodox claimed, to sin sexually as well as against God, Church, and State. The very name Family of Love left these enthusiasts vulnerable to sexual smear from the outset. Familists' "love" others freely translated into "free love" and promiscuity. Moreover, as with the Anabaptists, their group consciousness was inherent, which dictated private meetings, often in the dark, no doubt to escape detection. The very surreptitiousness of the movement and its community character encouraged suspicious minds to discover irregularities. The idea of keeping women in common dogged Familists throughout their history—it popped up in the trial of Anne Hutchinson in Massachusetts—and in this respect they were later compared with the Ranters of the 1650s. So too their kiss of greeting was a suggestive eccentricity about which much was made.[37]

By the early years of the seventeenth century the Family was fair game for anyone's picking. Thomas Middleton made the most of it in his bawdy play *The Famelie of Love,* published in 1608 but written a half-dozen years earlier. It is full of good and bad puns, innuendoes, and double-entendres, largely sexual and physical.[38] Primary action centers on Mistress Purge, appropriately wife of an apothecary, who is the very "cordiall of a Familist," an elder of the sect, in fact. Purge, her husband, has swallowed all the propaganda of Middleton's time about the Family of Love—"the house of Venery, where they hunger and thurst for't"—and believes he is cuckolded each time his wife leaves their home to attend meetings, which is frequently. Mistress Purge contributes to the suspicion, and when asked why the Family insists on gathering at night quickly replies that "with the candles out too, we fructifie best i' the darke." Purge attempts to follow her one evening, but fumbles the password— calls himself a "Familiar brother" instead of a "Brother in the Family"— and is denied admission. Again at home he ridicules the sect's outpouring of universal love with, "I shall expect my wife anon red hot with zeale, and big with melting teares; and this night do I expect, (as her manner is) she will weepe me a whole Chamberpot full, *Loquor Lapides.*"

Purge, his suspicions at a peak, takes his wife before a mock court of friends, where Dryfat, his crony, acts as his lawyer. If the Family is not punished and suppressed, Dryfat tells the court—as Middleton focuses again on what suspicious Englishmen expected of the Family of Love— "each mans coppy hold, will become free hold, specialties will turne to generalities and so from unity to parity, from parity to plurality, & from plurality to universalitie, their wives, the onely ornaments of their houses and of all their wares, goods and Chattell, the chiefe moveables wil be made common." "Speake *Rebecca Purge,*" demands the judge, "art thou one of this family? hast thou ever knowne the body of any man there, or elsewhere Concupiscentically?" Mistress Purge answers with a thumping "No," explaining, "I thank my spirit I have feare before my eyes, which my husband sees not, because somthing hangs in's light." "That's my hornes," interrupts Purge, "she flowts me to my face."

None too soon the mock judge brings the trial to an end, acquits Mistress Purge, and admonishes the apothecary to appreciate his faithful wife. "My counsell," he chides Purge, in typical Middleton manner, is "that you readvance your Standard, give her new presse money." But Mistress Purge has the last word and returns home with principles intact: "Truelie Husband my love must be free still to Gods creatures, yea neverthelesse preserving you still as the head of my bodie, *I* will doe as the Spirite shall inable me." Having had his fun at the Familists' expense, Middleton appears to leave Mistress Purge the winner; he salutes her unbounded faith in universal love and her unbending obedience to the motions of the Spirit, but all within the physical demands of husband and household.[39]

There are other Familist touches here and there. "Y'are my better in Barke and Rhyne," an apprentice boldly announces, "but in pith and substance I may compare with you: y'are above me in flesh mistrisse, and thers your boast, but in my tother part, we are all one before God."[40] Perfection and spiritual equality epitomized primary strains of enthusiasm which Thomas Middleton included in his coarse and funny play, but they were spiritual tenets the Quakers took up seriously and around them built another sect a couple of generations later—with debts to the Family of Love, if unacknowledged.

Separatists did not escape the charge of sexual immorality. Thomas White vigorously broadcast to Englishmen the "errors and abhominations" of Francis Johnson's congregation in Amsterdam. Not only were Johnson and the elders guilty of blasphemous doctrines, which were a "ground of familisme," but Johnson's people stood uncorrected in their uncleanness: Daniel Studley, an elder, not alone for his "filthinesse with his wives Daughter"; Robert Bayly "publikelye accused in their meeting for creeping in at a windowe to come to bed to another mans wife in her husbands absence"; Thomas Canaday "hath lived in *Sodometry* with his Boy." Besides, they held it unlawful for an innocent party in a case of adultery to continue to live with the guilty one, even though the wronged spouse forgave and forgot. This made it handy for husbands to accuse themselves and so be rid of their wives, as several had already done, White reported. "Are these the Saints then marching in such a heavenly and gracious aray"?[41]

The Brownists were the worst of the bunch, wrote a later defender of orthodox truth and moral rectitude. Their "private conventicles" were in obscure and secret places where the "Spirit enlightens the understanding to see a sister in the darke." They were a charitable lot, however. "Rather than their sisters shall want food, they will fill their bellies, and rather than they shall be naked, they will cover their bodyes," for "they are lovers of the sisters of the scaberd," and so on.[42] During the 1640s and 50s, when the radical sects showed few inhibitions, their opponents' propaganda insisted that sexual immorality was popular among them; even the Adamites reappeared, we hear, and everyone knew that they refused to hear the gospel or kneel to the sacraments unless they could do so stark naked and all.[43]

Enthusiasm may have pretty much shot its bolt (to use an appropriate Middleton expression) by the time of the Restoration, except among Quakers and a few others. But not all critics were convinced that the sexual nature of enthusiasm had run its course. Henry More warned of the "lurking Fumes of *Lust*," while Thomas Long linked Anabaptists and the Family as "Votaries to Venus" in his *Character of a Separatist: or Sensuality the Ground for Separation.* In a good many people's minds enthusiasm and sexual license were peas of the same pod. If the motions of the Spirit led to tearing down Church and State, they attacked also human institutions, and in their vital parts, too. Imagination ungoverned was a *"wilde* and a *ranging* thing," wrote the old Puritan Richard Sibbes; it set the *"baser* part of man above the higher," and it "maketh *evill* good, if it pleaseth the senses." Enthusiasts were beyond control; they knew no yoke, and they bred like rabbits.[44]

A reliance upon the Spirit alone left enthusiasts open to another charge— what we would call today anti-intellectualism. If the Word of God rationally culled from the Bible through a process of education meant little in comparison to visions, imagination, and revelation, then enthusiasts supposedly found little time for "humane learning," universities, and intellectual exercise. The heart subverted the mind; affections overhauled understanding; and the simple love of God and his creatures conquered theology. No doubt most enthusiasts would have agreed, for those who lived directly from the Spirit could not be tied to second-hand thoughts and the mental gyrations of pedants and legalists—even the stale revelations of first-century apostles and prophets. It was common knowledge that Hendrik Niclaes "made a divorce betwixt the spirite and the written word of God, which always are enlinked together."[45] Reading the Bible was not a spiritual duty. Still, one has to fit in the fact that Englishmen who became acquainted with the Family of Love learned a good deal about it from a dozen or more books by Niclaes, with the help of Christopher Vitell's translations. Granted, once the books were read true believers like Vitell and other members of the Family preached and persuaded and transcended Niclaes's words into "mystical fantasies" and "allegories," exciting their hearers to accept the Spirit and drop the forms. That they were successful is witnessed in the strength of the struggle against them by government, bishops, and local clergy.[46]

Books are for the scholar's idle times, wrote Ralph Waldo Emerson in 1837. An English enthusiast in 1600 would have said it only a little differently. He would tell us that he read books, if he could read, only when he was not in tune with the Spirit, for other people's thoughts, no matter how devout, were not the real thing, were not the voice of God in the heart. He might have gone on to say, "Don't give me books, don't read me the law, don't shut me up in a university—but give me Christ." Such a demand was a rallying cry of enthusiasts in England, and it would resound in the ears of Anne Hutchinson's friends in Massachusetts, where it received no better response from authority and the learned than it did at home.

Education and learning were burdens the enthusiasts could do without, for nothing should clutter the path along which the Spirit approached. Such a belief only added to the contempt hurled at them by the religious establishment and others whose religion was a balance between spirit and reason, zeal and knowledge. What outraged their enemies above all was that sectaries *unlearned* the doctrine of the churches as "abominable and corrupt" and substituted their own, which "they vaunt to be celestiall." And who taught these "pernicious errours" but "false prophets," "unlearned men taken out of some trade" to be "Teachers among the Anabaptists and Familists"? Some pleaded an honest heart, to be sure, but so did the heretics of old and all the cunning sectaries, who asked, "Hath not Hatmakers, Horsekeepers, Coblers, and Weavers as great abilities of the spirit, and as much holinesse as any Doctor of them all, that is bred up in learned Tongues and the Arts?" And remember, warned Thomas Fuller, it was the arch-Separatists Greenwood and Barrow who had suggested to Queen Elizabeth that she abolish the universities.[47]

When Thomas Edwards began cataloguing the heinous errors of the sectaries, anti-intellectualism scored high in his pantheon of heresies. Preachers of the Spirit scorned human learning and the reading of books. They were convinced that only from a "want of the Spirit" would "men write such great volumes, and make such adoe of learning." To study and premeditate were wrong-headed, for preachers ought not to "thinke of what they are to say till they speak, because it shall be given them in that hour, and the Spirit shall teach them." The Spirit moved George Whitefield in the same way a hundred years later and, we are told, has moved enthusiasts ever since. "I love to study," wrote Whitefield, "and delight to meditate . . . and yet would go into the Pulpit by no Means depending on my Study and Meditation, but the blessed Spirit of God."[48]

Sectaries defended their anti-intellectual freedom in different ways. Some, like Samuel How, the "Cobler," no longer preached in corners. In 1644 a London printer hawked his sermon whose title spoke for itself, if simply: *The Sufficiencie of the Spirits Teaching without Humane Learning. Or a Treatise tending to prove Humane-learning to be no helpe to the spirituall understanding of the Word of God.*[49] More sophisticated was *The Power of Love* by William Walwyn, who mounted a radical and bitter attack upon the established ways. Who cares for learning and education, he asked, "as learning goes now adaies"? What is it but an art to abuse and deceive men's understanding and lead them to ruin? If this is not true, why do the universities oppose the "welfare of the Common-wealth" and corrupt the judgments of the people? What good is it to have the Bible in our own language if we cannot be trusted to understand plain English but must rely on university men to interpret it for us? *The Power of Love* was a plea for liberty and a ringing call, like that of Emerson to Americans two hundred years later, for Englishmen to trust their "own considerations" in all that is necessary for "understandings and consciences." It was not the Anabaptists, Brownists, and Separatists who cried down learning and government in church and commonwealth, for the sectaries were enemies only of "usurpations, and innovations, and exorbitances in government" by others. Those who falsely accused the enthusiasts were the true enemies, the "Wolves in Sheepes' cloathing," the learned men who live upon the unlearned—words which Samuel Gorton across the Atlantic echoed time and again against the establishment of Massachusetts Bay.[50]

The argument here was strikingly different from that of ingenuous sectaries of an earlier period. At the height of Civil War dissent, even enthusiasts' dissent like Walwyn's took on edge as it merged purely spiritual opposition with radical social protest which flowered in the Diggers and Levellers.

While men like Walwyn tried to pull the world apart, their enemies, like Thomas Edwards, tried to hold it together. The battle against prelacy, said Edwards, which characterized the pre–Civil War struggle, had metamorphosed into a battle against heresy, and he was on the barricades against it. Prelacy was bad enough, but heresy might destroy the whole civilized structure of England as Edwards knew it in the 1640s. And the heretics were the enthusiasts whose blasphemous opinions and subversive practices threatened Church and State, society, yea civilization. This is their goal, he wrote, "that they might mingle Heaven and Earth, bring all Religion to nothing, abolish all learning, cauterize all mens consciences, and in the end, leave no difference between men and beasts."[51] As the Civil War progressed, as the monarchy toppled, as toleration increased and republicanism spread, many Englishmen were convinced that the enthusiasts had won the day.

3

Separatists and the New World: Plymouth's Pilgrims

O F ALL THE enthusiastic sects which plagued England and the King's Church, the Separatists were the most pronounced travelers. Holland, we have seen, received a good many, and English Separatists lived and worshipped there off and on for years. Still, there was a kind of homelessness about these people; somehow they did not seem to belong anywhere. "We are but strangers and pilgrims," wrote one of them, "warring against many and mighty adversaries."[1]

Although Englishmen generally abhorred Separatists, English opinion was divided whether they should be permitted to seek asylum in America. As early as 1597 Francis Johnson had little trouble securing approval from the Privy Council for possession of an island colony called Ramea in the Saint Lawrence River, where he and a small group of Separatists might settle and worship as they pleased. Despite the help of two London merchants and the efforts of a small reconnaissance party which visited the spot, the colony came to nothing. Trouble with both French and Spanish over trade and fur discouraged the larger contingent from ever leaving England, although not very much is known about either their plans or activities. William Bradford, once in the New World, looked back upon Johnson's people as harbingers of his own venture at Plymouth, which, we know, was a good deal more successful.[2]

Some Englishmen looked kindly on peopling America with sectaries, if only to get rid of them. At least this is the impression given by Joseph Hall, later Bishop of Exeter and then Norwich, whose heavy-handed satire *The Discovery of a New World* (1609) described their goings on in "Sectarouria, the second Province of Fooliana." Sectarouria swarmed with a variety of enthusiasts, from early Montanists to present-day Familists, and included "certain English Brownists, exiled into Virginia," where they had laid a plot "to erect themselves a bodie politique." Hall warned foreign potentates far and near of the contagious heresies of these people, suggesting strongly that to save their nations from fatal infections they might do well to banish such "damnable perturbers of holie peace" to Fooliana, where they could do little mischief. Better there than making trouble at home, warned Joseph Hall. He suspected also a connection between Francis Johnson's early Amsterdam congregation and the Scrooby people under John Robinson, who, he wisely guessed, might very well make their own attempt to find in America a foothold for homeless Separatists and "their hellish impieties."[3]

One would think, then, that Virginia held out to persecuted Separatists the best opportunity for escape. This was true only in part. William Crashaw, father of Richard, the poet, hardly welcomed such activity when he preached a farewell sermon to the Virginia Company in 1609, just before Lord de la Warre embarked for the infant colony as new governor. Besides warning against "Atheists[,] the Divels champions," in the same breath, as if equally obnoxious, he charged De la Warre to "Suffer no Brownists, nor factious Separatists." Let them hold their conventicles elsewhere and convert other heathens with ideas "fancied in their braines," but God forbid it should be in Virginia.[4]

The Reverend Mr. Crashaw did not speak for the whole Virginia Company, at least not after its reorganization in 1618. At that time the members in England elected Sir Edwin Sandys their treasurer and executive officer, and he made some thorough changes. The choice of Sandys smoothed the way for negotiations between the company in London and the Scrooby group in Leyden, which had been corresponding with Sandys for a couple of years about the possibility of settling a "particular plantation" in Virginia under the company's wing.[5]

Sandys was a prominent entrepreneur during the reign of James I. His father had been Archbishop of York and Lord of Scrooby Manor besides being an outspoken Puritan; his brother held the manor lease and employed the father of Elder William Brewster, a Plymouth settler and leader, as bailiff. Through this preliminary connection negotiations eventually matured between the Leyden Separatists and the Virginia Company. Agents in London carried the cause from negotiation to terms with Sandys's help and King James's permission. Edward Winslow, one of the agents, called Edwin Sandys a "religious gentleman," which no doubt meant that Sandys's religion was attractive to Separatists, or at least trusted, and maybe even vice versa. Politically, Sandys was a liberal, a staunch Parliamentarian, and a strong critic of the Crown's authority, which no doubt had something to do with James's outburst—"Choose the devil, if you will, but not Sir Edwin Sandys"—at the prospect of his reelection as treasurer of the Virginia Company in 1620.[6]

Beginning about 1618 a Puritan, even Separatist, tendency appeared in the Virginia colony, no doubt encouraged by Sandys. Its beginning, however, was a disaster. Francis Blackwell, an elder of Francis Johnson's old church in Amsterdam, led the bulk of the congregation to Virginia after Johnson's death. Cruelly overloaded, their vessel, the *William and Thomas,* after what must have been a nightmarish voyage, arrived in the colony with only fifty survivors of the 180 thought to have been aboard at Gravesend. Future migrations were more successful, chiefly in the early 1620s, while the Sandys faction retained control of the Virginia Company.[7]

Sandys's sympathy toward Separatists was not shared by all Virginia's friends. In fact, there were some who suspected him of harboring, besides unorthodox religious views, political ideas unfriendly to the governments of both England and Virginia. Some said his encouragement of Brownists, who already were suspected of subversive, even antimonarchical principles, was a means to erect a "free popular state" in Virginia. Such suspicions led Captain John Bargrave, who, like many an Englishman, equated schism in religion with resistance against sovereign power, to suggest that the plantation government suppress outright any colonists who professed doctrines contrary to those which were established.[8]

This kind of prejudice may help to explain why the Leyden Pilgrims gave Virginia a wide berth. It may also make clearer Henry Jacob's failure to establish a successful Separatist community in Virginia in 1622, which a Dutchman dubbed "Jacobopolis." Jacob was a zealous dissenter whose career in England and Holland was, to say the least, irregular. Strongly Puritan, he followed Johnson and Robinson into Separatism and Congregationalism, yet gave the King's Church its due. He insisted, however, on reform of the churches of England, which prelacy had led out from the true way. Only in one point of religion, he told James I in a petition of 1604, did he and his followers differ from their adversaries, and that was that "Gods written word ought to be our sole warrant for all things Ecclesiastical." For defending this principle, he said, we are maliciously called "Schismatikes" and accused of plotting subversion of Church and State. As a radical reformer, and like many other enthusiasts, Jacob harked back to the "original and first Plantation . . . of all Churches" before transgression crept in. There only is safety. For an attempt to return to the primitive church, he wrote, the prelates call our doctrine "Brownistical, Anabaptisticall, fanatical, dotage, phrensie, &C."[9]

In 1616 Jacob returned from Holland to London and established at Southwark the first Independent Congregational church in England. He gathered several friends who joined hands and covenanted with him in great solemnity, pledging in the sight of God to walk in his ordinances and ways "according as he had already revealed, or should farther make known to them," a loophole for ongoing revelation and inspiration, even enthusiasm. Historians agree that Jacob's new church was some kind of milestone in the history of Puritanism, Separatism, and Independency, that he and his followers in effect established a new sect, arising from a special agreement, complete with manifesto and consent of its members to church government, and a plea to the King for toleration.[10]

Henry Jacob held this congregation together for six years. That he was convinced his experiment stood for something new, an idea of truth worth preserving, even spreading, may explain his migration to Virginia in 1622. A new sect in a New World presented opportunities impossible in the England of James I. With but one church hanging on precariously, dependent upon a largesse the King disapproved of, Virginia no doubt looked attractive as a place to begin without the alleged corruption and wrong-headedness of the establishment. That he might gather under his wing the scattered Separatists and other Puritans already in Virginia probably encouraged him. For the most part, motives, even consequences, are vague. Jacob died in 1624—some say in Virginia, others back in London. What followers he attracted in his short stay in the colony fell away after his death, as did "Jacobopolis," if there ever really was such a place.[11]

In his six years at Southwark, before venturing to Virginia, Henry Jacob had managed to keep his congregation of "semi-separatists" out of trouble. This was not true of his successor, John Lathrop. From 1628 to 1633 William Laud was Bishop of London, and dissenters took a beating—one of the reasons for the heavy migration at that time to Massachusetts. Laud's people cracked down on conventicles. One of their many attacks occurred in 1632, when they broke up a meeting of Separatists at Blackfriars, seizing and imprisoning John Lathrop and his listeners, who included Sara Jacob, widow of the late Henry, and a Frenchman's wife, Abigail Delamar, described as a "deepe Familist & Brownist." Laud had them all up before the Court of High Commission in no time, where the Bishop himself presided. By what authority did Lathrop preach and keep the conventicle? Before the minister could muster an answer, Laud went after him again and brought to bear in his inquisition an accumulation of prejudices typical of the most severe critics of dissent and enthusiasm. "How manie woemen sate cross legged upon ye bedd, whilest you sate on one side & preached & prayed most devoutlie?" Lathrop managed, before the next question, openly to respond: "I keep noe such evill companie, they were not such woemen." How and by whom are you qualified; where are your orders? Laud persisted. Lathrop, who repeatedly was described as a "man of learning," although of "meek and quiet spirit," was ready for this one. In a statement which epitomized the presumption, the arrogance, yet paradoxically the hu-

mility, even dignity of the dissenter, perhaps enthusiast, Lathrop faced
Bishop Laud and answered simply, "I am a Minister of the Gospell of
Christ, and ye Lord hath qualified me."[12]

Lathrop spent the next two years in jail. Sprung in 1634 on a promise
to leave the kingdom, he sailed off to New England with about thirty of
his flock. Aboard the same vessel bound for Massachusetts were Anne
Hutchinson and her family. Tension at sea was high, we hear, and there
were repercussions later in Boston. But Lathrop steered clear of Winthrop's colony and instead took churches successively in Scituate and
Barnstable, both Separatist towns, under the jurisdiction of Plymouth,
where he lived until his death in 1653.[13]

After Henry Jacob's departure for Virginia in 1622, his Independent
church at Southwark became prone to schism. While Lathrop lay in jail,
John Spilsbury seceded from it and formed a second which was suspiciously Anabaptist. Five years later William Kiffin followed him, but the
new church shortly split also, one half led by Praise-God Barebones and
the other by Henry Jessey. The latter group was known as "Particular
Baptist," or Baptist with a strong Calvinist bent. Hanserd Knollys, by
this time a refugee from New England, where he had never got along,
joined Jessey in the early 1640s and then soon left to organize his own
Baptist congregation. By this means, a hiving out from the Separatists,
Baptist churches multiplied, encouraged, of course, by the heady religious
turmoil of the times.[14]

"Further Light" and Prophesying

That part of the Virginia colony which the Pilgrim Fathers sailed to in
1620 was a good deal farther north than the Virginia we know today.
Somewhere between Chesapeake Bay and the Hudson River, supposedly,
they planned what the Virginia Company called a "particular plantation," a settlement under the jurisdiction of, but apart from, the colony
itself. Inexplicably they touched first at the tip of Cape Cod and then
came to rest across the bay at what is now Plymouth, outside Virginia
and therefore free of its control.[15]

Plymouth Plantation was a Separatist community, although it dis-
claimed the name Brownist and tried hard to shake it. That it was a
colony of enthusiasts is something else again. Still, the Plymouth people
should be thought of as a sturdy segment out of the radical dissenting
tradition which sectarians had boldly nurtured in the late sixteenth and
early seventeenth centuries, and because of this they contained within
their religious ideas and forms of worship a degree of enthusiasm which
a number of dissenters shared. Several radical characteristics stemmed

from this tradition, and Separatists in Plymouth brought some of them to the New World in 1620.[16]

To Anglicans, but also Presbyterians, the most conservative of English Puritans, Christian truth was pretty much fixed. Religious ideas, organization, and custom were for the most part fairly rigid, and room to maneuver, to develop spiritual truths, was limited. Not so for the Separatists and several other sects in the first half of the seventeenth century. Independents stood somewhere in between, tied to the Word of God, as supposedly they all were, but sharing some of the less rigid habits of the sectarians. Separatists and other radical Puritans taught a different interpretation of God's ways with his people. Religious truth was not finite, not fixed or locked into the Bible for all time as establishments claimed. God's truths in the Scripture were universal, but they were not complete, and from them new truths were discoverable with God's help, for religious truths were progressive, successive, and they begged for an "experimental spirit," in A. J. P. Woodhouse's phrase, to unfold them. Radical dissenters, Separatists among them, welcomed the opportunity and acted upon it.[17]

"I am very confident the Lord hath more Truth yet to break forth out of His Holy Word," John Robinson preached to the Separatist Pilgrims departing from Leyden to America. And he charged them not to limit themselves in the New World to what they had learned from him. If God should reveal new truths by other means, he said, be as ready to receive them as you have truths from me. The trouble with the Reformed churches today, he went on, is that they have gone no farther than Luther and Calvin took them. Lutherans refuse to accept what God revealed to Calvin, and even Calvinists "stick fast where they were left by that great Man of God who yet saw not all things." Despite the fact that these church fathers were "precious shining lights" in their time, God had "not revealed His whole will to them." Were they alive today, Robinson told his departing Pilgrims, "they would be as ready and willing to embrace further light, as that they had received." And so it was with the Leyden Separatists, whom Robinson charged to receive whatever truth or light God should make known to them, being careful, of course, to weigh and compare it with other Scripture truths before accepting it. After all, he sensibly warned, the Christian world had barely emerged from anti-Christian darkness, and it was not likely that "perfection of Knowledge should break forth at once." It is clear that Robinson did not expect the Pilgrim Fathers in the American wilderness to be bombarded with a wealth of new and startling revelations. Still, true to the dissenting tradition, he taught them there was more to come. Christians should be ready to receive it, and Robinson wanted to be sure his Leyden Separatists were ready to receive it in the New World, where, he seemed to suggest, it might come more easily.[18]

John Goodwin of Coleman Street, London, as independent as they come and later a militant supporter of the Civil War, ran the gamut of dissent. In 1642 he carried some of John Robinson's ideas about "further light" to more radical conclusions. Because a religious idea was not accepted by the establishments did not mean that it was false, just as the fact that America was only recently discovered did not mean it had not been there for some time—say, as long as Asia, Africa, or Europe, a striking parallel which reveals something about the radical mind and its symbolic use of the New World. To cry down as error everything which is not taught or generally received was to "quench proceedings" toward further truth and was an indictment of "growth in the *Lord Jesus Christ*," and "growth in grace also." Truth was evolutionary, and the true Christian, as John Goodwin understood him, was ready to run it down when and wherever possible.[19]

How did simple Separatists and radical Puritans avail themselves of this experimental discovery of religious truths? Well, they did it democratically through what they called "prophesying," when church services were thrown open to the membership for discussion, the purpose being to lay bare the truth as it was determined by good Christians freely discussing it, guided all the while by the Holy Spirit. There was a risk, to be sure, for open meetings might be abused and false testimony promulgated; but Separatists took that risk, confident that liberty to talk over what they found in their hearts was a way to discover new truths from the Bible and to improve upon the old while enhancing their lives in grace and holiness.[20]

Lay prophesying was lockstep with the idea of "further light." One fed upon the other. *Prophesy* and *prophesying* are tricky words, and we ought to be sure we know what they meant at the time. Then as now, to prophesy was to foretell, to see into the future and describe what was unknown to others. In this sense the meaning was tied to the duties of prophets. But the words had an everyday, and no less spiritual meaning, one peculiar to evangelical religion. *Prophesying* meant to interpret and expound upon Scripture, to discuss and explain to others the Word of God, the divine mysteries, from experience with divine prompting, even inspiration, and usually at public meetings and services. During Elizabeth's early years prophesying was pretty much monopolized by ministers of Puritan tendency who met frequently to discuss theology and Scripture; but as the movement strengthened, church members with recognized "gifts" spoke up and increasingly participated. It became acceptable practice among many Puritans, chiefly the radical sects, and Separatists in particular received a good deal of new light and satisfaction from it. With biblical evidence in hand (1 Corinthians 14) John Robinson encouraged prophesying, and in defending Separatism in 1610 he specifically advocated it "for edification, exhortation, and comfort," although he questioned its appropriateness for women, except in extraordinary cases of direct revelation. A few years later Henry Jacob founded the Independent congregation at Southwark in 1616. A number of Separatists' practices rubbed off on the group which covenanted with him there, including the right of *any* church member to prophesy—except women. By the time John Goodwin took over Saint Stephen's from the New England–bound John Davenport, he too was a firm advocate of prophesying and, like John Robinson, warmly promoted it among his Coleman Street dissenters.[21]

But what of ordinary people in their congregations—church members, that is, believers, certainly, but common and uneducated people? What did they have to offer, especially in the presence of ministers and elders and the better sort? The answer, and a radical one, was that common and illiterate people frequently had more to offer than those above them, for God often planted in them insights to truth which he withheld from their betters. To exclude the "commonalty," warned Robinson, would be to divide God's people and undermine charity. What is more, it would extinguish the familiarity and good will between ministers and parishioners so necessary for the loving worship of God. To Hanserd Knollys, a dissenter among dissenters briefly in New England, then a Particular Baptist in London, only through ordinary people, the helpless and the poor, who were rich in grace, would the great changes, already begun in England, continue. Strongly defending prophesying, and for women too, Knollys went on and on about the virtues of the "contemptible," the "vulgar," and the "common people," through whom Jesus first spoke.[22]

According to John Goodwin, God deliberately sought out with "sweet consistence" the weak and those of little esteem, to whom he discovered and revealed himself, often holding back his truths from the "pillars" of the church. Goodwin approved of Zwingli's conclusion that what the "most abject and despicable" had to say in church ought to be listened to, examined, and closely considered, for, said one of Goodwin's contemporaries, *"they are not alwaies the learnedst men, that find out the greatest mysteries."* Separatists played down the ministry and listened to themselves, more so than did their fellow Puritans in England and later Plymouth's neighbors in New World Boston. Besides being spiritual nurture, then, prophesying was proletarian and fitted well into the radical ideologies of early seventeenth-century sectarians. Out of the mouths of ordinary people came words and ideas the whole world would do well to listen to—a very tolerant attitude to say the least, and a radical throw-back to the primitive church of Corinth.[23]

Not so tolerant were Anglicans and Presbyterians, who abhorred such liberties and called them enthusiasm. They linked prophesying and the blurring of clergy and laity with the Anabaptists and their wicked practices, and traced such goings on back to 1535, when two shiploads of these heretics fled Holland for England. It was they who let cobblers and felt makers preach, and mere women, too, whom Saint Paul had forbidden to speak in church, even to ask questions. It was they who met at night, they said, men and women together, sometimes stark naked, who promoted spiritual marriages and advocated a community of wives and goods; and now this dangerous foolishness had caught on and was spreading throughout the land. Ephraim Pagitt had no patience with the prophesying of "mad Prophets," a wild custom of "fanatick *Brownists,*" he said. Dragged up from the "mechanick trades," they publicly pretended to "open and shut heaven" itself. One would do as well to visit Bedlam, where madmen prated as wisely. And the confusion and contradictions they preached themselves into were notorious and sufficient to overthrow the whole idea of separation, according to several of their own ministers, who for some time now had had trouble keeping up with the prophe-siers.[24]

The Independents, with whom the Separatists had more in common, deplored the fanaticism and anti-intellectualism of the sectaries. Still, they were more flexible than the Anglicans and Presbyterians and looked more kindly on prophesying, at least at first, although they tended to keep it under wraps. Near the end of the century, when William Penn looked back upon religion in England since the Reformation, it was prophesying among the early Puritans that he admired most. Anyone could pray or speak in their meetings, wrote Penn, no matter how "low and mechanical." But unfortunately they failed to keep this liberty, and after they got a taste of "worldly empire" and the "favor of princes," they gave it up. Leave it to a Quaker to appreciate prophesying, for it was one of the customs which Quakers salvaged from radical Puritans lock, stock, and barrel, and developed as the heart of their worship. John Robinson and his followers openly encouraged both prophesying and ordinary people's roles in it. Through such practices they believed they came closer to the truths of God than their contemporaries. All the same, they suffered the charge of fanaticism, and some fled to Holland and then to the New World to begin again and escape the scorn and contempt of their enemies.[25]

It was this idea of "further light," of an evolving, progressive truth, which John Milton latched onto, enlarged upon, and defended in *Ar-*

eopagitica, published in 1644. Amidst the excitement of civil war Milton
saw God's hand in the greening of England, in decreeing "some new and
great period" for Englishmen affecting both Church and State. What
Robinson and Goodwin taught for the benefit of their flocks in the search
for a knowledge of God, Milton expanded to include a whole nation
whose civil war would reform the Reformation itself, and several other
things besides. Milton's civil war was a far-reaching, formidable undertaking, not confined to reordering the Church alone. Unfrocking a priest
or "unmitring" a bishop was only makeshift in the grand scheme of
building a "happy Nation" if other institutions as vital as the Church,
"both economicall and politicall," were not scrutinized also and reformed. Don't inhibit the truth, he warned Parliament in his plea for
freedom of the press. Expect and accept that "where there is much desire
to learn, there of necessity will be much arguing, much writing, many
opinions; for opinion in good men is but knowledge in the making."
Faith and knowledge throve on exercise, wrote Milton. Truth in Scripture
was a "streaming fountain," but "if her waters flow not in a perpetuall
progression, they sick'n in a muddy pool of conformity and tradition."[26]

"Perpetuall progression" was an on-going revelation of truth through
preaching and prophesying and exposure to the Holy Spirit, according
to Robinson and Goodwin. It was all these, argued Milton, but was
enhanced by a free exchange through an unlicensed press, by which all
men in the explosive era of the Civil War might read, write, print, and
discuss ideas no matter how unpopular they were with those who would
limit men's minds to the accepted truths of the past. By expanding and
liberalizing the pursuit of knowledge and understanding, Milton out-
distanced the Leyden Separatists and Plymouth Pilgrims; but both he and
they could look back to a dissenting tradition for the origin of a radical
reform which opened inquiry, encouraged participation, and tolerated
disagreement as a means of discovering "further light."

The dissenting tradition of which Separatists were a part was a radical
tradition. It defied set beliefs of the religious establishments and looked
upon the heart of religion as an evolutionary unfolding of progressive
truths which God discovered to them and which they shared with each
other. It was democratic, tolerant, and free, and in the seventeenth century
it was revolutionary.

Prophesying at Plymouth and Boston

Prophesying was prominent among the traditions the Leyden Separatists
brought with them. Plymouth people did not talk much about the custom,
but it obtained in the early years, fading eventually as the century wore

on and attitudes and conditions at Plymouth changed. It may be that it was not talked about because it was a common occurrence. Plymouth's leaders defended it when it was attacked and usually added that it was necessary anyway, for they frequently lacked ministers in the early years. John Winthrop described prophesying at Plymouth in 1632, when he and Boston's minister, John Wilson, traveled there on a friendly visit and worshipped with the people. Wrote Winthrop:

> On the Lord's day there was a sacrament, which they did partake in; and, in the afternoon, Mr. Roger Williams (according to their custom) propounded a question, to which the pastor, Mr. Smith, spake briefly: then Mr. Williams prophesied; and after the governor of Plymouth spake to the question; after him the elder; then some two or three more of the congregation. Then the elder desired the governor of Massachusetts and Mr. Wilson to speak to it, which they did. When this was ended, the deacon, Mr. Fuller, put the congregation in mind of their duty of contribution; whereupon the governor and all the rest went down to the deacon's seat, and put into the box, and then returned.[27]

Winthrop tells us only half the story. We have to wait until Cotton Mather's time before we get the rest of it. Roger Williams was a rigid Separatist, and the question he proposed was typical of his rigidity: whether an unregenerate man could be called "Goodman" by his neighbors. Both Williams and Pastor Ralph Smith insisted that the practice was unlawful, and they had worried the people of Plymouth about it for some time. Williams, who carried his Separatism sometimes to absurd lengths, spent two years at Plymouth between his residences at Salem, and it seems he was as reluctant to dub a sinner "Goodman" as he was to let him swear an oath.[28] In 1632 Ralph Smith, also a stubborn Separatist, had been minister at Plymouth for three years and would stay another four, but his career there was ineffective, and he easily gave over to stronger men like Williams and also John Norton, who preached in his place most of the winter of 1635 but refused a call to remain. Elder William Brewster had been right-hand man to Governor William Bradford since the start of things, and owing to his able leadership and "aptness to teach" was in many ways minister except in name, despite the intermittent presence of qualified clergymen. On this particular day in October 1632, John Winthrop came down hard on the liberal side against Williams and Smith and encouraged the Plymouth people to continue the use of "Goodman" in their goings and comings with one another. It was a "Civil Custom" in England for drawing juries together, he told them, and it was a pity to make such a stir in Plymouth about a harmless pleasantry "so innocently introduced."[29]

The issue is not as important as the means by which it was resolved, which was a splendid example of prophesying in the dissenting tradition. All told, Williams spoke twice, followed by the minister, Governor Bradford, Elder Brewster, and then "some two or three more of the congregation." John Winthrop and John Wilson added their bits when invited. The Pilgrim Fathers approved of the practice, in fact encouraged it, and were willing that prominent visitors participate.[30]

Winthrop described prophesying at Plymouth as "their custom." His remark seems to point out that it was more prevalent there than in Boston, although as a Puritan Independent he was familiar with it and prophesied himself occasionally in the early years of the Bay Colony's history. (*A Modell of Christian Charity* is perhaps one of the best-known lay sermons ever preached in America or, more correctly, on the high seas.) Prophesying had been Plymouth's custom since 1620 and earlier in Holland, but it was often doubly necessary owing to frequent lack of ministers. Gifted laymen such as William Brewster and other members of the congregation continued the Separatists' tradition whether there was a minister or not. Elder Brewster was particularly successful, often teaching twice each Sabbath, "both powerfully and profitably," and, according to Bradford, "many were brought to God by his ministry."[31] News of the practice blew back to England and contributed to the bitter criticism Separatists had suffered long since for what Anglican and conservative dissenters, many of them Puritans, called their blasphemy, heresy, and enthusiasm.

One of the first to broadcast Plymouth's primitive church customs in print was Thomas Morton. He was hardly an unbiased historian of New England. The people there twice had sent him packing, owing to his profligate life among the Indian squaws at Merry Mount and his selling firearms to their braves, who used them tellingly against good Christians. Every cow keeper in Plymouth, wrote Morton, had complete freedom to "exercise his guifts" at public worship as long as he spoke extemporaneously. They were all public preachers, Morton went on, and among them were some women who used their gifts at home in the company of other women, repeating and exhorting at length what they had learned on the Sabbath—which, if true, makes Anne Hutchinson's weekly meetings in Boston not so unusual and links her to the tradition of radical dissent which was damned as enthusiasm by a good many enemies.[32]

News of Plymouth's extravagances reached high places. Dissenting settlements in New England were thorns in the side of Archbishop Laud, who was elevated to Canterbury in 1633, and then shortly as Charles

I's chief minister pushed for uniformity in the Church and authoritarian policies over realm and colonies. When Plymouth's agent, Edward Winslow, waved a petition about in London which, if heard and granted, might have upset Laud's plans for handling New England's relations with her neighbors, the Archbishop had him thrown into Fleet Street Prison, accused not of interfering with his Lordship's schemes but, on Thomas Morton's promptings, of boldly preaching at Plymouth and marrying colonists as if he were a minister. Winslow's defense pointed out that without a minister it was either prophesying or no preaching at all. He also took pains to inform the Archbishop that according to his people marriage was a civil ceremony, and nowhere in the Bible was it tied to the ministry. What is more, he had been married himself by a magistrate in Holland, where Dutchmen and other Reformed societies in Europe had been doing the same for some time—and again there had been no ministers at Plymouth for several years at a stretch. Reasons of state forced Laud to drop the charges against Winslow and release him after seventeen weeks in stir; at the same time Plymouth's petition for more self-determination collapsed and was forgotten.[33]

It was easy to ridicule the primitive practices of religion at Plymouth for the entertainment of a stiff English audience, and William Rathband, an Essex Presbyterian, was good at it. At Plymouth they hold it lawful, he wrote, for "meere private persons . . . to exercise their gifts," preaching before the whole church with full authority, and all based on 1 Corinthians 14. Moreover, common people bless each other as does a minister, and before the meeting breaks up everyone present has an opportunity to speak his piece, questioning, propounding doubts and objections, and arguing for or against what has been said. What is more, reported Rathband, he had seen a sermon in print, preached at Plymouth, mind you, by a "Comber of wooll."[34] And so he had. Robert Cushman was the wool comber and one of the colony's agents; his sermon was preached on December 9, 1621, and published the next year in London. Rathband might have shocked his audience further. Cushman's texts were Romans 12:10 and 1 Corinthians 10:24: "Be affectioned to love with brotherly love," and "Let no man seeke his owne, But every man anothers wealth." To Englishmen already suspicious of Separatists and New Englanders, this suggested that Plymouth was a colony of fanatics and enthusiasts. They throve on brotherly love like the Familists; they shunned distinctions and opened their meetings to all their members high and low for prophesying like English enthusiasts and radical dissenters; and they listened to lay sermons by artisans, one of whom advocated an economic order based upon a community of property, as did the early Anabaptists. Besides, their women, silenced in church as Saint Paul and even John

Robinson had admonished, taught at home and propounded doctrine.[35] There was a fine line between prophesying and enthusiasm, between ordinary and extraordinary gifts, and dissenters were not always sure where to draw the line. Even the Pilgrim Fathers' location of it was not always fixed, while Anne Hutchinson and the antinomians ignored it.

Massachusetts Bay under John Winthrop ran hot and cold on prophesying for the first generation or so. The nonseparating Congregationalists were dissenters, to be sure, but they lacked some of the Separatists' habits and customs which characterized the old dissenting tradition. Moreover, there was never the same dearth of ministers in Boston and its surroundings as in Plymouth Colony. The incidence of prophesying in Massachusetts seemed more dependent upon circumstances than on commitment to principle and the inheritance of tradition. When John Wilson returned to England in 1631 to fetch his wife, he recommended prophesying in his absence but cautiously chose those he believed were most fit to do it: Governor Winthrop, the deputy governor, and the chief elder of the church. Winthrop, too, preached at Ipswich, where his son lived, when the church there had no minister. John Cotton's vibrant evangelical sermons in the early 1630s encouraged prophesying, which in turn encouraged conversions and confessions of faith; together they contributed to a little revival under Cotton's aegis—that is, until the disturbing outbreak of Mrs. Hutchinson's difficulties put a damper on it.[36]

The Antinomian Controversy in 1637 (to be discussed in the next chapter) was accompanied by a rash of prophesying. Prevented from expounding to the congregation by Saint Paul and the Massachusetts oligarchy, Mrs. Hutchinson prophesied at home to a growing audience until forbidden to continue. Her male followers spoke frequently, even insolently, in church and asked sharp questions of ministers, chiefly John Wilson, with whom they usually disagreed, all done with a "party spirit," but all part of the radical tradition in good dissenting fashion. With the collapse of the antinomians, prophesying pretty much collapsed, too, for a reaction to such freedom followed the outburst.[37]

Answers to English clergymen's probing questions about the reported goings on in the Boston church were cautious. Yes, wrote Richard Mather as spokesman, we think it proper for laymen to speak before the congregation, but only if they are "qualified," and then only "when occasion requires"—say, in the minister's absence. Yes, some still think it is acceptable for church members to ask questions, but ministers no longer call upon them to do so, wrote Mather. It was clear that the synod of 1637 had pretty much smothered the free exchange of ideas and the chance to pose questions after sermons because a number of people with "corrupt opinions" had sorely abused the practice. Since the departure of these factious people to Rhode Island, wrote Mather, we here in Boston may go a whole year and "not hear any man open his mouth in such kind of asking questions." John Winthrop did not conclude from the synod that the door was competely shut. Private members still might question ministers, he explained, but this ought only to be "very wisely and sparingly done," and then only with the elders' leave.[38] The English ministers pressed to know whether the Massachusetts clergy held that conversion of sinners resulted only from preaching by ministers, or whether lay people alike could effect it through the Word, as long as they were "gifted to preach." The colonial clergy's answer must have warmed the hearts of all New England's sons and daughters of the Reformation and persuaded them that as a result of the purge of antinomians, Massachusetts had not given over entirely to reaction, that the colony's Protestantism was still in part a people's religion and was not monopolized completely by those who seemed increasingly to call the turn. Said the Bay Colony clergy: to restrict the effectiveness of the Word of God in such a way as to hold that no sinner can be saved except he hear the Word from the mouth of a minister "is to limit the Spirit of the Lord where he hath not limited himself, who is free in working by whom he will and as he will."[39] A church member might well have asked, however, under what conditions such an opportunity existed.

The spark was alive, at least in principle. Still, prophesying from that time never recovered the freedom it had enjoyed before and during the antinomian revolt. Even John Cotton, whose congregation earlier had bloomed under the warmth of lay speakers, reported that it was "warily used." In 1642 he accepted prophesying by twos and threes in good Corinthian manner, but only "if the time permit," and when elders formally called upon the speakers. Limited questioning continued with Cotton's blessing, but again, "save onely for Women."[40]

The 1640s have been called Massachusetts's "Crucial Decade." There were difficulties on all sides, including the defiance of Samuel Gorton—a proper prophesier if there ever was one; Robert Child and his Remonstrance; and the spread of Anabaptists, who damned infant baptism, forced worship, and the lawfulness of war, besides denying the need for an educated clergy—all dear to Bay ministers and magistrates.[41] A synod sat on several occasions during the latter half of the decade, and along with all of these issues, and several more, it debated the practice of prophesying. Baptists were very good at speaking in other people's churches and interrupting services, just as Hanserd Knollys and Baptists like him taught in England. In reaction Ezekiel Rogers, minister at Rowley, blasted the practice as a menace to the ordinances of God and persuaded the synod to put a stop to it as official policy.[42] (For several years at Rowley "many Anabaptisticall Spirits" and "other base persons," including Samuel Sewall's grandfather, had made life wretched for Rogers.)[43] Out of this synod came the Cambridge Platform of 1648, which restricted preaching to pastors and teachers alone, silencing even the elders. The legislature then followed the synod's lead and prohibited prophesying by law, but not without some dissent, chiefly from Salem, where "certain fanatics . . . held forth" just like Quakers—"same fancies and whimsies"—before they had ever heard of George Fox or Quakerism.[44] But then, Separatists' sympathies had lingered at Salem from the very beginning, and already several Baptists resided there.

By the mid-1640s a number of ordinary Massachusetts people—tailors, shoemakers, and other "mechanicks"—had begun to "exercise their gifts" in private religious meetings here and there in the colony, where it was much appreciated among like-minded people. Not being able to express themselves freely in the colony's churches was frustrating, they said. In a couple of instances a handful of them, who were seized in Boston, confessed that one of the reasons for their defiance of the establishment was that it had suppressed prophesying. Their remedy was to become Baptists—or Anabaptists, as the colony called them—and attempt to carry on as they pleased. It was against these that the government cracked down with stiff laws lest such freedom and preaching and private meetings nurture a new Münster right there in the middle of the Bible Commonwealth.[45] Laws suppressing Baptists were really laws against prophesying.

Baptists confronted the Massachusetts oligarchy with a fundamental issue of the Reformation, an issue which probed a good deal deeper than the question of child or adult baptism. Did the Reformation free the individual to interpret Scripture for himself as the Holy Spirit directed, as the Anabaptists had argued, and the Baptists did now? Or had Protestants turned their backs on the Roman Church only to free the individual to interpret the Word of God as he was told, according to Luther, Calvin, Knox, and the rest of them? Put in this light, infant baptism seems almost a peripheral issue. The heart of the matter was whether each believer had freedom to prophesy, to act upon the Spirit within him, a volatile practice, to be sure, which occasionally got out of hand and spilled over into enthusiasm, if it were not already—which is exactly what the oligarchy feared and enacted laws to prevent.[46]

Neither John Clarke nor Roger Williams in Rhode Island ever forgave Massachusetts for turning thumbs down on prophesying. "Quench not the spirit," warned Clarke, in those whom it moves to speak; "despise not prophecyings" for them who have gathered to hear.[47] Roger Williams pushed the Separatists' custom in his attack upon a hireling ministry and claimed that, for every soul God saved through the efforts of a hired minister, countless others were delivered with the help of "Prophets & Witnesses" of "what rank soever," who have "knowledge & utterance of heavenly Mysteries." And then, as if to spite the learned Mathers and Cottons, he dragged in for praise the "despised and yet beloved" English cobbler and mechanic preacher Samuel How, an "Eminent Christian Witness & Prophet of Christ," who, without "humane Learning," but having a strong disdain for it, could run circles around all the "Rabbies" as a "Textuary of Scripture."[48] But then, Williams and Clarke were from Rhode Island, where prophesying already was carried to an art by Massachusetts's cast-offs, and shortly to perfection by a generation of Quakers.

While prophesying died out in the Bay Colony, it took a new turn at Plymouth. From Bradford's view of things, and that of the colony's leaders, few as they were, Plymouth suffered some sad, discouraging times in the 1650s. Chief among the difficulties was a decline in what old Separatists called true religion. There was plenty of activity, plenty of zeal, certainly, but of the wrong kind, said ministers and magistrates. An "epidemical disease" of sectarianism crept over the colony, prejudicing a good many people against a learned clergy. Prophesying accompanied it, and many former church members found more solace in listening to each other than to their ministers. In 1654 Plymouth church forced out John Reyner, who had been with them for almost twenty years. Other ministers were driven away by a lack of support and a contempt for their teaching. Strong leadership among the old guard declined. Elder Brewster died in 1643, and three years later Edward Winslow sailed for the last time to England as agent for Massachusetts to do battle against the likes of Samuel Gorton, Robert Child, and others in getting the ear of Parliament. When Governor Bradford, an "Irrefragable Disputant" against the Baptists, died in 1657, "religion itself had like to have died," lamented Cotton Mather when telling later the Plymouth story.[49]

In its place libertinism and a "Brownistick Spirit" prevailed, even strong talk about liberty of conscience, and prophesying discouraged the few clergymen who remained. When the Quakers struck in 1656, some of the less determined people were attracted to their errors; others gave up hope that enthusiasts ("Energumens," Cotton Mather called them) could ever be overcome. The election of Thomas Prence as governor and the tough laws he persuaded the legislature to enact strengthened the government's hand for a time; but like it or not, Baptists and Quakers were there to stay, and prophesying continued among them, if not those who had first brought it to Plymouth.[50]

Critics in England believed what they wanted to believe about New England, and it fitted their prejudices to conclude that all Separatists there were really fanatics. But ironically, experience at Plymouth was more sobering than exhilarating among original settlers, chiefly for those who were responsible for the religious purpose and political safety of the tiny colony. Separation, asylum, independence, "further light"—these were the Pilgrims' goals in the New World. But as time wore on Plymouth people found a wilderness and Indians and a grave need to be practical. Besides, Massachusetts, which dwarfed Plymouth from the start, was apprehensive lest religious experiment and discovery in the Old Colony lead to enthusiasm and heresy and spread infection to the Bible Commonwealth. The very littleness and weakness of Plymouth subjected it to pressure from its stronger and more prestigious neighbor; to "trot after the Bay horse" became not only a necessity but a humiliating commonplace in the smaller colony's language.[51]

William Bradford epitomized the shift from spiritual adventure to a safe orthodoxy. In his *History*, wrote William Haller, Bradford carried on "less and less like a Puritan preacher and more and more like the author of *Robinson Crusoe*." The "exaltation, the imagism, the mysticism" faded as the governor became increasingly occupied "with the practical problems of making a life for himself and his people, saints and sinners alike."[52] By the middle of the century Plymouth Separatists had turned their backs on the experimental practices of radical dissent. In doing so they became more like Puritans of the Bay Colony and really did "trot after the Bay horse." The more imaginative—those who continued to honor prophesying and a search for "further light"—looked outside New England orthodoxy and found what they needed among Baptists and Quakers, whose enthusiasm continued to spread.

Several generations later Thomas Prince of Boston tried to explain the conservative trend among the Separatists and concluded that the change had occurred because of an increasing awareness in the people at Plymouth that radical practices like prophesying were "peculiary accommodate to the age of Inspiration . . . which they never pretended to." By the time Prince picked up the Plymouth story this may very well have been the accepted explanation. But for the first generation the search for new truths played a vital role in their spiritual lives. Lay prophesying as part of this search was an established practice, indeed "their custom," as John Winthrop put it. "Further light" through prophesying by ordinary people was a legacy from the radical dissenting tradition which John Robinson had taught at Leyden, and it was grounded in the simple practices of the primitive church. Besides being popular with radical Puritans, it was a recurring characteristic among enthusiasts before and after the Plymouth episode, and it tells us something about how the Pilgrim Fathers regarded their God and themselves and the workings of the Holy Spirit in the New World.[53]

$\approx \sim 4 \sim \approx$

Anne Hutchinson
and the Naked Christ

SCRATCH an intense religious belief and you discover tensions, if you have not been aware of them already. Puritanism, of course, was no exception. There has been a good deal written about the struggle within the Puritan group, even within individual Puritans, to keep a balance between a driving thirst for the Holy Spirit and a rational and responsible regard for the role of Scripture and the law. Not all Puritans mastered the balance, which sometimes appeared finely drawn. On one side was the trap of enthusiasm, where the antinomian basked in his revelations and freedom from restraint and ignored the compulsion of Bible, sin, and church ordinances. Opposite, the Arminian reduced religion to rules and morality and set up the law as his host. Ideally, the good Puritan walked the "true middle way of the Gospel between the Legalist on the one hand, and the Antinomian (or loose Gospeller) on the other." Somehow he had to preserve a balance between the sovereignty of God and man's responsiblilty, the ecstasy of grace and the experience of everyday effort. "The way lyes very narrow," wrote Samuel Willard, between Arminian moralism and antinomian libertinism.[1]

It was not an easy task. Many Englishmen in Old England, as we have seen, fell into distortions, and, given the variety and strength of emphases in Puritanism before the Civil War, it is not surprising that the venture-some few who came to New England brought some of these varieties and emphases with them. God may have "sifted a whole Nation that he might send choice Grain over into this Wilderness," yet actually the choice grain included a few tares, some of whom were enthusiasts who made Massachusetts their first, if not their last, stop in the New World. This was true also of the clergymen who threw in their lot with John Winthrop's group of the 1630s. David D. Hall has pointed out that these ministers ranged from the likes of James Noyes, who soon fell out with Congregationalism altogether, to Hanserd Knollys, suspiciously tainted with Anabaptism, whose career before, during, and after his New England sojourn touched only the fringe of orthodoxy.[2] Stuffy John Wilson of Boston's first church satisfied the conservative middle, but what about John Lathrop, who only passed through Boston on his way to two successive churches in Plymouth Colony? There he had plenty of time to reflect upon his Brownist experiences in London, where, as successor to Independent Henry Jacob, he had spent a year or two in jail for holding "private conventicles" with women who "sate cross legged upon ye bedd" opposite him, or so claimed William Laud, then Bishop of London.[3]

Puritans were a diverse lot. Sometimes the diversity emerged in a single individual, which, I suppose, is only another way of explaining some of the basic tensions which were part and parcel of the Puritan mind—and heart. Thomas Shepard, who held together the church in Cambridge, Massachusetts, during the antinomian crisis, had been sorely tempted, while still in England, by the Grindletonians of Yorkshire, a group of perfectionists whose warm doctrines smacked of the very enthusiasm Shepard worked hard to suppress in Boston. Maybe his erstwhile sympathy for Familists had something to do with his sharp treatment of the Boston enthusiasts, since he knew better than most what dangers lay ahead. It might explain, too, his argument that although he and ministers like him offered Christ freely, and preached that the "riches of the mercy of God" were free, they pressed home terror and the law at the same time, in order to "wound the hart of sinners," who, Shepard claimed, "must first flee before they get into the city of refuge."[4] Thomas Hooker came to Boston all the way from Hartford to help John Winthrop and John Wilson defuse the antinomian threat; yet in England he had a reputation for zealousness which included direct revelation, an extremism contrary to the ordered Congregationalism he taught in the land of steady habit. "Sym . . . let itt be hott," he once advised a friend, Simon Ash, who stepped into an English pulpit to preach before him.[5] Nathaniel Ward was probably as orthodox and stodgy a Puritan as New England could boast, but his brother Samuel of Ipswich, Suffolk, in England, demonstrated a warmth and zeal in his sermons which came very close to breaching the barriers which confined his passion. In *A Coale from the Altar, to Kindle the Holy Fire of Zeale,* only at the last minute did he admit a temporizing need of Scripture to prevent his zealousness from exploding into enthusiasm. And it was the same Samuel Ward who helped pack ships at Ipswich with "such swarms" of good Puritans that Archbishop Laud's Commissary feared the migration to Massachusetts would decrease the "King's people" in Suffolk while filling New England with the Church's enemies and overthrowing trade. What is more, it was

Samuel Ward, one of the "breeders of these persons," said the Commissary, who had "caused this giddeness" in the first place, and the whole business ought to be stopped.[6]

Colonization offered release from several of these tensions. Escape from episcopacy into the wilderness presented a broad landscape on which to work out solutions without pressure from above, or so it seemed. To some, no doubt, refuge in America presented opportunities for change, the need for which was only partly recognized in England. Given the New World and a release from the hierarchy, it was remarkable, Robert Baillie of Glasgow later argued, that there were not "greater extravagancies" than what actually occurred in the early years of settlement, and he was no friend to Congregationalism.[7] No doubt a number of Englishmen were surprised how decorous the first few years were when common belief was that zealous dissenters chose a New World in order to indulge their passions and pleasures at will. A broadside called "The Summons to Newe England" was a reminder to Englishmen that strong dissent, if not actual enthusiasm, was probably immoral. The ballad must have embarrassed every man, woman, and child who found a home in Boston in the 1630s:

> Loe in this Church all shall be free
> To enjoy their Christian liberty;
> All things made common, t'voide strife,
> Each man may take another's wife,
> And keep a handmaid too, if need,
> To multiply, increase, and breed.
> Then is not this Foundation sure,
> To build a Church unspotted, pure?[8]

Migration to New England may have relaxed some tensions. But probably it aggravated others and even helped settlers to discover not only new ones but new dimensions of some they had brought with them. In the 1630s this last seems particularly applicable to the tenuous balance Massachusetts attempted to maintain between the Word and the Spirit, between legalism and enthusiasm.[9]

John Cotton—Trojan Horse

John Cotton migrated to Massachusetts in 1633. Before coming to New England he had won a splendid reputation as Vicar of Saint Botolph's in Boston, Lincolnshire. Strongly Calvinist, he fought Arminianism and preached a doctrine based on absolute grace, for which a good life was only partly material. Moreover, he laced this principle with the idea of conditional reprobation, which meant that men and women were damned not only because of Adam's fall but also because they tended to sin during their lifetime. Punishment was conditional on this misbehavior, which God had decreed anyway in his foreknowledge of it. Cotton's reputation did not suffer, however, for all this straight talk. He was a popular preacher, and his church remained full. Among his listeners on occasion was Anne Hutchinson, who journeyed to Boston from her home at Alford, also in Lincolnshire. She was wholly devoted to him and his doctrine, particularly his lofty interpretation of grace and his insistence on the indwelling of Christ's Spirit in those God elected.

John Cotton's theology helped to make up the diversity within the Puritanism which English colonists brought to Massachusetts. If Puritanism ideally claimed the uncomfortable position midway between antinomianism and Arminianism, then Cotton's beliefs led him out of the mainstream, particularly after arriving in Massachusetts. Once there, his Calvinism stiffened beyond that of most of his generation, for Cotton increasingly emphasized the helplessness of man before God's gift of conversion. While a good many Puritans in both Old and New England believed sinners were obligated through some kind of preparation to condition themselves for the planting of grace, Cotton taught a passiveness on man's part, magnifying God's initiative in the infusion. Christ entered more easily a prepared heart, Cotton's contemporaries preached; but Cotton divorced man's effort from the process of salvation and scorned the steps the sinner might take toward it. Even faith itself, which the orthodox agreed might emerge gradually as a by-product of human effort, Cotton disdained and relegated to good works. For faith and a good life were meaningless, taught Cotton, before the Spirit descended and took possession, before the fact of justification. Good works and a dutiful life meant little, least of all before grace. Even afterwards, contrary to what most Puritans believed, they were not, Cotton argued, a primary sign of sainthood, but only one of several, and not altogether trustworthy. Therefore, to relate good works to the grace of God was hypocrisy, besides being deceptive, leading a false saint to parade as the real thing.

Cotton's contemporaries had made God somewhat easier to live with when they admitted man's role—even if small—in the process of conversion. To be sure, God chose whom he would, but, as Perry Miller has told us, he was more likely to choose those whose hearts were prepared, who cultivated the means the church and clergy afforded them. Dangerous, said Cotton. There were no handles to God or Christ—neither good works nor pretended faith nor duties and graces, for none had meaning before the Spirit engulfed the soul of man and assured him of salvation. Cotton taught a loving Christ, but he was not to be possessed by fraudulent or superficial means.[10]

The above is stated baldly. It lacks the subtleties and nuances with which Cotton surrounded his theology in sermons and letters and, on a pertinent point, in his dialogues with Thomas Shepard, Peter Bulkeley, and the Massachusetts elders when the antinomian threat first emerged in the church of Boston. But Cotton held tight to the principle that a good life was no indication of saving grace. "Doth any good Christian," Cotton asked the elders, "take as much comfort from his faith, or from his hope, or from his love, or from his hungering and thirsting after Christ, as he doth from (the object of all these) Christ him self? Can any man take as much comfort in thirsting after the water of life as in drinking of it?"[11]

A good life meant little or nothing, then, respecting union with Christ. But Cotton played down good works after conversion, too, which must have been very upsetting to Boston's ministers. If one enjoyed the riches of grace in God and Christ, then one's belief in a converted state should remain unshaken "notwithstanding grievous sin." For, as Cotton explained, "justification and the faith of it doth not stand upon his good works, so neither doth it fall or fail upon his evil works." Although Cotton modified the statement slightly by pointing out that if the stronger the faith, the purer the holiness, and hence the weaker the corruption, the reverse was also true. To Mrs. Hutchinson and her followers, already breathing the fresh air of the New World—the Scot Robert Baillie claimed that the "free aire of a new world" had a good deal to do with the Hutchinsonian outburst—Cotton's teaching could be an invitation to antinomianism. Once assured of salvation, the law, duties, graces, ordinances, the lot, tended to become more courtesy than required.[12]

Cotton's arrival in Massachusetts, where he assisted John Wilson in Boston's church, was a feather in the cap of the struggling colony, for he was widely known for his theology and learning, his successful preaching and teaching. But Cotton's doctrine was strong dosage for a wilderness society straining to make good its promise, which Cotton himself earlier had helped to articulate.[13] For a couple of years Boston felt a spiritual upsurge owing chiefly to Cotton's presence and instruction. The release from tension and a liberty to prophesy—"tongues untied from the Prelates Injunctions," wrote Edward Johnson—along with Cotton's spiritual intensity, produced a kind of revival, a flow of conversions and new admissions to church membership. But like most revivals it soon dissipated, leaving a deflated state of mind and heart which in turn provoked dissatisfaction with churches and ministers, except with John Cotton. He continued to preach his version of distilled Spirit based on absolute grace and the helplessness of man, while denying that self-made faith and a good life were signs of salvation. It was heady stuff.[14]

Cotton was no enthusiast. But his potent doctrine laid itself open to the loose interpretation of others less learned and less subtle than he, and, at the same time, more demanding of assurance and of what the New World might offer them. Cotton's doctrine fell on sensitive Boston ears well conditioned to hear it. One pair belonged to Mistress Anne Hutchinson, and it was not long before the colony was in a great stir about what she and her religious friends made of it. How far Cotton was culpable in setting conditions for the outbreak of enthusiasm, and nurturing it once it began, have been issues which his contemporaries and historians then and since have attempted to resolve. That for several months during the crisis Cotton was less than acute in recognizing just what his followers were talking about led the colony's ministers to distrust his teachings, even to suspect the soundness of his doctrine. Early, Thomas Shepard identified these tendencies in Boston as Familism, "begun by Mistress Hutchinson," raised up by Henry Vane, whom the freemen "too suddenly" chose governor, and "maintained too obscurely by Mr. Cotton." The godly were grieved, wrote Shepard, "and many wretches hardened, deceiving and being deceived."[15]

A Desperate Enthusiasm

Anne Hutchinson was an enthusiast before she set foot in New England. Testimony at her trial—some of it her own—left no doubt of this, but there is no evidence that John Cotton recognized her as such until the very height of the controversy in Boston, and then for a time he was not sure. In England she had frequently heard him preach and marveled at the purity of his doctrine, which seriously affected her own beliefs. But from what one can gather, and according to her own report, she came also to a number of her conclusions by way of meditation and revelation, and from these the trouble sprang.[16]

Grindletonian Familism also played a role in molding her principles. At least so John Winthrop suggested, as have historians since then. Grindleton Chapel in Yorkshire was under the wing of Roger Brierley, who in the late 1620s won notoriety for his perfectionist teaching and Familist beliefs. Stephen Denison, a parish priest in London who lost parishioners to the Familists, catalogued and exposed for all to see the various branches of the sect, describing in some detail the Grindletonian errors. They believed that Scripture was for novices, and anyway, one ought always to try Scripture by the Spirit, not the other way around. Furthermore, to pray for forgiveness of sins after one was assured of God's love was "to offer Christ againe," which meant, no doubt, that Christ's first coming had erased the law, and so there was no sin for saints. Grindletonians were propelled not by motives but motions, said Denison, and they claimed that when God dwelt in a man, "he so fills the soule, that there is no more *sinfull* lusting." This was out-and-out antinomianism. How much of it Anne Hutchinson soaked up is anyone's guess, but at the peak of the troubles in Boston, John Winthrop and the General Court enacted laws drastically limiting immigration to newcomers with whose religious principles they agreed, lest Brierley's people invade and augment the Hutchinson party.[17]

Why did Mrs. Hutchinson come to New England? She volunteered the answer. God revealed to her, after she had undergone a long period of uncertainty, that Antichrist was not in Rome alone but right there in England in the form of clergymen, Anglican and dissenting alike, who denied in their preaching the overwhelming efficacy of the Holy Spirit and who tried to foist good works and dutiful lives upon sinners in search of grace. On top of this, God taught her to discern in whom the voice of Christ spoke, and she found it in the preaching of John Cotton and her brother-in-law, the Reverend John Wheelwright, of Bilsby in Lincolnshire, both of whom satisfied her lofty criteria as men of God. When they were "put by" or silenced, Cotton escaping to New England, God directed Mistress Hutchinson to follow him; and follow him she did with her whole family, despite the further warning that she would suffer in doing so. Wheelwright came along two years later.[18]

Several times during her trial unfriendly witnesses disclosed that they were aware of her earlier unorthodox views in England. Zechariah Symmes, who became minister at Charlestown, booked passage on the same vessel with her; he claimed she had slighted the ministers of God the one or two times he had been in her company in London. William Bartholomew, then a deputy from Ipswich, remembered her unusual curiosity about revelations as they once walked through Saint Paul's churchyard; she told him that never a "great thing" had happened to her but that it was revealed beforehand. Aboard ship, Symmes reported, Mrs. Hutchinson set up a "secret opposition" to his and John Lathrop's preaching. When Symmes took exception to the "corruptness and narrowness of her opinions," she let him know that he would hear a good deal more of that sort of thing once they got to Boston, for she had many things to say but he could not "bear them now." Mrs. Hutchinson's revelations continued during the voyage, to which William Bartholomew took offense. The gift was infectious, for her daughter reported that it had been revealed to her "that a young man in the ship should be saved, but he must walk in the ways of her mother."

Rumors of these events circulated in Boston after their arrival, but they were never really tied down until her trial. There was enough suspicion about her beliefs, however, to delay admission to church membership until John Cotton came to her aid and vouched for the soundness of her doctrine. Still, there was no doubt in a good many people's minds that Mrs. Hutchinson and her closest associates had brought these heretical ideas with them in their religious baggage.[19] "This woman had learned her skil in *England*," wrote John Winthrop in *A Short Story*, the colony's version of the affair published later in London, and carried her dangerous errors with her. Of course, testimony at her examination and trial pointed directly to the same conclusion. Other writers fell in line and parroted Winthrop with elaborations. "Certain Sectaries that were hither come," Edward Johnson called them; "fraighted with many loose, and unsound opinions," Ephraim Pagitt added, "which they durst not here [England], they there began to vent them." These were the *"Libertines, Familists, Antinomians,* and *Enthusiasts,"* chimed the Scottish Presbyterian Samuel Rutherford, probably the most ruthless of critics, "who had brought these wicked opinions out of Old England with them, where they grew under prelacie." To New Englanders who rallied around Winthrop and John Wilson in opposition to the Hutchinsonians, this was an invasion of error and enthusiasm. But it occurred to them that it was something more: a conspiracy to undermine the Bible Commonwealth.[20]

The story of Mrs. Hutchinson's activities in Boston is well known. She ingratiated herself with the community, performing many useful, mostly domestic tasks, midwifery among them. But she accompanied her household skills with guidance and advice in a variety of matters, chiefly spiritual. From this beginning she built up a following of intensely religious women and then men, frequently at meetings in her home, sometimes sixty or more present at a time, where she repeated sermons, explained doctrine, and added her own interpretations, which cast favorable light on John Cotton and John Wheelwright as the only clergymen in Massachusetts who were sealed with the Spirit, who taught a covenant of grace, and were the true voices of God.[21]

Most of Boston agreed at first that Mrs. Hutchinson did "much good in our Town." She was not only helpful and skillful as a midwife, but she discussed spiritual needs with her clients and friends and, according to John Cotton, rightfully dissuaded many from relying too much on external means and "sandy foundations," instead of a "saving Union, or Communion" with Christ. Still, her "spirituall estate" to Cotton was unclear, and even during the time of her helpful contributions to the community, he "dealt faithfully" with her about her faith, which, even he was surprised to learn, was not derived, or even strengthened, by public ministry or worship but rather by private meditations and revelation. Moreover, she clearly professed her salvation but neglected even Cotton's slight nod to good works as concomitant, according to Scripture. Lastly, Cotton admonished her for being "sharply censorious" of other people's spiritual states, a habit unbecoming God's servants, who ought to spend such time judging themselves, not others.[22]

Boston could probably have lived with Mrs. Hutchinson on these terms as long as her beliefs remained private and did not become strident. But it was not long before she "turned aside" and intensified in herself and chiefly in her many followers each of the faults John Cotton had recognized in her. Private meditation and revelation became public and broadcast. Union with the Holy Spirit occurred "without the sight of any grace, faith, holiness, or special change . . . by immediate revelation in an absolute promise." The earlier revelation about the prevalence of Antichrist she applied to the Boston clergy and accused them all but Cotton and Wheelwright of preaching a covenant of works, all the while encouraging her flock to turn their backs upon them, thus aggravating divisions which already existed. Taking their cue from Cotton's insistence that good works, even faith, were hollow signs of grace, she and the other "opinionists," as they were called, concluded, in Winthrop's words, that "no sanctification can help to evidence to us our justification." The "ground of all was assurance by immediate revelation." The whole Boston congregation, Winthrop lamented, "with the exception of four or five, closed with these opinions, or most of them." If Thomas Shepard and others preached terror and the law and tried to wound the hearts of sinners, they only convicted themselves of legalism, teaching works over grace, convincing the Hutchinsonians how far they were from an understanding of the Spirit, whose inundation freed the true believer from both law and the burden of works, even conscience. And what was more alarming, these ideas spread throughout most of Boston, sowing erroneous seeds "in the hearts of people of very good esteem," but also of "many prophane persons" who succumbed to her opinions, for, wrote Winthrop, "it was a very easie, and acceptable way to heaven, to see nothing, to have nothing, but waite for Chirst to do all."[23]

At bottom, Mrs. Hutchinson taught a "naked Christ." She and her Boston friends resisted any attempt to clothe him in respectable means, to hold out any hope for the sinner through his own efforts or anyone else's, for that matter. Faith, works, preparation—what the legalists taught—were false handles, for Christ alone did all. Cotton had told them that no Christian could take comfort from faith or love or a thirsting *after* Christ, but only *in* Christ himself. A few years later William Walwyn taught his antinomian Levellers in England that he was "not a preacher of the law but of the gospell." The law, he wrote, was given by Moses, whose minister he was not; grace and truth, however, came from Jesus Christ, whose minister he was.[24] The Hutchinsonian was overwhelmed by the same conviction, carrying it beyond John Cotton's theological subtleties, out of the range of a Wilson or a Winthrop, and into the limbo of enthusiasm. Theirs was a desperate cry, a plea for riddance of all encumbrances between the individual soul and the naked Spirit: "Here is a great stirre about graces and looking to hearts, but give me Christ, I seeke not for graces, but for Christ, I seeke not for promises, but for Christ, I seeke not for sanctification, but for Christ, tell me not of meditation and duties, but tell me of Christ."[25]

This intense desire for closing with the Spirit was the very heart of enthusiasm, and the colony's upheaval in the 1630s stemmed from its frustration. It was the basis of the Hutchinsonian appeal to anyone who would listen. It rose from the wilderness depths of enthusiasts' souls, which hungered for union with the Spirit. It cut though duties and responsibilities, the moral law, even Scripture. It was what Mrs. Hutchinson had come to the New World to cultivate, but it found the Bible Commonwealth as much a barrier to its consummation as the hierarchy, even the dissenting churches, in England. With the help of a few like-minded zealots, she enlarged her following among Boston believers, whom she persuaded that they, too, might expect more purity and less dross between themselves and the only religion which really mattered. She fought hard with a majority of the Boston congregation behind her, and she came within an eyelash of turning the direction of the colony of Massachusetts Bay.

Thomas Shepard, with his customary reticence, "found it a most uncomfortable time to live in contention." And well he might, since the Hutchinsonian challenge affected much of Massachusetts life between 1636 and 1638. It set a large number of the populace at odds with their ministers, with Mrs. Hutchinson calling the turn. It put young newcomer Henry Vane into the governor's chair, where John Winthrop was accustomed to sit. It even affected recruitment of troops for the Pequot War, since the government had appointed John Wilson chaplain of the contingent. And it divided the town of Boston into two parties, a fact which encumbered government and politics during a crucial period in the colony's relationship with Archbishop Laud and the powers that be in England. Truly, as Thomas Shepard reported, the "division in the church began to trouble the commonwealth." No wonder the orthodox party was convinced of conspiracy.[26]

John Wheelwright

Had it not been for John Wheelwright, the Antinomian Controversy might very well have turned out differently. During the troubles and several years afterwards he helped to define the issues, first by what he did and said, and later by explanation. Wheelwright, who was a graduate of Sidney-Sussex College, Cambridge, lacked the intellectual drive and spiritual appeal of John Cotton. Still, through their association in Lincolnshire, where Wheelwright had had churches at Bilsby and then Alford, neither very far from Boston, some of Cotton's religious intensity rubbed off on the younger man, whose preaching, like Cotton's, probed the indwelling Christ and ignored man's efforts toward salvation. Like Cotton, too, his reputation spread sufficiently to attract admirers who sought spiritual guidance. One of these was Hanserd Knollys of Humberstone, close by, a refugee from Henry Jacob's Independent church in London, whom God repeatedly directed to Wheelwright for spiritual sustenance. Admonished for building on good works instead of grace, Knollys pursued the Spirit with abandon. After an unhappy sojourn in New England, he returned home to become an ardent Baptist, hardly the direction Wheelwright had intended.[27]

At Bilsby, Wheelwright married Marie Storre, a distant relative of Anne Hutchinson by marriage. When she died he remarried in 1630 a closer in-law of Mistress Hutchinson and so was drawn into relationship with a family already intimate with the Holy Spirit—with John Cotton as overseer. Cotton left for New England in 1633, and the Hutchinsons followed the next year. Meantime, Archbishop Laud had silenced Wheelwright. After a couple of years of underground activities, he joined them in Boston in 1636, where Mrs. Hutchinson, and less deliberately John Cotton, were already dividing sheep from goats and preparing Boston's hearts and souls for an infusion of the Holy Spirit. Wheelwright did not fully qualify as such, but he helped enormously in whetting expectations.[28]

With Wheelwright's arrival the Hutchinsonians stepped up their campaign. When they tried to add him to Boston's church as coteacher with Cotton, John Winthrop objected, already apprehensive of Wheelwright's doctrine and suspecting a ganging up on his friend Wilson to offset his orthodoxy. Cotton politicly withdrew his support for the scheme in the interests of harmony, and Wheelwright took a church at Braintree, just south of the Boston peninsula, where a number of farmers had settled to be close to the lands assigned them.[29]

In January of 1637 the General Court ordered a day of fasting to promote harmony in the colony's churches, already creaking with dissent. Cotton preached, and then at his invitation, strongly supported by church members, Wheelwright prophesied, a primitive custom which the Massachusetts people soon laid aside but which Plymouth churches continued. Wheelwright came well prepared with a sermon in his pocket, and his prophesying turned into a notorious fast-day discourse which set the colony by the ears.[30]

Given the circumstances in Boston, it would be difficult to imagine a sermon more calculated to aggravate the schism already emerging. Wheelwright was a newcomer who by family ties, conviction, and temperament willingly fell into the Hutchinson camp, and his words, sometimes generally phrased, sometimes not, championed their cause. Besides describing grace as a closing with Christ "with whom we are made one," he took up the cudgels against a covenant of works and fashioned with strong strokes the plight of the "little flocke" of saints surrounded by the evils of Antichrist. Wheelwright's polemic was a call to arms, not carnal like those of the Fifth Monarchists but spiritual, to do battle against the "enimyes of the Lord" whom Saints must kill with the Word of God. Of course, it would cause a "combustion in the Church and comon wealth," Wheelwright warned, "but what then?" Did not Christ come to kindle the earth? The battle will be sharp, but with God on our side, one of you, he told the congregation, "shall chase a thousand"—a Biblical allusion Fifth Monarchists later exploited at their peril.[31]

Wheelwright was not prepared for the Winthrop party's reaction to his sermon. Each phrase, each figure he elaborated they related directly to the bitter struggle then going on between themselves and the Hutchinsonians. All the clergy but Cotton and Wheelwright were symbols of Antichrist, who taught a covenant of works and beleaguered the chosen few who must do battle against them. This was too much for Winthrop and his orthodox party. Given their inability to control the surge of enthusiasm by theological and ecclesiastical means or by rational argument, they turned to the civil power and cited Wheelwright for contempt and sedition as a threat to the civil peace. He was tried, convicted, and, after considerable delay in the hope he would recant, banished. Insisting that "hee delivered nothing but the truth of Christ," he claimed it was the ministers who applied his doctrine to themselves, not he. Wheelwright's attempt to appeal to the King was quashed at the very outset.[32]

It was the Hutchinsonians' turn to be outraged, and there commenced a battle of petitions and remonstrances, charges and countercharges, through the spring and summer of 1637 which only worsened the controversy. To avoid mass pressure in Boston, the General Court ordered the May election held at Newtowne, where, after many strong words and great unpleasantness over a petition in Wheelwright's behalf, Winthrop replaced Henry Vane as governor.[33] Shortly the General Court enacted legislation which threatened what civil peace remained when it drastically inhibited immigration lest Hutchinsonian supporters, supposedly Grindletonian perfectionists from Yorkshire, descend upon Boston in numbers large enough to carry the day against both government and churches. Defeated and disillusioned, Henry Vane in late summer took ship for England in plenty of time to revive his spirits and play a prominent role in the English Civil War.[34]

In the midst of the turmoil a synod met at Newtowne, and this proved to be a turning point in the controversy. Heretofore, John Cotton had never really recognized the exaggerated views of some of his congregation reported by his ministerial colleagues. When some eighty or more errors were drawn up against the Hutchinsonians for confutation, he was amazed to discover just how far apart he and they stood on a number of basic issues. As a result he joined the attack against them, and with this as a start he and the ruling elders found means to compromise their own differences in a statement of principle, an agreement which left the enthusiasts pretty much by themselves and devoid of official support.[35]

And so, with Vane's defeat for reelection and his precipitate departure, the government's successful use of sedition as a tool to suppress dissent, and then the synod's strong condemnation of the enthusiasts' extremism—with Cotton's consent—the Hutchinsonians' case bogged down. Several deputies to the General Court who continued to challenge the government's treatment of Wheelwright lost their places and were sent home. When church members persuaded a handful of prominent elders of the Boston church to condemn the Court's sentencing of Wheelwright, threatening to bring Winthrop to account for his role in it, the governor spiked their guns, pointedly telling them to keep their noses out of civil affairs. "Christ his kingdome," he informed them, "is not of this world, therefore his officers in this kingdome, cannot Juditially enq[uir]e into affairs of this world." And that ended that. So, it was off to New Hampshire for Wheelwright, where several members of the Boston church chose to follow him, and where he spent many of his remaining days.[36]

John Winthrop and Reason of State

John Winthrop and the elders wrapped up the controversy in late autumn of 1637. Authority to condemn and convict for sedition and contempt was a powerful tool in the hands of a government bent on ridding itself of enthusiasts who supposedly threatened to bring it down. Sedition and contempt were effective against John Wheelwright because the Fast-Day Sermon was fresh in the minds of his opposition. Mrs. Hutchinson's case was a little different: her offenses were less open, nonetheless more dangerous. Public exposure followed, however, and according to the orthodox party, the providence of God was responsible.

The General Court brought Mistress Hutchinson on the carpet in November 1637 after disposing of Wheelwright. The events of this momentous occasion in the life of the infant colony are well known. What needs to be brought out is the fact that her accusers, once she let down her guard respecting frequent revelations, quickly pounced on this most damning characteristic of enthusiasm and secured her banishment on the basis of it. Suspecting her since the start of the turmoil, some even earlier, the magistrates and elders found that Mrs. Hutchinson's own words convicted her. Already it was common knowledge that she believed God's direct intervention had brought her to the New World and had even warned her of the persecution she would encounter there from a ministry not sealed with his Spirit. Now in November she told them directly that she knew God would deliver her by miracle from whatever calamity they were about to thrust upon her, just as Daniel was delivered from the lions' den.[37] How did she know these things? the Court pressed. How was she certain that it was the Spirit which moved her in all her doings? Her response demonstrated the assurance of the enthusiast:

> *Mrs. H.*   How did Abraham know that it was God that bid him offer his son, being a breach of the sixth commandment?
> *Dep. Gov.*   By an immediate voice.
> *Mrs. H.*   So to me by an immediate revelation.
> *Dep. Gov.*   How! an immediate revelation.
> *Mrs. H.*   By the voice of his own spirit to my soul.[38]

That did it. The Court marveled at the providence of God, which reduced the impasse and permitted no doubt of her heresy. Like orthodox generations before and after them, the magistrates and elders held the line against direct revelation not tied to the Word. In confuting the antinomians' claims during the synod of 1637, the clergy's answer to

Error No. 40 stood out boldly: "Immediate revelation without concurrence with the word, doth not onely countenance but confirme that opinion of Enthusianisme, justly refused by all the Churches, as being contrary to the perfection of the Scriptures, and perfection of Gods wisedome therein."[39] And if the synod's refutation was not sufficient, pronouncements at the General Court which examined Mrs. Hutchinson only etched more clearly on the minds of those in authority that wild-eyed enthusiasm was the very basis of the upheaval. "Of all the revelations that ever I read of," Winthrop told the Court, "I never read the like ground laid as is for this. The Enthusiasts and Anabaptists had never the like." "I think it is a devilish delusion," chimed in Increase Nowell, one of the officials present, and the Court agreed, quickly adding that all their troubles since the controversy began came "out from this cursed fountain." Aye, Winthrop concluded, "it is the most desperate enthusiasm in the world."[40]

Now what did all this mean? Why was the enthusiasm of Mrs. Hutchinson such a threat to the Bible Commonwealth as Winthrop and the General Court insisted? Why could not a semichurch state of moderate Puritans in the expansiveness of the New World bear with a group of believers among them who differed only over the intensity of their relationship with God? John Winthrop gave his party's answers to these questions in full when he explained in *A Short Story* that Mrs. Hutchinson's opinions and practices "have been the cause of al our disturbances." In so doing he epitomized orthodoxy's age-old fear that religious fanaticism worked outside the accepted confines of theology and church polity and therefore was destructive of both. At the same time he expressed the Bay Colony's apprehension lest unbridled enthusiasm make chaos of civil order and propriety. Winthrop pronounced: "She walked by such a rule as cannot stand with the peace of any State; for such bottomlesse revelations, as either came without any word, or without the sense of the word, (which was framed to humane capacity) if they be allowed in one thing, must be admitted a rule in all things; for they being above reason and Scripture, they are not subject to controll."[41]

If these were the issues, there was no escape from the conclusion that Mrs. Hutchinson and her enthusiasts were subversives whose uncontrollable delusions struck at the very basis of the Bible Commonwealth. Already, claimed magistrates and elders, they had taught a religion based on motions of the Spirit which by-passed the Scripture, made a shambles of orthodox theology, and encouraged their adherents to ignore their ministers. They threatened the state, its peace and harmony; the allusions to the "Tragedy of *Münster*" throughout the crisis testified overwhelmingly to the fear of "suddaine irruption" upon "some revelation" whereby fanatics might turn on their enemies and tear down the commonwealth.[42] Such imagined threats actually led to the disarming of all Boston dissidents who refused to disown the petition signed earlier in Wheelwright's behalf. There would be no Münster at Boston. Chastened by the whole experience, Samuel Wilbore, one of the signers, recanted his contemptuous behavior and "unbeseming exspresyons" against authority. But why? He was no enemy to the state, he said, nor ever would be. Thomas Shepard, a true "legalist" in the Hutchinsonian gallery, claimed he understood the real antinomian catastrophe when he warned that it threatened to bring the whole state tumbling down around their heads, only to be reconstituted in the enthusiasts' image—again shades of Münster: "Would you have the State in time to degenerate into Tyranny?" he asked. "Take no care then for making Laws."[43]

According to the authority which eventually got the upper hand, the enthusiasm of the Hutchinsonians would turn society upside down. A lack of respect for ministers already had upset the ordered way of things so soberly protected by magistrates and elders. Moreover, it encouraged the "common people," said John Winthrop, to condemn the godly John Wilson, with whom they disagreed, and to teach and preach not only as if they had the right but as if they understood the issues. This was disrespect to ministerial authority and could lead only to disorder and heresy.[44] It was also a gross abuse of prophesying, which, in Winthrop's view, was already beyond control.

Bernard Bailyn has remarked that merchants "with striking uniformity" supported Mrs. Hutchinson. Emery Battis confirms this with facts and figures to demonstrate that merchants and craftsmen were more likely to join her dissent than were other colonists, and of these the wealthier were more susceptible to her appeal than the less well-to-do. Just why this was true is not altogether clear. Battis implies that the Hutchinsonians were less friendly to the "organic theory of commonwealth" and more entrepreneurial in their outlook than the magistracy, whose sympathies lay more with the needs of landed gentry. Mrs. Hutchinson's doctrine put less emphasis on harmony and cooperation through "good works" than it did on individualism and a willingness to disagree with the establishment, and this may have attracted merchants and craftsmen who were trying hard to get ahead in a new economy. But these suggestions do not make complete sense, for, even as Battis reminds us, "it would be a rash commentator . . . who would claim to know where religious motivation left off and economic began."[45] Maybe a simpler but deeper argument is one which merely stresses that an overriding drive for the freedom of Christ in the hearts of an intensely devout group of Puritans spilled over into an overriding desire to be left alone to seek their own way in all their pursuits—spiritual *and* material—and this among a people who expected more than they received from an experiment in the New World where communion with God, and maybe other necessities, proved to be as confined and regulated as they were in the Old.

The long-faced Court which confronted Mrs. Hutchinson had just as long memories about the reputation of Familists and other enthusiasts in England in the years before they migrated, and they would not let her forget it. What was her connection with the "Woman of Ely," that notorious woman preacher of the Isle of Ely in Cambridgeshire, whom Mrs. Hutchinson did "exceedingly magnifie" as one woman in a thousand? That the "Woman of Ely" was an enthusiast who preached—some said baptized—contrary to the laws of the Bible, there was no doubt— a "dayngerous Woman," full of "greevous Things and ferfull Errors"— and the Court tried hard to connect Mrs. Hutchinson with her, but without success. Her knowledge of Ely's most prominent enthusiast was all hearsay, she said; she "knew her not nor never sawe her." But Familists were sexual libertines, were they not, asked Peter Bulkeley; and did Mrs. Hutchinson "hould that foule, groce, filthye and abbominable opinion held by Familists, *of the Communitie of Weomen*"? Mrs. Hutchinson's answer was short and clear: *"I hould it not."* Although her accusers may very well have believed that at heart she championed the Family of Love, they got nowhere in attempting to entangle her with the free love which tradition told them was prevalent among sectarians and chiefly Familists.[46]

But Church and State, social structure, the economy, sexual morality— these were not the only institutions enthusiasts were suspected of subverting. What of learning, a respect for reason, the accumulation of knowledge which God directed good Christians to utilize, even Harvard College? How would these fare if enthusiasts had their way? There was evidence to suspect that the answer would not contribute to the glory of God, as the magistrates and ministers understood it, through an educated citizenry. No, there was scoffing at scholarly preaching, "rayling against learning," encouraging "both ignorant and unlettered Men and Women" to preach and teach to multitudes, who praised them for their nimble tongues. "Come along with me," said one of them to Edward Johnson,

> i'le bring you to a Woman that Preaches better Gospell than any of your black-coates that have been at the Ninneversity, a Woman of another kind of spirit, who hath had many Revelations of things to come, and for my part, saith hee, I had rather hear such a one

that speakes from the meere motion of the spirit, without any study at all, then any of your learned Scollers, although they may be fuller of Scripture (I) [ay] and admit they may speake by the helpe of the spirit, yet the other goes beyond them.[47]

Anti-intellectualism was as much identified with enthusiasm in the Boston of the 1630s as it had been in England for generations and would be during the series of revivals which later punctuated the eighteenth, nineteenth, and twentieth centuries on both sides of the Atlantic.

There was fear, too, of the spread of these wild ideas, first more widely in Boston, then by way of "itching eares" and "cunning sleights" into the surrounding countryside. Warn your ministers, Governor Winthrop charged son John, Jr., then at Salem, against admitting to their churches people who have swallowed "these newe opinions." They will dissimulate beyond belief, he cautioned, to insinuate themselves into the churches and then go to work as they have here, and with the same sad results.[48] Winthrop demonstrated at times a compassionate understanding of the difficulties confronting the colony, and in *A Short Story* he admitted that probably some of the church members then advocating "Familisticall opinions" were "indeed truely godly," deluded to be sure, but, he hoped, retrievable. The real danger of this, however, was that the next generation of New Englanders would suffer, being "trained up" in such doctrines, yet void of godliness, and in their own time, as scholars go beyond their masters, bloom as "plain Familists and Schismaticks," and this would be New England's demise.[49]

The burden of the crisis fell primarily on John Winthrop as chief magistrate. No doubt he felt it an awesome responsibility and no doubt he reacted to it as he believed a responsible magistrate should. This, as we have seen, was to quash the enthusiasts as a clear and present danger to the peace of Church and State.[50] The orderly lives of godly colonists, systematically nurtured by a godly ministry in public worship through God's Word, was what Massachusetts was all about. Colonists who scoffed at the Word and the law and luxuriated in ecstasies of the Spirit destroyed the Puritan balance of things, belittled the Scripture, and dishonored God. In addition, besides deceiving themselves in entertaining spiritual motions, they preposterously miscalculated the civil consequences of their actions—for which Winthrop was also responsible. Massachusetts banished Mrs. Hutchinson and those who would not recant, while her church excommunicated her for gross lies and several other things, and Rhode Island, like the Isle of Ely, became the New World's "Island of Errors."

Wheelwright and the Spirituall Chymists

Not until 1643 did John Wheelwright contest his banishment from the Bay Colony. In the meantime, he did a good deal of thinking—a "long and mature consideration of things," he called it—besides swallowing his pride, in view of the humiliation he had received. In that year he humbly confessed some of his mistakes and sought pardon from the General Court. He tried simply to clarify for the Massachusetts authority what precisely he thought his errors were in 1637 and to describe where he stood regarding the antinomians. A couple of years later Wheelwright was provoked into saying a good deal more about the crisis of 1637, and he argued a point of view about enthusiasm very different from that of the Hutchinsonians, the orthodox, and John Cotton. He offered an explanation all his own, illuminating a side of the controversy which has suffered from too little light.

Wheelwright told the Massachusetts authorities, through Winthrop, that the differences between him and them respecting good works as evidence of grace did not now appear as they had in 1637. For then, he admitted, he had scrutinized these differences "in the false glass of satan's temptations" and his own "distempered passions." He was unreservedly sorry for the "vehement contentions" he had raised, thus disturbing the churches, and it grieved him that the "censorious" parts of the Fast-Day Sermon and other writings had reflected dishonor upon ministers and magistrates. As far as the enthusiasts were concerned, he repented his adhering to them in their "corrupt judgment" and "errours of evil practices," none of which he had intended. Again, his "unsafe and obscure expressions" at the synod he attributed to the "buffetings of satan." For all these he craved humble pardon.[51]

Now all of this seems like knuckling under, and it was in a way, but really only to what he called his sinful conduct toward magistrates and clergy. A second letter to Governor Winthrop, thanking him for presenting the first to the General Court, revealed a much more subtle argument and to us a better insight into Wheelwright's mind and the issues. He reported to Winthrop that he would willingly go before the Court to ask its pardon, but if he did, he could not in good conscience plead guilty to all the charges against him—for instance, to "such capitall crimes, dangerous revelations, and grosse errors" laid at his door. In defending himself, he said, he must separate his own intemperate conduct, for which he was sorry, from the fanatical principles and the "many haynous offences" of the enthusiasts, from which, he insisted, "my conscience doth acquit me." Wheelwright trusted the General Court to make these distinctions, for making them himself was the only way he could bring himself to ask forgiveness.[52]

In May of the next year the Massachusetts General Court lifted the order of banishment against John Wheelwright and voted to readmit him to the commonwealth. The words of the order were revealing, for the Court based its reprieve upon the "solemne and serious acknowledgement and confession by letter, of his evill carriages and the Courts justice upon him for them"[53]—not a word about closing with Christ, a disregard for good works, the threat of Antichrist in the Bay Colony, or the probable "combustion" of the commonwealth when the saints girded their loins. It is probable that Winthrop and the General Court in 1643 had tired of theological dispute and convenant nit-picking, for the magistrates seemed to have mellowed in the intervening time. Was this true of John Wheelwright?

What he did not know was that in the years following the Antinomian Controversy, Winthrop had written a long account and sent it to London for publication. Its purposes were several but chiefly to broadcast the official colony version of the event and to offer propaganda on the side of English Independency against Anglicanism, on the one hand, and Presbyterianism, on the other, in the bitter fight for supremacy during the Civil War. Winthrop's tract would demonstrate, he hoped, that Independent Congregationalism in New England was a superior polity and could take care of itself despite attack by fanatics, successfully suppressing its enemies. *A Short Story* was something of a hodgepodge when it arrived in London in 1644, where Thomas Weld, a former Massachusetts minister and bitter opponent of Mrs. Hutchinson, took it upon himself to improve the contribution for wider appeal, writing an introduction and arranging the contents in a more effective order. When Wheelwright read the Winthrop-Weld *Short Story* he was outraged. In New England he had humiliated himself before Winthrop and the magistracy, confessed his guilt in acting contemptuously during the crisis, but he had taken great pains to distinguish himself from the enthusiasts and their wildly mistaken opinions. But here in *A Short Story* Winthrop and Weld had lumped him with Anne Hutchinson and the antinomians and published to the world an account of Massachusetts's struggle against enthusiasts which made Wheelwright not only one of them but one of the most misguided of the lot.[54]

His answer was *Mercurius Americanus,* published in London the next year. It was a penetrating explanation of the antinomian crisis in Boston, and it was a sharp refutation of *A Short Story.* It aimed directly at what Wheelwright believed was Thomas Weld's distortion of the facts, although John Winthrop came in for a few solid licks. It may be that Wheelwright was still unaware of Winthrop's chief role in *A Short Story*, for he concentrated on Weld and blamed him for the attack. It was also a defense of Wheelwright himself, and particularly against the charges of antinomianism, Libertinism, and other erroneous opinions.

What Wheelwright could not understand was why the powers that be in Massachusetts were so narrow in their conception of what they were doing in the New World. They had escaped the hands of the prelates, as all the colonists liked to phrase their coming, but having done this, why were they so *"prelaticall"* themselves in their treatment of a people who had left the bishops as well as they? Why did they refuse to permit a "freedome of spirit, and conscience which they came for"? At the very least, asked Wheelwright, why did they not hold off their suppression and graciously give these people a breathing spell to recover and collect themselves after they had so soon put persecution behind them? The newcomers came to the colony with a very good opinion of the people already settled there and the reformation they were carrying out, but in preparing themselves for the new experiment, Wheelwright explained, these newcomers too zealously focused their prayers and efforts on their new opportunity, because they expected so much from the New World—more than was spiritually or humanly possible. They elevated doctrine and discipline to so lofty a plane that the very act of sublimation left loopholes for errors which unfortunately crept in. However, these errors would never have advanced so far had it not been for the colony's vehement prosecution against them, provoking an *"Antiperistasis,"* or reactionary opposition, which soon took shape and then hardened into resistance.

Wheelwright boldly called the Massachusetts establishment to account. It did not have the good sense and largeness of view to accept wisely the imaginative expectations of these people and to recognize the opinionists "as men transported, through the fancie of practicall liberty"—which would explain why they spilled over into "Libertinisme." Had the Winthrops, the Welds, and the Wilsons recalled their own experiences when they were the objects of Anglican malice in Old England, they might have exhibited a "more moderate deportment" toward these good people rather than "fining, confining, imprisoning, disfranchizing, banishing, and as much as in [them] lay, killing." These were some of John Wheelwright's generalizations about the antinomian confrontation and its outcome after eight years in the wilderness north of Boston.[55]

But this was not all he had to say. Wheelwright devoted a good part of *Mercurius Americanus* to refuting Weld's conclusions while at the same time defending himself by explaining precisely what he had said in

1637 and what he meant despite Weld's distortions. That Wheelwright was the cause of the turmoil he denied with a good deal of evidence to show how divided Boston had been before his arrival. Far from being the *"Earthquake"* Weld had labeled it, the Fast-Day Sermon was nothing but a tremor of the spheres in the "New *Heaven*" of New England, and therefore blown up out of all proportion.[56] His listeners, he explained, already deeply divided, needed only a "beck from the Pulpit," to aggravate their "prepared *phansies*," taking this *"Idoll* of their own braines, for a *providence* of heaven" which Wheelwright "was not accessary to." As for their infatuation with a covenant of grace, he wrote, theirs was a pretended covenant only, composed of errors. The covenant he taught, although devoid of legalism, was unlike theirs, since it carried with it the *"grace of the covenant,"* and a "spirituall *prostration* of its opposites." This the enthusiasts had never understood, nor, more's the pity, had the magistrates and elders. For teaching these things, in a country supposedly renowned for its "charitie, Reformation, Christian liberty" in the "new Heaven and "new Earth," he was arraigned, imprisoned, and banished. And if this were not enough, he was defamed as a *"Heretique, Antinomian,* seditious person, what not," and all of it in print "with all possible disgrace and *diminution,"* and all for so small a matter. In his expansive mood of 1645, which enlarged on his own conceptions of the New World, Wheelwright was incapable of understading how the nursing fathers of the colony could take offense at these people for a little *"forwardnesse, freenesse,* and *irrespectivenesse* of discourse" and magnify them into *"sedition* and *contempt."* "Are a company of *Familists, Libertines,* &c. so *authentick?"*[57]

In *Mercurius Americanus* Wheelwright also got down to cases. He compassionately tried to explain away much of the enthusiasts' behavior. Like all who spoke of Mistress Hutchinson, he praised her good wit, judgment, and contributions to the community. In her spiritual life, however, her understanding had succumbed to the "power of suggestion and immediate dictates," leading to "strange fancies" and "erroneous tenents." But many of these strange notions he attributed to the problems of her pregnancy, producing—in good seventeenth-century explanation—a melancholy which the Devil took advantage of. (Enthusiasm was occasionally attributed to melancholy, a disease brought about by an imbalance of the bodily humors, which tended to promote visions and "fancies.") Her most grievous offense, however, was her pretended revelation foretelling the destruction of the Court, for which Wheelwright offered no defense. Still, his was a sympathetic picture of a deluded woman, but not an agreement with her or her principles. Like John Cotton, Wheelwright preached a theology which his pupils twisted into an unorthodoxy, and it was their undoing, even in a New Earth and a New Heaven.

Mary Dyer was as devoted to Anne Hutchinson as she was to her fancies. The monstrous result of her concurrent pregnancy Wheelwright said little about, refusing to comment, unlike her accusers, whether her egregious opinions were cause or effect of her grotesque offspring. Less serious were Wheelwright's arguments about the treatment of Sam Hutchinson, one of the tribe. Despite banishing him along with the rest to Rhode Island, the court saw fit to let him return to Boston once a month for business purposes. No doubt these visits occurred "in the waning of the Moon," Wheelwright tells us, in a rare mood of humor, "when his hotter fits (as they conceived them) were over, thinking that in some competent time, he might be perfectly cured of the *Lunacie,* which they supposed possessed him." Jane Hawkins, a midwife whom some called a witch, Wheelwright could call only a "poore silly woman." She stuck close to Mrs. Hutchinson's person, home, and instruction, and was always the first to acknowledge any new doctrine. By which means, claimed Wheelwright, she was on the receiving end of "some good victuals, insomuch that some said she followed Christ for *loaves.*"[58]

Wheelwright's attitude toward the substantial followers of Mistress Hutchinson, as it was to her, was a good deal more sober. And it is here that he speculated about the whole tragic event in a way that contributes significantly to an explanation of it. Granted he disagreed with their principles—or at least his explanation eight years after the crisis tells us so—he conceived of these people and their coming to the New World in a way wholly different from that of the Winthrops, the Wilsons, and the orthodox elders. Here are the reasons, he wrote, "which all these men might propound to themselves, for doing and saying what they did": "Alas, we must look at them as men who had left their estates, friends, pleasures of their native soyl, spirituall *Chymists,* extracting the sweetnesse of all into freedom of conscience, doubting not but they might find all in that *Elixar;* but as no *Chymist* yet got it, so they were many of them deceived; which when they surveyed, and see the result, it might trouble the weaker, and through melancholy fumes dispose them to strange fancies in Divinity."[59]

Over and above being an exquisite metaphor, bringing together religion and alchemy, not at all unusual for the time, what does Wheelwright's explanation tell us? Proving beyond doubt the diversity of Puritanism and the diversity of the pioneer Puritans who came to Massachusetts in the 1630s, there arrived in the early years a small group of intensely devout dissenters—call them zealots or enthusiasts—who believed they were on the way to extracting from the New World experience the holy presence of Christ, the philosopher's stone, which was denied to others. Unable to bring off the transmutation in Old England, they ventured to New England, believing that the liberty God led them to in the wilderness would allow them to distill and enjoy the essence of the whole. But deceived like the alchemist, who never quite transformed his base metal into gold, these "spirituall Chymists" fell short of the mystical union they sought. Like alchemists' gold, the oneness with Christ was a deception, a gradual realization of which led to disillusionment, particularly among the weaker souls, and so to a sadness which produced even stranger fancies in religion. They were enthusiasts whose appeal in Massachusetts attracted a good many who wished to be convinced that the New World held a new birth of Christ within them but outside authority. Confrontation with the Bay Colony, before they had quite proved or disproved their vision, disheartened them, and they fought back unsuccessfully against an orthodox Puritanism which in the end defeated them.

No Puritan writer save Roger Williams had expressed as strongly that differences of opinion might be accommodated in Massachusetts, and the government had banished Williams months before Wheelwright showed his hand. Early in the history of the colony the orthodoxy of Wilson and Winthrop had jelled into rigidity in opposition to dissenting points of view, let alone those of fanatics, regardless of the devoutness of their beliefs. In 1635 John Pratt apologized to the General Court for commenting that the gospel was as "dear here as in England," which appeared to him to be a great disappointment. But others, too, besides Wheelwright, looked to Massachusetts as a place where some variety of belief, at least, might be tolerated, if not welcomed. Henry Vane was one of these, and this was so before he went off the deep end into a sea of mystical abstruseness. Deeply offended by the General Court's arbitrary restriction on immigration at the height of the controversy, Vane argued that keeping out godly believers barred Christ himself. Moreover, said Vane, if the magistracy found Wheelwright's principle an affront to internal peace, then they had better be wary of the gospel itself, for it too was notorious for causing divisions, and did not Christ come with the sword?—all of which foreshadowed some of Vane's radicalism once he plunged into the English Civil War, to say nothing of Fifth Monarchy tenets of the 1650s.[60]

Despite his tussle with Roger Williams, John Cotton also contemplated differences of opinion in religious beliefs in Massachusetts, as long as they did not seriously disturb fundamentals. Could not a godly minister in New England say what he believed, and particularly should he not be free to disagree with his fellow ministers about, say, the efficacy of works, if these were honest differences? His holding out against the elders for so long—until he realized that fundamentals actually were at stake—was a prime reason for the seriousness of the antinomian crisis. Like Vane and Wheelwright, he abhorred the General Court's limitations on immigration and eventually struck out against them. What angered him most was that those refused settlement were the very people who agreed with him about Christ's Spirit enveloping the sinner before faith materialized and before good works had any meaning—differences which, from his theological perspective, did no injury to Scripture or to the Bay Colony's holy purpose. Because of the General Court's arbitrariness, Cotton came close to washing his hands of the whole affair and settling at New Haven in what became Connecticut with a group of followers, but he was dissuaded from such a drastic move in the interest of harmony in Massachusetts and among the colony's friends in England.[61]

In Cotton and Wheelwright there were gropings for an acceptance of legitimate differences of opinion which the Massachusetts orthodoxy under Winthrop refused to understand or accept. How much greater, then, was the desire for free scope of the Spirit among enthusiasts who went beyond their teachers into "unsound and unsafe doctrines." Such was the case with Cotton's congregation, as we have seen, and so it was with Wheelwright, one of whose parishioners, for instance, told him to his face that he preached "Antichristianisme," setting up Christ against Christ, and anyway, what was wrong with immediate revelations for those in tune with Jesus? Wheelwright's young scholar shortly joined Samuel Gorton's community of fanatics at Warwick in Rhode Island. Wheelwright was no antinomian, wrote Cotton, but the trouble was that his Fast-Day Sermon encouraged enthusiasts already "levened" that way. He spoke some things, said Cotton, which, had he recognized his listeners' Familism, he would never have uttered, a lesson Cotton applied to himself only at the last minute.[62]

The spiritual opportunities of the New World had looked bright to those who thought their "hunger and thirst" after Christ were stronger than the limits of an old and restrictive orthodoxy. But in Massachusetts legacies of the Old World, the law, and the Scripture were stronger yet; they either tamed the Spirit or banished the enthusiasts.

ᜒᜐ᜔ 5 ᜒᜐ᜔
New England Enthusiasts
and the English Civil War

J OHN WINTHROP and the Massachusetts authorities graciously accepted the demise and departure of the antinomians as the marvelous
work of God. A last stroke which helped dissolve the threat was the
discovery of the monstrous births from the bodies of Mistress Hutchinson
and Mary Dyer, which were equal only to their monstrous errors, and
became notorious not only throughout the colony but a "great part of
the world." These signs from heaven were blessings in disguise, for they
screwed the attention of the weaker sort to their duties and prayers.
Winthrop's hope was that the sordid results of the shameful affront to
God would open the eyes of Mrs. Hutchinson's sympathizers who remained in Boston so that "peace and truth" again might "flourish in
New England."[1]

Banishment and then settlement in Rhode Island failed to resolve the
problems of Anne Hutchinson and her friends. There was as much difference of opinion at Aquidneck as there had been in Boston, and this
led to the hatching of new delusions and "great strife and contention in
the civill estate" as well.[2] Troubles split the island colony into several
groups, according to Winthrop, with Hutchinsonians falling into "new
errors daily." Nicholas Easton sang the old song, claiming that gifts and
graces were nothing but Antichrist, while a true Christian was "united
to the essence of God." A chap named Herne turned up a good deal of
resentment when he went about the island denying that women possessed
souls. Mistress Hutchinson preached and prophesied, as did many others;
she and her people for a time discarded even the rule of magistrates,
confirming the threat to government earlier suspected by Winthrop in
Boston. God, it seemed, had given up the lot of them to delusions stronger
still than they had professed when under his responsibility.[3]

After her husband's death, Mrs. Hutchinson and her large family turned
their backs even on Rhode Island. Isolated primarily owing to her will-
fulness and an almost studied inability to get along with her supporters,

she left Portsmouth in 1642 for Pelham Bay on Long Island Sound, well into Dutch territory. The next year, besides taking their revenge against the Dutch, the Indians butchered her and most of her family and burned their home to the ground. The I-told-you-so's in Boston no doubt drowned out the earnest prayers of friends she had left behind. God's hand was the "more apparently seene herein," wrote Thomas Weld; and the Indian cruelty, greater than ever experienced before, did "pick out this wofull woman, to make her and those belonging to her, an unheard of heavie example." Again God had vindicated Massachusetts Bay against heresy, blasphemy, and primarily enthusiasm, so that New England might thrive in peace.[4]

Roger Williams's toleration and the antinomians' enthusiasm, plus other brands of heterodoxy which found resting places there, gave Rhode Island as wide a variety of religious opinions as any colony could boast, or in several cases lament. Since Massachusetts for a number of years fought off all kinds of enthusiasts, those who did venture to the Bay Colony usually ended up in Rhode Island, like the antinomians. And lest, despite "constant sedulity," they still attempted to settle in Massachusetts with their "phanatick Doctrines and practises," Nathaniel Ward proclaimed to the world in a much quoted warning, "that all Familists, Antinomians, Anabaptists, and other Enthusiasts, shall have free Liberty to keep away from us, and such as will come to be gone as fast as they can, the sooner the better."[5] Because Hutchinsonian enthusiasm, as we shall see, differed only in voltage from George Fox's inward light, a little theology excepted, early Quakers found a warm reception in the colony surrounding Narragansett Bay. By the end of the century Cotton Mather—not the most reliable chronicler of Rhode Island's religious heritage—could report that the colony contained "Colluvies"—a word he borrowed from Nathaniel Ward's *Simple Cobler*—of enthusiasts (I'll spare the reader the arm's-length list) and everything but "Real Christians." Mather's conclusion was "that if a Man had lost his Religion, he might find it at this general Muster of Opinionists" in Rhode Island—a clever if condescending remark George Berkeley echoed when he described the variety and vitality of sectarian beliefs there a generation or more later.[6] By the middle of the eighteenth century the Anglicans, who managed to take root in Rhode Island as well, claimed that the only principle the enthusiasts agreed upon was "pulling down the Church of England."[7]

Virginians were well aware of the antinomian upheaval in Massachusetts, according to George Donne, son of the poet John, who spent a handful of years in tobacco land as an agent for the King. Had they known of it Winthrop and his people would have been understandably upset to learn from Donne's "Virginia Reviewed" that their religion was a "ridiculous novelty" and their people "desperate E[n]thusiasticks" and "Fanaticks." In Massachusetts, wrote Donne, all would be kings in Münster, if not "Prophetts" or even "Christ the Messias." Maybe hardest of all for proud Puritans to bear was to be made fun of by Anglicans. George Donne described their "antick pranckes" and "unheard of Vanityes" in such a way as to move Virginians as much to laughter as to scorn. More serious was suspicion of their loyalty, for his report questioned whether they acknowledged the King at all, while at the same time whether it was worth the King's effort to acknowledge them.[8] Evangelical dissenters were historically wrong-headed, Anglicans agreed, but in New England they were enthusiasts and subversives besides.

The Antinomian Controversy made quite a stir in Civil War England. By the time the Winthrop-Weld *Short Story* appeared in 1644, dissenters there were already crowding churches to hear ministers whose doctrines were beginning to sound very much like those of the antinomians. Winthrop's purpose in writing the tract was to broadcast the colony's side of the story, to demonstrate how effectively it had suppressed fanaticism in Massachusetts. But enemies of Independency, whether Anglican or Presbyterian, utilized the same material to damn all New Englanders as a lot of Familists, antinomians, Anabaptists, Brownists, hypocrites, heretics, and enthusiasts, prone to repeat the tragedy of Münster. *A Short Story* was mined for propaganda by all sides. The antinomian upheaval in Massachusetts quickly worked its way into the high-spirited conflict of the English 1640s and proved advantageous to anyone who wished to benefit from it.[9]

In the 1640s attacks by both Anglicans and moderate Puritans intensified against the wilder forms of dissent. We make a good deal today of differences between Massachusetts Bay and Plymouth, and "nonseparating Congregationalists" comes quickly to mind as a convenient way to define Winthrop and his people.[10] But three thousand miles of ocean were sufficient to convince many Englishmen then that Separatism in New England was a fact, and less discriminating critics made few distinctions, lumping Plymouth Pilgrims with their Boston neighbors as one and the same. In fact, George Donne's idea spread in England that all New Englanders were enthusiasts as well as Separatists, a deplorable condition which would not be so bad if they stayed abroad where they belonged. But with the turn of events toward civil war, some New World enthusiasts were stealing back to the Old, where they spouted their new truths and threatened Church and State with their fanatical ways. The "lewd licentiousnesse" and "voluptuous wantonesse" of recent times, one report read, were owing in part to the "new wine lately come from

New England," carrying with it "new Spirit, new Revelations, & new Formes of Prayer." It was upsetting enough to read about Anne Hutchinson in the press, but here were some of her followers spewing the same sort of stuff from pulpits in London.[11] There was New Haven's Samuel Eaton, too, wholly acceptable in New England as pious and orthodox, even offered a pulpit in Boston if he would stay. Once back in England, fresh from the "New Jerusalem," Eaton was dubbed a radical and fanatic, a "supermystical" saint full of enthusiastic nonsense—and, alas, with teeming churches to hear him.[12]

The early years of the Bay Colony settlement turned up half a dozen enthusiasts, besides Mrs. Hutchinson, who gave New England a reputation on both sides of the Atlantic as a hotbed of fanaticism which it took years to live down. Massachusetts attracted offbeat devotees at the outset, but it was not always kind to them. Some it suppressed; others it banished. Still others, like Samuel Gorton, stood up to it and won places, if not in it, at least alongside it. Another few it sent blazing back to England either already burned, like Hanserd Knollys, or with torches to ignite all Christendom, like Hugh Peter, Henry Vane, William Aspinwall, and Thomas Venner. After Mrs. Hutchinson's demise and the beginning of the Civil War, several of these hotheads found New England too unexciting a place to fulfill their radical spiritual schemes.

Hugh Peter, at age thirty-seven, came to New England from Rotterdam by way of London in 1635—in the same vessel as Henry Vane. His six years in Massachusetts, spent in Salem, were packed full of a variety of activities. He took a hard line against the antinomians and openly reproved Governor Vane for his petulance on their behalf, chiding him about his youthful inexperience. Peter made clear that there had not been any trouble in Boston before Henry Vane appeared. Should not the young man be wary of "new opinions" and "notions"?[13] At Mrs. Hutchinson's examination he straightaway tried to identify her with the notorious "Woman of Ely," whom all of England knew to be the very caricature of an enthusiast and "woman-preacher" whose outrageous carryings on strengthened the Isle of Ely's legendary reputation as a haunt for the Family of Love and other fanatical sects. The trouble with Mrs. Hutchinson, Peter told her bluntly, was that she stepped out of line, that she would rather be a husband than a wife and a preacher than a listener, even a magistrate over a subject, and in doing so she tried "to carry all Thinges" in both Church and State for which she had not yet been humbled.[14] How far this strong talk contributed to her banishment and excommunication can only be guessed, but it tells us a good deal about

Hugh Peter and his rigid views of Church and State and the place of women in a community like Boston.

In other ways Peter showed a more liberal and humane side. He had plenty of imagination and applied it practically to some of Massachusetts's economic problems. He saw the value of the fishing and ship-building trades and devised schemes to encourage both at the outset of depression in the early 1640s. These and his generous distribution of much-needed provisions to deprived towns in time of want demonstrated a capacity for benevolence in sharp contrast to his shoddy handling of the spiritual needs of a few misguided enthusiasts like Mrs. Hutchinson.[15]

Hugh Peter was a man of affairs, and the colony recognized as much when it sent him and two others as agents to London in 1641. Their charge was ambitious: to improve economic relations with the mother country; to explain, too, the increasing debt owed English merchants; and not least, "to give any advice, as it should be required, for the settling the right form of church discipline." The beginnings of the Civil War opened up all kinds of opportunities for godly Puritans in England to act upon, and where better to get advice about furthering the reformation of churches than from Massachusetts, where the experiment was already underway? It looked as if investment in the "City upon a Hill" was about to pay dividends at home, and the Bay Colony sent three of its finest to help guide the payoff.[16]

Henry Vane was fifteen years younger than Hugh Peter. While the latter hounded the antinomians out of the colony, Vane was one of them and with their help had been elected governor in 1636, less than a year after his arrival. But as loser in both the next election and the religious crisis, he returned to England before the colony was quite rid of Mrs. Hutchinson and her enthusiasts.[17] His father was comptroller and treasurer of the royal household, and young Henry, a "Whelpe of the Old Curre," rose quickly in politics—joint Treasurer of the Navy, member and leader of Parliament, and knighted all in a few years.[18]

Vane was deeply religious, maddeningly so, and the enthusiasm he first exhibited in New England among the antinomians deepened and intensified in England beyond the comprehension of many. Friends and enemies found his writings cloudy and confusing, and a number wondered whether he understood them himself. He was a *"man above ordinances,"* wrote the Earl of Clarendon, indeed a "perfect enthusiast" who felt not the restraints and limits which bore on other humans. Henry Vane was also ambitious. These attributes added up to a Puritan revolutionary, half genius and half fanatic, whose rise and fall left Englishmen divided over whether they were blessed or cursed by his contribution to the whole.[19]

William Aspinwall also boldly challenged Massachusetts orthodoxy. He was an early comer to the colony and found no difficulty in working his way into public life: freeman, church member, deacon, selectman, and then in 1637 the Boston saints elected him deputy to the General Court in place of Henry Vane, who found several imperative reasons to return to England. But his public career was abruptly interrupted when the Court refused to seat him because he had signed the remonstrance justifying John Wheelwright's Fast-Day Sermon which had so outraged both clergy and magistrates and precipitated the antinomian upheaval.[20] There followed a striking give and take when the General Court called Aspinwall before it not only to dismiss him but to disenfranchise him, as it had a number of other participants. He would take none of it without a fight and defended Wheelwright, who, he claimed, was censured for nothing but "the truth of Christ." The Court had already dubbed Wheelwright and the remonstrance seditious, and it followed that anyone who supported either was guilty of sedition too. Aspinwall countered with two biblical precedents for petitioning, neither of which the Court found applicable, whereupon he fell back on the right of any English subject to petition his government. This also got him nowhere, since the Court insisted that what Aspinwall and the Hutchinsonians had signed was not a petition at all but a "seditious Libell." When the Court passed sentence, Aspinwall demanded chapter and verse, and the Court trotted out "*Hagar and Ismael*" who were "banished for disturbance." This time *he* found the Court's precedents inapplicable but was put down promptly with a pronouncement that the "Scripture calls it a casting out." Actually the Court had intended only to disenfranchise him along with several others, but it banished him, too, because his "behaviour was so contemptuous, and his speeches so peremptory." The Court's conscience was eased a bit the next day when it learned "by an overruling hand of God" that Aspinwall had not only signed the remonstrance but had drafted it in the first place and with "passages so foule" it had to be rewritten, all the while encouraging others to sign it, some of whose names appeared without their knowledge.[21]

Aspinwall joined the sectaries in Rhode Island, where he and the islanders approved the Portsmouth Contract of 1638. But life was no easier for him there. He fell into debt and was suspected of sedition—a more difficult task in Rhode Island than it ever was in Massachusetts. By 1641 he had returned to the Bay Colony and, like John Wheelwright, was allowed to clear himself of guilt by acknowledging his error. This he did, which restored his liberty and freedom of the colony, and before long the government appointed him "clarke of the writs for Boston" and then "publique notary." Despite his proficiency in this profession, borne out by the *Aspinwall Notorial Records* extant today, he got into trouble again over a particularly sticky case, and in 1651 the General Court suspended him. The next year he was in London as pamphleteer and enthusiast and a strong defender of the Fifth Monarchy.[22]

Actually Aspinwall commenced his publishing career before he sailed from Boston, which may have had something to do with his leaving. In 1647 he joined the debate, already vibrant in London, over the nature of the true Church. In a pamphlet published there but written in Boston, he challenged the legitimacy of ordination in both Presbyterian and Anglican ministry, making a strong plea for the Congregational way. He plugged its democratic character and pleaded the radical cause of those who accepted calls from the people to preach. Might they not do as well, he asked, in promoting salvation as those who stood on a weak foundation or none at all, claiming either Christ's authority through presbyters or succession from Romish priests? To preach out of love and good will, he insisted, was as acceptable as ordination, or what passed for it, in allegedly proper churches—an argument which smacked of Familism and Anabaptism and hinted at the ecclesiastical breakdown which England was then experiencing.[23] While he was still in Boston, Aspinwall's thinking had taken a direction which lent itself to the earthshaking tumult already making its mark in England when he arrived.

Samuel Gorton was an extraordinary man besides being an enthusiast and troublemaker. When he disembarked at Boston in 1637, he brought with him a healthy respect for English law and liberties, and, arriving in the midst of the Antinomian Controversy, he found both religious and civil liberty trodden underfoot. Winthrop and his people were about as ready to welcome him and his family and followers as Gorton was to embrace their habit of binding men's consciences. The Massachusetts authorities were already aware of these differences and promptly denied his group "the common benefit of the country"; hence, he tells us in a later defense of his activities, "we wandered."[24]

They did not wander very far, for their next stop was Plymouth. After a good beginning, giving promise as a "useful Instrument," Gorton soon betrayed "blasphemous and Familistical Opinions," which his critics claimed he tried hard to spread. On top of this, Plymouth's minister at the moment, Ralph Smith, took Gorton to court in a civil case, where he behaved so badly—"turbulent carriages towards both Magistrates and Ministers"—that the Old Colony banished him in no time, and he and his family were forced to wander again.[25]

One might think Gorton would have headed for Rhode Island in the first place after finding Boston uncongenial. But it was not until after the aborted stay at Plymouth that he came to Aquidneck, the island at the mouth of Narragansett Bay. Already the Hutchinsonians were at loggerheads. They may have agreed in Boston about infusion of the Holy Spirit, but once on the Island of Rhode Island, in neither church ways nor those of government could they get along. Gorton sided with the Hutchinsons at Portsmouth, while imperious William Coddington, a former Boston magistrate banished with them, seceded from the initial settlement and established what became Newport at the southern tip of the island.[26] Mrs. Hutchinson's leadership waned, and her husband, William, never had any to spare. When Coddington pushed hard in an attempt to gain control of the whole island despite promises of "Popular Government," the independent Gorton opposed him both politically and religiously.[27] Tried in a farcical court for denying authority and abusing the magistrates, he was convicted, whipped, according to several accounts, and banished. Legend has it that sympathizers, crowding the scene at the whipping post, volubly lamented, "Now Christ Jesus had suffered."[28] Rhode Island was blessed with a new sect "springing from the ashes of the antinomians." Gorton and the Gortonists "wandered" again, this time to Providence at the head of Narragansett Bay.[29]

Providence was not big enough for both Roger Williams's people and the Gortonists. Already divided, Providence lacked strength to combat Gorton and what looked like pure anarchy. He had abused "high and low" at Aquidneck, Williams complained, and was "now bewitching and bemadding Providence." His gross denial of Christian ordinances was the very "depth of Familism," and his defiance of government and authority, which unfortunately attracted too many of Providence's Anabaptists, brought the town to distraction, epitomizing the enthusiasts' tendency to subvert both Church and State. Before the townsmen quite came to blows, luckily prevented by Williams's mediation,[30] Gorton bought land from the Indians a few miles south and moved to what he called Shawomet on the western shore of the bay, leaving Providence in shambles.[31]

Massachusetts had its eye on the land around the bay where Gorton settled. At the same time, Boston people abhorred Gorton's religious principles—in fact, those of most Rhode Islanders—but found him difficult to dislodge since his settlement was not under the Bay's jurisdiction. Nevertheless, Massachusetts found means to interfere by challenging the sale of Indian land to Gorton and friends as fraudulent and by accepting a plea for help from colonists nearby who actually feared Gorton's unsettling presence. Governor Winthrop in Boston mouthed a rationale about rescuing helpless people from unjust violence and affording government to those who lacked it.[32] When Gorton refused with defiance to go to Boston to answer charges of blasphemy, heresy, and land grabbing, a small company of Massachusetts militia attacked Shawomet, captured Gorton and several close followers, and led them in chains to Boston through Providence, driving ahead of them eighty head of cattle as surety. From this proceeded Gorton's trial and punishment, which outraged his sympathizers not only in Rhode Island but even in England.[33] Winthrop did not lessen the outrage when he offered a further rationale that the land around Narragansett Bay would be altogether acceptable to Massachusetts since it afforded another outlet to the sea. Moreover, he explained, because "it came without our seeking, and would be no charge to us, we thought it not wisdom to let it slip."[34] Reason of state, no doubt.

While awaiting trial, the prisoners were forced to attend a Sunday service at which John Cotton preached. According to Winthrop, Gorton asked permission to respond to the sermon and, surprisingly, it was granted, giving Boston people another lesson in prophesying besides a strong dose of straight Gortonism. The church, he claimed, was really nothing but Christ, and therefore "ordinances, ministers, sacraments, etc., were but men's inventions for show and pomp."[35] He hinted, too, at one of his central convictions which his critics never forgave him for then or let him forget later. The Christ who lived eternally, died eternally, and this same Christ had been incarnate in Adam; in fact, he was the image of God in Adam. When Adam lost that image, Christ died; his birth and death later were only manifestations of his suffering and dying in Adam, and, therefore, the historical Christ, whom the churches worshipped, was a mere shadow, a resemblance only of what was really Christ in Gorton and in all true Christian men and women, restored there by regeneration.[36]

Blasphemous and wicked errors, said Winthrop; "delusion and mad Phrensies," Edward Winslow charged. He claimed he was "personally Christ," a "God-Man," Edward Johnson wrote a few years later in his history. All "Familistical Allegories," another added.[37] Next in seriousness to the Gortonists' wild and heretical views was their condemnation of public worship in Massachusetts. They damned all ordinances, labeled baptism an "abomination," likened the Lord's Supper to a magician's skill in turning "the juice of a poor silly grape" into the blood of Jesus, and dubbed all sermons "tales" and the sermonizers "Necromancers."[38]

Already set against the liberating tendencies of the English Civil War, against liberty of conscience generally, but specifically against the fanatical foolishness this liberty encouraged in England, the Massachusetts oligarchy turned on Gorton and his fellow enthusiasts with a vengeance. Rather than let their trial testimony stand—since they "excel the jesuits in the art of equivocation," said Winthrop—the Court convicted them on the basis of their earlier writings, not their explanations.[39] Boston's ministers, John Cotton and John Wilson, were for stringing Gorton up on the spot, but he escaped hanging by a handful of votes and ended up in Charlestown to work out his sentence by hard labor in irons at the Court's pleasure. His friends received similar sentences and were distributed separately to other towns.[40] But Gorton was more dangerous tethered on a Massachusetts farm than loose in Rhode Island—even Salem felt reverberations of his heresy, John Endicott lamented—and after six months or so the Court released him and his friends and back to Rhode Island they went, but not for long.[41] In 1644 Samuel Gorton, Randall Holden, John Greene, and one or two other followers, grossly offended by Massachusetts's ill treatment, sailed for England to complain directly to Parliament.

Antinomian exiles to New Hampshire lacked some of the exciting qualities of enthusiasts like Samuel Gorton, who were drawn to Rhode Island. An exception was Hanserd Knollys, a Cambridge man and an English friend of John Wheelwright's. Knollys's difficulties in England, like Wheelwright's and John Cotton's, had begun under Bishop Laud, and Knollys spent some time in jail as a sectary, lodged there by the High Commission Court. But unlike the other two, Knollys came to New England just late enough to be met at the wharf by Massachusetts magistrates who scrutinized closely his religious beliefs. They found them too close to those of Mrs. Hutchinson and her "familistical opinionists" and in no time ran him off to what became New Hampshire, where his short but turbulent life in the New World began and ended.[42]

Knollys got off on the wrong foot with John Winthrop and the Bay Colony government for reasons over and above his supposed antinomianism. Piqued by his shoddy welcome at Boston, he wrote a letter home which Winthrop intercepted—Winthrop had a way of getting hold of "seditious" letters—a letter slandering the government as worse than the High Commission, and accusing it of outright oppression. Called to account, Knollys obsequiously apologized for his harsh words, but not before Hugh Peter, minister at Salem, and Captain John Underhill of Boston, came to his aid and pleaded with Winthrop for leniency.[43] Peter had helped get rid of Mrs. Hutchinson, and no doubt his advice was respected. The same was not true of the unstable Captain Underhill, an ardent backer of the Hutchinsonians, who, on another occasion, had the temerity to boast that his first pangs of assurance respecting grace came as he lighted a pipeful of his favorite tobacco. John Underhill promptly joined Knollys in New Hampshire.[44]

After several difficulties first in Pascataqua, Knollys formed a church in what became Dover. A serious confrontation occurred between him and a competing clergyman, Thomas Larkham, not only over supremacy in the church but over Knollys's hard line against "prime evidence" as proof of grace and the godless sins of the legalists—"the controversie is not new, you know," Larkham reminded Winthrop. Taking a different line, Larkham admitted all comers to church and baptized any and all children. The result was conflict and high farce. Knollys and his people excommunicated Larkham, who in return tried to beat up Hanserd Knollys. Before the magistrates arrived to keep the peace, Captain Underhill and a number of Knollys's friends marched on Larkham's house, one hoisting a Bible on a pole as an emblem and Knollys himself brandishing a pistol.[45]

Some unsuspected discoveries emerged from the fracas. News of Captain Underhill's adulterous life in Boston arrived in time to prejudice somewhat his position at Dover. Larkham "suddenly discovering a purpose to go to England," left behind a very handsome but very pregnant housekeeper, who was finally persuaded, once Larkham had vanished and the evidence was beyond dispute, to divulge the name of the father. And Hanserd Knollys was ignominiously exposed as "an unclean person," having "solicitated the chastity" of two of his maidservants, enjoying "filthy dalliance with them." Knollys admitted as much before his church, which promptly dismissed him. The occasion was doubly notorious, according to many, since the discovery of his indiscretions occurred at the very time he was exhorting his people, with a finger on the Bible, to commence proceedings against Captain Underhill for his bedwarming in Boston.

John Winthrop was not one to gloat effusively over this second vindication of the Bible Commonwealth's righteousness. But he could not restrain himself from recording in his journal that it was indeed observable how God had given up these people who had stuck with Mrs. Hutchinson's opinions, and that it was not hard to understand why they had fallen into "these unclean courses," laying open to the world their own misdeeds and erroneous opinions.[46] After all, according to tradition, not only did Familist enthusiasts undermine Church and State, but sins of lust were as much a part of their subversion of society as heresy and blasphemy. Hanserd Knollys was known as a sectary before he came to New England. His experience there did nothing to lessen the intensity of his dissent or enthusiasm, although it did seem to frustrate his spiritual schemes, and back to England he went in 1641.

When Samuel Gorton arrived in London three years later, he defended not only his actions in New England but his religious beliefs as well before an audience considerably more sympathetic than he ever found in Massachusetts. *Simplicities Defense* (1646) was his major piece, laying out for all to see his side of the war with the Bay Colony, complete with documents. From these and writings which followed, we get a better idea of Gorton's particular kind of enthusiasm and some strong hints, too, of what he believed the New World promised for Gortonists and people like them.[47]

Christ was the center of his system. He had a past and a future, to be sure, but most of all he had a present, and it was this "present being" which was the heart of Gorton's inspiration.[48] The trouble with conventional religion was that it stifled the open spirit of inspiration and prophesy; Gorton's job was to release that spirit. "We don't want the Lord bottled up" or the "fountaine of life" inhibited, he wrote. Such demands led him to continual warfare against clergy and priesthood. There is a "doore open, another way," he wrote, "yea a nearer & shorter cut to the Kingdom of God, then the common ministery of this world driveth at." The outward forms alone were momentary and carnal, "but the words of Christ, they are spirit and they are life."[49]

Gorton was largely successful in his mission to England. He had gone at the right time, for, like Hanserd Knollys, he found Englishmen ready to listen to him. This was first true of his pleas for help in keeping the Massachusetts government out of his affairs in Rhode Island. Parliament treated him with respect, and when he was ready to come home, he brought with him the Earl of Warwick's pass, which saw him safely, if grudgingly, through Boston and back to Shawomet, whose name he promptly changed to Warwick.[50] He was successful, too, in a religious way, for Englishmen, many of them anyway, were enjoying a ripe freedom of conscience and inquiry unheard of earlier and were a good deal warmer than ever before toward enthusiasm during these intense Civil War years. The Independents were more than cordial and bent on enlisting the support of dissenters, even Gortonists from Rhode Island. He preached frequently, enjoyed it immensely, and claimed later that his experience in England, particularly his acceptance as a "preacher of the gospel" by illustrious clergymen and zealous people, confirmed a belief that his call to preach was as good as any man's.[51]

After his sojourn in England, Gorton gradually settled into a more peaceful life in Rhode Island. At least one assumes this to be true, since information about him is thinner after 1650 than before. When Massachusetts Bay clapped into jail the Quakers who first visited Boston in 1656, Gorton wrote a tender letter, sympathizing with their lot and sharing with them some of his insights about "conversing with God face to face, as a man talks with his friend." Quakers seemed to be of two minds about Gortonists. The first response from the "Common Gaol" was cordial enough,[52] and a few years later William Edmundson, a widely traveled Quaker missionary, held a meeting at Warwick, where he found the people "very loving, like Friends"—although he failed to mention Gorton. But in the same year John Burnyeat and John Stubbs reported something very different. The Gortonists, they recorded, were "filthy, unclean Spirits" who argued that "Creaturely Actions" could not be sin—not even whoring and drunkenness. Burnyeat and Stubbs dismissed them as *"Ranters"* and hurriedly went on their way.[53] Gorton, the cantankerous, spiritual freebooter, had trouble getting along with many people. It may be that his familiarity with God, the Moses-like face-to-face encounters he wrote about, his beholding the "glory of the Lord, as in a mirror," was too dazzling an image even for children of the inward light to bear.[54]

Warwick remained for him and his handful of followers the "Isle of Patmos" he earlier described, where a forlorn people, still not wholly acceptable to all their neighbors, were singled out "for other ends and uses." There God would reveal to them, as on Patmos he had revealed to the Apostle John, the "mysteries of his Kingdome"—the "further truths" enthusiasts were so eager to discover—that their children's children might learn of the "noble Work" God "hath Wrought" for them in the Lord Jesus.

Samuel Gorton was no run-of-the-mill enthusiast. Radical in his ideas about Christ, assured that he was right, arrogant in his criticism of others' beliefs, defiant of their ordinances, religious and political, yet insistent that he be left alone to work out his convictions, he established a thorny reputation as an arch-heretic and bizarre character. No one, not even Anne Hutchinson, seemed more subversive of reformed Protestantism and civil order in New England than Gorton of Warwick, Rhode Island. His enthusiasm, which equated the true Christian with Christ, was a presumption even the tolerant and long-suffering Roger Williams could not forbear. He was everything the orthodox Bay Colonists feared might undermine their Bible Commonwealth, and his very presence in New England was an affront to their reason for being. Yet he survived the vicious enmity of his opponents, and he outlived most of them as a self-proclaimed "Professor of Christ."[55]

After the debacle in New Hampshire, Hanserd Knollys threw himself into the rush of religious changes then occurring in England. He soon confirmed his reputation not only as an antinomian but as an early Baptist and rabble-rouser as well. He preached a kind of universalism, if not equalitarianism, to the poor, the common people, not the noble and the wise. It was only through the poor and helpless, who were "rich in grace," he claimed in Leveller fashion, that the great work just begun in England might go on.[56] He seized pulpits when he found the opportunity and preached in open churchyards when they were denied him, which was frequent, often provoking "riots and tumults." An inveterate prophesier, he doggedly answered directly to sermons without invitations in what soon became good Quaker practice.[57] A close reading of his *Christ Exalted* points directly to antinomian principles of which the Hutchinsonians would have been proud: "We are delivered from the law," he wrote, and we "serve in the newnesse of spirit and not in the oldnesse of the Letter."[58] Caught up in the religious and social upheaval of the Civil War, he encouraged women to prophesy as well as men, and argued against tithes and a state-supported ministry so that Christ might be served freely—ideas which also appealed to Levellers and later Quakers and became, too, common substance among Baptists.[59] Thomas Edwards happily enshrined Knollys in *Gangraena* and reported, as did others, his primitive practice of combining prayer with anointing the sick in the process of healing, including himself. In and out of jail, Knollys lived to a ripe old age and, like Samuel Gorton, survived most of his enemies, besides succeeding before his death at ninety-two in making Baptists almost respectable. Despite Knollys's clownish few years in New England, Cotton Mather had the grace to speak well of him in *Magnalia*—if only as an "Anabaptist."[60]

In London William Aspinwall's enthusiasm, which Massachusetts had succeeded in keeping under wraps after the Hutchinson crisis, burst out in Fifth Monarchy fanaticism. Less interested in economic and social reforms than the Levellers and Diggers, Fifth Monarchists strove to convince Englishmen that the prophecies in the books of Isaiah and Daniel were to be fulfilled in their time. There was no King but Jesus, there were no laws but his; and the sooner they all realized these truths and put them into effect, the better able they would be to prevent the prophesied calamities and prepare themselves for Christ's coming.[61] Aspinwall wrote England into the biblical revelations of world history. The prophetic books justified defeat of the Stuarts and the beheading of Charles I, and at the same time pointed to the imminent rise of the Fifth Monarchy over the Fourth, which was Roman and Antichrist, a victory for the Kingdom of Christ through Oliver Cromwell, God's "choise Instrument." The saints "did not assume power, before it was given them," he wrote, for "God gave them a just occasion to take up Armes for their owne defence." Leave not a "stump of *Baal*," not "anything that bears the stamp of Prerogative, either in Church or Commonwealth." Let all be "consumed with the fire of Zeal."[62] Let nothing impede the building of Jerusalem. God has said it shall be built, "and shall it not come to passe"? And then, as if impatient with the slowness of things and the burgeoning pamphlets, tracts, and books on several sides of the question, Aspinwall asked, "What is become of our faith, if a company of poor Historians can turn us besides our path?"[63] "*Daniel* did foresee all these things," he wrote, despite the fact that the prophet had no actual knowledge of England, Scotland, or Ireland.[64]

Like most enthusiasts, Fifth Monarchists turned their backs on any religious institution which bore the stamp of human authority and which challenged the supremacy of Scripture, prophecies and all. But like many enthusiasts of this very enthusiastic period, a strain of mysticism lined their beliefs and turned them inward to illumination, visions, dreams, and the like. The first half of the seventeenth century was rich in this sort of thing, and there were plenty of opportunities to consult the writings of such men as Paracelsus (1493–1541), who mixed medicine and religion in large doses, and the works of Jacob Boehme (1575–1624), the mystical German of a generation or more earlier, both of whose writings found English translations in the 1640s and 50s. Familists, Ranters, Quakers, and Fifth Monarchists, fed up with the failures of Church and State and other products of man's reason, turned to the irrational, the fanatic, and found comfort, even ecstasy, in the promises of revelation, magic, and mysticism.[65]

Twenty-two years in New England—Jerusalem, he called it—had convinced Aspinwall that it, too, had a role in the drama of events being played out in the mother country. The calamities foretold were England's, no doubt of that, but New England must be warned, and Aspinwall was the man to do it, to apply "analogically" the prophecies whose fulfillment was imminent in England. What should New England do? Aspinwall had a ready answer. Put itself under Christ the King, which could be done easily by accepting directly God's laws. And where better to find them than in those drafted earlier by John Cotton, "an old Prophet of the Lord," who had collected them "out of the word of God."[66]

In 1636, at the request of the Massachusetts General Court, John Cotton had drawn up a code of laws—"Moses His Judicials," it was commonly called—for use by the Bay Colony. Actually, as it turned out, the Court passed up Cotton's draft and a few years later enacted the Body of Liberties as its guide, finding Nathaniel Ward's compilation more English and less Mosaic, and therefore more to the deputies' liking. Cotton's code found its way to New Haven, in what later became part of Connecticut, and then Southampton on Long Island, where settlers were more appreciative of God's laws undiluted than in Massachusetts.[67] In 1641 it was published in London, erroneously titled *An Abstract of the Lawes of New England, as they are now established*—which, of course, they were not, but they were readily in print for Fifth Monarchists' admiration and use when the proper time came.[68] And in case there was any question of their availability, Aspinwall republished in London his own edition of Cotton's laws in 1655 and in the same year made his strong plea to the people of New England to accept them as the way to salvation—in fact, chided them for not having done so already. Accept the Lord Jesus, he urged, in "civils as well as in spirituals," and you will become an example for all Christian nations. New England's reluctance so far to incorporate Cotton's code of laws had "greatly impeded" Christ's work not only there but in England, too, for if the laws of Christ the King were not shown to be a sufficient guide for a small colony, how could they be an *"adequate rule"* for great nations? Had the saints of England enjoyed a similar opportunity to establish a New Jerusalem, "they would ere this have set up Jesus Christ as King, and not only in their churches, but in the commonwealth also." And then in words which echoed those of John Winthrop, Aspinwall admonished his former church fellows: "You are as a Beacon set on a Hil. Great things God hath done for you, and great things he expects from you." Mind how you dishonor his son by "withdrawing your necks from under the yoak."[69] England and New England had lessons to teach each other, according to Aspinwall, and their people could do no better than to recognize that *The Legislative Power is Christ's Peculiar Prerogative.*[70]

Biblical law and Mosaic codes appealed to Fifth Monarchists of the 1650s. They were not only what God had commanded and, therefore, eternal; they were right and good and a "perfect standard to admeasure all judicial actions and causes, whether civil or criminal, by sea or by land." And besides, they appealed to the radical reforming instincts of Fifth Monarchy Men, who appreciated the objectivity of such laws, which were applicable to the poor as well as the rich and, once in effect, would challenge the greed of lawyers in a society which used the law as a means to oppress the lower classes. How these Mosaic laws might have fared in the England of the 1650s is another question, but the fanaticism and enthusiasm of a few Fifth Monarchists in this regard drew attention to much-needed legal reforms. John Cotton's "Judicials" contained some of the positive characteristics which were lacking in the legal codes of the time, and he and his laws have won praise in our own century for their grasp of the principles of good government and the protection of civil rights in an earlier century not well known for either.[71]

Now, was John Cotton an incipient Fifth Monarchist as early as 1636? That he was a strong millennialist, stronger than most in Massachusetts, there can be no doubt. That Fifth Monarchy Men were also millennialists is obviously true, too, and both were convinced that a nation or a people would be closer to the time of Christ's second coming were they to live by the laws of God. Further, Fifth Monarchists probably found Cotton's laws more attractive than the biblical code enacted by the Anabaptists at Münster in 1535, given the outcome.[72] And Fifth Monarchists in the 1650s had two editions of Cotton's laws to guide them, the second edited and published by a Massachusetts refugee, now one of their own, whose writings contained, as Aspinwall said, "what the Lord hath imparted to me for the publick good."[73] New England had contributed to the Fifth Monarchy cause both a constitution and a pamphleteer to show its leaders the way.

William Aspinwall may have answered Fifth Monarchists' need for a polemicist, but this was as far as he would go. He was no plotter or conspirator. Spiritually subversive, yes, but he made no attempt to undermine the Protector's government, being content to work through its existing forms, hoping to persuade the authorities in England and Massachusetts to accept Jesus as their King, who would then rule through his saints. In stark contrast was Thomas Venner, another New Englander who headed for London soon after the death of the King. While Aspinwall thumbed his Bible and listened to God, Venner preached and prayed and led Fifth Monarchists into the streets and straight to hell. Who was Thomas Venner, and what did New England mean to him and the Fifth Monarchy on the brink of eternity?

Venner had lived an unexceptional life in both Salem and Boston, Massachusetts, as a wine cooper. He seemed not to have sought public life except to serve on juries and as constable, buy land, sue and be sued in court a few times, and head a company of coopers in Boston and Charlestown which the General Court incorporated in 1648. At one time he was zealous to lead a platoon of New Englanders to Providence on the island of Grenada in the West Indies to strengthen a church already there, which may show some dissatisfaction with his religious lot in Salem, but nothing seems to have come of it. Unlike Aspinwall, Venner took no part in the Antinomian Controversy, which was increasing in intensity when he arrived in Massachusetts. What his opinions were would be difficult to determine. They seemed orthodox enough; he signed the church covenant at Salem and saw his children baptized there and in Boston, where he moved probably in 1644. Soon he becaᵐ member of the Artillery Company; one wonders how much of the militarʸ prowess he demonstrated later in the streets of London he had learned while training on Boston Common.[74]

What turns a New England Puritan into a Fifth Monarchy Man, and a wild and bloody one at that? At least Aspinwall had shown his colors earlier when he supported John Wheelwright and the antinomians, besides defying the government of Massachusetts and being banished to Rhode Island for his pains. If Venner shared these feelings or even more intense ones, he kept them to himself in New England. Once in England, however, he blossomed with the Fifth Monarchists and preached to a meeting of like-minded zealots in that nest of dissent and fanaticism, Coleman Street, London.[75]

Exposure to historic events in England provoked an abrupt turn in Hugh Peter's religious thinking. Had the Puritan oligarchy in Massachusetts foreseen the change, it might have kept him closer to home, and so might the people of Salem, who had given him only a reluctant release. The turnaround was a surprise to Roger Williams, too, who earlier had felt the brunt of his narrow orthodoxy. Peter had filled Williams's pulpit at Salem and spent a good deal of time in that distracted church smoothing feathers and avoiding quarrels among the saints after Williams's hurried departure. When Salem Church got around to excommunicating Williams, he already had disappeared into the wilderness in search of Providence before it could inform him of the action. Peter was all for chasing him down with the document, such was his doggedness, "after the manner of Popish bulls," said Williams. And yet this was the same Hugh Peter who greeted Williams in London a few years later and warmly embraced him, boasting that he, too, "was for liberty of conscience" and proudly preached it regularly.[76]

And so he did, and a lot more. Probably no one threw himself more completely into the English Civil War and argued and acted more strenuously than Hugh Peter. He became the best-known chaplain in the army, often Cromwell's right-hand man, really his secretary for a time, and as forward as any in the trial and execution of the King.[77] Not only did he preach liberty of conscience but he acted upon it, and reports found their way to Massachusetts about how he "too much countenance[d] the Opinionists"—some of the same people the colony had cast out a few years earlier. On top of this, Peter himself wrote back to the Winthrops, exhorting the colony to treat dissenting consciences tenderly. Devise a way for them to live with you, he admonished, and you will increase your number of friends here markedly, for now "none will come to you because you persecute. Cannot you mend it?"[78] The way Massachusetts Puritans were treating Anabaptists at the moment and would treat Quakers a few years later was answer enough to Hugh Peter about how things stood with sectaries in the Bay Colony.

From persecutor to libertarian, from orthodox Puritan to Civil War enthusiast, these were changes worthy indeed of a major reversal. Peter's hitch in the New Model Army was one grand exercise in prophesying in which he both preached and listened. It was a revolutionary experience, and it convinced him that the Spirit of Jesus was in the common, the contemptible, and the poor, just where Hanserd Knollys, John Goodwin,

and William Walwyn had said it was. The experience changed Hugh
Peter from a Puritan oligarch to a Christian democrat—among believers,
at least.[79]

There were gainsayers on all sides of Hugh Peter. As early as 1643 a
Royalist who heard him preach was grossly offended by his "zealous
Doctrine," the "new Gospell," which taught Englishmen to "rebell and
resist the King." Not only was the lesson offensive, but so too was any
minister who brought it from that Land of *Canaan*, New England.[80] As
a man of "great use," Peter was subject to ridicule as he dashed here and
there on Cromwell's business and other matters of great import. Hardly
an army victory was won but Hugh Peter delivered the news of it. He
was active enough before 1646 to win several pages in Thomas Edwards's
Gangraena, that volume of invective by a disgruntled Presbyterian who
would have given over a whole book to him had he had the space and
the time in his catalogue of errors and heresies. It was Hugh Peter, right
out of New England, mind you, who now pleaded the cause of antinomians and Anabaptists and toleration for the sects—the very "Solicitor
Generall for the Sectaries"—and who would lead the nation to anarchy
and confusion if he had his way, warned Edwards. Peter fared even worse
from authentic radicals like John Lilburne, the Leveller, who had given
up long since on Cromwell and dismissed Hugh Peter as a hypocrite and
the "grand journey- or hackney-man of the Army."[81]

Gilbert Burnet later described Peter as "sort of an enthusiastical buf-
foon preacher." This was never more apparent than in December 1648,
when he preached to the House of Commons a few weeks before the
trial and execution of Charles I. At a dramatic moment in the sermon
he buried his head in the pillow and then bounced up with a "Revelation"
that "this Army must root up Monarchy, not only here, but in *France,*
and other Kingdomes round about; this is to bring you out of Aegypt."
And to those who objected that such an earthshaking event was unprec-
edented, he reminded them that so too was the virgin birth. After all,
said Peter, "this is an Age to make examples and precedents in."[82]

Despite such prophetic flights about England's deliverance and the
army's role in precipitating the millennium, Peter gave Fifth Monarchists
and Thomas Venner a wide berth and, in fact, helped to protect Cromwell
against their daring. One wonders whether he ever met Thomas Venner
face to face in a bustling London street, as he certainly must have earlier
in the quiet lanes of Salem. Peter's "being so useful a man" in many
different ways convinced Independent ministers that for sake of the cause
he could not be spared to return home despite a "peremptory call" from
his Salem church.[83] Massachusetts had brought out Hugh Peter's Puritan
orthodoxy, and there he hewed to a line close to New England's way.

But in England, during very exuberant times, an enthusiasm emerged which dissolved spiritual restraint, and he rode high with the saints until the Restoration dragged him down along with several others.

Henry Vane and Oliver Cromwell parted company in 1653. A firm believer that the people were the origin of political power, Vane accused Cromwell of usurping that power from Parliament and betraying their trust in him. At the same time the Protector grew weary of Vane's dogged faith in the people and his fuzzy enthusiasm, neither of which got the work done as Cromwell saw it.[84] Vane returned to a life of meditation and prophesying. His spiritual friendships stretched wide among enthusiasts from Familists to James Nayler of the Quakers to Fifth Monarchist John Rogers. Several Quakers found him "drunk with imaginations," and he disappointed George Fox, who called him "vaine" and proud and "not the man he once had been." But most Quakers were loving friends, for they, like him, preached liberty of conscience and an end to tithes, and questioned the taking of oaths.[85] According to the Reverend John Ward, a rare humorist in this unfunny age, one Quaker dubbed Vane the "Lord's anointed," and proceeded to pour a "botle of stinking oil upon his head, which made Sir Henry shake his eares." In his writing Vane soared high into ecstatic prophecies and "flights of enthusiasm," when not burying himself in Jacob Boehme, like other fanatics of his generation.[86] The death of Oliver Cromwell and the political demise of his son Richard yanked Vane back into the limelight at the head of the Puritan fanatics and sectaries who hoped to return to the business of the millennium. The Restoration of Charles II throttled their expectations; it throttled, too, several of the enthusiasts who had made the Civil War possible.

For all their beliefs in prophecy, Fifth Monarchists became disillusioned extremists in the latter half of the 1650s. Oliver Cromwell may have been God's "choise Instrument," according to Aspinwall, but Jesus as King and a government led by saints were no nearer than before. In fact, Cromwell, and later his son Richard, seemed as much a drag on the unfolding of revealed events as had been Charles I, and we know what happened to him. It was not for want of scheming that Cromwell did not end up like Charles, or at least dead—if not by a court's verdict and public execution—for there were several rumors about blowing up the Protector's chapel with him in it and "some like design upon his son *Richard*."[87]

By the spring of 1657 Fifth Monarchy Men were convinced that their time had come, that the "saints must do it," they argued; they must pull down Babylon and bind "kings in chains." And so they plotted in April of that year.[88] But someone leaked the scheme to the government, whose troops smothered their meetings, and Thomas Venner, a "principal actor," ended up on the carpet before the Protector, where he "behaved himself with as great impudence, insolence, pride and railing, as . . . you ever heard of." Several other names appeared on lists of conspirators, and it was strongly rumored that they included Sir Henry Vane, who, if not a Fifth Monarchist, believed like them that Cromwell frustrated the emergence of Christ's Kingdom in England. Venner spent the next year or so in the Tower of London and when released after Cromwell's death promptly returned to his Coleman Street pulpit. He preached there to what after 1660 was a "conventical," since the Restoration government and Charles II opposed in principle all dissenting sects, although they indulged some of them for the time being.[89]

Venner and his fanatics tried again in January 1661, this time against the restored King and country. Using first old Saint Paul's as a base, they succeeded in getting into the streets, their intent being to overthrow Charles's government and any and all who opposed them and reform the world, beginning with the City of London. Having been spurred to the peak of enthusiasm by a Venner sermon summoning them to "fight for King Jesus," between forty and fifty of them burst through the old City, killing indiscriminately any who offered resistance, giving as much as they took from the trained bands who attacked them, and showing great discipline and order besides "mad courage." Venner had assured them that each was a match for ten, and that "ten should chase a thousand." "No weapon formed against them should prosper," he counseled, "nor hair of their Head be touched." After three days of sporadic street fighting, the King's troops eventually wore them down, and when the last skirmish, fought in a public house, dissolved, about twenty-two of His Majesty's subjects were dead on each side. Venner was badly wounded and captured. Most of his followers refused to take quarter, and the rest, who were not shot, were made prisoners. The government dealt with them in short order, as we shall see.[90]

Samuel Gorton had returned to Rhode Island long since, where he continued to profess the mysteries of Christ. Hanserd Knollys overcame his dubious start in New England, and while promoting the poor and vulgar as God's anointed in England led Baptists into a tolerable dissent. Fifth Monarchist William Aspinwall disappeared in the late 1650s and may not have survived the Restoration. The new government of Charles II was left with Hugh Peter, Thomas Venner, and Henry Vane on its hands. All were notorious civil warriors in one way or another, and no time was lost in disposing of them.

Hugh Peter had been so much in the public eye that after 1660 London's reaction against republicanism, confusion, and enthusiasm focused on him. There was no way to argue that he had not been conspicuously forward in the New Model Army, the trial and execution of Charles I, and the government of saints. What is more, not only had he "been in *New England*"—telling evidence—but "was employed out of New England" to "destroy the King and foment war," his enemies argued.[91] As a result an angry House of Commons placed him outside the act of pardon which let the notorious John Goodwin of Coleman Street escape. Peter was soon a prisoner in the Tower and six weeks later was tried, a man without friends, or at least friends who dared show themselves, even many sympathizers. On October 16, 1660, Hugh Peter was ignominiously hanged, drawn, and quartered for treason before a taunting crowd at Charing Cross. In New England "many godly men" lamented, Roger Williams among them.[92]

Only six weeks elapsed between the seizure of Hugh Peter and his execution. Justice was even swifter against Fifth Monarchists. In just a few hours after their capture the Crown brought the "possessed enthusiasts" up for indictment and trial. Thomas Venner pleaded not guilty, but only after he had delivered a "wild Phanatique discourse" about the coming Fifth Monarchy under Jesus. He accompanied this with reciting what he called his "conversation in New England" and the "testimony within him above these 20 years." These two phrases, or something similar to them, appear in several of the sources which describe the Fifth Monarchy rising, and particularly Venner's demise. What actually did he mean? His death speech a few days later is no help, for it was a statement of his absolute trust in the God who had bidden him to set up Christ and his saints in the place of Charles II's new government. The "bottomless discourse" at the indictment was different, and save a fuller explanation, his words seem to tell us that the dozen or more years in New England were a training ground for the enthusiasm which exploded in January 1661—that he was conversant with the workings of New England, and the experience there was crucial in the formation of his Fifth Monarchist zeal. What is more, the evidence or testimony of this heightened faith had been locked up in him for twenty years, and finally, under a Fifth Monarchists' banner, it had burst into bloody rebellion. "Whom man judges, God will not condemn," he declared to the court after its sentence of death upon him.[93]

Venner was dragged on a sledge to a scaffold constructed in Coleman Street just outside his meeting house on January 19, 1661, only twelve days after the rising began. Carried to the ladder because of his severe wounds, he stood with his head in the noose and uttered his last words, which included, "What I did was from the Word of the Lord," who will "speak more by my death then by my life." Like Hugh Peter he was hanged and butchered along with his fellow preacher, Roger Hoskins (or Hodgkins); half of his surviving comrades suffered the same punishment in several parts of the city that day and the rest two days later. Their heads adorned London Bridge on poles in company with Hugh Peter's. All had remained adamant in denying the charge of treason and war against the King. If we were deceived, they insisted, it was God himself who deceived us.[94]

Like the Anabaptists at Münster, the Fifth Monarchists in London under Venner remained the epitome of enthusiasm for a long time to come, a "Continuation of the bloody History of the Fanaticks." That Venner's period of gestation was in New England only confirmed what archcritics in Old England already believed. "We'll never deny his New-England testimony," wrote one chronicler, for it has "made Old England smart, having been the nursery and receptacle of sedition too long"; and don't forget, Gough and Whalley, two of the regicide judges, are not only there but thriving.[95] A few years later Edward Randolph, New England's royal customs officer and general nemesis, reported from Boston to the Lords of Trade that the Bay Colonists, besides having no regard for the Acts of Trade, "held fast the anti-monarchical principles spread among them" by such as Henry Vane and Hugh Peter, and, added Randolph, by Thomas Venner, who "had his education here also."[96]

Anabaptists and other sectaries in England ran for cover. Lord Clarendon persuaded Parliament to draft several bills suppressing them despite dissenters' pleas of innocence and lack of complicity in the Fifth Monarchy uprising. The Anabaptists published two apologies protesting strongly against the "Principles & Practices" of the fanatical Monarchy men, but they were unable to prevent passage of the Clarendon Code, which bore heavily upon them all. Several sects went underground, while the Quakers, claiming nothing to hide, continued to meet openly and suffered the brunt of the Restoration government's reaction to a conspiracy to enthrone King Jesus.[97]

New England also felt the taint and scrambled to remove it. Apostle John Eliot's *Christian Commonwealth* was published in London in 1659, although he had written it several years earlier when Cromwell was riding high in England. It smelled strongly of millennial promise and Fifth Monarchy reforms. The structure of government he prescribed in it and recommended for England derived from Exodus. Already he had introduced it to his praying Indians—hardly persuasive to Englishmen, even fanatics.[98] The news of Venner's explosion arrived in Boston in the late spring of 1661. Not long afterwards the Bay Colony forced Eliot to disown the antimonarchical principles in *The Christian Commonwealth*, and the book itself was burned by the public hangman on Boston Common.[99] Thus Massachusetts tried to purge itself of any hint of Venner's fanaticism, acts which later failed to convince Edward Randolph of the saints' love of monarchy, as we have seen. But most Massachusetts Puritans prided themselves on their ability to distinguish between Christian truth and outright enthusiasm. Despite his "conversation in New-England," Thomas Venner went down in their books as another John of Leyden, and good riddance.

Venner's bloody rising astounded Englishmen in and out of court by its fanatical daring. At the same time it made Charles's government wary of Sir Henry Vane, the only man of stature still alive who had written recently, if confusedly, and in dead earnest about the immediacy of Christ's rule in England. If a New England wine cooper like Venner could stir up nightmares, what might a man of "such vast Parts" yet "so much Madness" as Henry Vane accomplish? Moreover, he too had lived in New England, was even governor there for a time, and his well-known belief that political power originated in the people and ought to be used for their benefit was a far cry from Restoration principles of monarchy. "Certainly he is too dangerous a man to let live," Charles wrote to the Earl of Clarendon, "if we can honestly put him out of the way." Against these odds Vane had little chance in a Stuart regime. Once sentence was passed at his trial, Vane comforted himself and his party with the promise, "Whom Man judges, God will not condemn," the very words Thomas Venner uttered to the court which convicted him, an association not lost on Vane's judges. Just before execution Vane told friends that he would die secure in the belief that the "Cause shall have its Resurrection," again echoing Venner, who also believed he died a martyr. Charles and his government concluded that if there was any resurrection of the "good old cause," they would rather face it without Henry Vane. Although "much interrupted in his final speech" by the King's drums and trumpets, "because he reflected on his judges," he faced the headman's ax with great composure, most agreed. This was in 1662; Vane's execution closed an era, for he was the last in England to pay with his life for the enthusiasm of Civil War.[100]

By the time of the Restoration, Anne Hutchinson's revelations and the crisis she and her antinomian followers provoked in Boston must have seemed like pretty small potatoes. What is surprising is that several New Englanders who made life difficult for John Winthrop and the Bible Commonwealth played even more troublesome roles in the wholesale outbreak of enthusiasm which surrounded the English Civil War. New England zealots, at least, did not go unnoticed; in fact, they stirred up a good deal of excitement, and enthusiasm was at the heart of it.

~~~ 6 ~~~
Quakers of the First Generation:
The Martyrs

W HAT AN AGE for unconventional Protestants! What a time for radical Puritans! In the 1640s and 50s England was on the verge of something extraordinary, and such times called for extraordinary measures—all the more reason for breaking out of the confines of orthodoxy and convention and worshipping the Spirit close at hand. There was a general stirring up of religious extremism, whose adherents found events a good deal easier to accommodate to prophecies of old than ever before: civil war, regicide, a New Model Army, a major breakdown of ecclesiastical authority, and the appearance of God's grace flowing abundantly. The English Civil War and the Interregnum gave confidence to a number of enthusiastic sects whose lineage by this time was veteran—Anabaptists and Familists, for instance. But these explosive years also turned up new sects which attracted old- and newcomers to them. Quakerism under George Fox was one of these and, as things turned out, by far the most successful. If enthusiasts were those who believed they were closely in touch with God through personal revelation, were guided in all things by light of the Spirit within them, then Quakers satisfied the criteria.

Englishmen on the side of burgeoning dissent varied in degrees of enthusiasm and intensity, no doubt of that. They ranged from moderate Puritans, like Presbyterians and Independents, to Ranters and Quakers and Fifth Monarchy Men; but at heart they were all Puritans who felt called to remodel the establishment into something new, or at least different, each according to his light. That the Quakers' light was strong and demanding goes a long way toward explaining the direction and means the sect took under the leadership of George Fox.

Contemporaries differed, as historians do today, about the origins of Quakerism. To orthodox opponents like Richard Baxter, the times simply had gone from bad to worse, provoking a descent of dissent from Anabaptism to Separatism to Quakerism. Some called the Quakers the "Spawn of the Jesuites," while others thought George Fox and his followers merely built on a number of ideas already worked out by the early Anabaptists. The recent unhappy events of the 1640s and 50s, wrote another, "piled up such materials" that it was "easie for Quakers to arise as the scumme of all." Take the malice out of the metaphor, and we may be close to the truth—that Quakerism was derived from the turmoil surrounding radical Puritanism, which included Anabaptists, Familists, Levellers, Ranters, Seekers, and several more enthusiastic sects which the times had cast up. It was the genius of George Fox to present the inward light in such a way as to attract a number of these extremists who discovered in Quakerism a vehicle for the Spirit and a language for expression which appealed to their radical needs.[1]

George Fox wrote that Quakers were "in the Power of God." He meant that Quakers looked inward for Christian truths which God revealed to them directly. Fox read the Bible only to discover in its pages truths he already knew "experimentally," a key word he frequently used and one which became central to enthusiasts' understanding of spiritual life. To be a minister of these kinds of truth, God told Fox, one did not have to be bred at Oxford or Cambridge, to be book-learned, or dependent upon the forms or ordinances of conventional churches, for these were externals, the human trappings of religion and not the divine. To be a recipient of these truths one had only to be open to them, wrote Fox, for every man and woman could be "enlightened by the divine light of Christ."[2]

Quakers were a difficult people to live with. What do you do with an increasing body of fanatics who spout at length about an inward light and direct revelation, a spirituality which flies in the face of any kind of organized religion? The Restoration government had even more trouble with Quakers than Cromwell's people. It came down hard upon them at the very outset, associating them—wrongly, it turned out—with Thomas Venner's Fifth Monarchy Men, and in so doing aggravating their sense of martyrdom. Add to this their growing aversion to war and to swearing oaths, and the subtle equalitarianism which the ubiquitous light of the Spirit suffused. Given all these, the governments which had to put up with the first generation of Quakers had their hands full, to say nothing of their jails, Fox included. Quakers were a frustrating and disarming lot and never more so than in their early years.

To Anglicans and moderate Puritans, to most respectable Christians, the arrogance and presumption of the Quakers' enthusiasm was astounding. Their belief in an immediate call, and that the light of Christ was sufficient for salvation with little outward help from Scripture, books, teaching, or even a professional clergy, were woeful delusions and fundamentally opposed to gospel worship. Quakerism denied the Trinity, played down Christ's role in the flesh as nothing but a figure or example. It dismissed the sacraments as "types," even "shadows," which faded before the light of the Spirit. And what of the boast of infallibility, the claim of perfection? More than one report went abroad that George Fox possessed a "discerning spirit," while his friend George Whitehead pretended to "know the hearts of men."[3] Quakers preached that the patience with which they suffered for their beliefs was itself a sign of holiness and justification. The truth is, wrote Ephraim Pagitt, Quakers believe that their people can be so possessed of the light that they become "Prophets, Christs or Saviours," and what they speak and write is really a declaration of the word and mind of God, as authentic as any part of Scripture. "O a woefull delusion this is." Any one of these "pernicious tenets" was subversive of true religion; together they were notoriously heretical and destructive of church order. They were the embodiment of enthusiasm. Religion "admitts of no eccentric motions," John Norton warned his Massachusetts congregation, but with Quakers we are confronted with "Raging Waves" and "wandering stars."[4]

So full of the Holy Spirit were these people that they sometimes were unable to contain themselves. One report tells of a group from the North of England which visited Wales in 1653 and after long silences at meetings fell into trembling and quaking and to shrieking and howling and yelling and roaring, so much so, in fact, that they scared the wits out of their curious Welsh spectators, besides causing the "dogs to bark, the swine to cry, and the cattel to run about." At other times and places men, women, and children were "strangely wrought upon," falling down, foaming at the mouth, and even swelling in their bodies.[5] Such goings on occurred early in the course of Quaker history and would occur again; they were descriptive, too, of later enthusiasts—French Prophets, for instance—and victims of evangelical revivals in the next century.

If Quakers plagued Puritans and Anglicans with their blasphemous errors and spiritual presumptions, what about the Ranters and Fifth Monarchists who plagued Quakers? Quakers were radical Puritans, but they were not as radical as some who roamed the Commonwealth in the 1640s and 50s. The inner light guided Quakers and freed them, they said, from dependence upon Scripture, book learning, ordinances, church discipline, and magistrates when they got in the way of the Spirit. It justified and, according to some, perfected, but it did not deify; possessed with it, Quakers did not equate themselves with God. Quaker enthusiasm went just so far. It did not "runn out," as George Fox would say. There were boundaries based on Christian ethics and morality and common sense, and these Fox and some of his followers began to define in the 1650s.[6]

The difference between Quakers and Ranters was that the latter exceeded even the limits Quakers drew during and after the liberating business of the 1640s and 50s. Although very like the Ranters in doctrine, Richard Baxter wrote, Quakers lacked the profane and blasphemous abandon of the more extreme group. The series of drastic events, chiefly the killing of the King, was sufficient to convince some volatile believers that the political and spiritual revolution had turned the moral world upside down, that God was in every man and woman and his grace flowed so abundantly that it eradicated sin. No thought or activity was sinful because there was no sin. While Quakers reduced the Scriptures and human reason to externals, they still believed them aids of a sort to religious life, although not its substance. Ranters denied this, accepted the Spirit as all there was, and as perfectionists in spiritual things lived as they pleased. Ranters were infallible and amoral libertines and sinned in public to prove it. The Blasphemy Act of 1650 cut down some of the wilder carryings on, such as masquerading as God and committing murder and adultery, and the prison terms the act prescribed had a way of prompting recantations. But Ranterism lived on, and its adherents took malicious pleasure in taunting Quakers.[7]

George Fox kept running into Ranters and, according to his journal, straightening them out. At Coventry Jail, where he visited, he reproved them and quite "brought them down." At a meeting Fox arranged with Ranters to "Try their God," they sang, whistled, and danced, but the "Lord's Power so Confounded Them" that they shut up and listened, and many were convinced. A particularly "Rude Company" of Ranters disturbed the meeting at Southampton. They lived communally not far from the meeting house, and one of them, who "gloried in his wickedness," publicly declared "at the Market Cross" his fornication with a woman who lived with them. Fox was moved to rebuke the lot, promising plagues and judgments from God. Shortly afterwards they all were seized and jailed and he "that had lain with the woman" stabbed the jailer and later hanged himself, while the woman "had like to have cut a Child's throat." Fox appreciated retributive justice and was certain to report it.[8]

Their wickedness and their disturbances at meetings were bad enough. Worse for Fox was that "People of the World" failed to distinguish them from Quakers, and the Lord moved Fox "to Clear Friends and Truth of these Lewd People." Ranters would have inundated the nation, according to some reports, had it not been for the Quakers, who were successful in persuading many of them to change their ways and join them. As

Quakerism spread, the Ranter movement subsided and soon withered away. The battle between the two was continued in the colonies. Fox was successful against the Ranters in Old England only to find more of the same and just as "rude" in New England, and chiefly Long Island when he visited.[9] Quakers were enthusiasts, but they were not out of control. Fox saw to it that an anchor was buried in the Christian tradition, albeit a radical part of it, and although it allowed them plenty of leeway to swing with the Spirit, it prevented them usually from running out with the Ranter tide.

Quakers had as little respect for Fifth Monarchists as they did for Ranters. Fox met a group of them while in prison in 1656 and listened to their prophecies about the immediate and literal coming of the Kingdom of Christ. Poor deceived people, he recorded, who failed to realize that Christ had already come and now reigned in the hearts of Quakers and those like them. And they here, out of the truth, said Fox, have become his enemies and enemies to us who already possess him. The poor deceived people in 1661 tried desperately to provoke fulfillment of their prophecies and prepare Restoration England for King Jesus. In London, Thomas Venner and his crew struck in January of that year and "put the City and Nation in an Uproar." Following the bloody rising, all radical dissenters took a beating from the new government. "It was dangerous for sober People to stir abroad for several weeks after," warned Fox, so great was their harassment. This was true despite the fact that Venner and his platoon of extremists were kind enough to deny openly just before their executions that Quakers had anything to do with their plot or even knowledge of it.[10] Fox and his Quakers had "reasonings" with Monarchy Men and with all the "sects" they found ways to confront in England. None of these dared to affirm that it manifested the same spirit and power that suffused the Apostles, and so, wrote the presumptuous Fox, in giving us that power and spirit, the Lord gave Quakers "Dominion over them all."[11]

Restoration religion and politics inhibited the unhinged enthusiasm of the Ranters, and they quickly faded from sight only to reemerge—or something like them—in America a few years later. The Fifth Monarchists barely survived the Restoration itself, and despite complaints by Edward Randolph, who believed the New England wilderness was full of them, they never really got a start in the colonies. But Quakers and Quakerism endured; they seemed to thrive on persecution, and in both England and America they got plenty.[12]

Quakers shared with most Englishmen the belief that the finger of God pointed in the direction of America. In fact, Quaker propaganda in the second half of the seventeenth century sounded very much like that of an earlier period, if often with a Quaker twist. A "divine Influence" upon Columbus, George Fox claimed, had no doubt moved him "so zealously" to search out his "new found World." William Dewsbury wrote of the light (he called it "Lightening") which nature herself drew from east to west as a symbol of the "son of Man" whose "Children of Light" set their faces toward "Sion in the New Jerusalem." Once Pennsylvania was a reality, Fox carefully described the responsibility belonging to the Lord's "Instruments" for enlightening both Gentile and Jew in "God's English Israel." *Plantation Work,* he charged, was the "work of this Generation."[13]

Quakers tended to bear out, too, the idea that between enthusiasts and the New World there existed a unique relationship. Before any of the sect set foot in the colonies, they had decided that English America should not be an extension of Old World institutions but rather a base for new Quaker institutions—a "peculiar and special Work appointed for many in our day," said Fox. Once settlement took hold, the conclusion became even more fixed. God has chosen you "to be a Peculiar People to himself," Josiah Coale charged New England Quakers in 1667, "to be Witnesses for him in the midst of a Crooked and Perverse Generation." The "majesty of Truth is great here," a new settler wrote home from early Pennsylvania. It will grow and increase to the "ends of America." Quakerism and the New World deserved each other, they seem to be telling us.[14]

It is difficult today to comprehend the assurance, the presumption of first-generation Quakers who equated incidence of their inward light with absolute Christianity. They insisted that those who shared this conception actually participated in the primitive spiritual relationship which existed between God and man before the Scriptures, before man encumbered it with fine-spun theology, ecclesiastical furniture, and other human inventions. So overwhelming was the belief in the immanence of the Holy Spirit that Quakers saw no earthly reason why their view of things should not prevail over the beliefs of those who were mistaken, once the errors were pointed out, explained, and corrected. Those who were a part of it, who shared in the "Light," presumed that Quaker ideas would eventually dominate, for this simply was how God meant things to be. It was this assurance, this arrogance, besides their revolutionary enthusiasm, which first-generation Quakers brought to the New World.

American colonists, chiefly in New England, were as ready for the arrival of Quakers as they always were for the Devil. When Ann Austin and Mary Fisher disembarked in Boston, the Puritan fathers clapped them into jail, where they kept them for several weeks. While the women languished there, the colony government rifled their baggage and burned their books. On suspicion of their being witches it stripped them naked and subjected them to such inhuman searches that one of them, a mother several times over, reported that she had never been so done to even in the birth of her children. They were soon back aboard the vessel which brought them and packed off to Barbados whence they had come.[15]

George Bishop, a Foxian missionary, never let the Massachusetts authority forget its treatment of Mary Fisher and Ann Austin. These were two simple, loving women whom God had directed to your shores to bring you truth and light, but they shook your peace and order "as if a *formidable* Army had *Invaded your Borders.*" Why? he asked. "What are you afraid of?" "May not the *Lord* of Heaven and Earth send *His* Messengers among *ye*, without your leave?"[16] Given the disarming nature of Quaker enthusiasm, these were questions which provoked Massachusetts Puritans more to exasperation and frustration and blind force than to reason, argument, and comprehensive answers, and they were the losers for it.

Beyond the danger to religion, beyond the "uggly Disturbances" which occurred repeatedly in meeting houses in both England and the colonies, Englishmen feared Quaker subversion of established governments and even the fabric of society. This "phanatic sect," wrote diarist John Evelyn, showed respect to no man, least of all the magistrate, besides being "exceedingly ignorant." Their errors and heresies not only disturbed the public peace and the safety of the state but were "subversive of all governments." It was all attributable to the "Sun-shine of too generall toleration" during the hectic years just past, according to one bitter pamphleteer who equated new Quakers with old Anabaptists.[17] In England during a public dispute at Cambridge in 1659, Richard Blome put it right up to George Fox and his friend George Whitehead. Was it not true, Blome asked, "that you teach doctrines that break the relation of Subjects to their Magistrates"? Blome did not record Fox's answer, if he gave one, but the next year, when Fox lay in Lancaster Jail, the charges against him were that he was a disturber of the nation's peace, an "Enemy to the King," that he and others of his "Fanatick Opinion" had lately tried to "raise Insurrection" and embroil the "whole Kingdom in Blood." Moreover, he was the chief "Upholder" of the sect called Quakers. Fox denied the charges, except the last, as any Quaker might. And then in humble Foxian manner he explained in his journal that he was a child with respect to these things; he was ignorant of war, for his weapons were spiritual, not carnal. Anyway, he recorded, he followed him who said his "Kingdom is not of this World."[18]

For years history had demonstrated that enthusiasts undermined the

peace and order of society. Perfectionism and antinomianism led people
to believe that their sinlessness eliminated the need for moral law, for
authority, for states to govern. Massachusetts Puritans were good historians, and it was easy to liken Quaker carryings on to those of John
of Leyden and the wild men and women of Münster. The fear of subversion was behind John Winthrop's hurried riddance of the antinomian
enthusiasts in 1638. It was the cause of Massachusetts's harassment of
the Baptists before the oligarchy had ever heard of Quakers. Enthusiasts
were impossible people to come to grips with in matters of either Church
or State. Winthrop's remarks about Anne Hutchinson and her followers
fitted the Quakers, too; they were "above reason and Scripture [;] they
were not subject to controll."[19] From the time Mary Fisher and Ann
Austin disembarked at Boston in 1656, the Massachusetts government
and clergy marked Quakers as enemies to civil peace who provoked
rebellion and sedition in the very face of authority. They reviled magistrates, spoke evil of "dignities," and by their insidious teaching withdrew the hearts of the people from subjection to just government. Believing
as they did, what was to prevent their "stirring up mutiny, sedition, and
rebellion" but strong laws and banishment? And then in justifying the
death penalty against them, the General Court went out of its way to
explain that these people suffered not because of their many crimes, such
as blasphemy and heresy, however capital, but because of their "super
added presumptuous and incorrigible contempt of aucthoritie."[20]

Plymouth found Quakers, their doctrines, their very "carriages" wholly
"destructive to the peace" of the country; while the government of Rhode
Island, which, as we have seen, refused to coerce them, admitted to
Massachusetts that Quaker doctrines, if generally taken up, tended to a
"cutting downe and overturninge relations and civill government among
men." New Haven whipped and banished Quakers who refused outright
to submit to the laws and whose profane and "disorderly ways," if not
suppressed, would certainly overthrow government and order.[21]

The tolerant Roger Williams believed Quakers were subversive of the
liberties and mercies which God specifically had bestowed upon Rhode
Island and which Quakers who settled, even visited, there enjoyed for
the first time in their lives. In his week-long debate with them in 1672
they so rigged the ground rules that only speakers who championed
Quakerism had an opportunity to open their mouths. Still, they broke
even their own rules, he said. When the Quaker governor Nicholas Easton
tried to join the debate—on their side, mind you—against Williams,
"Pope Edmundson" shut him up with a "Whist Whist," over which there
was no appeal. If they treat their Quaker friends this way, asked Williams,

what "will they say or Thunder to their Enemies if ever they get up into the Papal Chair"? He found them an imperious lot who had set their brazen faces against kings and magistrates without any English reverence or civility, and they based this imperiousness on a "horrible and lying pretence" that even in civil matters the amity of Christ was no respecter of persons. Subversive, yes, Williams would agree, not by gradually undermining Church and State, "creeping (like Hercules) out of the Cradle," but, more startlingly, by trampling outright over all mankind like gods. Watch out, he warned them in a debate which was not in the least friendly: "You do infringe not only upon our Souls but upon our *Temporal Liberties*."[22]

One of the few books Williams ever published in Boston resulted from this debate with the Quakers, which occurred first in Newport and then continued in Providence, Rhode Island. Of course, Williams could hardly say anything critical of Quakerism with which Massachusetts Puritans did not heartily agree, and so Bay Colony authorities judged it safe to publish *George Fox Digg'd out of his Burrowes,* Williams's detailed reconstruction in 1676 of the confrontation. There was no winner, for once Williams had given his side, George Fox and several friends in England published a rejoinder heavily weighted against him. Williams may have had the last laugh, however, for shortly after his book appeared, Rhode Islanders went to the polls for their spring election and refused to return the Quakers to office.[23]

Quaker beliefs subverted other institutions besides Church and State, opponents insisted. The same wild doctrines which undermined connections between subjects and their magistrates made a shambles, too, of relations between husbands and wives, parents and children, servants and masters. And did not Quakers talk of dividing up men's property and "having all things in common"? asked Richard Blome at Cambridge in 1659. Other sharp questions arose, and Quakers found that they were subject to the same kind of suspicion that had plagued enthusiasts since the time of the Donatists and Montanists in the early years of Christianity. Englishmen wanted clear answers to questions about the dangers of women preachers and the whole sect's disdain for learning. Like most conventional Christians when face to face with radical beliefs, they showed an almost prurient interest in attitudes toward sex and morality. Was fornication sinful? Did Quakers approve the "doings of those Men and Women, who lye naked in the Streets, fathering it upon the Spirit?" And did Hugh Bisbrowne sin or not when he "committed buggery with a Mare"? George Fox drew together a variety of radical sectaries when he preached the doctrines of the inward light. He also drew the focus of a nation upon Quakers and Quakerism, a nation which concluded that the heart of Quakerism was enthusiasm, "a Mother and a Master-Error" to the many mistaken and heretical beliefs they held.[24]

Most Puritans in Massachusetts believed that Quakers there tended to destroy the holy purpose behind the colony's mission in the New World. Fanatics all, they sought to "alter the received laudable customs" of the nation and turn upside down the customary respect given in society to equals and the reverence owed to superiors. And even more disturbing, they insinuated themselves into the hearts and minds of the simpler folk, who, because they were the meaner sort, were less attached to social order, the discipline of commonwealth and churches, and so far Quakers had succeeded in drawing off a number of these people to their pernicious principles.[25] Plymouth authorities feared for civil respect habitually given to one another, to magistrates, but also to masters and parents and to the aged and revered. Troublesome too was the increase in the infection; by 1659 Quakers had taken over almost the whole town of Sandwich on Cape Cod. Virginians also were apprehensive. There these turbulent and unreasonable people met daily and spewed their "lies, miracles, false visions, prophecies, and doctrines" which could only tear down religion and law and all the "bonds of civil society."[26]

Most American colonists were as determined to stifle Quaker enthusiasm as Quakers were to give vent to it. Massachusetts led the way, encouraged by the New England Confederation, which already was anxious about Anabaptists and their radical notions. The Bay Colony's laws were notoriously severe. They struck at Quakers for being Quakers, not waiting often for them to show their hands, or their hearts, and disseminate their principles. On top of this the laws fined ship captains for bringing them and colonists for keeping them, and punished local people who joined them. Magistrates burned their books and papers, misused them in jail, whipped them unmercifully, and then sent them away. When laws and cruel punishments failed to deter the invasion of either newcomers or repeated visitors—usually through "back door" Rhode Island—the legislature banished them on pain of death.[27]

Hardly less severe was Virginia. Several acts, beginning in 1659, suppressed the sect, including one similar to Massachusetts's, which demanded death for return after the second banishment. If no hangings actually occurred, Thomas Jefferson wrote more than a hundred years later, it was not owing to moderation of either the colony's legislature or the Anglican Church. Sir William Berkeley's government imprisoned "many Quakers," and a number lost their estates and were banished for refusing to swear they would not meet to worship in their own way, contrary to the establishment's practices.[28] Despite an earlier act of toleration in Maryland, Quakers ran into plenty of official trouble there in the 1660s. "What torturing, and prisoning, and whipping and scourging," wrote Francis Howgill, to say nothing of the government's seizing people's goods for not doffing their caps before superiors, or more important, for refusing to take oaths or go to war. Maryland Quakers, most of whom were converted in Maryland despite this treatment, or maybe because of it, had their share of cattails as they were switched from one constable to another on their way to the colony's boundaries.[29]

There were fewer laws and more proclamations in New Netherlands, where Governor Peter Stuyvesant ruled without an assembly. He seemed moderate enough at the outset when half a dozen Quaker missionaries disembarked in August 1657. But when two of them, young women in their twenties, paraded about the streets of New Amsterdam declaring Quaker versions of truth to startled burghers, they were taken up and soon sent away. In defiance of Stuyvesant's orders, Quakers continued to arrive; most were packed off to Rhode Island, the home of "errorists and enthusiasts," and the only colony which tolerated them. But Stuyvesant fought a losing battle, particularly on Long Island, where Quakerism prevailed and continued to spread. By 1663 the directors of the Dutch West India Company suggested moderation; but Englishmen after the conquest in 1664 were no more sympathetic than colonial Dutchmen, and persecution continued, questioning Quaker marriages late in the century and Quakers' right to vote well into the next.[30]

Connecticut enacted its share of suppressive laws from the first appearance of Quakers there and extended its proscription to include Ranters and Adamites. Like Massachusetts's, Connecticut's laws aimed at ridding the colony of the "loathsome Heretickes," but the legislature stopped short of hanging as a means of accomplishing it. The procedure, based largely on fines and whippings, must have worked, for in 1680 the colony reported only a handful of Quakers in the whole population.[31] New Haven Colony, which in 1662 became part of Connecticut, ordered branding and tongue boring for repeated Quaker offenses, but like her larger neighbor failed to exact the death penalty. Proximity to Shelter Island near the eastern tip of Long Island was a worrisome problem to New Haven people. Like Rhode Island, Shelter Island afforded an asylum where Quakers might lick their wounds before returning to battle in Boston, New Haven, and other hostile New England towns. Practical New Havenites made exceptions for well-stocked Quaker merchants, who were free to come among them to conduct "lawfull business," although they carried on under close surveillance and "at their charge." The laws prohibited possession of Quaker books as well as writing them.[32]

Some colonies and colonists resisted Quakerism more strongly than their neighbors. Or, one might say, in some colonies Quakerism took root more easily than in others. The incidence depended, it seems, on colonists' susceptibility to a free, unhinged brand of spiritual religion, or, as chief persecutor John Norton of Boston knowingly put it, "The strength of false prophecy lay not in the argument of the speaker, but in the affection of the hearer."[33] In Massachusetts and Connecticut, where a disciplined Puritan Congregationalism obtained, Quakers ran into stiff resistance, and it was many years before colonists there felt hospitable to them, even comfortable with the newcomers; some never did.

In Maryland, Long Island, Plymouth Colony, and, of course, Rhode Island, the story was different. In these places either lack of ministers or lack of interest in a strong ecclesiastical discipline left people more receptive to what Quakers had to offer. John Yeo, an Anglican priest in Maryland, blamed negligence on the part of the King's Church for the sad state of religion in his colony. Many people, he wrote home to Canterbury, were daily falling "away either to Popery, Quakerisme or fanaticism," leaving Maryland a "Sodom of uncleaness and a Pest house of Iniquity."[34] Separatists had always looked more kindly on inward religion and inspiration than either Anglicans or Puritan Independents, and in several colonies Separatists of one kind or another held sway. Seventeenth-century England seemed to have its share of men and women who sought more emotional, more open, less regimented religious experiences than what establishments could offer. Transfer a number of them to the New World where restraints in many parts were necessarily few; assume, too, that one of the reasons for their willingness to migrate was to rid themselves of religious restraints at home. All together these might explain why the hearts and minds of some colonists were prepared for the intuitive, imaginative, and emotional character of Quakerism. Cotton Mather insisted that there were Quakers in Salem before any of the real thing appeared in Massachusetts, meaning that there emerged in Salem a group of enthusiasts very much like Quakers except in name— same "fancies and whimsies"—and so prepared the ground for those who arrived in the late 1650s.[35] Where people of this temperament settled, where religious organization and discipline were thin, Quakers found willing converts. Plymouth and Rhode Island were two such places— Plymouth less so, to be sure, but certainly a case could be made. "Many unstable people" there, wrote Nathaniel Morton, "were leavened with their errors, and proved very troublesome."[36]

Plymouth, Connecticut, New Haven, and New Hampshire all responded to warnings and harsh recommendations by the New England Confederation and Massachusetts Bay about dangerous Quakers and what to do with them. Rhode Island answered, too, but in a very different way. The colony, least liked of any so far settled, was now the home of Separatists, Seekers, Gortonists, antinomians, Anabaptists, and just plain heretics, and it soon won a dubious honor as a place to dump Quakers who had been run out of Massachusetts, Plymouth, and New York. Because of its toleration of anyone in these years, it had become the "Latrina of New England," as a couple of Dutch domines indelicately put it.[37] To complicate matters, Rhode Island was never admitted to the New England Confederation and yet was on the receiving end of strong demands from the commissioners to rid the colony of all Quakers and Ranters and other "notorious heretiques" who either lived there, visited, or might some day crop up among the settlers there. All the more galling to Rhode Island was the Confederation's not so subtle threat to use any further means God might call for should the mischief continue.[38]

Rhode Island, under its governor, Benedict Arnold, took a brave stand against Quaker-hating New Englanders surrounding it. In so doing it read Massachusetts a Jeffersonian lesson about persecution and martyrdom and how to rid New England of both through toleration. In letters to the Massachusetts Bay authorities and the New England Commissioners, Rhode Island pointed out that it had never passed laws to punish people for what they believed about the "things and ways of God," about salvation and eternity. We have found, the letters explained, that when people such as Quakers are left alone to speak freely what they believe and are opposed only by argument and debate, they lose their desire to remain, in fact, come to "loath this place." Far from being opposed by civil authority, they are left free to mouth their "pretended revelations and admonitions"; no one pays much attention to them, nor are they likely to gain many followers. You see, Rhode Islanders explained, these people "delight to be persecuted," because they are apt to gain more converts through their "patient sufferings" than they ever could win by their "pernicious sayings." Although we admit that their doctrines, should they be widely taken up, might undermine society and civil government, still we are convinced that the damage these people can do to you and neighboring colonies, while we tolerate them here, will be nowhere near as dangerous as the consequences of what you are doing to them yourselves. We shall see to it that they behave and perform the duties necessary to our charter demands, and if they do not, we shall refer the problem to authority in England, where, we are sure you know, Quakers have been "suffered to live" for some time, "yea even in the heart of the nation."[39]

For several years Massachusetts Bay steeled itself against such silly advice as came from the soft underbelly of New England. The message from Rhode Island did seep through to a few here and there. Surprisingly,

John Hull, who heretofore had taken a hard line toward heretics and even dissenters, seems to have had an inkling of its meaning. He confided to his diary that Quakers appeared to "suffer patiently," in fact, "take a kind of pleasure in it." Where they are free to speak as they please, as in Providence and Warwick and other parts of Rhode Island, they don't tarry very long, for they find them "dry places."[40] But Hull never shared his insight with the Bay Colony government. In Plymouth, too, there was some recognition of the connection between persecution and Quaker successes. A letter from a sympathizer went back to London full of reports that the remarkable patience demonstrated by those who were monstrously beaten was sometimes the occasion for their drawing more followers than if they had openly tried to do the same through preaching. Quakers flourished in Dover, New Hampshire, too, the only town in that province where they were physically mistreated. The irony of it all remained a secret from Governor Sir William Berkeley in Virginia, who was as hard on Quakers as were his Massachusetts contemporaries. The harsher his treatment of them, the more they burgeoned. When the English government clipped his authority to persecute, Quakerism tended to fade.[41]

George Fox and his Quakers believed themselves to be prophets. While radical Puritans and dissenting sectarians prophesied and expounded on Christian truths in their churches with the help of the Holy Spirit, Quakers carried the practice beyond their contemporaries. They made prophesying the very center of their worship. They were prophets, they said, full of the same inspiration God had showered upon the Old Testament fathers, on Isaiah, Amos, Jeremiah, and Ezekiel. At God's commands, like their biblical forebears, this early generation of Quakers dealt in signs and symbols in order to convince those "out of the truth" of their poverty of spirit and wickedness. James Nayler's Christlike procession into Bristol City in 1656 was just such a sign, although those not privy to the Christ in him pronounced it blasphemy. Quakers used portents and symbols to denote the evils and wickedness and the judgment and doom which lay ahead, while those to whom the signs and symbols were directed read them as compounded evidence of enthusiasm, even madness.[42]

Next to hanging, public nakedness was probably the outstanding sign Quakers had at their disposal. Nakedness had a long history among enthusiasts. It began with the Adamites, whose aim was to return to the primitive innocence of Adam and Eve before the Fall. They met in conventicles in subterranean places and worshipped entirely nude, men and women together, some say in purity, some not. The idea sprang up again in the sixteenth century among Anabaptists in Amsterdam, who occasionally streaked through the streets of that city crying woe to the ungodly. Some fifty years later, in 1580, another Dutch Anabaptist sect was dubbed Adamite by contemporaries when it customarily stood its prospective members unclothed before the congregation as a way of demonstrating a lack of lustful desire in their devotions.[43] (There were strong suggestions that Shakers in America did the same in the late eighteenth century.)[44] Rumors of nudity among Baptists spread to the colonies. There was something about total immersion which suggested lasciviousness and promiscuity, and Obadiah Holmes suffered for it in 1651 when Governor John Endicott and Massachusetts Bay clamped down on the sect. Holmes's defense against the accusation that he had baptized Goody Bowdish naked was simply that he knew "better than to do such a thing," and anyway, her husband was present—that is, to testify that she was plentifully clothed with "comely garments."[45]

Scattered charges were heard that some of the new sects which mushroomed during the English Civil War also incorporated nudity into their worship. Of course, rumors flew suggesting that all kinds of wanton and lewd exercises accompanied these practices, including community of wives and outright promiscuity. Ranters were included, and one of them broadcast that the maid of one of John Milton's friends had lately got into the Ranter spirit and "stripped herself naked and skipped" at one of their meetings.[46] Roger Williams claimed that nakedness was a lively Ranter custom, and he could name names, too, if needed, of those who had made a big stir recently about the necessity of settling colonies in warmer climates where they might more conveniently carry on the Lord's ordinance "of Nakedness of men and women in Gods worship."[47] How much of all this, if any, rubbed off on the Quakers would be difficult to determine. They claimed strictly biblical precedents for their practices, of course, and patiently suffered when other possibilities or purposes were suggested, as frequently they were.

Quakers' nakedness was an unnerving example of uncompromising enthusiasm. If, at God's bidding, Isaiah could "loose the sackcloth" from his loins and for three years walk naked "for a signe," symbolizing the shameful captivity of Ethiopia and Egypt, then Quakers could do the same to expose the wrongheaded wickedness and eventual doom of Cromwell's government, the Anglican Church, or the Puritan oligarchy in Massachusetts, all of which persecuted them. Quakers made it a point to tell posterity that "going naked for a sign" was never an easy thing to do. William Simpson, like Isaiah, "went three years Naked and in Sackcloth" in the days of Cromwell and stalked through markets, courts, towns, cities, and great houses. The burden was heavy, and he would rather have died, he said, but once God spoke, "Go on and prosper," "it was sweet unto me, as the honey and the honey-Combe." Outwardly his reward, wrote Fox, was "whippings with horse whipps & coach whipps[,] stoneinges & Imprisonments."[48]

During the great plague of 1665 Solomon Eccles strode stark naked through Smithfield Fair with a dish of fire upon his head to bring home to suffering London God's judgment upon it. Given the circumstances, the plague and all, the effort seemed hardly necessary, or any more effective than his surprising the Irish one Sunday morning in Galway, where he demonstrated unclothed against a Catholic Mass, all the while balancing a pan of fire and brimstone on his head. Eccles exhibited other eccentricities in the Lord's service such as commandeering the pulpit and communion table of a local London church, where he set up shop as a shoemaker in a fit of contempt for Anglican forms. A call for this kind of demonstration struck Robert Barclay, the Quaker apologist, in 1672, when he traipsed through the streets of Aberdeen, some say stark naked, others in sackcloth and ashes, warning people there to repent their evil ways.[49]

Quaker signs and symbols did not change the direction of English or Scottish society or initiate ecclesiastical reforms in the 1650s and 60s. Fox lamented that instead of taking to heart their own "nakedness from the image of God & righteousnesse," Englishmen merely whipped and abused and imprisoned the Quakers who tried to convince them of it. Yet Quakers seemed unaware how futile the actions were in pressing their message upon others. It was sufficient only to convince themselves, to clear themselves of a duty laid upon them by God, and this they did and were fulfilled, if not understood. The Restoration government interpreted these events as signs of increasing discontent, which, of course, they were. "In all great towns," one report read, "Quakers go naked on market-days through the town, crying" woe to this and to that, "and declare strange doctrine against the Government."[50] But it was the Fifth Monarchists' bloody uprising which was crucial in provoking the Restoration government's reaction against fanaticism in the form of the Clarendon Code, not the parading of a few shivering Quakers through streets and marketplaces as signs and symbols of judgment and doom.

Geoffrey Nuttall tells us that the liberating forces of the Civil War and Interregnum and the unbuttoning of religious life at the same time had its effect upon Quaker sexual habits. Among some it signaled sexual liberation, too; the highly emotional content of the inward light was reflected in moral attitudes, and some of Fox's people took advantage of the new freedom.[51] But such liberation had been an inherent part of the history of enthusiasm from the very beginning, although it often existed, as we have seen, more in the minds of unfriendly observers than in fact. Today, given their reputation as a sect, it is difficult to smear seventeenth-century Quakers with sexual immorality, let alone promiscuity. Still, the sexual life of all enthusiasts at the time, even Quakers', was suspect. One of Richard Blome's pointed questions to Fox and Whitehead at Cambridge in 1659 was whether Quakers believed the moral law and the Ten Commandments were rules to walk by.[52] About the time of James Nayler's notorious pageant at Bristol, rumors spread about his "committing of fornication," although Willem Sewel, the first Quaker historian and contemporary of William Penn, wrote that he had been "very inquisitive" about Nayler's habits and could not find "that he was in the least guilty thereof."[53] Quakers seemed to have pretty chaste ideas about marriage, albeit the ceremony itself was unorthodox. When Fox was newly married to Margaret Fell in 1669, both of them in middle age, an old Puritan had the nerve to ask him what he wanted to do that for when the purpose of marriage was to have children. Fox told him he only thought of these things "in obedience to the power of the Lord," for he "judged such things below" him.[54] "Such things" may have been beneath George Fox; other Quakers felt up to them. Although they never lay "naked in the Streets, fathering it upon the Spirit," like the Anabaptists, they set no precedents for the celibate Labadists or Shakers, either. Quakers were enthusiasts, and like enthusiasts then, earlier, and later, some drifted into perfectionism and antinomianism and felt free of the morality which bound their contemporaries.

Massachusetts remained impervious for several years to the blessings of toleration as Rhode Island understood them. The more persistent Quakers became in attempting to teach their truth in the Bay Colony, the more severely the government reacted against them. As a result Quaker prophets soon became Quaker martyrs. "I have ordained Thee a Prophet unto the Nations," God announced to Marmaduke Stevenson, a Quaker missionary to America, and then directed again his steps to Boston in 1659. William Robinson told Governor John Endicott and the Massachusetts Court the same year that God had commanded his return to Boston, his life to lay down at God's will. Together from their Boston prison, Stevenson and Robinson confessed that they spoke as the voice of God; they condemned the Puritan "children of anti-Christ" who refused the truth which God had sent the Quakers to unfold to them, who cruelly oppressed the innocent, even Christ himself, and who soon would be consumed by God's righteous anger.[55]

Mary Dyer of Rhode Island joined Stevenson and Robinson in the summer of 1659. Boston was well acquainted with the "comely" Mary Dyer and had banished her as an antinomian close behind Mrs. Hutch-

inson in 1638. Since then she had lived at Portsmouth on the Island of
Rhode Island with her family—that is, until 1651, when she and her
husband, William, accompanied Roger Williams and John Clarke to
London to undo the machinations of William Coddington, who had
succeeded in separating Newport from the rest of the colony. While in
England, Mary Dyer became a Quaker. Whether succumbing to the inward light was much of a shift from subjection to the antinomian Christ
within is a nice theological question not much discussed at the time. In
her case there seemed to be little difficulty. George Fox's strong leadership
carried many enthusiasts along with him and even pushed some ahead.[56]
But upon Mary Dyer's return to the colonies her ship landed in Boston,
from which she was soon banished again to Rhode Island, this time as
a Quaker. It was not long before she returned and as a result lay in the
same jail as her Quaker contemporaries Stevenson and Robinson. In
pleading her release her son boldly challenged Massachusetts's laws against
Quakers and likened her treatment to that of the saints in Queen Mary's
time and the persecution of the Waldenses in southern France. Besides
being a Quaker, the charge against her was that she affirmed the "light
within her to bee the Rule." Does Massachusetts have a law, young Dyer
asked Governor and Council, "that s[ai]th the light in M. Dyer is not
M. Dyre's rule"?[57]

Massachusetts Bay's severe punishment of Quakers derived from its
frustration in the face of stubborn enthusiasts who were as sure of their
commission as the colony was to forbid them it. As their laws directed,
John Endicott and the courts tried the Quaker prisoners and condemned
them to hang. "And well they deserve it," added John Hull, the "godly
goldsmith," all the while rejoicing that God had so strengthened the
colony magistrates "to bear witness against such blasphemers." Two
hundred soldiers were thought necessary to protect the people of Boston
from the trio as they were led to the gallows on October 17, where Mary
Dyer, standing on the scaffold, watched the hangman turn off her two
companions. And then, in what could only have been a humiliating
gesture, the authorities denied Mary Dyer her martyrdom and banished
her yet again. Relatives and friends saw to it that she hurriedly departed
from Massachusetts within the two days allowed.[58]

Now a martyr manquée, there was probably no one as determined as
Mary Dyer to die for the Quaker cause. Unknown to her husband in
Newport, who had lost sight of her for six months or so, she left Shelter
Island off Long Island, where she had fortified her resolve for some weeks,
and worked her way through Rhode Island, then secretly into Massachusetts, and finally in broad daylight to Boston, where she was promptly
seized. Near the end of May 1660 her husband this time pleaded for her

life. The tone of his plea was less assured than his son's, less convinced of her mission, and it damned her people who encouraged each other to hazard their lives for he knew "not whatt end or to what purpose." Let your pity and your favor overcome her great zeal, he petitioned the Massachusetts General Court. Let not your compassion be overturned by her "inconsiderate madnesse," for through compassion you will be victorious.[59]

The last thing the Puritan oligarchy felt for Quaker enthusiasts in 1660 was compassion. Mary Dyer's short trial proceeded immediately, and as it drew to a close Governor John Endicott asked her outright whether she believed she was a prophet. She answered simply that "she spake the words that the Lord Spake in her; and now the thing is come to pass." As she started to "speak of her Call," Endicott shut her up and waved her off. Old John Wilson, who had hounded Mrs. Hutchinson out of the colony and who had thumped for stringing up Samuel Gorton, accompanied Mrs. Dyer to the gallows tree and pressed her to repent. "Be not so deluded and carried away by the deceit of the Devil," he charged her. "Nay, man," she replied; "I am not now to repent," and she did not. There was no disappointment this time, and she was hanged on June 1, 1660. The next year William Leddra received the same treatment.[60]

They brought it upon themselves, the colony argued in justification of the executions. Their design was apparent; our experience in the past and the "example of their predecessors in Münster" were enough to warn us that they aimed at overturning the peace and order of the colony. They knew the law; "they would not keep away, but came again, and run themselves upon the Sword point." Yes, they came again, and again, said Edward Burrough, another of Fox's missionaries, not in contempt of Massachusetts's lawful authority but "in the Motion of his Holy Spirit." When God and man command things differently, said Burrough, Quakers follow God.[61]

Mary Dyer "did hang as a Flag for them to take example by."[62] Both persecutor and persecuted agreed; one saw her death as the fanatical end all die-hard enthusiasts usually come to, or ought to, and the other as a sign of an indomitable faith which would eventually conquer the world. If, like English Quakers, those in New England wished to advertise their opponents' total lack of Christian love and spiritual truth, no symbol more graphically expressed it than Mary Dyer's corpse swinging in the breeze on Boston Common.

After William Leddra's death in 1661 there were no more hangings. Charles II got wind of what Massachusetts was up to and ordered it stopped and the Quaker prisoners sent to England, although not in time to save poor Leddra. Massachusetts insisted, however, that the Crown did not wish to prohibit other Quaker punishments but actually encouraged them—wholly a deliberate misconstruction of all the King's letters, reported the Royal Commission of 1664—and the legislature went on to pass a cart and whip act in 1661. By its means, the commissioners charged, "they have beaten some to jelly"—including Alice Ambrose (later Alice Gary), who held the record for being horsewhipped in more towns than any other Quaker visitor or native from Maine to Virginia and back.[63]

Quakers resisted in the only way they knew. To protest the wickedness of minister and magistrates at Newbury, Massachusetts, Lydia Wardel succumbed to the "leading of the Lord" and attended church stark naked as a sign of "ignorance and Persecution" in the town fathers. Her appearance so outraged the magistrates, to say nothing of the minister and elders, that they had her up before the next court, which ordered her tied to the tavern fence, stripped to the waist, "her naked Breasts to the Splinters of the Posts," and thoroughly whipped, "tho' it miserably tore and bruised her tender Body." She was a sign indeed, wrote George Bishop, of the wicked state of unreasonable men who in the name of religion were blinded into cruel persecution. The burden of suffering heaped upon Quakers affected Deborah Wilson similarly a few years later at Salem. A young woman, modest and retiring, she "was constrained" to walk naked through the town in 1669, accomplishing a good half of her task before being seized. The court at Salem added a new twist to her punishment. Fastened to a moving cart she was whipped with her mother and sister tied one on either side "that they might counsel her to what she had done," said the court. Robert, her husband, followed closely behind, "clapping his Hat sometimes between the Whip and her Back."[64]

Signs and symbols were a prophetic language through which Quakers spoke to their contemporaries about poverty of spirit and the cruelty of persecution. American Quakers were as expressive, as eloquent as their English cousins, although they spoke less frequently. Probably both English and American Quakers would have agreed that their painful efforts went a good deal farther to satisfy themselves, to clear the truth, than to change attitudes toward them, the inward light, or, one might add, enthusiasts generally.

The effect of Margaret Brewster's sudden presence in Boston's Third Church one Sunday morning in 1677 would be difficult to determine. She had journeyed all the way from Barbados for the purpose and appeared during sermon time in sackcloth, hair disheveled and gray with ashes, her face blackened with soot, led by a pair of Quakers with two following behind. Her appearance in shocking get-up "occasioned the greatest and most amazing uproar" Samuel Sewall had ever seen, but he did not explain its meaning, if he knew. And he and others might very well not have understood what Quakers were trying to tell them, although the macabre figure seems to have unnerved and upset, but also exasperated, the whole town of Boston.

Suspecting that Bostonians had missed the point, George Fox spelled out to the governor of Massachusetts that Margaret Brewster had come as a sign of his government's *"Shame* and *Nakedness,"* its dearth of God's armor and spiritual weapons, which lack it proved by its *"Blows* and *Prison,"* its *"Whips* and *Stocks,"* its "Diabolical Spirit." The same year George Bishop explained that she had visited Boston as a sign of the black pox, a judgment which shortly settled upon the town and cut off a number of its people. For this timely warning, said Bishop, she was "stripp'd and whipp'd."⁶⁵

Margaret Brewster's whipping was the last punishment of that kind inflicted upon a woman in Massachusetts. Was the shift in treatment the result of changing times, or was the Quaker spirit getting through to Bay Colonists? Quakers had a way of wearing down their opponents. Gilbert Burnet in England drew this conclusion about the time Massachusetts stopped beating women. When English Quakers were forbidden by the Conventicle Acts to meet and worship, he wrote, they met anyway. When the government locked them out of their meeting houses, they gathered in the streets before the doors, for, they said, they were not ashamed to worship God publicly. A good many Englishmen called this just plain obstinacy, while others admired their pluck and devotion. By their perseverance, wrote Burnet, they "carried their point: for the government grew weary of dealing with so much perverseness, and so began to let them alone."⁶⁶ Conditions in Boston were not those of London, to be sure, but for a variety of reasons Puritan persecution of Quakers eased. Besides King Charles's demands, Quaker "perverseness" probably helped.

Few colonists accepted the naked sign business, although some resented it more than others. No matter how much Roger Williams and his colony tolerated the carryings on of Quakers, he, at least, never forgave them their "whorish and monstrous Immodesty," as he called it. In fact, in his debate with Quaker leaders in 1672, he harped upon the subject so frequently that they turned the argument against him. When had he seen any of their women naked? they demanded; never had they thought he "wouldest have been such a wicked man." Williams quickly changed the subject.⁶⁷

In Maryland, George Alsop was grateful that Fifth Monarchy Men and Ranters stayed away. Maryland was free of the worst kinds of enthusiasts, he said, although a large part of the people there were "desiredly

Zealous, great pretenders to Holiness," and "very apt to be catcht." So far, among the enthusiasts, only Quakers had made any headway, and most of them seemed to behave themselves. He was particularly thankful that no "dancing Adamitical Sisters" had put in an appearance, those who "plead a primitive Innocency for their base obscenity, and naked deportment." Anyway, they would never take hold in Maryland, he said. One blast of the northwest wind in January and February would not only cool off such "cract-brain Sots" but "convert the hottest of these Zealots from their burning and fiercest Concupiscence."[68] Going naked as a sign was restricted to Massachusetts, despite the colder weather, among Puritans who least appreciated it.

Like other enthusiasts, Quakers played down intellectual pursuits. George Fox in the early pages of his journal repeatedly reminded his people that study at Oxford and Cambridge did not fit men to be ministers of Christ. It was not "Latine, Greek or Hebrew, that teacheth to understand the Scripture, but it is the Spirit of God," wrote Edward Burrough, one of Fox's missionaries.[69] Puritans and Anglicans alike had always insisted that education keep pace with religious insight, for the two worked hand in hand, or in Massachusetts what was Harvard College for? Quakers believed the inward light was a shortcut to true religion, eliminating the intellectual baggage which so bogged down orthodox people; it offered an unencumbered passage for inspiration which really had nothing to do with "humane learning" anyway. When the work of the Lord prospers, wrote Alice Curwen from Barbados, it is because "he is turning back the Wisdom of the wise," permitting truth to triumph over those who would bait and ensnare the innocent. Roger Williams called Quakers "Ignorant Praters" who willingly shut their eyes to reason and common sense. They and the Catholics would be burning Bibles next and substituting "infallible spirits" and silly traditions. "Ah, poor cheated Souls."[70]

Quakers went even farther. Not only were they wary of learning and intellectual endeavor which dimmed the light, but they were suspicious too of teaching, for like learning, it was secondhand. This suspicion was shared by other enthusiasts. Historically one can trace a wariness among some of these people against gathering disciples and forming cults, for the nature of enthusiasm usually worked against dependence on teachers and prophets, and this was particularly true of Quaker enthusiasm.

George Fox was an "original . . . no man's copy," wrote William Penn. What he knew he learned from no one, least of all from study, and his teachings and writings were practical and sensible truths, neither "notional [n]or speculative." They encouraged "conversion and regeneration and the setting up of the Kingdom of God in the hearts of men."[71] In the spring of 1673 Fox visited Rhode Island for several months. There his successes included a good deal of organizing and a huge six-day meeting of loving colonists who flocked from all over to hear him. In the midst of his stop at Narragansett, Fox learned that several local magistrates were scheming to scrape together enough money to hire him as their minister. News of this pulled him up short. It was time to move on, he said; if they have their eyes on me or any of us, they will never teach themselves. They understand neither us nor our principles. Our job, he explained, is "to bring every one to their own Teacher in themselves"—and off he went.[72] Like Fox, like most enthusiasts, Penn also attempted to bring people to the "principle" within themselves. The same message was clear and direct even to nineteenth-century Transcendentalists, who borrowed from Quakerism, particularly the likes of Ralph Waldo Emerson. In speaking and writing, Emerson jotted in his journal, he had no wish to bring men and women to himself but to themselves. He delighted in driving people from him; it was his boast that he had "no school follower."[73]

Quaker ministers entertained no self-interested or personal design, wrote Penn, and here he hit upon a major theme which helps to explain the enthusiasts' intense sacrifice and often lonely search. How could they be personally interested, asked Penn, when as missionaries they left themselves vulnerable to abuse and scorn, when they turned their backs on father and mother, brothers and sisters, wife and children, and all they held dear in order to follow Christ?[74] Penn's words echoed the Bible (Luke 14:26), but Samuel Gorton and George Fox had said as much and together set a pattern for Margaret Brewster, Patience Greene, and the Transcendental Emerson, besides countless other wandering enthusiasts. Patience Greene, a "public friend" from Rhode Island, felt divinely called in 1771 to desert her family and preach against slavery in the southern colonies. She returned to find one child dead and another dying but soon left again for England, Scotland, and Wales, hoping for an audience with George III to persuade him to free slaves in the dominions.[75] (Nathaniel Hawthorne's Catharine in "The Gentle Boy" owes a good deal to Margaret Brewster and Rhode Island's Patience Greene.) "I shun father and mother and wife and brother when my genius calls me," wrote Emerson. "I would write on the lintels of the door-post, *Whim*. I hope it is somewhat better than whim at last, but we cannot spend the day in explanation."[76] Enthusiasts, whether Cassandras, prophets, abolitionists, or reformers, had a lot in common and still do.

Conventional society found enthusiasm one sided. It destroyed that studied balance between emotion and reason around which most sensible people attempted to fashion their Church and their State—in fact, their social institutions. It exaggerated the emotional, intuitive side of men's and women's natures and played down the rational, external forces which also helped to form their beliefs and direct their actions in religion and society. This balance between emotion and reason was difficult to maintain. While enthusiasts found the emotional side primary, orthodox believers tended to emphasize the reasonable and external, and it was this side of Old World institutions which a majority of colonists, by force of habit or inertia, were bound to establish in the New. But Quakers were Christian enthusiasts who knew another way, a different way, a disarmingly simple way in which to build a New Jerusalem, a way in which God spoke directly to individuals independently of manmade institutions of Church and State. It was a way which subverted by its very nature customs, habits, traditions both religious and civil, which the Old World taught the New to respect. To Quakers, America was a new and different world, to be built on different premises—premises which Quakers looked inward to discover.

❧ 7 ❧
Quakers from William Penn
to John Woolman

HISTORIANS agree that the 1660s were a turning point in the course of Quaker history. They do not agree specifically on the year, but a number of things occurred which in retrospect we can see signaled a change. James Nayler was dead, and in the more staid days of the Restoration there was a reaction to his kind of fanaticism among many. John Perrot, who had given George Fox so much trouble as an enemy of "hat honour" and other "forms," died in 1665, and even extreme Quakers began to look differently upon his upsetting contributions to their history. The next year a group of weighty leaders met in London and drafted a circular letter, setting down a policy for all Quakers which played down individual spiritual vagaries and emphasized coordination within the group around common principles of "Truth." Later that year George Fox was released from prison and began a diligent campaign of correspondence and organization which resulted in a network of permanent meetings, lending Quakerism something of a structure and direction it had not known earlier.[1]

Outside of Quakerism England itself took a turn with the Restoration. In government, politics, and imperial affairs 1660 marked a reaction to the republicanism of the Civil War and Interregnum, which historians have described and analyzed at length. In both religion and science there were serious second thoughts about the fanaticism and irrationality of the previous generation. The restored government reestablished the King's Church and launched a campaign to suppress dissent. Natural philosophers organized the Royal Society and attempted to establish more acceptable foundations for modern science—chemistry in particular—questioning the Helmontian and Paracelsian amalgam of religion and science which heretofore had characterized their endeavors. It is easy to make too much of turning points and this one in particular, but the 1660s lend themselves to this kind of analysis, and historians need all the help they can get in making sense out of the past.[2]

Despite its origins in the sectarian enthusiasm of the 1640s and 50s, Quakerism was not immune to these changes. Quakers were enthusiasts still, but beginning in these years they tended to moderation; nakedness and sackcloth were pretty much things of the past. William Penn was a good example of this shift in temperament. He was twenty years younger than George Fox, and unlike the founder was an educated and sophisticated gentleman with good connections in high places. Both were outspoken, to be sure, but Penn gave Quakerism a kind of respectability it never won under Fox.

Faith healing was forgotten along with Fox's 150 "successes" in that profession. His manuscript on miracles lovingly left to posterity curiously disappeared, although a version of it, reconstructed from a calendar of Fox's writings, was published only as recently as 1948.[3] Quakerism was still a horrible delusion, wrote Puritan Richard Baxter, but he looked forward to Penn's reforming it and establishing a proper ministry. Even Cotton Mather changed his tune, if only a little, recognizing Quakerism under William Penn as "quite a new thing," a refinement of the old "Foxian follies" by "more sensible sort of men." Still, the old Puritan prejudices hung on, and Mather continued to damn the sect's fundamental conceptions of God, Christ, light, and seed as idolatry.[4] One of the early Quaker settlers of Pennsylvania seemed almost surprised that New Yorkers openly welcomed Penn on his first visit there, after dropping his baggage in Philadelphia. He was "well approved of," wrote Thomas Paskell, and "extraordinarily entertained," behaving himself quite nobly.[5] There was still plenty of opposition to Quakerism, but some of the sect's crudeness had worn off, or as historians have put it, it was on its way to becoming a religious society instead of remaining an unhinged sect.[6]

Always a prolific writer, William Penn outdid himself after George Fox's death in 1690 and spent a good deal of time distilling what he and his second-generation Quakers understood to be Quaker truths. Penn remained an enthusiast, but he expressed Quaker beliefs in less arrogant and presumptuous ways which, if they were not more reasonable, at least appeared less wild and less heretical than ever those Fox had preached. Penn called Quakerism "Primitive Christianity Revived" and explained its "Ancient, First, and Standing Testimony": that through Christ, God had planted in everyone a "Principle" which not only taught him his duty but enabled him to do it. The measure or standard was the light of Christ in one's conscience. This principle divided sheep from goats, for those who lived up to it were God's people, and those who did not were not, despite what they made outwardly of religion. That which was divine Quakers understood through this principle, and though it was "in Man" it was not "of Man, but of God." Moreover, it led to God all who wished to be led by it.[7]

Penn felt the need to answer critics about Quaker views of Scripture, Christ, and revelation. Granted Quakers asserted the sufficiency of the Christ within, they never dismissed outright the Bible or any other external means. Nothing they taught opposed what God afforded outwardly for comfort and edification. In a remarkable letter of advice to his children, Penn referred them to the light of Christ within and to the truth of Scripture *and* to any exterior testimony which bore on eternal truths. Quakers did not play down the physical appearance of Christ, wrote Penn, or the efficacy of his sufferings and death as some had charged. They continuously confessed the historical presence of Christ who was like man in all things but sin, and then Penn rattled off the events in his life which orthodoxy had made creedal.[8] And what of revelations? Penn had a justification and defense for them, too, which, he wrote, were not "Whimsical Raptures" and "Prodigious Trances" as enemies insisted and ridiculed. He denied any Quaker share in "vain Whimsies and idle Intoxications" but modestly tied Quakers' understanding of revelation to the light within. Revelation was a "solid and necessary Discovery from the Lord" of all those vital things which bore on the conditions of daily life respecting the honor owed to God and care of their own souls.[9]

Penn's Quakers were more respectful of orthodoxy than were the martyrs of the first generation. Without giving up the essence of their belief, his explanations smacked enough of conventional religion, if not to take the curse off enthusiasm, at least to relieve it of some of its wildness, although Quakers were not always as careful of the world's feelings as Penn.

When railing priests and Anglican critics insisted that visions and revelations had ceased in the early years of Christian history, Quakers argued that indeed they had ceased for those who remained in a "dismal state" and knew them not. But without them, claimed James Dickinson to a Virginia audience, there was not true knowledge of God, for, as many had said before him, "Where there is no revelation, the people perish."[10] Although times changed and Quakers looked differently upon their own society and its organization—that is, their outward lives—the heart of their beliefs survived into an eighteenth century which looked more askance at enthusiasm than had the Restoration. But new truths kept erupting in America. Samuel Bownas marveled at the uncommon "Supply of new Doctrine every Day" which the Spirit fed him as he spoke at Philadelphia's huge meetings. In New Jersey he was inundated with "fresh Matter," he said, free from all human contrivance, books, and writings, which, among ministers of the letter, brought only death.[11] In America, "further truths" were disclosed to Quakers in abundance.

Surprisingly, William Penn looked backward, too, for he admired the early Puritans. He saw in them a "softer temper" than they later exhibited, a temper which recommended the love, goodness, and mercy of their religion. Most of all he admired their prophesying, the discovery of "further truths" in ordinary people, and the openness with which they permitted high and low, laity and clergy, liberty to speak and pray and discuss pressing issues at their meetings.[12] Along with the early Puritans' prophesying, Penn picked up Fox's idea of experimental religion—another firm fixture among enthusiasts at any time—and argued frequently for the practical and realistic nature of Quakerism. One can search and talk of God all one wants, but to know him is actually to be impressed with his truths. Quakers learned God's justice from his reproofs, patience from forebearance; through his forgiveness they became acquainted with mercy, and holiness from sanctification in their own hearts. These were the "grounded knowledge of God," the experience, the "realities of religion."[13] Quaker ministers "directed people to a principle in themselves" so that what they preached might be accepted "through experience." They pressed these truths, repentance, conversion, and holiness, upon their listeners through words, to be sure, but they did it "knowingly and experimentally," too, leading them to the "principle," telling them where to find it, how they might recognize it, experience it, enjoy it, and understand its effectiveness. This was no speculation and theory, wrote Penn; it was a "bottom upon which man may boldly appear before God in the great day of account."[14] George Whitefield hardly said it differently two generations later. Experimental religion was as much a part of revival enthusiasm as it was of Quakerism. Practical knowledge through religious experience was a key to both, although Penn's Quaker and Whitefield's revivalist were different, too. But they may not have been as different as we have imagined. Granted Whitefield was unusual among his breed, and certainly ecumenical, he had respect for Quakers, at least for their experimental piety. After being entertained by a Quaker in Wilmington, Delaware, in 1740, Whitefield told the world in his journal that his host had a "right spirit within him, and could speak as one experienced in the things of God."[15]

Quakers, like other enthusiasts, had a way of making anti-intellectualism a virtue, for it led to a practical piety. "Have but few books," William Penn told his children; rather, "measure both religion and learning by practice." Meditation and reflection were far more rewarding than reading, he advised them: "Much reading is an oppression of the mind and extinguishes the natural candle, which is the reason of so many senseless scholars in the world." Leveller William Walwyn and Samuel How, the cobbler, had said as much in the 1650s.[16] Penn reviewed the evidence and agreed. Human learning could be useful, Thomas Story confessed to the Harvard students who gathered about him one afternoon under a "large spreading Oak" close to the college yard, but only when the "Spirit of Truth" had subjected the mind. Don't sin against God, he warned them, by depending upon what was acquired at the "Fountain of human Learning." Drink rather at the "living Fountain," the "River of living Water." John Woolman has told us that he was always on his guard not to let his own will or the wisdom of the world get uppermost and cause him to depart from the Truth that was clearly fixed in his mind.[17] The advice was pretty much the same all along the line, and it continued throughout the eighteenth century. Human learning and worldly wisdom were reluctantly acceptable in their places, but, as Thomas Story rather clumsily put it, "not to be preferred as the chief Qualification in that Service." "Books are for the scholar's idle times," wrote Ralph Waldo Emerson in 1837, a very Quakerlike assertion in "The American Scholar" with which William Penn would have agreed heartily.[18]

Treatment of Quakers improved in the latter years of the seventeenth century, given a strong goad by the Toleration Act of 1688. Progress was not always consistent, however. In several colonies and among certain people, prejudices endured for some time. Although Quakers had never proved quite the threat they promised to be, still their kind of dissent seemed disloyal, chiefly in colonies where strong churches existed. At a Quaker meeting in Black Creek, Virginia, a sheriff confronted the traveling James Dickinson with a sharp inquiry about who had given him commission to preach. In words which matched those of Separatist John Lathrop, when cornered by Bishop Laud in 1632, Dickinson replied, "I have my commission from the great God." Astonished, the sheriff backed off and then hurriedly disappeared when the missionary boldly asked him by what law he persecuted Quakers.[19] At Nevis in the West Indies, the governor there treated Dickinson and his companion, Thomas Wilson, like spies until he learned they carried passes from the Secretary of State in London. He backed off, too, and from being "very high" suddenly became "very kind" and gave them the run of the island.[20]

The Quakers' stickiest problem was still Massachusetts. Governor Simon Bradstreet reported to the Lords of Trade in 1680 that there were probably some fifty Quakers in the colony—whom he lumped with beggars and vagabonds—but, he explained, most people did not count them Christians. Outright suppression of Quakers had pretty much ceased by this time, although there had been talk of it a few years earlier during King Philip's War, when some people suggested the colony ignore White-

hall's orders to desist and trust God with the outcome. Most orthodox
Puritans listed the grudging toleration of Quakers in Massachusetts as
one of the war's causes. After revocation of the colony's charter in 1684
the government annulled the death penalty for Quakers who returned
after banishment—and well it might since this and several other discriminatory laws had contributed to loss of the charter in the first place.[21]
James Dickinson found considerable resistance to the Truth at Plymouth
and people "hard and set against" it in Boston when he visited in 1692.
Samuel Bownas had much more success at Nantucket in 1703, where
islanders were drawn to the "primitive Purity" of his message. On a
second tour several years later he ran into trouble at Newbury, where
the local "priest," unable to prevent townspeople from attending the
meeting, attacked Quaker principles, or the lack of them, such as the
role of Scripture, baptism, communion, and resurrection. He put up very
weak arguments, said Bownas, who was happy to confute them and turn
his own people against him. But on another occasion the Newbury congregation appointed a day of humiliation and among other things asked
the Lord's help in preventing the spread of Quaker errors among them.[22]
A change in attitudes already had commenced when Thomas Story felt
at ease among the Harvard boys, whom he found a good deal more
"solid," more attentive, and "more like Christians" than any students
he had met at Oxford or Cambridge, Edinburgh, Glasgow, or Aberdeen—
and this despite his lecturing them on how far New England had strayed
from its glorious past when *"Gifted Brethren"* dominated.[23] Story, like
William Penn, looked back to the days of early Puritanism as a golden
age before corruption of truth set in and ruined the holy enterprise.
Samuel Sewall carried his prejudices against Quakerism well into the
eighteenth century, called it a profane heresy, and voted in council against
permitting construction of a new Quaker meeting house in Boston; he
"would not have a hand in setting up their Devil Worship," he said.[24]

Ranters

American Quakers had no James Nayler to play the role of Christ and
embarrass them. They did put up for a while with John Perrot, who
stirred things up in Virginia and Maryland and perhaps even farther
north. About the time official persecution began to fade, Quakers suffered
from schism in their own ranks in the form of Ranters and "New Quakers," "Young Quakers," and "Singing Quakers" who popped up here
and there but chiefly on Long Island to worry the Truth and harass its
messengers. Some of the extremists had been Quakers at one time or
another, but others merely were attracted to antinomian freedom and

found pleasure in plaguing the main body of Quakers, whose enthusiasm by this time recognized some bounds, although very different from those of orthodoxy.

It is difficult to determine just what these Ranters' purpose was. They struggled against Quakers chiefly, not conventional churchgoers. Colonial governments intervened only when they got out of hand and began taking off their clothes or making nuisances of themselves, for example blaspheming God publicly. Long Island had the highest incidence of Ranter carryings on, particularly at Oyster Bay and Flushing, which were also Quaker centers and remained so for years to come. George Fox met some there during his visit in 1672 and claimed he put them down. John Burnyeat had struggled with them the year before, as did William Edmundson three years later. Fox met more in Rhode Island, some of whom had come to his meetings just to heckle, but with the Lord's help, he tells us, the Spirit won out over them. Roger Williams never complained of Ranters in Rhode Island, although several attended his debate with Quakers—the same year Fox visited—along with Presbyterians and Baptists, besides a preponderance of Quakers in that "very great Gathering of People."[25] Fox and his missionaries frequently made it a point to meet specifically with troublesome individuals and groups like Ranters, always with the hope that God's power would subdue them, and, according to Quaker journals, it usually did.[26] Alice Curwen found the Ranters very wicked at Oyster Bay, where they disrupted her meetings with "Ranting, Roaring, Singing and Dancing." She and her flock, like Fox and his in England, learned that the "World" often mistook Ranters for Quakers, which put her and her people on the defensive and made it difficult to separate themselves—who are "Instruments in the hand of the Lord," and a "Song among a Wild Generation"—from their wicked opponents, thus hindering recruitment and setting the "World" against them.[27]

Oyster Bay was headquarters for Ranter operations, for there Thomas Case and his crew hung out. Case had a diabolical way about him, wrote Cotton Mather, and with an evil eye drew people to him, usually young women. Such was the explanation of Ann Rogers's truancy when her husband found her in Case's company after two weeks' absence from home. The law sent her back to be a good wife, but the next morning she was again at Case's place, carrying on in a "dancing quaking manner, with silly insignificant discourse." "Close custody" followed in New York City, where neither Case nor her husband enjoyed much of her company.[28]

Sometime in the 1680s the Ranters drifted into what New Yorkers called "New Quakers"; Thomas Case, now a perfectionist, remained in charge. "New Quakers" were very much like old Ranters and continued to turn their contempt upon ordinary Quakers, whom they criticized bitterly for inconsistencies and a refusal to go the whole way with Truth. Theologically they denied resurrection of the body and argued that resurgence of the light within the heart was sufficient for their purposes, and anyway it already was attained by them. Carrying this theological profundity to a conclusion, they turned away their wives, claiming that "Children of the Resurrection" had no need to marry. And if that was not enough to condemn marriage, they supported their denial of it by arguing that marriage was the Devil's own institution, proof being that people of the "World" married, and so it was not for them.[29]

Critics were prompt to point out that although "New Quakers" shunned marriage, they loved sex and took to heart George Fox's claim that good Quakers were blessed with the primitive innocence of Adam and Eve. Mary Ross of Long Island was quick to agree, and, after walking off with another woman's husband, she stripped herself stark naked, claiming "that it was a sign of *Guilt* to be asham'd of one Part of ones Body more than of another"—a change in rationale, one might add, from the "naked for a sign" routine so devoutly suffered earlier by the martyrs. But the wife was not easily done out of her husband; she tracked down the unclothed Mary and beat her unmercifully, so much so that had the victim not needed her clothing for cover, one report disclosed, she certainly could have used it for "Armour."[30]

Cotton Mather made a good deal of a similar story in which Mary Ross played again a bare but prominent role. This time she fell in with a pair who had led astray the wife of a Plymouth man—thus Mather's concern. Taking on a demonic power earlier reserved for Thomas Case, Mary Ross in a short time burned her clothes, called herself Christ, dubbed her companions apostles—one Peter, another Thomas—"died" for three days, rose and danced "naked altogether" with the other three, and managed several "stupendous blasphemies" while she and the lot were carried off to the magistrate. Cotton Mather told the story well.[31]

Quakers were scandalized, of course. They disassociated themselves from both Ranters and "New Quakers," and reproved them as antinomians, claiming their real purpose was to commit sin without thought or control. The extremists continued their antics for several years—carrying on much longer than their counterparts in England—interrupting Quaker meetings with singing and dancing, with shouting and howling and "lewd and lascivious" behavior.[32] Although Oyster Bay remained the focus of much Ranter activity, there were reports of eruptions in New Jersey, Connecticut, and New Hampshire.[33] James Dickinson ran into Ranters in Philadelphia, but they were soon "chained down by the power of God." There were "troublesome Spirits" in Maryland, where

William Edmundson helped to "set truth and it's Testimony over them." Thomas Story found in Elizabeth's Town, Virginia, "airy, wanton" scoffers who leered out from under their hats to mock him and the sober people who came to hear him. But Story and his companions cleared their consciences in spite of them and left persuaded that God's seed had taken hold. "Singing Quakers" vexed an unbelieving Milford housewife in Connecticut when they descended upon her, "humming and singing and groneing after their conjuring way." Here, she greeted them, "take my squalling Brat of a child . . . and sing to it says she for I have almost split my throat wth singing to him and cant get the Rogue to sleep." This tale tickled Sarah Kemble Knight in 1704 and helped to relieve her tedious journey, encumbered by bad roads and noisy taverns.[34]

Like their English cousins, American Ranters were out-and-out libertines, perfect antinomians. So convinced of their grace were they that sins were no sins, since every deed or thought was dictated by Christ— in fact, was the action of Christ within them and therefore could not be sin. This left them free, then, to do and say what they pleased regardless of laws, churches, and social conventions. English Ranterism had risen out of the breakdown of these institutions and the heightened enthusiasm which accompanied the English Civil War, and it faded with the Restoration's authoritative reaction to freedom and license. In America, the Ranters took the Quakers' enthusiasm one step farther, encouraged by spotty restraints in a New World setting. Theirs was a new dispensation, a freedom to soak themselves in the Spirit regardless of Old World legacies, a yearning for the perfect Christianity in which Christ did all. Conventional society damned them as Quakers, while Quakers insisted they were madmen or devils or both, and bitterly reproved their religious and moral nihilism. Ranters scoffed at Quakers for falling short, for giving up the spiritual revolution within sight of victory; they called their meetings, their prayers, their marriages, their very accountability carnal "set Forms" and contemptuously threw dust in the faces of their ministers. By 1700, in contrast to Ranter anarchy, Quakers spoke of how settled they themselves were under the "most concise, regular, and reasonable Constitution of Discipline that ever was established in the World,"[35] a conclusion which later events proved premature, but good propaganda, at least, in the struggle for New World souls against Ranterism.

George Keith

If Quakers acquired a more formal and reasonable look in the presence of Ranters, they lost it when Keithians emerged upon the scene. Quakers thought Ranters had "runn out," but Keithians, they believed, were reactionaries, on their way back to orthodoxy or already there. To Quakers, Ranters had dangerously carried the spiritual revolution to antinomianism and anarchy, while Keithians were still stuck with the Word and the externals of religion. Quakers were threatened from both sides, and the Keithian challenge was probably the more serious because it hit them squarely in a vital part.

George Keith was an Aberdonian and Scottish Presbyterian who became a Quaker in the 1660s. A graduate of the university at Aberdeen, he was a serious scholar (Bishop Gilbert Burnet was once his student); in fact, Keith was doubtless the most educated and scholarly Quaker the seventeenth century could boast. Outspoken and a strong writer on Quaker subjects, he spent several months of his early life in tollbooth prisons in both Aberdeen and Edinburgh and a stretch later at Newgate in London. Keith was friendly with both George Fox and William Penn, but his writings put him more in the moderate camp of Penn, despite his earlier start. Penn's toned-down discussion of revelation and the inner light suggests that he learned a good deal from Keith, as did Robert Barclay, whose *Apology* benefitted from some of Keith's ideas.[36]

To Keith in the 1660s immediate revelation, which he defended, had little to do with foretelling the future, or the discovery of new ways to heaven, or similar extreme claims. Revelation to Quakers, according to Keith, was not an audible voice of God to the outward ear, or an external appearance to the eye, or even visions, or dreams, or trances, and least of all miracles. Immediate revelation, wrote Keith, prefiguring the language of Emerson, was an "intuitive knowledge" of supernatural things. It was the discovery within the mind and heart of a seed, or "birth of God," an appropriate principle or instrument through which supernatural and divine things could "be sufficiently and satisfyingly, that is to say, intuitively known." All true Christians, then, daily, even hourly, enjoyed "Manifestations, Revelations, and Influences of the Life eternal[,] fresh and new from the Fountain, as the *Israelites* gathered the *Manna*, new from Heaven every day"—"further truths" in Quaker fashion.[37] Keith, like Penn after him, wrote of the practicality of Quaker principles, and despite his education and scholarship, he argued the simple and experimental character of Quaker religion. Like the woman preacher of Samaria, taught by Christ himself, who "saw more into the reason of the thing, than all the University men have done unto this day," like the woman of Samaria who left her jugs at the well and went into the city to tell others her story, Quakers taught Christ from their own experience.[38]

George Keith was a Quaker enthusiast of a moderate stamp. If he did not walk naked through the streets of Aberdeen alongside Robert Barclay, neither did he knuckle under to authority, State or Church. Rather, he preached an "intuitive knowledge" of God and the experimental Christianity of Quakers and went to jail anyway for his pains. In the early 1680s he sailed to the colonies, first to New Jersey, where he won prominence as a surveyor, and then Pennsylvania to oversee the schooling of children in the new Quaker province. After a year or so as an educator, Keith became sharply critical of the direction Quakerism was taking in America, and in pushing his criticism he provoked in the early 1690s a major schism among Quakers in the New World.[39]

Enthusiasm was at the heart of the Keithian controversy. While Ranters held Quakers in contempt for not having enthusiasm enough, Keith and his followers condemned them for having too much. After thirty years as a Quaker, George Keith had second thoughts about his fellows, or about how his fellows practiced Quakerism in Pennsylvania. In the early 1690s Keith left his schoolmastering to preach and to write against the laxness of Christian discipline in American Quakerism and for a stiffer use of theology in its religious thinking. Keith was a more orthodox Christian than the Quakers he found in Pennsylvania, and he argued, often impoliticly and intemperately, in favor of a better balance between the Spirit within and a Christ without. He claimed Christians needed both, that Quakers emphasized the light within at the expense of a faith in the outward Christ, and were, therefore, deceived and misled. Keith insisted that they were dead wrong about the body of Christ after resurrection, that they dismissed it in their thinking, even lost it somewhere in heaven, and this was heathenish. Quakers needed something besides the light for salvation, and Jesus the man, his suffering on earth, and his mediating in heaven were this something. Those who relied simply on the Christ within, wrote Keith, had turned their backs on the true light, had fallen "into Imaginations," which was really Ranterism.[40]

After several years in the colonies, Keith came to see Quakerism in a way he had not seen it before, to discover in it what earlier had been hidden or kept from him. In America, in a home of their own, Quakers found themselves "far out of reach" of conventional churches and religious ideas. Moreover, in Pennsylvania Quakers were their own bosses, not subordinate to an orthodox culture, and so "they spoke out their mind plainer." Once Keith had talked and worshipped with them in the New World, he concluded that they had turned Christian doctrine into simple allegories, most of all those doctrines which had to do with the "death and resurrection of Christ" and the way sinners were reconciled to God "by virtue of his cross."[41]

Keith never convinced most Quakers of his "Christian Quakerism." But he split the society wide open and drew to himself a healthy following of Pennsylvanians who helped to spread his doctrine to several spots in the colony besides Philadelphia and across the river into New Jersey. Ordinary Quakers fought back in their meetings and through the press, claiming Keith taught two Christs, one inward and one outward, and in so doing denied their principal tenet. Faith in the external Christ, argued Thomas Lloyd, and a belief that he died for man's sins yet rose again, "was not necessary to our Salvation." There was no doubt, according to Lloyd, that "Christ within did all." To challenge the essence of their belief was bad enough, but to do so immoderately, as Keith did, to accuse them of gross ignorance and blasphemy, and to smear them with Ranterism won him an unenviable set of epithets, including "Brat of Babylon," "Primate of Pennsylvania," "Father Confessor," and just plain "Pope."[42]

The Keithian controversy went beyond the issues of the role of Christ and the Scriptures. In his bitterness Keith tangled with one of the colony's magistrates in a name-calling fracas which brought Keith a charge of sedition in company with others, including William Bradford, printer of his pamphlets. The conflict spread to several fundamental questions about Quaker life in America such as the use of coercion in government, worldliness in a Quaker culture, and the Quakerliness of slave holding—Keith and his followers opposed all three. Before the issues were settled, the court convicted Keith and Bradford of sedition. What began as a struggle between two kinds of enthusiasts, respecting the "nearest and most direct way to Heaven," ended as a quarrel between conflicting factions over the meaning of Quakerism in the New World.[43]

In suppressing him Keith believed Pennsylvania Quakers had acted no differently from Puritans in Massachusetts. He advertised the similarity in a sharp piece of propaganda called *New-Englands Spirit of Persecution Transmitted to Pennsylvania,* printed not in Penn's colony but necessarily at New York in 1693. There were several besides Keith who concluded that there was little difference between the difficulties he found himself in and those of Roger Williams sixty years earlier. Although fined only five pounds after conviction, a fine the government never bothered to collect, Keith washed his hands of Pennsylvania for the time being and returned to England, while William Bradford, his printer, settled in New York, taking his press with him.[44]

The fact that Keith was shocked by the direction Quakers had taken in the colonies tells us something about their New World beliefs. Granted upon return to England he found fault with Quakers there, too, his discovery of the depths of Quaker enthusiasm occurred in America. He found they had "runn out" in much the same way James Nayler had strayed from George Fox's principles, that in the colonies, where no state

Church or orthodoxy kept an eye on it, Quakerism showed its true character, which Keith claimed was ignorant, superficial, and blasphemous.[45] The spiritual revolution which Quakers survived and then epitomized in England took a new turn in America, where it knew no restraints. It had forgotten its foundation, which Keith believed was a balance between pure Spirit, on the one hand, and an indispensable, physical Christ, on the other, supported by Holy Scripture. The American experience brought home to Keith that the inward light so stressed by colonial Quakers was an *ignis fatuus* unless it corresponded with the outward Christ of orthodoxy. Together they were the essence of Christianity. Reliance on the light alone made fools and infidels.[46]

New World Quakers who opposed Keith did so because in their view he tried to drag them back under the canons of the Old World. They had carried their spiritual revolution farther than he, although they lagged behind the Ranters, as we have seen. They had cut through and eliminated the theological and ecclesiastical trappings of orthodoxy and the state's control of religion which so bogged down Old World institutions. For ten years they had enjoyed complete freedom in a colony which encouraged their experiment in primitive Christianity, a colony they themselves had founded. And then along came George Keith, one of their very own, who suddenly turned on them and called them ignorant heathens and tried to smother their light with theological wraps and suffocate them in manmade dogma.

Back home English Quakers were not all friendly to Keith when he asked for support against their Pennsylvania cousins. The London Yearly Meeting disowned him, deciding that he had departed from the unity of the Spirit and had divorced himself from its fellowship. Keith soon set up for himself at Turner's Hall in London, still outwardly a Quaker but using every bit of evidence he could lay hands upon to prove that Quakers were rank enthusiasts and not really Christians at all. Actually, few Quakers came to hear him, but plenty of others obliged, and so he lectured them on Quaker absurdities.[47]

In 1700 Keith threw in his lot with the Anglicans and published an elaborate denunciation of the Quakers' "extravagantly Wild and Frenetick Delusions." The King's Church shortly ordained him priest. Gilbert Burnet applauded his reconciliation and was certain he could only do good service in "undeceiving and reclaiming some of those misled enthusiasts."[48] Already Keith had taken aim at William Penn as the archenemy of orthodoxy. When Keith first commenced the controversy in Pennsylvania, Penn was inclined to back him, for they had been missionaries together, traveling with George Fox on the Continent, and both had preached a moderate Quakerism, perhaps a reflection of their education and intellectual interests. But once Keith left the fold, Penn turned his back and supported the main body of Quakers against him.[49]

Quakers could talk all they wanted, said Keith, about the Spirit as the wine which "refresheth and cherisheth them," but if the Spirit was the wine, the Scriptures were the flagons in which it was conveyed. "Stay me with Flagons, comfort me with Apples," was no idle song for an honest Christian. The Scriptures were both means and rule "by which the Spirit doth Teach," claimed Keith, besides quickening, comforting, and strengthening the believer.[50] No more talk about "Immediate Revelation" and "intuitive knowledge" as an Anglican. It was means and rules and a Christ who was crucified. That was what true Christians were made of.

Even before Keith donned Anglican robes, he increased the tempo of his crusade against the Quakers. The attack upon William Penn was only one step along the way. In 1702 he became a missionary and began his proselytizing in, of all places, the colonies. Objective observers, if there were any, must have marveled at the nerve of the man. Keith's ship landed in Boston, where Samuel Sewall, on the wharf to greet Massachusetts's new governor, Joseph Dudley, was "startled" to find George Keith disembarking with him, sent by the Bishop of London, no less, as a missionary from the Society for the Propagation of the Gospel (SPG)—with an annual salary of two hundred guineas.[51] Before returning to Philadelphia, Keith took a swing through New England, where he was about as welcome as the Pope. But he seems to have spent less time arguing with Puritans and comforting scattered Anglicans than with confronting Quakers, whose enthusiasm and false beliefs he continued to ridicule—that is, when they let him speak, for they repeatedly and rudely interrupted him in much the way Ranters had abused Quakers a few years earlier. His line was the same: the insufficiency of the light within for salvation "without any thing else." Did the inward light, without Scripture, he continued to ask opponents, teach that "Jesus Christ was born of the Virgin Mary?" In Hampton, New Hampshire, up popped a woman among his listeners who claimed perfection; she had no sin, she said, not even a taint of original sin, for she was born of holy parents. Keith got nowhere with her and had to be content with lamenting in his journal that this was the kind of stuff George Fox and Edward Burrough had left behind them in America. At another meeting in Hampton a chap named Talbot read a treasured copy of George Fox's will, describing how Fox had bequeathed his boots and spurs and "Clyster-pipe" to one of his followers, implying all the while, Keith added, that the father of Quakerism had graciously left them behind as "holy Relicks."[52]

Before returning again to England in 1704, Keith met "abusive entertainment" from New England to Maryland, chiefly at Flushing on Long Island. In Philadelphia there was opposition from some of his old Christian Quakers, or separates, one of whom, a preacher, disputed with Keith whether Quakers like them, already "in Christ," ought to worry about hell. Keith was sure they should, for it was an "antinomian notion" not to, but he failed to convince the preacher of it.[53] Keithian Quakers had carried on by themselves for a while, but without a leader some drifted into Baptist churches, some to Anglicanism like Keith, and the rest returned to the Quaker fold. After scolding the lot about neglecting family prayers, and after dogging the steps of Samuel Bownas, who had called him a "Heathen Man and a Publican," Keith set sail for England and eventually settled into a comfortable parish at Edburton in Sussex.[54]

Comfortable or not, Keith did not cease his campaign against Quakers. *The Magick of Quakerism* brought together all his arguments in 1707: their "natural Enthusiasm" and their refusal to distinguish between "extraordinary Inspirations," which God had given only to a few in the days of prophets and apostles, and the ordinary, which he still discovered to the faithful through Scripture and other outward means. Without faith in an external Christ, without Christ revealed in Scripture, Quakers fumbled about in ignorance and spiritual blindness, despite their pretended or imagined light. Deism, infidelity, ignorance, and, of course, enthusiasm—with these Keith set a pattern for orthodox criticism of Quakerism which the eighteenth century echoed again and again.[55]

One of these echoes resounded in the preaching of George Whitefield, who began his evangelical career in the 1730s. Much as he admired the purity of the Quakers' spiritual side—and he referred to it frequently— he found their foundation all wrong. Quakers mistakenly equated the light of conscience with the Holy Spirit; they taught an inward Christ as the fundamental of their faith, and not the Christ without. That Jesus had imputed his outward righteousness to true Christians, Whitefield insisted, was the "sole fountain and cause of all the inward communications which we receive from the Spirit of God." Alas, if Quakers only had the sense to realize this! Otherwise, they presumptuously "make [their] own holiness." At the height of the Great Awakening in 1741, when Jonathan Edwards of Northampton, Massachusetts, defended the Revival and himself from charges of enthusiasm and extremism, he sharply distinguished between the Jesus who appeared in the flesh, the outward Christ, upon whom all men and women were dependent, and the "mystical, fantastical Christ," the light within of the Quakers which led them away from the Spirit of God.[56]

The Evangelical Lutheran Henry Melchior Muhlenberg spent some forty years in Pennsylvania among his own German people but surrounded by Quakers, and again and again he threw up his hands at their lack of Christian teaching, their total ignorance of God. For the orthodox Muhlenberg the wounds of Jesus had healed his wounds; the "Merit" of Christ's death breathed life into his soul, and the "Dogmatics, Exegisis, Morals, Homiletics" he had studied strengthened his weak faith. Of all these, he concluded, Quakers were hopelessly innocent.[57]

Samuel Seabury put it a little differently in 1759 after being assigned to an SPG mission on Long Island. Flushing had been the "ground seat of Quakerism" a generation or more ago, he wrote home to England, but now it was the "seat of Infidelity." He found this a natural transition. Nothing was more clear than that where Quakerism had taken root, there was basis for a loss of faith. Having trusted only the light within, these people neglected their children's religious education, and the youngsters now looked with contempt upon the church and disavowed even a need for redemption. In back-country Carolina another SPG missionary, Charles Woodmason, grudgingly put up with Quakers and a variety of other wild and enthusiastic dissenters, disliking them all. Quakers, he reported, were a "vile, licentious Pack—Absolute Deists unfit the Title of Christians."[58]

Had Quakers "runn out" in the New World? Had colonizing beyond the seas feathered the edge of spiritual revolution begun by the first generation—the "Publishers of Truth," as George Fox had called them? Quakerism never succeeded in becoming a majority force anywhere but in Pennsylvania, and its majority disappeared there in mid-eighteenth century, followed by withdrawal from government altogether over the realities of war it could not control. It was outnumbered on all sides and had long since lost its drive to convert the world, settling for a Society of Friends with its own habits and customs, jargon and restraints.

Still, Quakerism never denied its original spiritual insight, which, its members believed, was the true way to salvation, despite ridicule and contempt and attempts by others to rescue it from enthusiasm and heresy. Faith in the principle helped Quakers contribute to colonial life in their own way. A devotion to the Christ within continued to dictate how they reacted to the course of events, although their responses were not always popular with their neighbors. Along with their drift to a "peculiar people," there remained among Quakers an independence which offended conventional society and in some instances subverted, or was thought to subvert, several institutions inherited from abroad. Whose "truth" was Truth? The Quaker version was God's, they said; it was an intuitive, experimental Truth, and the New World had helped to shape it.

Pacifism and Antislavery

Quakerism was the hardiest of the enthusiasms to come out of the English Civil War years. Since God's Spirit lived in them, Quakers believed they were in an excellent position to judge the truth of manmade institutions which surrounded them. As a consequence Quakers challenged two of these institutions in particular as infamous scourges which had afflicted mankind throughout recorded history and which contradicted Christian truth as they came to experience it. The light within never shone brighter than when Quakers protested against war and slavery. At the same time it was never more subversive than when it impugned a British colonial society whose very existence rested on an imperial venture which provoked wars between European nations, to say nothing of the Indians, and depended on the forced labor of black human beings from another continent.

Quaker Christianity diffused a kind of equalitarianism, for God had "made of one Blood all Nations of Men." The inward light encouraged love of all creatures, which Quakers expressed through compassion, benevolence, and humanitarianism, all irreconcilable with war and slavery. Love and patience surpassed the weapons of war, wrote William Penn, and they in the end will have the victory.[59] "Thou shalt not kill" Quakers took literally almost from the start; gradually, as time wore on, they added the equally strong injunction against slavery.

William Penn defended eloquently the Quakers' peaceful tenets. Just as speaking the truth succeeded the need for oath taking, so patience and faith succeeded war in the practice of Quakerism. And then in what seems today a tongue-in-cheek statement, Penn added that he failed to see why Quakers should be obnoxious on this account to governments anywhere; if they would not fight *for* them, they would not fight *against* them either, "which is no mean security to any state." After all, wrote Penn, you cannot blame a people for not doing for others what they scruple to do for themselves.[60]

John Woolman was a working tailor from Mount Holly, New Jersey. As his religious insight and Quaker sensitivity deepened, he became increasingly alarmed about slaveholding and slave trading by a people whose religious principles, he insisted, opposed both. In good Quaker fashion he broached the subject at meetings, not very successfully at first, and then traveled among slaveholders near home and in the southern colonies, where he talked with planters and expressed his conviction politely but firmly within a Quaker context. Woolman published his first tract against slavery and the slave trade in 1754, although he had written it several years earlier but was reluctant then to see it in print. Eight years later he published a second part with the same title, and then after his death his journal and other writings appeared. Through gracious but determined agitation in preaching, visiting, and writing, Woolman, more than any other individual, was responsible for directing Quakers' attention to the evils of slavery, resulting eventually in its elimination from their society altogether.[61]

In the second half of the eighteenth century Quakers appeared to raise their sights respecting war and slavery and to address an audience larger than their own people. Anthony Benezet, who first made his mark as a Philadelphia schoolmaster, was half a dozen years older than the uneducated Woolman. Their antislavery campaigns overlapped by several years, and after Woolman's early death in 1772 Benezet carried on for another generation. His struggle against slavery continued after the Quakers had washed their hands of it, and his appeal against war during the Revolution was broadcast beyond Quaker meetings to all Christendom.

Woolman and Benezet brought plenty of peculiarly Quaker evidence to bear on the wrongness of slavery: that it obstructed the channel through which the "perfect Plant" within them took nourishment, that it corrupted minds and debased the morals of those it touched, and that it shut out the Holy Spirit of love, meekness, and charity which were the very nature of Quaker Christianity.[62] But they made full use of broader arguments, too—Christian virtue, the Golden Rule, equality and liberty, benevolence, brotherhood, and the rest of it—all of which they shared with an increasing number of Quakers and non-Quakers as the eighteenth century wore on.

Quakers said little about color as an ingredient in the complex of conditions surrounding slavery. But Woolman argued openly that black and white availed nothing respecting equity and right, yet slavery and black were as fatally related as were white and freedom. Only with difficulty can we disentangle the "false ideas" which our minds are apt to twist together, he explained, demonstrating a surprisingly clear understanding of the basis of prejudice. Neither slavery nor war stood alone in their gallery of evils. In condemning slavery in his saintly way, Woolman damned war, too, and blamed man's selfishness for both. "Wealth is attended with power," he claimed, and we who abhor war and believe we walk in the light, ought to take a closer look at the motives and foundation of owning great estates.[63] Slavery, wrote Benezet, "proceeds from the same corrupt root as War": an "unwarrantable desire of gain, a lust for amassing wealth." In describing the relationships between selfishness and sin, Woolman came very close to damning eighteenth-century capitalism and made a strong plea for the rights of the poor and oppressed in a society based on an unequal distribution of property—thus endearing himself to nineteenth-century socialists. Not only was greed for wealth and property the origin of slavery and war; it was evil in its own right and a fit subject for radical reform.[64]

Quakers believed it was Christ's task in life, death, and in spirit to conquer this wordly attraction, to turn men and women from it to the truth within, to wean them from selfishness to love and benevolence, with which war and slavery were incongruous. Having had a hearty glimpse of these truths, Woolman and Benezet felt driven to help others find them. It was not easy; neither the enthusiast's nor the reformer's lot was ever easy; it was often "mortifying," and it was frequently lonely. But the stakes were high. Should colonists not listen—and the prevalence of war and slavery in eighteenth-century America was good evidence that many did not—judgment and then calamity would follow, and saints like John Woolman and Anthony Benezet foresaw plenty of both.[65]

Quaker enthusiasm was subversive and revolutionary. It rejected accepted institutions such as orthodox Protestantism, uniformity of belief, and established churches, but also war and slavery. It found them incompatible with Christian principles anywhere, particularly in a New Jerusalem where men and women enjoyed exceptional opportunities to form societies based on God-given truths which were discoverable by all. But Old World institutions died hard, too well entrenched to give way, and Quaker enthusiasts were suspect for questioning them.

8

Continental Strains:
From Plockhoy to the Benezets

ENTHUSIASTS in early America were not all English, nor even all British. Their story would hardly be complete without a nod to other Europeans of that breed who ventured to the New World with high hopes of spiritual fulfillment. Religious unrest, and in some cases outright persecution, as well as political dissatisfaction, had sent English dissenters to the colonies since the 1620s. Similar conditions, some of them worse, made the New World look inviting to Continental radicals, religious and political reformers, and refugees. Asylum and utopia, a chance to carry out unconventional spiritual experiments, were attractive chiefly to Dutch and German and then French Protestants, many of them touched by different shades of Calvinism, Lutheranism, Behmenism, and simple pietism. The variety of the reformed in Europe was reflected in the variety of reformers who put the Atlantic Ocean between themselves and their difficulties. This was a historic migration. No words fit better its cosmic dimension than Tom Paine's in *Common Sense* (1776), when he marveled that the discovery of America had preceded the Reformation, as if the "Almighty graciously meant to open a sanctuary to the persecuted in future years."[1]

Still, these newcomers had more in common than just enthusiasm. But it, too, differed in intensity from, say, the peaceful quietism of the Moravians to the militant fanaticism of the Dutartres. Despite these differences, they shared several characteristics. They all came from the Continent; they embraced a primitive Christianity based on direct inspiration; and they were prepared to struggle in their own fashion to cultivate spiritual insights and derive from them new truths which could lead only to heaven. Most settled in the middle colonies, where toleration preceded them. Several established communities, enjoyed common property, and in various degrees regulated the religious, social, and economic activities of their members. Not many put as permanent marks on colonial society as the Moravians or the Benezet family. Yet they were a curious lot of heady Protestants who contributed colorfully, if not indelibly, to the rich cultural diversity of colonial life.

Plockhoy on the Horekill

Ronald Knox called the Mennonites "shy repositories of the old Anabaptist tradition." The tiny clutch of forty-one who came to Zwaanendael, near the mouth of the Delaware River in 1663, really had no time to be shy or anything else before they disappeared altogether. Mennonites may have risen "on the ruins of Münster,"[2] but the handful who disembarked "at the Whorekill" under Pieter Cornelius Plockhoy were a far cry from King John of Leyden's people, the explosive and fanatical Anabaptists whom the Mennonites had chosen to forget.

Jacob Arminius, who died in 1609, would have been surprised to know that his modification of Calvin's theology had something to do with Plockhoy's enthusiastic dissent a couple of generations later. When Arminianism came under fire from officialdom, there emerged in the Netherlands a group of "Remonstrants" who defended its principles until 1619, when the Synod of Dort dislodged them from the Dutch Church and cut them off from official and academic recognition. Left to organize themselves, one radical group, the "Collegiants," gathered and worshipped and spread a kind of equalitarian simplicity, pacifism, and the enthusiasts' habit of prophesying to several Dutch cities, including Amsterdam. There Pieter Plockhoy and his followers, already at odds with the Mennonite Church owing to its reaction to their attempts at liberal reform, mixed freely with the Collegiants, several of whose principles rubbed off on them, including, besides an enthusiastic bent, an ecumenical Christianity and broad emphases on religious freedom and economic and social justice. Despite their radical social reforms, the Collegiants were moderates in their way—not wild-eyed enthusiasts, neither disorderly nor emotionally irresponsible—and some of this moderation rubbed off on Plockhoy, too.[3]

As a universal reformer and something of a busybody, Plockhoy visited England in the late 1650s, apprehensive lest Oliver Cromwell and the English take a wrong turn in their search for the Kingdom of God. Full of advice, he had audiences with the Protector and later wrote a series of letters all aimed at persuading "His Highness" to give an "ear to the Poor," shun the sectaries, and set up a universal church which would treat all Christians alike. Cromwell died before the letters reached him, and so Plockhoy published and sent them to Parliament. That the Restoration of both monarchy and Anglican Church occurred the very next year tells us something about the English reception of Plockhoy's suggestions. As a result he retreated to his homeland and schemed at implementing his universal church in America. Most Englishmen saw Plockhoy as one of several "foreign quacks" and Continental enthusiasts who mistook "every wild reverie of their own brain to be the immediate inspiration of the Divinity."[4]

Plockhoy first put together his plan for a communitarian experiment while still in England and published it in 1659 as *A Way Propounded to Make the Poor in These and Other Nations Happy.* It was a strong call for righteousness, brotherly love, and social harmony. It rested on a brand of socialism which would return merchants' profits to members of the community, who in turn would guarantee backing for all capital ventures. It afforded medical care for everyone, along with social security of widows and children. Permeating the whole was a universal Christianity based on happy families and the Holy Spirit.[5]

There is little doubt that Plockhoy has earned a place in a book about enthusiasts. Still, the articles of confederation on which he based his community at Zwaanendael curiously warned off headstrong Puritans and Quakers, "besides all obstinate, present-day pretenders to revelation," a legacy, no doubt, from the moderate Collegiants, or maybe still a reaction to Münster. He saw in the New World, however, a chance to shape a society which was religiously oriented to the radical side, a tolerant, freethinking Christian community based on freedom, love, and equality—or so his tracts tell us. His *Short and Clear Plan,* published in 1662, made plain a scheme for economic betterment by relieving fellow craftsmen of their burdens. His goal "on the South River of New Netherlands" was to "lighten the Labor, Unrest, and Difficulty of all Kinds of Handicraftsmen" through the establishment of a "Mutual Company or Colony." With the backing of the City of Amsterdam and the promise of exemption from tithes and import duties for twenty years, Plockhoy and his two score radical Christians hoped to make a go of it in America by farming, fishing, and simple manufacture. They settled on the Horekill in May 1663 and as far as we know made a decent start, disturbing as they were to Peter Stuyvesant and his intolerant Dutchmen along the Hudson—and to the English who soon replaced them.[6]

Labadists at Bohemia Manor

The Frenchman Jean de Labadie, unlike Plockhoy, never set foot in the New World. Still, he was responsible, indirectly at least, for settling a more successful and certainly a longer-lasting colony of enthusiasts there than the Dutch Mennonites were ever permitted. Unable to reform the Church of Rome through Jansenism, Labadie, as early as 1650, read

Calvin and deserted Rome—and France. Like many new converts, he attempted to reform the reformers and suffered for it, treatment which did nothing to lessen his conviction that he was divinely inspired and destined to lead others similarly illuminated. The Reformed Church in the Netherlands, where he next settled, was not then a healthy institution for a visionary; his expulsion from it was only the beginning of his travels, during which he gathered about him an exclusive church of saints, chiefly Calvinist in theology, who entertained, they claimed, a special covenant and communion with the Holy Spirit.

The well-traveled Labadie died before his community came to rest at Wieuwerd in Friesland, a northern province of the Netherlands. There it reached its greatest strength in discipline and hierarchy. And there the Labadists attempted to live down some of the notorious rumors which had followed Labadie and them through their pilgrimages, both theological and geographic. Not only did they hold a community of property, said the gossips, but a community of women, too. Despite the rigor of their organization and theology, Labadists resembled Quakers in their emphasis on the rule of the Spirit, which freed them from restrictive laws, hardly disguising an antinomianism. To both, the Bible was a secondary source of inspiration, and as early as 1667 William Penn, visiting them on the Continent during one of his journeys, encouraged their joining his society. But the rude treatment Labadie gave Penn and his friends, besides some of the wild tales still circulating about the Labadists' ecstasies and shocking conduct—murder and adultery included—prevented it.[7]

Labadists at Wieuwerd found community living more successful in religion than in economy. There was a tendency to hive out in small groups, the better to work, feed, and clothe their members. It was such a hiving which brought a splinter group to Maryland in 1683. They did not come unprepared. Several years earlier Jasper Danckaerts and a colleague, Peter Sluyter, had visited the English colonies to reconnoiter the land and find a spot to settle. Both took assumed names in order not to raise suspicion—which they did anyway—while they pursued their search from colony to colony. They chose Bohemia Manor, several thousand acres in what became Cecil County, Maryland, which they persuaded a zealous convert, Ephraim Herrman, to deed to them. Herrman was the son of Augustine Herrman, a Bohemian from Prague, to whom Lord Baltimore had granted a handsome estate—some 24,000 acres—in return for fashioning an up-to-date map of Maryland and Virginia, drafted to help his Lordship keep the colony's borders intact from aggressive Quakers and New Yorkers. Danckaerts and Sluyter returned home by way of Massachusetts, where they were thought to be Jesuits; elsewhere they were suspected of Quakerism, Brownism, and even Familism. Once among their friends at Wieuwerd they reported Bohemia Manor a likely place, and in 1683 the Labadists planted a community there, Sluyter but not Danckaerts among them.[8]

In its heyday Bohemia Manor never numbered much more than a hundred souls. Its exclusiveness may have had a good deal to do with its small size, since its members were all saints, all inwardly directed by the Holy Spirit, a requirement which ruthlessly divided families, saints from sinners, even husband or wife from spouse and children. The recently married Ephraim Herrman left his bride to join the Labadists, a rash act he later regretted and reversed and for which his father never forgave him. (The old man reworded his will in such a way as to prevent forever the community from acquiring any more of the Herrman estate.) At Bohemia Manor all property was common, as it had been among Plockhoy's followers; members dressed alike; they lived in families when all were believers, but men and women chastely took their meals separately. Rumors of sexual freedom appear to have been left behind in Europe. Despite an early promise to convert the Indians, they tended to ignore them and concentrate on the spirit within and the cultivation of corn without, along with tobacco, flax, hemp, cattle, and the manufacture of linen. Contrary also to early expectation, they bought black slaves and worked them for profit like most other colonists.[9] Had it not been for selfish leadership, the Labadists' colony in Maryland might very well have survived, at least for a time. It certainly got off to a better start than had Plockhoy's people on the Delaware, as we shall see, although the course of communitarianism in America, with or without the help of the Holy Spirit, is littered with good starts which for a variety of reasons became croppers.

Rosicrucians

Plockhoy's Mennonites and the fanatical Labadists had grounded their economies on the needs of their communities. The Rosicrucian mystics who descended upon Germantown, Pennsylvania, in 1694 were more a community of souls than an experiment in Christian communism. Their mundane needs were supplied more conventionally from the Pennsylvania countryside. They were German, they were highly educated and deeply pietistic, and they came in a symbolic number of forty to minister to the religious needs of colonists and Indians, all the while hoping, like Moses or Elijah, to grow perfect in the wilderness in anticipation of the Second Coming. Johann Jacob Zimmerman had gathered them first from Württemberg and the neighborhood and led them to Holland, where one of

William Penn's Quaker agents warmly encouraged them to settle in Pennsylvania, and where too Zimmerman had the misfortune to die. Johannes Kelpius from Altdorf in Bavaria assumed leadership and brought the holy band first to London, where they mixed generously with Jane Lead and the "Philadelphians," a band of English enthusiasts whose origins, some said, was in the Family of Love, and who shared with Kelpius's people a mystical insight and devotion to the writings of Jacob Boehme.[10] From London they sailed for the New World, stopping with the Labadists at Bohemia Manor before they arrived in Philadelphia on June 23, 1694. That evening, on the highlands outside the city, they celebrated the summer solstice with a huge fire of pine boughs and brushwood, according to the mystic rites of Saint John's Eve—all of which must indeed have perplexed Philadelphia's staid Quakers. Next day they walked the few miles to Germantown, where they were expected and welcomed.[11]

Now, what are we to make of these theosophical enthusiasts? Right out of the Revelation they called themselves the "Order of the Woman in the Wilderness," and they settled above Wissahickon Creek hard by what is now Fairmont Park. They were nominally Lutherans, but they differed considerably from one another in their beliefs and practices, agreeing, of course, on the need for personal illumination. Some taught school; others preached here and there among Lutherans, Quakers, and Anglicans. Kelpius, who took this wilderness business seriously, built himself a proper cave to live in on the banks of the Wissahickon. He preached love and benevolence to all denominations and worked toward uniting New World Germans in a single church of brotherhood, possibly a germ for some of Count Zinzendorf's plans for Moravians a generation or more later. Strangely they mixed orthodox Lutheranism with a good deal of half-baked science, medicine, alchemy, and astrology, showing a strong link to earlier enthusiasts, but particularly to Jacob Boehme, the German mystic, who had flourished almost a century before and had had such great influence on Familists, Ranters, Fifth Monarchists, Quakers, and countless others, including Sir Henry Vane. (Kelpius and company's baggage contained several complete sets of Boehme's works in a recent edition. But then, all enthusiasts read Boehme—George Whitefield, William Blake, and Ralph Waldo Emerson among them.) According to Justus Faulckner, one of the forty, Kelpius's plan for a universal religion fell far short, for Faulckner wrote home regularly, lamenting the "spirit of errors and sects" which already had found asylum in Pennsylvania. He blamed Quakers for most of these troubles, an ungracious charge, given the warm welcome and complete freedom the Rosicrucians had received in the Quaker colony, so necessary, they believed, to pursuit of the millennium in the New World.[12]

Seventeenth-century enthusiasts from the Continent did not leave very promising records in America. Among the several characteristics they shared was an inability to survive, let alone attract new followers and thrive.

The year after Plockhoy's Mennonites built their tiny haven on the lower Delaware the English struck at New Netherlands. Sir Robert Carr, who was commissioned to destroy all Dutch settlements along the river, or so he claimed, fell upon the helpless community with a vengeance. Destroy he did, and plunder, too, all that belonged to the "Quaking Society of Plockhoy to a very naile," scattering the handful of communitarians widely over the map. Plockhoy barely recovered sufficiently to resettle near what is now Lewes, Delaware, and he lived there for some thirty years before finding his way to Germantown, where a sturdy group of Mennonites had helped to start Pennsylvania on its long career of piety and religious freedom. He died there in 1700 as a public charge and blind to boot, sadly leaving unfulfilled the religious and economic ideals of *A Way Propounded to Make the Poor in These and Other Nations Happy*.[13] His stab at a return to primitive Christianity in the New World was met head-on by the imperialism of the Old. Had Plockhoy any consolation, he could lay his defeat not to his people's enthusiasm or their radical social reforms but to their being Dutch and settling smack in the path of English conquest.

At Bohemia Manor Peter Sluyter outlasted the handful of Labadist leaders, who one by one made over their rights to him—Jasper Danckaerts as early as 1693. Sluyter not only emerged as bishop of the community but improved upon the already authoritarian and hierarchical government. By 1698 individualism had overcome community ideals, and when Wieuwerd in the Netherlands faded away, so too did the spiritual ideals of Bohemia Manor in Maryland, leaving little trace. Sluyter lived on until 1722 and by this time had won himself a lavish estate from what was once common property. Poor leadership at home and abroad, an ineffective economy, and the mercenary demands of Peter Sluyter combined to undermine the efforts of a community which had attracted at best only a few outsiders, and these mostly Dutchmen from New York.[14] When the Quaker missionary Samuel Bownas first visited Bohemia Manor, he found a devoted, industrious, and frugal "Family," each of its members bent on following "some inward Motion." At his return a few years later, "these People were all scattered and gone," he reported, "and nothing of them remaining of a religious Community in that Shape."[15] Maryland easily survived the invasion of Labadists and turned its attention to Quakers spreading from the north, who, early and

late, seemed more of a threat to social stability and his Lordship's property than a few Dutch fanatics who kept pretty much to themselves.

The Labadists' legacy in America was meager and died with the demise
of the community—with the exception of *The Journal of Jasper Danckaerts,* kept while he scouted the land in 1679 and 1680. Danckaerts was
a little aloof and stiff-necked as he traveled up and down the coast,
looking for a likely spot to plant his fellow enthusiasts. He saw much
that he liked and a lot he disliked, and described both, but one respects
his comments about people and places and learns a good deal of the
primitive quality of life most colonists confronted in a society not yet
formed nor very sure of itself.[16]

The Rosicrucian community of souls barely outlived the death of Kel-
pius in 1708, but already the symbolic circle of forty had been broken.
Henrich Bernhard Köster withdrew with several other dissatisfied sepa-
ratists to nearby Plymouth, where they formed their own community.
Before returning to Germany at the end of the century, Köster played a
role in Pennsylvania Quakerism's first serious schism when he joined the
"Christian Quakers" under George Keith on the side of stricter doctrine.
Unlike Plockhoy's Mennonites and the severely disciplined Labadists, the
Society of the Woman in the Wilderness left more than a trace despite
its demise in the early eighteenth century. Several of its offshoots or
"insinuating sects," which Justus Faulckner complained about, were per-
manently touched by its spiritual inwardness, giving to Pennsylvania
pietism mystical and enthusiastic qualities which endured for some time.[17]

One legatee was Conrad Beissel. In and around his home near Hei-
delberg he had become strongly affected by German pietism and brought
a healthy bit of it to the American colonies when he migrated there in
1720. There is a good chance that he spent some time with the few
remaining Labadists in Maryland before settling in Pennsylvania, where
he searched out the surviving Rosicrucians left over from Kelpius's circle.
It was Beissel who gathered about him a number of devotees in 1732
and formed in Lancaster County the Ephrata Community, whose deep
piety and ascetic living soon won for their retreat the name Cloister. Like
Kelpius, Beissel was a disciple of Jacob Boehme, whose immanent God
directed affairs at Ephrata as he had those of the Rosicrucians on the
banks of the Wissahickon near Germantown.[18] Revivalist George Whitefield also found Boehme an inspiration. His writings are "truly evangelical," he wrote a friend, affording "sweet nourishment to the new-born
soul." On Whitefield's first visit to the colonies he preached at Germantown and with several "dear disciples" sought out Conrad Mattheus,
then a reputable hermit, who was probably the last survivor of the Rosi-

crucian community and, in fact, has been called the "successor of Kelpius." "Our hearts were knit together," Whitefield reported of his encounter, "and the God of love was with us of a truth." In 1748 Quaker diarist John Smith of Philadelphia visited the Swiss Mattheus, accompanied by his friend Anthony Benezet—Smith not for the first time. Unlike Whitefield he came away disappointed, for he failed to find in Mattheus "that depth of Experience in religion" which he had expected in one who for so long had lived in solitude, his mind withdrawn from external distractions. But then, Smith was a Quaker.[19]

Not very far away lived the "New Mooners," a small lateral sect identified by its practice of meeting when the new moon appeared each month. Fittingly the leader was John Zimmerman, either son or grandson of the John Jacob Zimmerman who had collected the mystical forty destined for Pennsylvania in the first place. Despite the elder Zimmerman's death in Holland, his wife and children had brought his brand of enthusiasm to the colony not long afterward. Forty years later it blossomed again in Conestoga Swamp with the "New Mooners," understandably at the height of the Great Awakening.[20]

Plockhoy's people on the Delaware, the Labadists of Maryland, and the handful of Rosicrucians in Pennsylvania, had they sat down together and talked things over, probably would not have agreed on a creed, or how they should worship God, or even how to organize their communities. Like Quakers, however, they would have insisted that religion was more heart than head, that the Bible was helpful if not the prime source of inspiration, and that the true saint was inwardly guided by the Holy Spirit. No doubt these communal livers would have agreed, too, that the New World afforded a splendid opportunity to indulge both their enthusiasm and their pietism. And when the religious revival of the 1740s reached Philadelphia and the middle colonies, enthusiasm and pietism were the vehicles by which it traveled.

Moravians

The Moravians, who settled in Pennsylvania and later North Carolina, had much more staying power than did their fellow European enthusiasts of the seventeenth and eighteenth centuries. Certainly their numbers were larger, and that helped, but they came not as a community so much as a brotherhood, the *Unitas Fratrum*. Like Plockhoy's friendly people, the rigid Labadists, and Kelpius's misty Rosicrucians before them, the Moravians remained pretty much separate from the English establishment, both Church and State. Unlike them, however, they built on strong foundations which have supported their church and their unity for over two hundred years.

Moravians came from Bohemia, in what is now Czechoslovakia, where they claimed lineage back to John Hus. Proper dissenters, they and the Waldenses have been called Protestant sects which predated the Reformation. Their genealogy runs thin in spots over the long pull since Hus's time, but supposedly apostolic succession was clear. When Christian David brought them together in the early eighteenth century, the "hidden seed" was intact, or at least salvageable, despite the Reformation, Counter Reformation, several wars, and many years of persecution. David led them to German Saxony, where they accepted the hospitality of Count Ludwig Zinzendorf and his huge estate at Bethelsdorf. They attracted there not only more refugees like themselves from Bohemia but other Protestant Germans who needed a religious home, and they called it Herrnhut. Zinzendorf, probably the eighteenth century's best known pietist, was ecumenical in his strong religious bent and schemed to establish under his wing at Bethelsdorf a united brotherhood of Christians which would forever light the world. From that time Moravianism bore something of the Zinzendorf stamp, although the comprehensiveness he sought was never wholly achieved.[21]

Still, Moravians avoided the confines of a single creed, and one would never call their beliefs rigorous or doctrinaire. With the help of Zinzendorf, who encouraged them to resist a sectlike form and to become truly a "united brotherhood," they managed to maintain a kind of universality which made it easy to worship with others. James Logan of Philadelphia described them as full of "universal charity" and not bound to any form. They would join with other persuasions, he wrote, "Papist or Protestant," as long as they were "inwardly guided by the Spirit of Christ." Granted they abhorred the "fopperies of the Roman service . . . saints, images, etc.," they easily forgot the "exteriors in worship," "if the heart be right." Moravians embodied piety, if eccentric sometimes; in their emotional approach they shared the warm spiritual feelings of other pietists and successfully vented it in several directions, most memorably in their splendid music. Like most enthusiasts they assumed that learning was secondary to a rule of the Spirit, as was the Bible; but like Quakers they encouraged elementary education in order to help their people get on in the world as farmers, merchants, and mechanics.[22]

With their pietism Moravians embodied a kind of discipline which impressed their contemporaries and historians who followed. Geared to a hierarchy, they worked within a framework which kept them separate, discouraging litigation in secular courts, demanding marriage within the fold, and exercising surveillance over the conduct of their people. The *Unitas Fratrum* was not for run-of-the-mill Christians. It was a religious life without celibacy, wrote Ronald Knox, and even marriage was subject to the elders' consent. Moravians would have liked to fashion a city of God on earth, and in trying to do so they bred a religious elite which many other enthusiasts have envied.

Above all was a spirituality which punctuated Moravian life and gave it its peculiar quality. So intense was this, along with a belief in the interposition of Providence, that they developed a passivity, a kind of quietism, much like that of their Quaker contemporaries, in which state they waited for the Spirit to act upon them. Providence governed all, and when it was slow to act, they cast lots to determine it, even sometimes the selection of mates in marriage, for a people so closely in tune with God had no apprehension about the gamble. Moravians were not merely pietists; they were pietists of a particular order, and enthusiasm was a strong current in their make-up.[23]

Moravians played a decisive role in the origins of Methodism, which helps to explain the enthusiasm of both. True, John Wesley's group at Oxford, already called the "Enthusiasts" and the "Holy Club," was active before the Moravian Peter Boehler came upon the scene. Still, it was Boehler, whom Wesley met in Georgia and then again in London, whose glowing pietism had such an effect upon the father of Methodism. It was Boehler who in 1738 helped Wesley turn his attention inward to discover a new wellspring of religious feeling, and it was Boehler who suggested establishing the Fetter Lane Society in London, which Wesley patterned after several Moravian meetings already in existence. The next summer Wesley and several friends visited Herrnhut in Germany and quickened their own pietism. Late that year and early the next, Wesley, George Whitefield, and other incipient Methodists held meetings with the Moravians at Fetter Lane, which Whitefield could only describe as "love-feasts," where more than once he "spent the whole night in close prayer, psalms, and thanksgiving," and where his "heart greatly united with the brethren." Whitefield was convinced that the Spirit which he felt revived among them was akin to that of the primitive Christians.[24]

From these meetings emerged organized Methodism as well as new Moravian societies. But they emerged separately. Love feasts at Fetter Lane marked the high point of a Moravian and Methodist marriage in London. By the next year the joint spirit of primitive Christianity, which had so excited Whitefield, fell asunder. Wesley and the Moravians parted company over the latter's quietism, which annoyed, even offended Wesley, who brought a strong activism to Methodism besides a genius for organization. To be up and doing was good Methodist practice, but

Moravians experienced holiness passively and waited upon the Lord. Their custom of casting lots, however, did rub off—much to the disgust of many, including George Whitefield—for Wesley sanctioned this method of exploiting Providence in important decisions for years to come. There may have been jealousy between the two groups; Wesley was never one to take a back seat in spiritual matters. Several years later George Lavington, Bishop of Exeter, who spent a good deal of time criticizing the enthusiasm of both Moravians and Methodists, claimed that contention rose over "who should be the greatest." Soon Wesley and the Methodists withdrew and left the Fetter Lane Society to the United Brethren, who at this early period outnumbered the Methodists anyway. There never again was rapport between the two groups.[25]

Differences between Methodists and Moravians in 1740 laid bare at the same time differences between Methodists—that is, between George Whitefield and John Wesley. How long these had simmered is less important than that they existed and that they were theological. Despite Methodism's break with the Moravians, Whitefield discovered several of their errors in Wesley himself. They boiled down to some of the main points of Calvinism, to which Whitefield adhered and, ever so politely, accused Wesley of dropping. In letters from the colonies he made clear to Wesley and others the critical danger in advocating universal redemption, for in doing so, he wrote, you "plainly make salvation depend not on God's *free-grace,* but on man's *free-will,*" and for Christ's sake, warned Whitefield, "consider how you dishonour God by denying election." But this was not all. According to Whitefield, Wesley preached a "sinless perfection," setting up a mark which he could never reach until he came "to glory." Much as he himself lived in God's presence, Whitefield immodestly confessed, he never dared pretend he was "absolutely perfect." What was Wesley trying to do—"drive *John Calvin* out of *Bristol*"?[26] When he returned to England the next year, Whitefield complained that his "spiritual children" who earlier "would have plucked out their own eyes" to serve him, now turned their backs, so prejudiced were they by the Wesley brothers' "dressing up the doctrine of Election in such horrible colours." Universal redemption was bad enough, but "sinless perfection" was the earmark of an enthusiast, an accusation frequently leveled at Wesley during his Oxford days and again in Georgia, and one he would have to live with for the rest of his life, despite frequent denials. Whitefield suffered, too, from charges of enthusiasm, but never for assuming he was sinless. Even Jonathan Edwards associated the Wesleys with the same heresy, along with "some other high pretenders to spirituality in these days," but never Whitefield.[27]

A split between Whitefield and the Moravians occurred about the same time, although it was somewhat different in nature. Moreover, it emerged while Whitefield was in America following what had been a close association. After the initial "love-feasts" at Fetter Lane, Whitefield sailed for Georgia, intent on establishing an orphanage for children of parents who had not survived the proprietors' philanthropy. In Georgia he met Peter Boehler and Auguste Spangenburg, both later Moravian bishops, and Whitefield and they and the handful of Moravians there discovered considerable congeniality. But Georgia, a buffer colony, was not a healthy place for Moravians, chiefly after the outbreak of war between Britain and Spain in 1739. Like Quakers, Moravians were pacifists and balked at taking oaths of allegiance to government; in a short time they had worn out their welcome in proprietary Georgia, which was then under the imperialist governor and general James Edward Oglethorpe. Whitefield came to their rescue and offered them passage to safer ground in tolerant Pennsylvania in the sloop *Savannah*, fitted out for him by a wealthy benefactor in London. They promptly accepted.[28]

Despite the large numbers of Quakers who had little to do with revivalism, Whitefield found Pennsylvania Germans and other colonists there attracted to his brand of pietism. On several occasions he and Boehler preached in tandem to large audiences, Whitefield in English and Boehler in German, and their double-barreled evangelicalism was an effective means of spreading revivalism. Moravians were the gainers, for Whitefield's preaching added a good many Pennsylvanians to the Moravian fold. For several months he and his new-found friends seemed destined to fulfill Count Zinzendorf's schemes of a universal Christianity.[29]

For the first year or so of their association, Whitefield was a great admirer of the Moravians. In words that almost defined pietism, he wrote, "The order, seriousness, and devotion of these people in common life, is most worthy of imitation." Besides an intense piety, Whitefield and the Moravians shared, too, a missionary spirit which in Georgia had focused on the colony's blacks. A similar concern was equally intense in Pennsylvania, reflecting Whitefield's earlier success in ministering to slaves there. Financed by the same benefactor who provided him with the sloop, Whitefield purchased a 5,400-acre estate above Philadelphia at the Forks of the Delaware River for the purpose of erecting a school for Negroes. He called the place Nazareth and left his new Moravian friends in residence to get on with the building while he fulfilled his role as the Grand Itinerant.[30]

This was in 1739, but within a year something happened to the relationship. Whitefield gave up the joint scheme and sold Nazareth to the Moravians. He made it clear to all who would listen that the Moravians were theologically unsound, and he wanted as little to do with them as possible. This change of mind, no doubt, was the result of recent news regarding the split between John Wesley and the Moravians in London, and probably, too, it occurred after Whitefield had scrutinized more closely what Peter Boehler actually preached and the Moravians swallowed. From both he concluded that what he objected to in Wesley he found redolent in the United Brethren: a loose Arminianism about redemption and a tendency to perfectionism, even antinomianism. The Moravian belief "that Christ died for them that perish," that all "damned souls would hereafter be brought out of hell," appalled Whitefield, as well as did a "sinless perfection"—the old enthusiast's trap—that "a man hath no real salvation till he literally cannot commit sin." "Take heed, brother," he warned a friend who had touted Peter Boehler as a sinless saint; "though he has been washed in the blood of the Lamb . . . yet like me his feet want washing still, and will, till he bows down his head and gives up the ghost"—really the advice he was giving Wesley at the same time. Whitefield probably could not bear to pick a fight with Wesley ("Do not oblige me to preach against you; I had rather die," he wrote home to his fellow Mehodist) but he could wash his hands of Count Zinzendorf's pietists, and he did so in 1740. "I cannot for my soul unite with the *Moravian Brethren,*" he wrote to Wesley, and the same year he sold Nazareth to them and packed his bags for London.[31]

With the purchase of Whitefield's estate at Nazareth the Moravian pietists established a firm foothold in British America. Count Zinzendorf made a grand tour of the New World and took charge of Moravian operations. Under his supervision they expanded from Nazareth to what the Count called Bethlehem (he arrived there on Christmas Eve) eight miles away. There was great talk of absorbing all the land between the two centers to a width of two miles, really an enclave organized in small settlements which derived their names from villages found on maps of the Holy Land. Small colonies of brethren organized abroad sailed for Pennsylvania. One, the "Sea Congregation," arrived in late spring 1742, the first of several to follow. The small invasion delighted the Pennsylvania proprietor, who was eager to sell land in large chunks, for the Count spoke of transporting more than ten thousand people to settle on land for which they would pay the going price. This was an ambitious undertaking, but it fell far short of its goal in the early years, for by the middle 1750s, despite all the talk, the total Moravian population was nearer a thousand. There were, of course, many times that number of Germans in several parts of the colony.[32]

To English-speaking colonists the Moravians must have seemed larger in number. Those in Pennsylvania were a highly mobile people. They were warm and friendly pietists, and they sought out other warm, friendly pietists, making visits to the Ephrata group at the Cloister under Conrad Beissel, to the Mennonites in Germantown, and the "New Mooners" in Conestoga Swamp.[33]

Soon after settlement they began their missionary work among the Indians, a chief cause for their coming, and they were probably more successful in this endeavor than any other group of colonists. They spread out a number of thinly established missions, one of the most successful, if short lived, was at Shekomeco in New York, several miles up the Hudson in Mohican country. Bethlehem remained the center of their network, and there was constant travel between headquarters and missions by both missionaries and Indians.[34] Pietism was exportable from the Old World, and within Moravian pietism was an enthusiasm equally exportable, even contagious. Some of its victims were colonists, as the Great Awakening would demonstrate; others were Indians, whose acceptance of Christianity and enthusiasm as well was not altogether appreciated by many white colonists who entertained the Holy Spirit only through the Bible, and an English one at that.

French Prophets

While Moravians were enthusiasts, and pietists, too, no one mistook them for Ranters or militant fanatics. Strong enthusiasts, to be sure, given their intimacy with the Holy Spirit, their pietism nevertheless dictated a modesty and decorum which were the envy of many of their contemporaries. Not so the French Prophets of the early eighteenth century. They were, indeed, a different breed, whose strident irreverencies and bizarre antics harked back to the days of the Ranters, even to the Anabaptists at Münster. No wonder the ecumenical Moravian Count Zinzendorf contemptuously dismissed them as the only Christians he could not stomach.[35] Who were these Prophets, these Camisards ("short shirts"), as they were called, and what, if anything, did they have to do with the American colonies?

French Prophets were a militant band of Huguenots who, unlike their more peaceful comrades, refused to succumb to the religious tyranny of Catholic Louis XIV. They were Languedocians, already alienated historically, religiously, and linguistically from the powers that be in France. When in 1685 Louis attempted to bring them into line by revoking the Edict of Nantes, they resisted, took to the hills—their own Cévennes in the South of France, refuge of their spiritual forebears, the Albigenses, five hundred years earlier—and waged guerrilla warfare against the King's troops. They suffered severely for their stubbornness, as did whole villages of Cévennois who befriended them. Besides being militant, they were fanatically religious, and years of official oppression and cruelty only intensified their enthusiasm. The bloody resistance hung on for much longer than anyone thought imaginable, despite terrible odds. The King threw thousands of troops against them, unsuccessfully as it turned out, while the Camisards numbered only about four thousand fighting men, sometimes only half armed and half clothed. Gilbert Burnet, Bishop of Salisbury in England, admired their "courage and confidence" and eagerly read reports which described them as "full of a sublime zeal and piety" but "without any learning." Educated or not, their zeal admirably sustained them; deprived for years of a ministry, they traditionally were nurtured on inspiration and prophecies of ultimate deliverance and thus were dubbed "Prophets." The Camisard War came to a vicious end in the early years of the eighteenth century only after wholesale burning of villages, execution of resisters, and finally negotiation.[36]

Englishmen were sympathetic to the Huguenots and admired the patience and constancy they exhibited despite intense suffering. The Anglican churches and particularly the Bishop of London contributed thousands of pounds to ease the lot of the refugees, many of whom found asylum in England, while the bulk were funneled through to the colonies.[37]

The arrival in London of a handful of French Prophets in 1706, straight from the Cévennes, made a great stir. They were notorious for their visions, revelations, and attempts to heal the sick and resurrect the dead, to say nothing of prophecies of revolution, Christ's second coming, and the end of the world.[38] A number of volatile and easily impressed Englishmen were bowled over by them, among whom was the well-to-do John Lacy, who not only became a spokesman in defense of the Prophets but also one of them. Lacy made public that the same immediate inspiration which had risen "out of the Ashes of those of *Languedocq*" bore a message "suitable to Englishmen likewise and to all the world." The "New *Jerusalem*" was "now even at the Door," and in three years' time it would be manifest over the whole earth.[39]

These were not the prophecies of "Impostors or Enthusiasts," wrote Lacy, but of prophets sent by God to London. Lacy swallowed them whole and published them, too, for all to read. Next came his own prophetical warnings, and blow-by-blow descriptions—symptoms and all—of the intense, physical, but involuntary agitations which seized him. God spoke through him—his best days for this sort of thing were Sundays. Lacy merely mouthed and wrote, his "fingers forceably moved," what God directed him to express in his ecstasy—and frequently in Latin and Greek, too, although some critics were so ungracious as to fault the Holy Spirit's syntax.[40]

Hostile critics kept the presses busy, and 1 John 4:1, about false prophets and a need to try the spirits, got a good going over in the many pages of tracts and pamphlets.[41] The most sophisticated piece provoked by the Prophets in London was the Third Earl of Shaftesbury's *Letter Concerning Enthusiasm,* published in 1708. It was a clever essay from an articulate deist who refused to become excited about the extremism rampant in London—and spreading northward. "All Nations have their Lymphaticks of some kind or another," he wrote; "and all Churches (Heathen as well as Christian) have had their Complaints against Fanaticism." Shaftesbury's antidote to enthusiasm was "Good Humour," which was the "best Foundation of Piety and True Religion"; otherwise, he warned, "the Remedy itself may turn to the Disease." Several virtuous souls who mounted the attack against the Prophets saved some of their resentment for Shaftesbury, whose deism and skepticism were equally as offensive as the enthusiastic presumption of the Prophets.[42]

Samuel Keimer

"Good Humour" may have satisfied Shaftesbury as the proper antidote for the enthusiasm of John Lacy and the Frenchmen. It was not a matter of "humour," good or bad, to Samuel Keimer of London, who succumbed to the Prophets in 1707. When still apprenticed to a printer in Threadneedle Street, young Keimer attended his first meeting in Southwark and there discovered the jumping, shaking, and hiccupping John Lacy as he laid hands on a kneeling woman in performance of the *"Gift of Blessing."* Within a short time his sister, followed by his mother, and finally Samuel were drawn into the Prophets' circle, he being "blessed" by Elie Marion himself, one of the handful of fanatical Frenchmen who had first initiated Englishmen into the world of the inspired Camisards the year before.[43]

Keimer married a young woman of similar religious convictions and set up shop as a printer, only to run afoul of the law by printing a variety of treasonable and libelous pamphlets besides a newspaper offensive to most Londoners. He was in and out of jail repeatedly, but his soulmates, the Prophets, failed to succor him—in fact, ignored him. Deserted by his spiritual guides and confronted with overwhelming difficulties in the printing trade, Keimer "cry'd to the Lord" for some sign of help in his distress. It came, he wrote, in a sharp and clear discovery that the whole French business from beginning to end was "only a Mixture of human Contrivance, join'd by Satan's transforming himself into an Angell of

Light to deceive Mankind." His increasing disillusionment cured him of the Prophets forever. "I am e'en quite tir'd in raking in this Dunghil of a Religion," he wote.[44]

In 1723 Samuel Keimer sailed for the New World, leaving his wife behind in London. "I am seeking a country not made with Hands, eternal in the Heavens, whither I am bound," he had confessed to the Quakers a few years earlier.[45] It is improbable that Pennsylvania ever came quite up to the mark, but his lack of success in the printing business, his distress over his experience with the Prophets, and his sympathy toward Quakers doubtless combined to make Pennsylvania look petty good, if not eternal.

And whom did Keimer meet at the outset in Philadelphia but young Benjamin Franklin, fresh from Boston. It would be difficult to conceive of two more different people. That their paths did cross Keimer probably called a sign or portent of Providence, while Franklin no doubt attributed it to plain bad luck. The fullest account of Keimer's short career in Philadelphia comes from Franklin, written later, and therefore perhaps not wholly accurate. Franklin comes off very well, while descriptions of the older man make him out to be something of a clown.

Keimer was already set up in the printing business when Franklin arrived, and he took him on as a helper. In fact, they lived together for a time, and Franklin has several amusing tales to tell at Keimer's expense. He was still full of his "old enthusiasms," Franklin wrote, and he could act out the Prophets' "enthusiastic agitations" at will. Keimer loved to argue, and Franklin frequently indulged him, taking great sport in forcing him into "difficulties and contradictions" by way of the "Socratic method." Keimer marveled at the young newcomer's forensic ability and once suggested that they collaborate in establishing a new sect, he "to preach the doctrines" while Franklin confounded all opponents. But when Keimer attempted to explain the doctrines, young Ben poked so many holes in them that they gave up the idea.[46]

Keimer's full beard and seventh-day Sabbath—which some claimed was the whole of his religion—annoyed Franklin. But he traded off the inconvenience of both for Keimer's accepting a vegetarian diet, which he held him to despite protestations. Sometime later Keimer could stand it no longer and ordered a repast of "roast pig" for dinner at their home, inviting a couple of lady friends to enjoy it with them. The scrumptious meal arrived earlier than expected, and before Franklin and the doxies appeared, Keimer had eaten every scrap.[47]

He was "very ignorant of the world," wrote Franklin, "and had, as I afterward found, a good deal of the knave in his composition." Keimer might have said the same of Franklin, for while they were working together, unknown to his boss, Franklin schemed to set up his own shop.

Once he and his partner established it, he wrote articles attacking Keimer with the intent of putting him out of business. At the same time the naive Keimer subcontracted a printing job to Franklin's press, giving him and his partner their first real bit of work. But the enthusiast was not a good businessman. Soon Franklin had his way when Keimer packed up and sailed off to Barbados, where he managed to scrape along for several years, as Franklin explained, "in very poor circumstances."[48]

It would be difficult to determine what mark, if any, Samuel Keimer made upon the New World. His enthusiasm, however intense, was not the kind which posed a danger to society. It wanted the militancy of the Prophets' and it did not lend itself to the organization and togetherness of Quakers or Moravians. Keimer was a loner, an outsider; he lacked sophistication and know-how; he was not even a very good printer; and he was eccentric and gullible and something of a slob, if we can believe half of what Franklin tells us. The enthusiasm which had warmed to the ecstasies of the French Prophets in London deserved a better vessel in America.

The Dutartres

For a time it looked as if the Dutartre family of South Carolina would fill the bill. If they were not actually French Prophets, they should have been, for they carried on in similar fashion. More Huguenots migrated to South Carolina than to any other British colony, although there was a sprinkling in all of them. Proposals to give asylum to French Protestants in America were talked about as early as 1679—not counting a sixteenth-century attempt they themselves made nearby in the face of the Spanish—and when Louis XIV revoked the Edict of Nantes, their numbers swelled, many, as we have seen, traveling by way of England. Of course, this was not wholly a selfless gesture on England's part, for Huguenots brought with them a number of useful trades and crafts which New World colonies needed; besides, they were solid Protestants, and a number drifted to the Anglican Church as time went on.[49] Governor Francis Nicholson of South Carolina welcomed a boatload of them in 1700 and helped settle all 207 men, women, and children some twenty miles above the falls of the James River at a place called Manikin Town. They found good land there where they could remain in a group and, as Nicholson pointed out, "be astrengthing to the Frontiers"—after all, South Carolina in 1700 was a border colony. Whether any were enthusiasts is unknown. A François du Tartre was among them, and he may have been patriarch of the family, whose notoriety in the 1720s stamped it as the epitome of enthusiasm in colonial America.[50]

By the early years of the eighteenth century South Carolina already had a reputation for religious irregularity. Most reports about it came from Anglican clergymen who found their own church weak in the face of dissenters, and also found that very little could be done about it owing to the lack of a bishop. Commissary Gideon Johnston was shocked by what he saw in Charlestown in 1708. In a letter to Gilbert Burnet he described Charlestown's people as the "vilest race of Men upon the Earth . . . a . . . Hotch potch . . . of Bank[r]upts, pirates, decayed Libertines, Sectaries and Enthusiasts." The largest number were Anglicans, but the rest were a "Mungrel Race."[51]

Some of this irregularity rubbed off on Saint Thomas's Parish in the Orange Quarter, where the Dutartres lived. According to one report, a couple of Prophets either emerged from the several families there or merely visited and found the ground fertile. Anyway, in 1715–16 "two pestilent fellows" caused a great stir in the parish with wild tales of the true Prophets who had electrified London a few years earlier. The Orange Quarter, it appeared, was vulnerable to enthusiasts' notions, which may have helped prepare the way for what was to follow.[52]

This was even more obvious at another time, not fixed on the calendar, when Christian George, called a "strolling Moravian," appeared and distributed to the Dutartres and their neighbors the writings of the German mystic Jacob Boehme, along with others of the same stamp. The Reverend Alexander Garden, then Anglican priest at Charlestown, was not sure whether Christian George was Dutch or Swiss—he was sure he was an enthusiast—but never mind, the newcomer's conversations and the mystical writings he handed about soon filled the Dutartres' heads with "many wild and Enthusiastick Notions."

The effect was startling. They soon withdrew from the Church and the community and indulged themselves in the extraordinary idea that God had chosen their family alone from all others as the cradle of his truth and grace. There followed impulses, signs, tokens, and then open visions and revelations to this holy family. Peter Rembert, who had married old Peter Dutartre's eldest and widowed daughter, pronounced himself a prophet to whom God revealed his will to destroy wicked mankind as in Noah's day and start all over again with but one family, the Dutartres, from which the good seed would spread. The family had less trouble accepting this revelation and its implications than it did the next, in which God commanded Rembert the prophet to "put away" his wife and begin a new family with Judith, her youngest sister, a virgin, as mother of the new seed. (His wife's first husband God would resurrect for her once the "wicked Generation" was destroyed.) Old Peter, father Dutartre, had difficulty accommodating himself to this command until

God, as the prophet said he would, gave him a sign which dispelled his anxiety, and he dutifully led his youngest daughter by the hand to the bed of the prophet. Thus they lived, said Aexander Garden, in open adultery and incest.

Besides moral convention they defied the civil magistrate, too—in fact, all manmade laws. This became apparent to the neighborhood when they refused to bear arms or work their bit upon the highways. Unconvinced that they were "holy Seed," South Carolina justice moved in, issued warrants for their arrests, and sent a constable to bring them in. The God who refused to let them shoulder arms in defense of the colony permitted it in defense of the family, and they drove off the constable with defiance and gunfire. When the officer returned with Magistrate Symmons and the militia, they stormed the well-defended family home. Justice Symmons was shot dead in his tracks and several of the militiamen wounded before the rest of them forced the citadel, where they took the Dutartres prisoner, all except a *"Mrs Lesad"* who was found already dead of gunshot wounds. The militia packed them all off to Charlestown, where were promptly arraigned, tried, and convicted, except young Judith, the "Prophet's Revelation Wife," who was well on the way to having a child. To adultery and incest were not added rebellion and murder.

Conviction failed to shake their assurance that God had called them out, that they did all by his express command and order. They defiantly faced hanging, convinced that God would either deliver them beforehand or resurrect them afterward in three days' time to carry on as before. When Rembert, old Peter, and one other were turned off and proved unreliable either of God's options, two remaining Dutartre sons, whose executions had been delayed, confessed their delusion and were pardoned. Not yet free of his "Enthusiastick Notions," one of them a few years later killed a man at God's command and died shortly on the gallows.[53]

From what occurred it would be difficult to believe that Rembert and the Dutartres were not acquainted with the doings of the French Prophets in Languedoc or in London or both. Their inspirations were of the same stripe, and Rembert's renouncing his wife to cohabit with a disciple on God's command smacked of the Prophets' carryings on in London which won them a reputation for promiscuity. Bishop Lavington lumped them with the Anabaptists at Münster, the Family of Love, and several other extremist groups whose history demonstrated that a "Multiplicity of Wives and promiscuous Use of Women had been the *Favourite Tenet* of most *Fanatical Sects*." Having said this, the good Bishop went on to imply gratuitously that "there was no reason to think [the Methodists] were any better then their neighbors."[54]

Samuel Keimer seems pretty much forgotten except in the writings of Benjamin Franklin. The Dutartres' "Tragical Scene of Enthusiasm," however, lived on in the minds of a good many colonists as a remarkable example of the extreme to which "Extravagance, Folly, and Wickedness . . . will hurry the poor Sons of Men."[55] Like the Anabaptists at Münster for Europe, the Dutartres of South Carolina became the epitome of wrong-headed enthusiasm in the New World.

Before the opening salvo of the Great Awakening, New England seemed not very interested in the Prophets. No family like the Dutartres exploded on the scene to horrify the saints of the North. But by the spring of 1735 their notoriety had spread far enough to persuade Edward Wigglesworth in Massachusetts to forewarn his fellow colonists against similar devices of the Devil, who delighted in deceiving people into thinking they were inspired directly by the Holy Spirit. One wonders whether Jonathan Edwards's convulsive revival that very year at Northampton—over three hundred people struck down—had anything to do with the cautious Wigglesworth's "Seasonable" warning to "try the spirits whether they are of God." After all, he reminded his audience, "many false prophets are gone out into the world." During the Great Awakening a half dozen years later its opponents were not at all reluctant to smear New Light revivalists with the enthusiasm of the Prophets, and it may be that Wigglesworth was just a little ahead of his time, as was, truth to tell, Jonathan Edwards.[56]

But the French Prophets left other legacies to America; one in particular differed strikingly from either Samuel Keimer's or the Dutartres', chiefly because of its positive and constructive character.

The Benezets

Samuel Keimer left Philadelphia just four years before the arrival of a French family intimately related to the Prophets. These were the Benezets, whose father, Jean Étienne, had been one of them at Calvisson in the heart of Languedoc about ten miles southwest of Nîmes. Once schooled in the Prophets' extremism, he threw in his lot with a particular branch of Camisards called Congéniès Quakers, really a group of Huguenot enthusiasts who, unlike the Prophets, although derived from then, had renounced war and the use of force. Because Benezet was now an enemy of the state, or, as a son later explained, because he interpreted the Bible differently from the priests, the French government confiscated his estate in 1713.

He and his family, including two-year-old Antoine, hurriedly left France for Holland and then England, where they lived for the next sixteen years. In London the Benezets became friendly with both Quakers and Moravians, with Peter Boehler, right-hand man to Count Zinzendorf, and also the young George Whitefield a year or two before he went off to Oxford. While in London, Antoine, now Anthony Benezet, became a Quaker at the age of fourteen, and this commitment, along with the older Benezet's dissatisfaction with the Anglican hierarchy, no doubt had something to do with the family's move in 1731 to Philadelphia, where John Stephen and Anthony joined a Quaker meeting. Their large home on Second Street became a haven for itinerant enthusiasts. Count Zinzendorf visited for some time when his own rented home was under repair, and George Whitefield repeatedly stayed with the Benezets while stopping in Philadelphia during his frequent travels. Meanwhile, Zinzendorf sent Peter Boehler to the American colonies; he promptly renewed acquaintances in Philadelphia with the family he had known in London, and John Stephen, with a new friend, Benjamin Franklin, attended Boehler's ordination in the Moravian Church, presided over by the Count.

John Stephen, along with three of his daughters, became a Moravian in the early 1740s and shortly moved to Germantown. The daughters soon married Brethren at Bethlehem; the youngest, Susan, chose John Christopher Pyrlaeus, an Indian missionary, and the couple lived for a time with Conrad Weisser in Mohawk country, where Pyrlaeus studied the language and they both taught school.[57] Anthony Benezet remained a Quaker the rest of his life and chalked up a splendid career in Philadelphia as schoolmaster and then worthy successor to John Woolman in the struggle against slavery and war, a struggle both men based solidly on Quaker principles.

From the Cévennes to London to Philadelphia to Germantown, from French Prophet to Quaker to Moravian, John Stephen Benezet ran the gamut of enthusiasms. Friendly with Quakers everywhere, with the ecumenical Count Zinzendorf, and with Calvinist George Whitefield, Benezet and his son, Anthony, symbolized the openness and the interrelatedness of an inward experimental religion which Pennsylvania attracted and welcomed. When John Stephen died in 1751, Quakers and a wide assortment of sectarians, besides orthodox believers, flocked to Germantown in tribute, where revivalist Gilbert Tennent spoke at grave side to a "great number of people."[58]

From Plockhoy's Mennonites on the Horekill to the Quaker Benezets in Philadelphia and Germantown, the history of Continental enthusiasts in the American colonies is a history of religious experiments and experiences, some as different as the enthusiasms which provoked them. Communitarians, singletons, ecumenists, mystics, pietists, and fanatics, some more, some less, they shared beliefs in spiritual immanence and radical piety, besides a conception of America which invited and encouraged both.

None of these individuals or groups seriously changed the course of history, although several presumptuously expressed the intent. But whether they were successful or not on anyone's terms, many colonists suspected the worst of them and found their enthusiastic religions threatening, even subversive. The very interrelatedness of enthusiasm, despite its diverse origins and expression, aroused mistrust, particularly when it expanded and intensified and became a radical vehicle not only for revivalism and communitarianism but for Christianizing blacks and heathen Indians.

꿈ᵕ쩍 9 ᶜᵕᵕ쩍

The Great Awakening
as Enthusiasm

*I*T IS NOT surprising that advocates of the Great Awakening in the
1740s were called enthusiasts. There was no need to explain to eighteenth-century colonists the meaning of the heresy which by that time was
traditional and recognizable and reminded them of the Anabaptists and
Familists of the sixteenth century. It recalled, too, tales of Anne Hutchinson and the antinomians in early Massachusetts, the Ranters and Quakers of the English Civil War and after, and the French Prophets in both
France and England, to say nothing of the Dutartres of South Carolina.
Whether this great revival was a genuine religious movement is a question
which does not really worry most historians today. What does concern
them is how people at the time regarded the Awakening and whether
they thought it was genuine or false. Colonists' responses help to explain
why the Revival occurred and, at the same time, why it provoked such
intense emotion—emotion which its champions defended as true religion
and tied to New World opportunities, and which its opponents scoffed
at as enthusiasm, wild-eyed and destructive.

Thirteen colonies had carved a good deal of territory out of the "howling wilderness" by 1740—several were already at least one hundred years
old—and settlement had blunted some of the sharp edges of the frontier.
The first half of the eighteenth century was a period of expansion and
development—no quarrel with that. But in the midst of material progress
and prosperity something was not as it should be. Was America not
worthy of its earlier promise? Was it degenerating like England and the
Old World into materialism and self-satisfaction? The danger seemed to
lurk in a moral and rational approach to religion, tending to Arminianism
and even deism, which was offensive to most colonists whose religion
and world view were largely Calvinist.[1] "Whatever is, is right" may have
fitted Alexander Pope's sophisticated world in Augustan London,[2] but it
was not compatible with the religious attitudes of Puritans in New England and Scotch-Irish and Germans in the middle colonies and Virginia.

For those who honored the covenant or a more vague, yet advantageous, conception of their relation with God, a slackening of religious endeavor was not only sinful but disastrous, because more was expected of New World colonists than of less privileged people elsewhere. That this was the "best of all possible worlds," as Voltaire's Pangloss was to tease the century,[3] may very well have satisfied enlightened rationalists in France and England, but it was a far cry from the conclusions reached by a good many settlers who were embarrassed by the religious decline they observed about them. The vital link with God which the New World had promised was much weakened, if not already broken. The seventeenth century had enjoyed it, or at least in retrospect had seemed to, but in the 1730s many people experienced a "general deadness," and God's spirit appeared to be withdrawn. The Great Awakening was an attempt to do something about this state of affairs, to promote a radical return to the purity of an earlier condition when the grace of God had abounded in the hearts of his people.

A number of religious leaders were successful in convincing a large segment of the colonial population that not only was America different from the Old World, but religion itself was different in America. They held that a vital relationship demanded a "vital religion," and that a vital religion was an experimental religion which affected the hearts or emotions of the people. In fact, the emotions, or "affections," were a vehicle for the new religion. This was a radical breakthrough for the colonial clergy who participated, for previously emotions had been carefully kept under wraps lest they misdirect and lead to enthusiasm.

According to the new psychology, which Jonathan Edwards both understood and championed and which other revival preachers found would work, colonial ministers of evangelical temperament appealed to the emotions of their people as the quickest way to conviction of sin and conversion. In this way they produced a revival which swelled into a general awakening.[4] Everyone damned enthusiasm, but the advocates of the Awakening refused to recognize the revivals they produced (or provoked) as anything but remarkable outpourings of God's grace. They insisted that this movement was something new and different which must be understood on its own terms, that extraordinary times demanded extraordinary methods. God in America was working outside the accustomed forms. After all, God could work in any way he chose, and in the New World he chose to work by new means, some not acceptable to those who insisted on Old World, even seventeenth-century, criteria.[5]

What a time to be alive in America! To Josiah Smith of Charlestown, South Carolina, it looked as if some remarkable happy epoch were just beginning—another Reformation perhaps. "Some great things seem to be upon the anvil," he wrote, "some big prophecy at the birth."[6] Visitor George Whitefield early caught the revival promise and helped marvelously to sustain it. Besides being an "excellent school to learn Christ in," he wrote, America was an "excellent soil for christianity." What, he asked, is Jesus about to do if the "beginning is so great"? Look to your holy laurels, Old England, for surely the "divine Herbert's prophecy is now being fulfilled":

> Religion stands a tiptoe in our land,
> Ready to pass to the American strand.

(The next year Whitefield offered his own metaphor on the same subject which fell a little short of the "divine Herbert's" but expressed a similar promise: "Surely the candlestick will shortly be removed from *England*.") Then from Boston, he asserted with determination, "GOD shews me that *America* must be my place for action."[7]

It was a brave and strange New World. For the revivalists the movement was a revival of an original purpose and an awakening to new means of fulfilling it. In spite of their theology and church order, which had previously restrained their zeal, they found a surprising quickening of religion through the "affections" or "passions" of their people. What to their opponents was enthusiasm and deception was to the revivalists the unique characteristics of an extraordinary outbreak of divine grace.

If proponents of the Awakening were radical in their emotional and dramatic approach to religion, they were, for the most part, orthodox in theology. After all, they were Calvinists at heart and had no doubt about the fundamentals of Christian doctrine. None of the revivalists felt that they had any cause to question these assumptions, although Whitefield tended to relax doctrinal rigidity. What the revivalists did question were the traditional means of grace, for these, they claimed, might better be utilized to promote God's plan for America. Thus, in handling these means the revivalists were radical and further laid themselves open to the charge of enthusiasm. The revival experience gave a new gloss to orthodox doctrine and practice. Since men were sinful, they must be convinced of it before they could expect God to reach out and save them. Therefore, revivalists stressed more strongly than ever the "terrors of the law" to bring men and women to an absolute surety that they were evil in God's eyes and deserved the death and punishment the Bible promised. Once convinced of this, despairing of any hope, they could look for no escape but to throw themselves on God's mercy—"shutup to Christ," as Gilbert Tennent put it—wholly persuaded of their unworthiness to receive it. To bring about conviction, New Light preachers painted stark pictures of hell and the likelihood of man's falling into it. They placed sharp emphasis on fire and brimstone and played heavily on emotions of their listeners as the surest means to dissolve all support concealed in complacency and good works.[8]

Some ministers were more skillful than others in striking terror into the souls of the unregenerate. Gilbert Tennent was a "son of thunder" who had "learned experimentally to dissect the heart of a natural man." After hearing him preach, even Whitefield admired and marveled and regretted his own softness in dealing with sinners.[9] Jonathan Edwards surpassed all other ministers in sheer ability with words; he bombarded the senses of his listeners with simple ideas of damnation and hell, well aware of the psychological effect upon their understanding.[10] Unlike Tennent, whom opponents repeatedly called an enthusiast, Edwards spoke very naturally in a "low and moderate Voice," never letting his gestures, only his words, excite the attention of his listeners—words which he delivered with great solemnity as if in the presence of God.[11] Conviction was a part of God's plan for conversion. The ministers were altogether willing to help him promote it by literally scaring the hell out of their people. And scare them they did, producing at times mass physical reactions from whole congregations—further evidence of fanaticism—and a universal lament about what people could do to be saved. The intensity of the reaction was often, but not always, in proportion to the zeal of the minister. An extremist with a dramatic flair and a good pair of lungs might provoke outright frenzy among his listeners and come close to bringing down the roof.

To strike terror into the breasts of the unregenerate or to convict them by other means was not the only duty of the ministry, even in revival time, for ministers preached the gospel as well. Without hope of reward, with hell staring them in the face, sinners were prepared for God's act of grace, should he choose to manifest it, and the 1740s demonstrated that conversion was likely to come in connection with a revival and strong preaching. During the Awakening there was no dearth of preaching, for churches and ministers kept land-office hours. Even as some hearers were struck down, others were lifted up, and in countless meeting houses the moanings and groanings of the condemned were offset by cries of ecstasy, even holy laughter, of those experiencing pangs of the "New Birth," demonstrations which could only convince opponents how deeply embedded enthusiasm was in the whole process of revival.

Conversion in the 1740s, however, differed from what was usual and customary. It was frequently telescoped into a short period of time and was less the planting of a seed to be slowly nurtured by the believer than a "circumcision of the heart," just as the Bible said it was,[12] or even a cataclysmic encounter like Paul's on the road to Damascus. Under revival conditions the process of conversion became more hurried and concentrated. An inability to cite the precise attributes of one's conversion was sometimes accepted as evidence of none at all.

The very nature of grace also tended to shift during the Revival. A seventeenth-century saint had an inkling which side of God he stood on, but he never could be absolutely sure. Often after minor transgressions he experienced a gnawing doubt as to the condition of his soul and retired to his closet to search his heart for renewed evidence of salvation. But those of the "New Birth" boasted confidence in grace. The new character of conversion afforded saints an assurance of salvation which at times smacked of the antinomianism of Anne Hutchinson and her enthusiasts and was, therefore, heinous in the eyes of old-guard Calvinists. Once sure of salvation, it was not much of a jump for new saints, having judged themselves, to judge others, even ministers, on the state of their souls, a practice which led to accusations and resentment, often schism and separatism.[13]

Had itinerant preaching attracted only the skills of ordained ministers, objections to it from the Revival's opponents might have been less severe. The Awakening also encouraged exhorters whose credentials for their holy tasks were often no more than heated devotion, enthusiasm, and a call to preach. Some thought that the prestige of the ministry suffered with rank amateurs loose in the field, but the criteria among the religiously aroused were not college degrees and proper ordinations; instead they were grace and a zeal—often called enthusiasm—to promote it.[14]

The same dispensation which dictated a new look at conviction and the "law," at conversion and the means of grace, that demanded a converted ministry and encouraged itinerants and exhorters, permitted also a change in traditional ideas of education and ministerial control, particularly if they tended to inhibit the Revival. Although previously a minister needed a degree from a European university or a recognized colonial college, New Lights accepted products of the Log College at Neshaminy, Pennsylvania, where, in reaction to the formalism and head learning of the universities, Gilbert Tennent's father had trained a generation of revival preachers for what he felt really mattered and sent them out to awaken the world.[15] Opponents of the Awakening, in addition to insisting upon formal learning, demanded proper ordinations according to traditional ecclesiastical procedures. No wonder they looked askance at Isaac Backus of Norwich, Connecticut, who, a year or two after his conversion, felt directly summoned by God to preach the gospel and promptly did, itinerating, exhorting, and finally settling at Middleborough, Massachusetts, after being called there to shepherd a Separatist congregation. Backus was minister at Middleborough for over sixty years, the only change in arrangements being that he led a shift to the Baptist Church with a part of his congregation a few years after his arrival. In the opinion of Old Lights and Anglicans, besides being an enthusiast he was an ignorant nobody, an impostor, without rightful claim to pursue God's work. That he championed the radical idea of separating Church and State, a conviction he formed from his galling experiences as a Separatist, was further proof of his enthusiasm and did not endear him to Congregational Massachusetts, where public worship of God had been protected by law since the 1630s.[16]

Like other outbursts of enthusiasm throughout history, the Awakening had its share of anti-intellectualism. It reached a peak with James Davenport's notorious book burning at New London, Connecticut, in 1743. Besides books, he and his flock were ready to throw in their gaudy clothing and other superfluous apparel when one of the more moderate among them called a halt, and luckily, too, for Davenport had already topped the pile with his "old, wore out, plush breaches," his only pair.[17] Not long before the great fire of New London, some of Connecticut's extremists founded nearby what they called the Shepherd's Tent, a makeshift colony for revivalists' meetings and the instruction of exhorters, which flew in the face of orthodox Congregationalism in the "land of steady habit." Once the book burning was over and the burners humiliated, the Shepherd's Tent suffered by association as a further example of radical enthusiasm; it soon quietly folded, and its shepherds slipped away.[18]

Isaac Backus's splendid *History of New England* in three volumes certainly belied any hint that he opposed intellectual activity. Backus was outraged by Davenport's book burning. What disturbed him most, however, was that some of Davenport's critics did not fully appreciate the true meaning of the event: that the book burners, by their destruction of outward things, had completely ignored their own evil within. "If we could burn all the *idols, books* or *heretics* in the world," he told his readers, "it would avail us nothing without *charity* in our souls."[19] (A century later Nathaniel Hawthorne improved both Davenport's fiery deed and Backus's moral to give us a delightful tale called "Earth's Holocaust," published in 1844.) Whitefield was no book burner; instead, in one instance he had thrown "bad books" overboard, beyond reach of susceptible sailors, after ransacking the vessel which first brought him to the colonies in 1738—replacing, of course, what volumes he found with "good ones." "But what are books without Thy Spirit, O Lord?" asked Whitefield. Like George Fox before him and Ralph Waldo Emerson after, he believed books were for the saint's idle times, when the enthusiast was not in tune with the Spirit. But, then, they ought to be "good ones," and he frequently recommended to his followers the works of Jacob Boehme and William Law, whose mystical writings enthusiasts have never ceased feeding upon since they were first published in the early seventeenth and early eighteenth centuries, respectively.[20]

Most New Lights accepted learning as part of a minister's "baggage," but they were careful lest it dominate at the expense of the heart. "I love to study," wrote Whitefield, "and delight to meditate . . . and yet would go into the Pulpit by no Means depending on my Study and Meditation, but the blessed Spirit of God."[21] The majority of revivalists undoubtedly preferred a nice balance between intellect and emotion, but as itinerants and exhorters quickened the tempo, their emphasis fell less on learning and more on the heart and its needs. Tennent, his critics complained, "roar'd more fiercely" than Whitefield "against Colleges, Human Reason and Good Works."[22]

If, as Whitefield suggested, he entered the pulpit full of the "Spirit of God," there was no need, it seemed, for written sermons. "*Extempore* preaching*," always a trademark of the enthusiast, became as much a part of the revivalist's style as an appeal to the "affections"; in fact, they were intimately related. A minister read the pulse, or sensed the mood, of his listeners and tailored his message accordingly. The Spirit moved quickly in the 1740s, and a clergyman had to stand ready to move with it, not be tied to a stuffy sermon written in the cool of his study. A sermon had to smell of brimstone, not of the lamp. "Feed on this promise," Whitefield encouraged an exhorter in 1740 in words his critics jumped upon: "It shall be given you in that hour what you shall say." Forget your sermon notes, he advised another; just remember Christ's words, "Lo I am with you always, even to the end of the world."[23] In the heat of the Awakening a good many ministers ignored their written sermons, even their notes, and preached on the spot as the Spirit moved them. Their method was both exciting and effective, lending to their sermons and prayers an emotional appeal which was the very essence of revival—and of enthusiasm.

One of the new means was the dramatic style of Awakening preachers—Edwards excepted, as we have seen, who pretty much tended to business and produced his effect by the words he used. Whitefield was a man of remarkable voice and gesture. In his twenties during the 1740s, he was a slender individual (later in life he rounded up considerably, which was a source of embarrassment to him) of medium height and a fair complexion, and as anyone knows who has seen his portraits, hopelessly cross-eyed. Still, his overall appearance was attractive and his movements agile and sprightly. Contemporaries spoke of a piercing lively imagination. Whitefield possessed a striking memory w' course, enabled him to take full advantage of what appeared to be extemporaneous preaching. His voice was "perfect music," said Sarah Edwards of Northampton, Massachusetts, and he commanded it expertly. Equally effective were his gestures, which he graciously related to a beautiful intonation and used both unaffectedly. One contemporary commented that if his delivery was the product of art, "'tis certainly the Perfection of it," and later John Adams made no bones about his skill as an actor. Despite mastery of words, his speech was plain, lacking conceits.[24] Even his most bitter critics among the clergy marveled at his voice and "agreeable delivery" and accused him of using both to rob them first of their character and then their audiences.[25]

Whitefield's expressions and gestures were famous and memorable. The Evangelical Lutheran Henry Melchior Muhlenberg has told the story of the German woman in Philadelphia who was drawn by accounts of Whitefield's preaching and walked forty miles to hear him at the height of the Awakening. Once back home she told her friends of her experience, that never in her life had she been so quickened, so awakened as she was in listening to that man. Of course, this frau understood not a word of English, but Whitefield's presence, appearance, voice, expressions, gestures left a vivid impression of his spiritual message upon her. Muhlenberg was an admirer of the "sainted" Mr. Whitefield, but not a blind one, and he occasionally pointed out where he thought he was wrong, if only in his journal.[26] He too was impressed by Whitefield's manner of preaching and tried to understand what there was about it that turned people into limp rags or wailing converts. Several years later Muhlenberg commented on an episode in 1740 and added an explanation. It seems that Whitefield was once late for a huge service where he was to preach, and to fill the time "another saintly" minister spoke in his place on a particularly "powerful Scripture passage." The large crowd was politely quiet—no stirring, no tears or emotional response. Whitefield arrived in the middle of the other chap's expounding, and the latter gave over immediately, placed the Bible in Whitefield's hands, and pointed out the text from which he preached. Within a moment's time Whitefield had the place rocking; the whole "*auditorium*" was deeply moved. There were tears, hand-wringing, weeping, sighing, and shouting. Was it not possible, Muhlenberg shrewdly asked, that "name and fame, preconceptions and fancies," had played a strong role in the "synergism"? After all, he added, laughing, weeping, sneezing, and yawning were infectious; they were like electricity. In looking back on the Great Awakening, Henry Muhlenberg concluded that enthusiasm was contagious, too.[27]

Gilbert Tennent could not have been more different, although he too was a "Man of considerable Parts and Learning," and like Whitefield was wholly acquainted with experimental religion. But he took no care to please his listeners with his gestures or delight their ears or their fancies with his voice or language, and John Adams certainly would have been disappointed in his acting. Tennent aimed directly at their hearts and consciences and laid bare their delusions and deceptions, their "numerous, secret, hypocritical Shifts." He left no refuge unsearched; he seemed to recall afresh the terrors of the law when he brandished them before the eyes of sinners while he pierced the hearts of even the most stubborn.[28] His enemies called him madman, fanatic, and, of course, enthusiast, who preached the reason right out of his listeners and left them raving.[29]

Proponents of the Awakening insisted that revival activities were an extraordinary manifestation of Christ's Spirit upon the land, exempting them from customary ecclesiastical restraints, sometimes even scriptural guidelines. Opponents, whether Old Light, Old Side, Anglican, or rationalist, stigmatized these same activities as fanaticism and lumped together as enthusiasts moderates such as Jonathan Edwards, the crazy extremist James Davenport, and contentious Gilbert Tennent. Old Lights and the Old Side objected to the Awakening on other grounds, too. Certainly there was honest disagreement over the nature of religion, the meaning of conversion and grace, and the efficacy of reason and learning. There were decorum and tradition to be considered. Besides, established means had always existed through which God's grace worked, and anything else was considered suspect as enthusiasm, particularly if it opposed the principles of logic and formal theology. Perhaps more important was the Revival's affront to the established clergy, who were often looked upon with contempt, and whose offices and duties were frequently disregarded when itinerants swooped down on likely spots and congregations flocked to hear them.[30]

There is no doubt that the Awakening disrupted organized churches, whether Congregational in Massachusetts and Connecticut, Presbyterian in Pennsylvania and New Jersey, or Anglican in Virginia and South Carolina.[31] Whitefield generally ignored denominational lines; although he was nominally an Anglican, he preached mainly in dissenting churches to mixed audiences or in the fields and marketplaces, where ecclesiastical divisions meant little. Moreover, he frequently spoke in ecumenical terms, lamenting the differences between dissenters and conformists: "Oh, that the partition-wall were broken down, and we all with one heart and one mind could glorify our common Lord and Saviour Jesus Christ!"[32]

The established denominations fought back as best they could against the blending of congregations and revivalists' fanatical practices which disturbed the accustomed order. Most severe was the response in Connecticut, where the Old Light clergy persuaded the legislature to clamp down on the activities of itinerants, foreign and domestic.[33] Samuel Davies in Virginia had to contend not only with the colony government but also with the Bishop of London and his Commissary in order to keep revival channels open in Hanover County and other back-country places. Had Davies preached only to his own Presbyterians, the government might have left him alone; but many of his listeners were former Anglicans—with more coming over every day—who were bored with the "languid harangues" and "insipid speculations" mouthed in the Church of England.[34] The Massachusetts government took action against such men as James Davenport, whose conduct, most Yankees agreed, constituted a public nuisance—singing in the streets and all that—and whom Charles Chauncy liked to call the "*wildest Enthusiast*" he had ever encountered. Accused of slandering and reviling his opponents in print, Davenport was tried by the Superior Court; rather than find him guilty, it compassionately declared him insane and gladly sent him away.[35]

Those hostile to the Awakening had various reasons for opposing it, ranging from contrary views of religious temperament to fears of encroachment upon privilege and class. However, all the opponents of the Awakening agreed upon one thing—its enthusiasm. No charge against the Revival and its participants was more frequent; to no other charge was the "New Way" more vulnerable. According to critics, God worked in accustomed and reasonable ways, as the Bible taught and ministers had preached for some time. The use of terror, they claimed, played upon people's fears rather than convicted them of sin; it thus tended to drive sinners from Christ rather than toward him. What passed among revivalists for conversion experience, no matter how vivid and dramatic, was considered contrary to God's usual means and opened the door to impulses and visions and other forms of enthusiasm which impressed the gullible but cheapened the revealed Word in the Bible. No man was more presumptuous than he who was overconfident of obtaining grace and judged his neighbors and the clergy on his own terms, not God's, at the same time claiming divine guidance. The ministry was a noble calling and instrumental in saving souls. Therefore, when New Light clergymen established themselves as a "holy band," and separated their people from those whom they rashly judged and called unconverted, this was thought to be the height of arrogance and enthusiasm, which could only provoke factionalism, schism, and contempt. Itinerants and exhorters distracted the people, upset the traditional churches, and destroyed gospel order and respect for the clergy. And all this was done from a false spirit, said

Jonathan Mayhew, by "enlightened Ideots" who made "inspiration, and
the Spirit of truth and wisdom, the vehicle of nonsense and contradictions."³⁶

Critics with a historical bent delighted in describing the Awakening
against a background of enthusiasm culled from the Christian past. The
Anglican Commissary of Charlestown, South Carolina, in his ridicule of
George Whitefield, ransacked church history for all the "instances of
enthusiasm and abused grace" he could find. And with the "grand itinerant" seated in a pew before him, he compared him to "the *Oliverians,
Ranters, Quakers, French Prophets,*" and even the notorious Dutartres,
who had outraged Carolinians a few years earlier with their trances and
visions, their incests and murders.³⁷ A bitter pamphlet published in Philadelphia in 1741 dubbed the enthusiasm of the Awakening a "Wandering
Spirit" and likened it to the lodestar which guided Jacob Boehme, the
German mystic, in writing his "Jargon and dark Nonsense." It was the
very same spirit which had inspired the bloody fanatics at Münster and
Ranters everywhere.³⁸ A Salem Anglican wrote home to England that the
illusions of the French Prophets were nothing to the "confusion, disorder,
& irregularity" of Boston, and if something very soon did not put an
end to the fanaticism, 1741 would be as memorable for enthusiasm as
1692 was for witchcraft. The converted, he wrote, "cry out upon the
unregenerated, as the afflicted did then upon the poor innocent wretches
that unjustly suffered."³⁹

The French Prophets were a favorite comparison, probably because
their notorious activities were still within the memory of a good many
people in the 1740s. Boston's Charles Chauncy was doubtless the most
learned—and the most bitter—critic of the Revival; more than once he
taunted New Lights with the Prophets when he was not likening them
to Mrs. Hutchinson and the antinomians or the Quakers.⁴⁰ In 1742 there
was published in Boston a lengthy tract called *The Wonderful Narrative,*
which faithfully traced the history of the Huguenot extremists; in a revealing appendix the author—who may or may not have been Chauncy—
related what he saw at his doorstep in Boston to the "*Raptures and
Ravishments*" of the French fanatics.⁴¹ Chauncy's most significant work,
Seasonable Thoughts on the State of Religion in New England, published
the following year, was a full-fledged attack upon Jonathan Edwards and
the Awakening and the extraordinary use the New Lights made of the
various means of grace. A religion whose substance is merely passion,
warned Chauncy, finds itself vulnerable to the wildest temptations, chiefly
fancy and enthusiasm.⁴² The effect of divine truth upon the soul should
be a reasonable "Solicitude," not the loose shenanigans of New Lights.
Chauncy was the Old Lights' rational man, and his book was a careful

exposure of the Great Awakening to the light of reason. But in addition to its criticism, Chauncy's volume was a splendid explanation of what the revivalists were rebelling against.

It was much easier to make fun of the Awakening and hurl charges of enthusiasm than to defend it. A positive view of the Revival was difficult to impress upon its enemies since most were religious rationalists, like Chauncy, who delighted in ridiculing emotion, or Anglican moralists, like Alexander Garden in Carolina, for whom religion was formal and professional. At the same time the hard-core New Lights, who found an enduring spiritual essence in the Awakening, were forced to protect this essence from outright fanatics within their own group, like James Davenport, who made fools of themselves. The very attempt to guard the Awakening from these people was accepted as an admission that enthusiasm *did* accompany the Revival. Its supporters had the difficult job of arguing that, despite the lunatic fringe, the heart of the Awakening was pure and beyond all argument a wonderful, "new and extraordinary" work of God's Spirit.[43]

The defense went about its tasks in several ways. One method was to deny outright that the movement was centered on enthusiasm and to brand all who claimed it was as carnal and unconverted and enemies to God. At the height of the Awakening this was Gilbert Tennent's chief weapon, and in his hands it did little to convince his opponents that they were mistaken.[44] To dismiss the Revival in New England as enthusiasm, argued Whitefield, was as useless as the Roman attempt to brand the Jewish religion with the "hated Name of Superstition."[45] Another means of defending the Awakening was to cite biblical precedents for irregularities. The lamentations, the groanings, the faintings, said Tennent, were "no more than what the Scriptures inform us did happen in the apostolick times."[46] Harvard College accused Whitefield of speaking like a man who believed he had direct communication from God and as much intimacy with him "as any of the Prophets and Apostles." Whitefield answered the Harvard people guilelessly: certainly he had communion with God, he said, "to a Degree," and had he not, he never would have become a minister. In what other way are saints chosen, he asked? "To Talk of . . . having the Spirit of God without feeling it, is really to deny the Thing." The charge of enthusiasm missed its mark on Whitefield, for he claimed no "false spirit" but declared his communion with God to be the real thing.[47]

Jonathan Edwards has left us the most profound defense of the Awakening. One of his efforts was a commencement sermon which he delivered at Yale College in the spring of 1741, called "The Distinguishing Marks of a Work of the Spirit of God." Edwards argued calmly and subtly that, although physical manifestations were not necessarily a sign of God's Spirit, neither were they necessarily *not* a sign. What Edwards attempted to do, and what most advocates of the Awakening had difficulty accomplishing, was to place the Awakening in an acceptable perspective as an extraordinary work of God. It was clear from Scripture, Edwards told his Yale audience, that God had certain things he wished to accomplish which had never yet been seen—"further truths," the Pilgrims' John Robinson would have called them. Therefore, deviations from what men understood to be usual ought not to be used as evidence of enthusiasm— that is, if they did not violate God's prescribed rules. Certainly, said Edwards, "we ought not to limit God where he has not limited himself." The extraordinary means used by God at the time could very easily produce "extraordinary appearances." Given the weakness of man's nature, these "effects" should be expected and excused, not made the center of controversy and condemned wholesale by the doubters. If we look back upon church history, wrote Edwards, "we shall find no instance of great revival of religion, but what has been attended with many such things."[48] He held that physical effects had little to do with what was really going on and, therefore, should not be used to support or attack the Awakening. Gilbert Tennent grasped this part of the argument, and although he undoubtedly was one of the worst offenders against a reasonable "solicitude" and decorum, he and his Log College friends could ask, "What if there were some things exceptionable in the conduct of some of the instruments and subjects of this work? Is this so strange an incident in a state of imperfection, as to give us ground of surprize or prejudice against the whole work?"[49]

Proponents of the Awakening found themselves on the defensive for several years. Surprisingly, Tennent and Davenport shifted courses to preserve the purity of the movement. Friends had convinced them that the Awakening suffered seriously from extremism. In order to rescue the substance of the Revival, they argued, the crackpots should be quickly isolated. By 1744 both Tennent and Davenport had confessed their "misguided Zeal" and retreated from a number of radical positions taken earlier and defiantly held. Tennent spoke first and included a severe condemnation of Davenport.[50] Even Whitefield pulled in his horns—at least a little—not about the supernatural force behind the Awakening but about his own carryings on. In 1749 he conceded that there had been some wildfire in his zeal, that he had written and spoken from his own spirit too much, when at the time he had thought he was "writing and speaking entirely by the Assistance of the Spirit of God."[51] But it was too late. Opponents seized upon the confessions as admissions not only of enthusiasm but also of guilt, which more fully convinced them of the disingenuousness of the movement.

The charge of enthusiasm dogged Edwards until his death in 1758. At times he seemed as interested in protecting "true experimental religion" from some of the revivalists as in defending both from the charge of enthusiasm. In 1747 for a number of reasons Edwards chose to review the life of his friend David Brainerd, a young New Light minister from Connecticut who had died that year in his thirties. Since Brainerd was widely known as a saintly minister and a successful Indian missionary and had been an active revivalist during the Awakening—although he had experienced religious conversion a year or two before the Revival— Edwards found his career to be a perfect example of the good "effects" of experimental religion. He used Brainerd's life—almost exploited it— to distinguish the "New Birth" from enthusiasm by editing Brainerd's memoirs, adding a revealing commentary, and publishing them together in 1749.

Edwards was certain that the life of his friend proved there was indeed a truly vital religion, a religion which arose from "immediate divine influences, supernaturally enlightening and convincing the mind, and powerfully impressing, quickening, sanctifying and governing the heart." The fact that "immediate divine influences" were evident in Brainerd's life was reason enough to accept these influences even though they seemed contrary to traditional means God used in dealing with his saints. And this was true despite many "pretences" and "appearances" in others which had "proved to be nothing but vain, pernicious enthusiasm." After reading his memoirs, if anyone still insisted that Brainerd's religion was enthusiasm, a "strange heat," a "blind fervor," Edwards then asked, were his *virtues* the "fruits of enthusiasm?" (Here he listed about a page of these virtues, really an Edwardsean catalogue of the attributes of grace.) If these were the fruits of enthusiasm, "why should not enthusiasm be thought a desirable and excellent thing? For what can true religion, what can the best philosophy do more?" If "vapors and whimsey" make men and women thoroughly virtuous and lead them to the "most benign and fruitful morality," helping them to maintain both through a life of many trials while in the meantime opposing the "wildness, the extrav- agances, the bitter zeal, assuming behavior, and separating spirit of en- thusiasts" (all the bad "effects" of the Awakening), if vapors and whimsy can do this, Edwards declared, the world has cause to "prize and pray for this blessed whimsicalness, and these benign sort of vapors!"[52]

The logic here is tricky, and Edwards's readers might easily miss the point. Hardly condoning enthusiasm, Edwards shared his century's mis- trust of it. Nor was he flippantly asking, "If this be enthusiasm, who needs grace?" for he found no time to be amusing. The key to the argument is probably the phrase "the fruits of enthusiasm," which Edwards twice used in this passage, along with a "fruitful morality" maintained "through a course of life." If the fruits of enthusiasm were "true virtue," then there was working in the converted person something quite apart from enthusiasm as it was understood at the time—obviously, the grace of God, which supported these virtues throughout life in the saint's pursuit of his kingdom. Others might see "vapors and whimsey," but if the fruits were the virtues of a Brainerd, let the world call "true experimental religion" what it will—even enthusiasm.

What Edwards seems to be telling us is that maybe the eighteenth century was all wrong about enthusiasm—that, given the remarkable spiritual conditions of the 1740s, what people called enthusiasm was really something else. Maybe the word's meaning ought not to be as pejorative as the century had insisted. Edwards had read John Locke and Shaftesbury and knew that they in their treatises and tracts had distinguished between true inspiration, on the one hand, and enthusiasm, on the other, or so they said. After describing what Whitefield had stirred up in Charlestown, South Carolina, Alexander Garden called the flagrant impulses, motions, and impressions "proper and direct *Enthusiasm*," and then added, in the "bad Sense of the Word to which it is now commonly restricted."[53] Edwards would lift that restriction, or maybe do away with the word altogether if its meaning in people's minds no longer served the overwhelmingly spiritual experience of loving Christians who surrounded him. But besides being a reader of other people's ideas, such as Locke's and Shaftesbury's—and he was a great one for that—Edwards was a practitioner of experimental religion right there in Northampton, Massachusetts, where he saw and felt his own parishioners profoundly affected by God's spirit and grace. Sarah Pierrepont Edwards, his wife, was no enthusiast as the world understood that term, according to Edwards. She had neither grown up in nor had she been educated in "that enthusiastical town of Northampton"—as some called it—and yet, Edwards explained, she had experienced the "sweetness and ravishment of soul, that has been altogether inexpressible." If these things were enthusiasm, if this was distraction, declared Edwards, "let my brain be evermore possessed of that happy distemper" and "glorious distraction!"[54] George Whitefield had the same doubts about enthusiasm as his contemporaries used the term, mostly in attacking him. In defending New England's experience during these heady times, he insisted that the Awakening's enemies damned it in vain. If what occurred there, he wrote, was "truly *Enthusiasm*, then we have been wholly mistaken in the Meaning of the

Word," for what they have called enthusiasm was a "glorious and blessed Work of GOD."[55]

It was left to Edwards to salvage the meaning of the Awakening for New Lights who survived him and the evangelical generations which followed. Despite the century's penchant for rationalism, the "affections," said Edwards, primarily those related to "fear and sorrow, desire, love or joy," were *bona fide* channels for transmission of religious truth. That an appeal to these emotions produced what some people called enthusiasm and occasionally "extraordinary effects on persons' bodies" meant little in Edwards's large view of God's plans. What mattered was that the new "means" encouraged conviction and conversion and therefore grace and virtue, and it encouraged them sweepingly throughout the colonies in the form of an Awakening.[56] Related to Edwards's understanding of the remarkable outpouring of grace was his conception of America's peculiar Providence in God's overall scheme for redemption. His lucid explanations of conviction and conversion, of grace and true virtue, were laced with a millennialism, a manifest destiny, which, he claimed, the Awakening foreshadowed. "And if these things are so, it gives us more abundant reasons to hope that what is now seen in America, and especially in New England, may prove the dawn of that glorious day: and the very uncommon and wonderful circumstances and events of this work, seem to me strongly to argue that God intends it as the beginning or forerunner of something vastly great."[57]

When the New World first swam into the ken of the Old, the gospel, like the sun, soared from east to west, and, as Thomas Bastard explained in *The Marigold and the Sunne* (1615), it was "making day to the Indians and Antipodes."[58] To Edwards, what the Awakening foretold was "vastly great" enough to turn the course of things around. In the "new heavens and new earth" the sun of righteousness will be "wonderfully altered," changing the "course of nature"; the "light will rise in the West, till it shines through the world, like the sun in its meridian brightness."[59]

A manifestation of the Kingdom in the New World meant also the conversion of Indians to Christianity. John Eliot had taught as much almost a century earlier. Such a promise had drawn John Wesley to Georgia in 1735, where, he wrote, a great opportunity faced him; disappointingly he fell short, finding the Indians debauched and not yet ready for the gospel.[60]

Whitefield repeatedly spoke of the churches' responsibilities in America and prayed God to "open a door amongst the poor heathen." Christ died for Indians as well as white men, Whitefield reminded the world in his letters and journals, and may he have them for his inheritance.[61]

Edwards marveled at the way the Awakening had spread to the barbarous and ignorant, to Indians and Negroes, and foresaw a time when all nations and countries "shall be full of light and knowledge." When the Northampton people dismissed him from their church in the late 1750s, he took over the Indian mission at Stockbridge, Massachusetts, and experienced some of the practical problems of converting Indians, not least of which was resistance from white people nearby who shared little of his vision.[62] Daniel Marshall of Connecticut caught fire under Whitefield and in a fit of millennial enthusiasm dashed off to the Mohawks, where he hoped to hasten the *"latter-day glory,"* the "blissful period." Only an Indian war sent him home after eighteen months; he soon became an itinerant preacher and exercised his gifts for all to hear as far south as Georgia.[63] At about the same time, Edwards's friend David Brainerd had begun his short-lived stint with the Indians in New Jersey. He was amazed to discover that there was little for him to do, for God worked upon them supernaturally, he wrote, and he was scarcely conscious of being an instrument at all. Brainerd stood still and watched God's grace descend upon them.[64] God would work with extraordinary means in America, and the Awakening was his sign. Who could doubt the auspicious beginning?

Although most American colonists agreed that enthusiasm was a "false spirit" and therefore evil, they could not agree whether the Revival breathed a true spirit or enthusiasm. However, whether colonists approved or disapproved of the Awakening depended often upon their own religious temperaments, on the manner in which they believed God manifested himself in human society, and on what they understood to be the meaning of their purpose in the New World. Those who accepted America religiously and intellectually as a logical extension of the Old and applied Old World criteria to religious experience, who believed that theology, religious expression, and ecclesiastical institutions, as they were, gave reasonable form to the means of grace, to worship, and church government, these people were shocked and offended by the extremism of the Awakening. They pronounced it damnable enthusiasm and particularly resented its threatening spread to blacks and Indians.

For others, America was a radical chapter in the history of Christendom. They demanded a vital link between themselves and the God who sustained them in the new circumstances. Traditional religious convention frustrated their emotional drive to press close to God, to experience "further truths" and the "New Birth" which the New World promised. To these people new means were necessary. To them the Awakening was a blessing; it was far from false, it was not enthusiasm, and it was as free to Indians and blacks as it was to whites.

~~~ 10 ~~~

The Great Awakening as Subversion and Conspiracy

A WIDESPREAD reason for opposition to the Great Awakening was the belief that it posed a threat to social and political stability, besides undermining orthodox religion. According to opponents, the enthusiasm of religious radicals was subversive of established institutions, and one had only to look at the course of history since the Reformation for evidence of the troubles it had caused in the past. To these opponents the Revival was openly vulnerable to such criticism, for its revivalists were a clear and present danger to society at large, as well as to the well-being of Church and State.

Books, tracts, sermons, letters, and newspapers condemned the "New Way" and spoke of the ignorant, the rabble, the "admiring Vulgar," and Negroes, all of whom revival ministers and exhorters aroused and made restless and kept from their callings.[1] Virginia Anglicans accused Samuel Davies of "*holding forth* on working days," contrary to the "religion of labour," and causing Virginians to neglect their duties in providing for their families. Davies certainly did not increase his popularity in either Williamsburg or London when he replied that his people spent less than half as many working days listening to him hold forth on the "Word of Life" as Anglicans were "obliged to keep holy according to their calendar." Davies's quip made little impression; not long afterwards the Virginia governor and council intervened in support of orthodoxy and by proclamation prohibited "all Itinerant Preachers whether New Light men, Moravians or Methodists" from preaching or holding meetings.[2] Connecticut's government claimed that James Davenport's wild behavior had a "natural tendency to disturb and destroy the peace and order" of the colony. In response to these disturbing tendencies in this "Land of steady habit," the legislature, like Virginia's, put a stop to traveling preachers through severe laws to protect the good people of the colony and shelter the established Church.[3]

That the "peace and order" of the American colonies generally were disrupted by the Awakening there can be no doubt. Itinerant preachers and lay exhorters provoked "Ministers against Ministers," church against church; they upset ecclesiastical harmony, tending to schism, confusion, and disorder. A telescoping of the conversion process and a mindless play upon the emotions of its victims distorted theology and misrepresented God's relationship to man. But the "wandering Spirit" of enthusiasm also set husbands against wives, children against parents, servants against masters; it made a shambles of that reverence traditionally due the "Aged and Honourable," precisely what had been said in both England and the colonies about George Fox and his Quakers.[4] When George Whitefield preached from colony to colony, day laborers threw down their tools and mechanics shut up their shops to follow him, shirking their responsibilities and abandoning their families. The same was true of Gilbert Tennent. If only he could be persuaded to release the "Strollers" who tagged along after him and let them get back to their looms and lasts, their packs and grubbing hoes, the world might return to peace and quiet and an orderly face of affairs. Enthusiasm, charged Charles Chauncy of Boston in a tone reminiscent of the seventeenth century, always filled the church with confusion and the state with disorder. The boys at Harvard, despite all the holy talk, said another critic, received nothing but enthusiasm from Whitefield and Tennent, along with large doses of pride and a "Contempt of their Betters."[5]

Enthusiasm harbored radical behavior which also challenged custom and convention, obedience and morality. The heart when brimful of Christ's Spirit often found itself perfect and sinless and free from control and discipline. To some in whom the Spirit dwelt this meant sexual license, and the Awakening had its share, recalling the immorality of the Anabaptists and Ranters and other antinomian perfectionists. Enthusiasm, wherever it appeared, supposedly betrayed strong tendencies to promiscuity and communal marriage; it tended to destroy property, Chauncy claimed, and not least "to make all things common, *wives* as well as *goods*."[6]

Jonathan Edwards several times warned of what he called a "counterfeit of love" to which the "wildest enthusiasts" were vulnerable. Love and affection within an isolated group often became indistinguishable from mere attraction between the sexes, which easily degenerated into the gross and criminal. The early Gnostics suffered this kind of decline, as did the Family of Love, and no doubt, Edwards suggested, it was this decay of affection which led to the community of women we hear so much about among several of the sects. The practice of "mutual embraces" and "holy kisses" could only turn "Christian love into unclean and brutish lust." Right there in Northampton, Massachusetts, at the height of the Awakening, Edwards saw the risk of unchaperoned young people in mixed company meeting for religious services. Although at the moment the youngsters' minds were taken up with a "sense of divine things," this would wear off sooner or later and offer plenty of opportunities to "consort together in couples for other than religious purposes." Who knows, soon some might attend such meetings merely for the sake of "company-keeping."[7]

This all seems pretty chaste; it appears that Edwards was unnecessarily alarmed. But the history of enthusiasm, at least, warned him about "future dangers" set up by the Devil. Revival enthusiasm grew in some places to perfectionism and antinomianism, as it had countless times before. There were several instances of putting away wives and taking up with more fitting soul mates, a reordering thought permissible, given the dispensations which accompanied sinlessness—in the style of French Prophets and the Dutartres' holy household in South Carolina. Pregnancy aggravated one such couple's live-in arrangement in Cumberland, Rhode Island, although the father of the young lady (already married) earlier had explained that he saw no harm in his daughter's home away from home since she and her spiritual companion always "lay with a Bible between them." A similar occurrence shocked the people of Canterbury, Connecticut, when it ended in the tragic poisoning of a cast-off wife and two children. An accompanying difficulty in both these cases and one other, according to Isaac Backus, was that the orthodox clergy blamed the scandals on Separatists like Backus, who, they preached, were notorious for schism and faction and the destruction of communities.[8] Outbursts of enthusiasm were associated historically with subversion of convention and morality, let alone Church and State, and the Great Awakening of the 1740s was no exception.

Religion and Slavery

A universal complaint against enthusiasts was that they undermined society. But just as the Great Awakening had its indigenous causes, so too a peculiarly American brand of subversion emerged from it which tended to disturb established colonial customs such as the enslavement of blacks and prejudicial treatment of Indians.

Since slavery's beginnings in seventeenth-century Virginia, there had been a question in many colonists' minds about converting Africans to Christianity. Supposedly it was a godly duty to do so, just as it was to spread the gospel among the Indians. But there was some hesitation, even refusal, among slave owners, who never could be sure how black salvation would affect outright ownership, and many suspected the worst in reaction and revenge. Conversion might be interpreted as a step in the direction of equality with whites, which was an absurdity and incongruous with the whole institution of slavery.[9] King Charles II had encouraged the English Church and the gospel in the New World as a demonstration of his regard for American souls, black as well as white. But he blasted as gross "impiety" the slave owners' habit of prohibiting baptism "out of a mistaken opinion" that it made slaves "*ipso facto* free."[10]

Quakers were among the first to take notice of the religious needs of black slaves. Teaching the enthusiastic principles of Quakerism to anyone was bad enough, but teaching them to slaves was doubly subversive. Several extremist women spread their heretical beliefs among blacks in Virginia as early as 1661. Because of opposition to their meetings, Quakers in York County began holding them in out-of-the-way places to which they invited neighboring blacks. That the governor and the county authority were convinced that something more than religion was at stake in these clandestine assemblies is clear from the oaths of supremacy and allegiance demanded from likely disturbers of the peace. Mary Chisman, wife of a prominent planter and already a Quaker, attended these meetings with her slaves, for which the government stepped in and charged her husband to prevent her, their slaves, and other members of the family from such suspect activities.[11]

The ubiquitous William Edmundson found blacks at Barbados receptive to, even eager for, nurture of the inward light—so much so, in fact, that whites became apprehensive. A suspicious Anglican priest confronted Edmundson, and, besides damning Quakers as usual for blasphemy and heresy, he accused Edmundson and them also of making blacks Christians, a condition which could only teach them to rebel and cut the throats of whites. As the government was about to seize Edmundson for fomenting rebellion, he first, in good Quaker fashion, called upon the governor, who echoed the accusations. He told him that the only way to keep blacks *from* cutting white throats was to make them loving Christians; if they did rebel, it would be owing to the whites' denying them a "Knowledge of God and Christ Jesus," besides keeping them hungry.[12]

Quakers would not become outright abolitionists for three or more generations, but they were well prepared to share their light with blacks, and blamed whites for preventing it. In the 1670s Alice Curwen sounded very much as George Whitefield would in the 1740s when she taught what Christianity would do for the souls of blacks, besides making them better slaves and less likely to cut anyone's throat. But when Curwen and her missionary friends actually preached Quaker truths to enslaved

Negroes in Barbados, white society smelled racial equality and bloody rebellion.[13]

In South Carolina, where blacks outnumbered whites by the early eighteenth century, masters were adamant almost to a man against including them in the gospel promise. They claimed slaves grew worse for being Christians despite laws which plainly disassociated baptism from freedom. Assembling blacks for worship was foolhardy, they believed; it would give slaves a sense of their strength and tempt them to rebel despite bloody consequences, particularly on isolated plantations. Anyway, religious instruction took precious time away from work and would cut deeply into profits, besides drawing slaves away from their own gardens from which many fed and clothed themselves, freeing planters from the expense of both. These were strong reasons for not encouraging religion, although the SPG missionaries reported that planters would never admit the selfishness of the arguments. Slave owners insisted instead that Negroes were a wicked and stubborn race and therefore could never become true Christians.[14] Several years later Samuel Davies, who spent a good deal of time with Virginia slaves as a Presbyterian minister, sensed a real need on the part of some of them for religious instruction and worship to relieve their habitual uneasiness. The chief trouble was the masters' neglect of them, as if their condition necessarily deprived them of immortal souls. Still other slaves, he found, looked to religion and particularly baptism as a step toward equality, an urge Davies learned to discourage.[15] Apprehension remained among whites, however, lest religious education and eventual baptism become dangerously disruptive; converted blacks, who looked forward to a heavenly kingdom, might take steps to inherit an earthly one as well.

George Whitefield was no crusader against slavery. In fact, he was so far from attacking slavery as an institution that in 1741 he agreed to testify before Parliament in support of it in Georgia and later lamented that the trustees had deprived the colony of slave labor these many years. What a flourishing place it might have been, he commented, and think of the white lives their efforts would have saved! As late as 1751, when slaves became legal in Georgia, he regretted not possessing them at Bethesda, his orphanage—for their own good, of course—where he might make them comfortable and breed into their posterity the blessings of the Lord.[16]

The moral issue of slavery aside, Whitefield did preach a God who was no respecter of color; therefore, his sincere desire to include blacks in his promotion of God's grace made many South Carolinians uneasy and got him off to a bad start in their colony. No emancipator, Whitefield pushed for better treatment of Negroes, chiefly proper care of their souls.

Early in his colonial career he charged planters throughout the South with abusing their slaves and keeping them ignorant of Christianity. This he did in a series of published letters, and it did him no good either with the powers that be in South Carolina or the Anglican Commissary, Alexander Garden, who was already suspicious of Awakeners purely on religious grounds.[17] Garden publicly accused Whitefield of "enthusiasm and pride," and lumped him with all the fanatics he could think of, including the Ranters, the Quakers, and the notorious French Prophets, as a bad lot. He claimed Whitefield's letters incited insurrection among blacks, and for these reasons by themselves, let alone enthusiasm, Whitefield was suspect. To compound the uneasiness, Whitefield talked of establishing a Negro school in the colony, and he would have, too, he reported, had he found the time and proper schoolmasters.[18] When word spread later that he intended to convert "Whitefield's Folly," his orphan house at Bethesda, Georgia, into a college, his esteem in the South suffered badly. Because climate and isolation dictated severely against it, such a proposal suggested that there were devious designs, "some Venial Views," a "particular Scheme" up his sleeve, and southern planters wanted none of it.[19]

What Whitefield had no time for, Hugh Bryan, a devoted follower, tried hard to accomplish. The story of Bryan bears out the truth of a revealing contemporary charge against Whitefield: that he "unhinged many *good sort* of people." Bryan was a well-to-do Carolina planter, officeholder, and Presbyterian. With Whitefield's advice and the help of his wife and brother he resolved to establish a school for blacks on his own plantation.[20] But several events occurred which cast some doubt on Bryan's usefulness to Whitefield's crusade. As a result of his conversion and a measure of his zeal, he boldly attacked the Anglican priests in South Carolina, claiming their churches woefully neglected Christian duty to the colonists there. Full of "Decrees and Cannons," wrote Bryan, the orthodox clergy persecuted Christ's faithful ministers—meaning revival preachers—for not conforming, while "they themselves break their cannons every Day." Whitefield beamed approval and helped to see Bryan's charges in pamphlet form through Peter Timothy's press at Charlestown in January 1741. This was too much for Commissary Garden, whose shoddy treatment of Whitefield was obvious in Bryan's transparent indictment. The Commissary slapped a libel suit on all three—author, printer, and reverend agent—which detained Whitefield in South Carolina for some time, where he played the martyr and indulged himself in a "scene of suffering," delighted to call it "persecution." Whitefield posted bond, but the affair soon blew over when an appeal to England eventually stopped the proceedings.[21]

Meanwhile, Bryan's wife died, with a testimony to Whitefield on her lips.[22] Whether her death unstrung Bryan or whether too much of White-field's enthusiasm rubbed off on him would be difficult to determine. Under guidance of the Spirit, Bryan soon began prophesying the fiery destruction of Charlestown by blacks and their violent escape from slavery to freedom. Rumors spread quickly that he was holding encampments in Saint Helena's parish surrounded by "all sorts of people," most of them blacks in large numbers, gathered under the pretext of worship. What is surprising is how calmly the government seemed to take these wild claims, particularly since they followed by less than three years the notorious Stono Rebellion in South Carolina, which was put down only after the killing of forty blacks and half as many whites. Still, lest the black majority get wind of Bryan's "enthusiastic Prophecies," the government issued a warrant for his arrest. By this time he had recanted, calling the whole thing a delusion of the Devil rather than the bidding of the Holy Spirit, and begged forgiveness. But before his abrupt change of mind, he had lived for a time barefoot in the wilderness where the Spirit bade him attempt several miracles, including a smiting of the river waters that they might divide and let him pass. Undaunted after a thorough soaking, he foretold his own immediate death, and when that fizzled, too, he was persuaded to go home and retire from the prophesying business, shamefully confessing his delusion.

Great Awakening revivalists were not protoabolitionists. But like Whitefield they prayed and preached for the conversion of black slaves, who, if they could not win freedom, might win salvation. Most Carolinians, however, were convinced that slavery and religion, most of all enthusiasm, did not mix. Although they blamed Whitefield for Bryan's ominous fanaticism, like their government they came eventually to take the crisis in stride, and before long got a good laugh out of the outrageous episode.[23]

Not so funny was the case of Anne Le Bresseur, a "Widow Gentlewoman of considerable Fortune" and a "prime Disciple of Mr. Whitefield's." Mme. Le Bresseur had difficulty settling down in a Charlestown communion once Whitefield began preaching there, and not many weeks after Hugh Bryan confessed his delusion, she shot herself with a brace of pistols. Just before her death a couple of hours later, she made clear her absolute assurance of salvation and her longing to enter the "blessed mansions which she knew were prepared for her."[24] Whitefield, indeed, "unhinged many *good sort* of people," besides a good many others.

The Negro Conspiracy in New York

George Whitefield admired the Quaker colony's toleration and its open society. He found there a "greater equality between the poor and rich than perhaps can be found in any other place of the known world"—high praise, indeed. In fact, he thought so highly of Pennsylvania that he visited it frequently, finding appreciative audiences in a variety of Christians, although not many Quakers among them. He decided in early 1740 to establish a school for blacks there, going so far as to buy a huge tract of land near the Forks of the Delaware and planting it with a few Moravian friends to get on with the building while he traveled and preached.[25]

Whitefield brought to New York the same solicitude for souls, black as well as white, that he had shown in South Carolina, and he ran up against some of the same difficulties, too. New York City presented as many social tensions as the southern colony—maybe more, or so it seemed—which Whitefield and other revivalists aggravated. Already he had quarreled with Commissary William Vesey when he first visited there in November 1739, and although at the time he blessed God "for such success at New York," early the next year he found it a "very secure place"—that is, complacent and assured—where he and his revivalism were "mostly opposed."

It did not help matters that he became friendly with the notorious James Davenport from Long Island, whom the New York ministry already had contemptuously dismissed as an "enthusiast and a madman." Still, while preaching on several occasions, Whitefield reported that the Spirit "came down like a mighty rushing wind," which, besides alarming his congregations, resulted in a good deal of "crying, weeping, and wailing" from many members of his audience as they collapsed into the arms of friends who tried to comfort them. To conventional Anglicans, even Presbyterians, Lutherans, and Dutch Reformed churchgoers, Whitefield stirred things up in New York, and no wonder, he lamented: a "work of God had never been carried on" there since it was first settled.[26]

At the peak of the Revival, New York City experienced a severe jolt of another kind, a near catastrophe, which some colonists believed Whitefield had helped to provoke. New Yorkers called it the Negro Conspiracy of 1741, which, we are told, was a sudden attempt by blacks to plunder and murder the white inhabitants and burn the city. Mysterious and destructive fires, one at the Fort, the seat of government, accompanied by a series of robberies, were more than sufficient evidence to convince the powers that be that New York City, whose population of about twelve thousand included some two thousand blacks, was the victim of a horrid conspiracy and that slaves were at the bottom of it. The fingering of a tavern keeper, who not only sold rum to slaves at will but served as a fence for their stolen goods, along with the alarming testimony of a few frightened blacks and a handful of self-serving whites, added to the frenzy and brought the city close to panic. A dramatic drawn-out trial followed through the spring and summer of 1741.[27]

Several pieces of evidence convinced the credulous that religion in more ways than one was a cause, if not *the* cause, of the Negro rebellion. Supposedly New Yorkers had learned their lesson about catering to black souls when a similar but less serious revolt broke out in 1712, led by a handful of Coromantee slaves, already notorious for their fearless fanaticism. Forming a cult for resistance and revenge, these Coromantees successfully recruited a number of New York blacks who swore bloody reprisal upon their oppressors. Their ambush of whites failed miserably, for they were soon overpowered and scattered, but not before they had set a destructive fire, killed nine or more New Yorkers, and wounded several more.[28] The city's reaction, besides execution of the leaders—nineteen in all—was not to inquire into the causes of the bloody uprising but to attribute it out of hand to foolhardy attempts to Christianize blacks. Elias Neau, a French Anglican priest of Trinity Church, who indefatigably catechized blacks at his church school with the blessings of the SPG, took the brunt of the blame. Despite the fact that only two of the three dozen or more blacks indicted had anything to do with his classes, and despite Governor Robert Hunter's continued support and praise of Neau's efforts, New Yorkers stubbornly insisted that religion was the cause of the outburst. Their legislature supported them by restricting further blacks' freedom after working hours in order to prevent their attending religious instruction. Like Carolinians, many New Yorkers as early as 1712 believed salvation and slavery were dangerously incompatible, and encouragement of one could only undermine the other.[29]

Whitefield was not in New York during the immmediate crisis of 1741, but no matter, said his opponents. Reports went home to England that "his imprudence and indescretion" in pushing conversion of slaves during his very recent visit had given "great countenance" to the mutiny.[30] And from the trial of one of the white defendants came testimony that it was Whitefield's "great encouragement" of the blacks which was the cause of the whole trouble. A day earlier another witness informed the court that the same defendant had insisted that attempts to convert Negroes were useless. Leave them to God, he said; it is their nature to be slaves, and furthermore, "give them learning, do all the good you can, and put them above the condition of slaves, and in return they will cut your throats." A good many New Yorkers were inclined to agree with the witness, who, of course, may have had his own reasons for trying to shift blame for the plot to the likes of Whitefield and others who treasured black souls. Still, there was plenty of sentiment circulating that the Great Awakening stirred up blacks as well as whites, that Whitefield "unhinged" the black sort as well as any other sort of people,[31] and that New Yorkers paid the price for all this enthusiasm with several months of terror.

As the trial of the New York conspirators wore on into the summer of 1741, it became apparent that the plot, whether as serious as it was blown up to be or not, contained religious ingredients of another kind, which also involved George Whitefield. The issue was Catholicism. The dread of it and its spreading, so strong in Leisler's Rebellion of 1689, had not lessened by the middle of the eighteenth century and would not for several generations to come. Great Britain and Spain went to war in 1739, and Georgia, settled a few years earlier as a buffer between the Protestant English and the Catholics of Spanish Florida, among other reasons, rose to its first test under General James Edward Oglethorpe, a proprietor and at the same time governor of the new colony. Between laying siege (unsuccessfully) to St. Augustine in 1740 and turning back a Spanish attack upon Frederica in 1742, Oglethorpe busied himself with affairs of Georgia and the empire, most of them military.[32]

Suspicions that a Catholic plot was a part of the New York uprising of 1741 had surfaced earlier. But it was not until the last of July that such figures as Lieutenant Governor George Clarke and magistrates Cadwallader Colden and Daniel Horsmanden insisted that "popery was at the Bottom" of the "hellish conspiracy."[33] The turning point came when a letter from General Oglethorpe to Governor Clarke was read in court as telling evidence of the plot. It seems that Oglethorpe had learned from a Spanish prisoner that the Spaniards, in an improbable scheme worthy of Cervantes, had dispatched among the British colonies a number of priests disguised as physicians, schoolteachers, dancing masters, and other professionals, to sabotage magazines and forts and disrupt colonial cities. These spies in disguise were to insinuate themselves with the colonists and gain admittance to their homes, the better to carry on their villainous deception. Oglethorpe, it was admitted, was not certain the report was true, but never mind.[34] In the New York court his letter became prima facie evidence of a Catholic plot to burn the city and murder its people. From the time it was first read other pieces of evidence, according to His Majesty's prosecutors, fell nicely into place to spell out a huge conspiracy instigated by whites but performed by blacks. In no time at all the court brought before it four "suspicious school-masters," two of them "professed" papists, along with John Ury, a "Romish Priest," and "principal promoter," some said, of the whole horrid business. Dragged in, too, were a renegade tavern keeper, whose public house was headquarters for hatching the plot, several other suspected whites, and two dozen or more black slaves who supposedly did the work.[35]

Now, where and how did George Whitefield fit into all this? Not directly, to be sure, for he led no blacks on the rampage, burned no buildings, and fenced no goods. But given the frenzied state of affairs in New York City in the spring and summer of 1741, there were plenty of people, some of them highly placed, who were willing to believe the worst of George Whitefield. They suspected that his flitting about the colonies as an itinerant minister, holding noisy revivals and stirring up misguided colonists into orgies of enthusiasm, was only a pretense, hardly distinguishable from Oglethorpe's priests and dancing masters who were the heart of the conspiracy. The very witness whose evidence connected Whitefield's encouragement of blacks to the slave mutiny testified in the same breath that his informant also believed "Whitefield was more of a Roman than anything else," having come abroad in the first place "with no good design."[36]

To twentieth-century ears this sounds pretty far-fetched. But some eighteenth-century attitudes toward enthusiasts, revivalists, pietists, and Methodists—and Whitefield was all of these—make such suspicions, if not factual, at least plausible. Enthusiasm had been linked with Catholicism off and on for many years. Good orthodox Protestants had difficulty thinking of two worse manifestations of false religion, unless they were antinomianism and Anabaptism, which were really other forms of enthusiasm. During the 1740s colonial revivalists sometimes suffered the ignominy of popish accusations, often finding the charge easier to deal with than the frenzy of enthusiasm, although to some they were identical. The *South Carolina Gazette* ran a clever tract in October 1740 called "The Wiles of Popery." It explained in detail the cunning casuistry of the Catholic Church to recall Protestant heretics to the fold, but the tactics described were patently those of George Whitefield and the revivalists—"bold Pretences to *Illumination*," and the "*Indwelling* of the Spirit," besides "Mechanic *Impulses* and violent *Movings*"—really all attributes of enthusiasm.[37] At the height of the Awakening, Philadelphians read of "The Wandering Spirit" of enthusiasm, which, when not in Quaker, antinomian, or Anabaptist dress, was disguised as a "Fryar or a Monk," reminiscent of the "Holy Necromancers" and "Spirit of Delusion" in the dark times of "Pope Gregory or Hildebrand."[38] And are they not just like papists, another Philadelphia tract queried, when Whitefield and his people made "Parties, Factions and Confusions" up and down the land, and all this "in a Time of War with a Foreign Nation," and a Popish one at that?[39] When "Enthusiastic Preachers" swooped down on Hanover County, Virginia, the Anglican priest there suggested they be suppressed, for, he warned the Commissary, "they may be Jesuits for any thing we know."[40] Methodists in England were just as suspect to the establishment—maybe more so. Bishop George Lavington, having taken about as much as he could stomach from Whitefield's and John Wesley's carryings on, smeared the Methodists first with enthusiasm, then Catholicism, and for good measure wrote a lengthy pamphlet, *The Enthusiasm of the Methodists and Papists Compared.*[41]

In late February 1741, when the burglaries were spreading in New York, the mysterious fires crackling, and the accusations multiplying, Whitefield was already on the high seas and headed toward home. New York's Awakeners blessed him and the Revival and gratefully talked of the grace of God among them. Their government all the while damned Whitefield as an inciter of riots. In the long hot summer which followed, it hanged the white conspirators and in a notorious fit of discrimination burned fourteen blacks at the stake besides hanging eighteen more and jailing and deporting hundreds of others.[42]

The powers that be in New York wanted very much to believe that "Mr. Whitfield that Arch Enthusiast" and his "Vagrant, Stroling Preachers," his "itinerant enthusiastical teachers," had "debauched the Minds of the people with Enthusiastical Notions." These "New-fangled principles or Tenents," once they had infected restless blacks, along with the "Vilanous Practices of disguised Papists" who had treacherously infiltrated the heart of the city, were responsible for the New York crisis, or so the government reported.[43] Whitefield, enthusiasm, revivalism were bad enough, but when they were laced with Catholicism and Spanish intrigue, they were notoriously subversive of the state and white supremacy. They could only be at the bottom of New York's slave conspiracy of 1741, to which New Yorkers reacted with panic, then hanging and burning.

Moravians and Indians

War with Spain had heightened suspicions about the interrelatedness of the Great Awakening, slave revolt, and Catholic intrigue. During the war with France, which began in 1744, George Whitefield's revivalists, although still suspect, were joined by Count Ludwig Zinzendorf's Moravians, who doggedly strove to share their piety and enthusiasm with American Indians. We left a handful of United Brethren at the Forks of the Delaware, where they had purchased Nazareth from George Whitefield in 1740. As their numbers increased under the aegis of Count Zinzendorf, they went on to settle nearby Bethlehem and the surrounding countryside. Unlike the Labadists before them, who pretty much forgot an original intention to Christianize the Indians, the Moravians immediately seized the opportunity, and their missions, along with their music, have become historically two of their most memorable legacies.[44] Bringing God to the Indians was not an easy task, as John Wesley had learned to his surprise in Georgia. Moravian missionaries, unlike the earlier Rosicrucians outside Philadelphia, were not an educated cadre but ordinary people—farmers, mechanics, and artisans—whose religious zeal, which had brought them to the colonies in the first place, was reflected in their devoted missionary work. They taught Christianity in German, sometimes through interpreters, and their only text was the Bible. Very few learned the Indian languages.[45]

One of the best known and most successful was Christian Rauch. Just five weeks after his arrival from Germany, he planted a mission at Shekomeco, near a village called Pine Plains in Dutchess County, New York, and began work there among the Mohicans. They were a hard-drinking, tough lot of Indians, said Count Zinzendorf, both fierce and vindictive. They had little respect for Rauch at first, thought him a fool, and once threatened to kill him. Little by little he broke down their prejudices, and his devoted teaching turned the tide in God's favor. Rauch married an Indian woman, which may or may not have helped the cause; her mother proved difficult, her "machinations" causing a good deal of vacillation in his wife and daughter.[46] Still, by perseverance he overcame even this, and in February 1742 had the satisfaction of baptizing his first three converts, Abraham, Isaac, and Jacob, at Bethlehem in the presence of Count Zinzendorf, who just previously had ordained Rauch and two others as Moravian ministers. By the end of the next year the congregation at Shekomeco under Rauch had grown to over sixty baptized Indians, and services there drew even a larger number of "regular hearers."[47] Rauch traveled widely, too, visited Bethlehem frequently, and made other trips to Philadelphia, Germantown, and wherever Moravians and Indians resided. By 1743 he and John Pyrlaeus, who was a student of Indian languages, pushed their preaching into the Mohawk Valley as far as Schoharie and Canajoharie, but Shekomeco remained Rauch's home ground, and it was there that he had his greatest success in the early 1740s.[48]

Moravians were a mobile lot. Bethlehem, settled in 1740, was the center of their activities, to be sure, but several years later a Pennsylvania governor reported that of the 1,062 settlers who called it home, forty-eight were attached to missions elsewhere among the Indians, and another fifty-four either preached or taught school in other colonies. There was constant coming and going, and the scattered missions looked to Bethlehem for inspiration, regulation, and support. Missionaries received no salaries, but when they needed assistance, the congregation at Bethlehem, headed by Peter Boehler, usually supplied it.[49]

American colonists were divided in their opinions about Moravians. In fact, they were not unanimous in the way they viewed the increasing German population. As early as 1727 the Pennsylvania Council discussed the influx of Germans and resolved to require of them an oath of allegiance in the future. Complaints centered around their burgeoning numbers, their ignorance of the English language and laws, and their settling in communities distinct from Pennsylvania's other colonists. All of these posed questions of security in a colonial society and set a lot of people thinking. The imminence of war intensified such feelings, as did factional politics, and Benjamin Franklin used the Germans for purposes of propaganda in both instances to their disadvantage. Still, their numbers increased, and by the time of the American Revolution there may have been as many as 150,000 colonists of German origin in British America.[50]

Granted the Moravians were a tiny part of these; but not only were they Germans, or adopted Germans; they were pietists and enthusiasts. There was plenty of dissatisfaction with them on religious grounds alone. The Maryland Scot Dr. Alexander Hamilton, whose grand tour took him through several colonies in 1744, came across a number of Moravians in both New Jersey and the Hudson River Valley and dubbed them a "wild, fanatick sect." He resented their living in common, "men and women mixed," in great barns or houses where they sleep, eat, drink, and "preach and howl." It was all started by that "German enthusiast," Count Zinzendorf, and he and they, like all enthusiasts, thought their "religion of the Lamb" to be the only true religion. But maybe they were right, Hamilton concluded, insofar as some, no doubt, were "wolves in sheep's clothing."[51]

George Whitefield disengaged himself from the Moravians in 1740 over their loose doctrine of election and the presumption of perfection, after a short honeymoon celebrated in London, Georgia, and at the Forks of the Delaware.[52] Gilbert Tennent of Pennsylvania and New Jersey had counted largely on Moravians for the success of his revivals, but when the zeal of the Awakening slackened, he backed off, took a sober look at the damage enthusiasm and fanaticism had done to evangelical Protestantism, and turned on the Moravians as scapegoats, damning them as confused and deluded and dangerous.[53] Whitefield believed Tennent was unnecessarily severe in his condemnation of the Brethren and suggested that maybe some of Tennent's own "wild fire" was mixed with the sacred zeal which came only from God. Both revivalists agreed, however, that Moravian beliefs were mistaken, although Whitefield described himself as more temperate in his criticism than Tennent; in fact, in a fit of messianism, he compared himself to Jesus, who "sees all the quarrels . . . of His children, and yet bears with, and loves them still"—even Moravians.[54]

As if to deflect attention from his own extravagances, which he regretted, Gilbert Tennent in 1743 lit into the Moravians with a fury, sounding very much like Charles Chauncy against New Lights in New England. He resented their endeavors to conceal real opinions and distrusted their pretensions to simplicity. He questioned the ancient history of the sect and suggested strongly that its "whole system" was of recent origin, framed in 1725 at Count Zinzendorf's home in Saxony. He scoffed at their beliefs in the assurance of salvation and "sinless perfection." Their authoritarianism in church and society, their regulation of marriage, their unhealthy grip on children, and surveillance of converts all impinged, he said, on religious and civil liberty. They were worse than the Labadists in their "Mixture of many Errors." To await the voice of the Lord, like Quakers, only encouraged enthusiasm, and Zinzendorf's insistence that the elders and ministers of the church spoke only what "Christ works in them" smacked of "Immediate Inspiration." Not to be subject to the law, as the Count described his ministers, was rank antinomianism. And on top of this, they scorned learning and slighted human reason. Their beliefs and carryings on, Tennent concluded, were "Nonsense, Contradictions, and mysterious Gibberish."[55]

Charles Chauncy in Boston had little sympathy for either Gilbert Tennent or the Moravians. At the peak of the Awakening, Chauncy claimed Tennent had welcomed their swelling numbers and succeeded in confusing them as well as other victims of the Revival. Now that he had changed his mind, said Chauncy, becoming apprehensive "lest the Churches should be undone with a *Spirit of Enthusiasm,*" he cut himself off from the Moravians and then blamed them for all the trouble.[56] By 1743 both Whitefield and Tennent, two of the Awakening's leading figures, had turned their backs on the United Brethren, and the issue ironically was enthusiasm. Evangelical piety could get out of hand, they now confessed; when it did, it easily spilled over into enthusiasm, as it had with the Moravians, and as such it was subversive of true religion. These German pietists, then, were suspicious characters, and true believers ought to be wary of their "Unreasonableness, anti-evangelical, and licentious Religion."[57] There were probably many people besides Charles Chauncy who were convinced that the pot was calling the kettle black.

Suspect in religion by both Old and New Lights, Moravians became objects of even greater suspicion when war broke out with France in 1744. New Yorkers found all matter of reasons for driving their missionaries out of the colony. The government dragged several to Manhattan for questioning. By what right did they preach to the Indians without the governor's leave? Who called them to the ministry? Why did they refuse to take oaths of allegiance? Some of their answers hardly satisfied a colony government whose geography seemed to invite French invasion from the north and whose people believed it was imminent. It was the "Saviours pleasure he should be a Minister," claimed one, while another confessed guilelessly that he had no idea whether the Indians wanted teachers, but he did know "that all the Earth was to be Subject to the Lord," and so he did his part. Still another claimed his commission to preach came from the Moravians at Bethlehem, and all of them, of course, refused oaths as contrary to the principles of their church. Public resentment against foreign-speaking busybodies, who consorted with the Indians in out-of-the-way places, led to claims against their land and tales of complicity with the French, even Jesuit relations.[58]

As a result of these suspicions, the colony legislature put its foot down decisively in late 1744 with an "Act for securing of his Majesty's Government of New York." It demanded oaths of allegiance when called for, the licensing of Indian preachers, and registering of houses of worship. As a warning the council gave notice to all "Moravian & vagrant Teachers" that if they did not cease their preaching and teaching and leave the province immediately, the government would promptly enforce the new law against them. The Moravians who had not departed already either to Bethlehem or Connecticut, owing to increasing antagonism, were forced out, breaking up completely the mission at Shekomeco.[59] They were no safer in Connecticut than they had been in New York. Resentment had spread there and beyond to Massachusetts, where John Sergeant complained that his Indian congregations at Stockbridge had suffered from Moravians nearby who left their converts "enthusiastick and bigoted." They have made themselves so suspect in New York and Connecticut, he explained, that the governments there will not tolerate them further, since they refused to take oaths of allegiance to the King or even a "Solemn Declaration" like the Quakers. Two of them spent several weeks in a New York jail for just these offenses.[60]

News of harassed Moravian missionaries in New York reached Count Zinzendorf, then living in England. In defense of his people he bitterly complained about their "injurious treatment" to the Board of Trade in London, where the Church of England and the government then and later were sympathetic to the Moravian Church and encouraged its people to settle in America. The Board got busy and questioned Governor George Clarke in New York about discrimination against the sect, and the governor in turn asked his council for an explanation of the legislature's act and why it had mentioned the Moravians specifically.[61] Daniel Horsmanden was head man of the council—the same Daniel Horsmanden who shortly before had published a lopsided history of the Negro revolt of 1741, in which, he concluded, notorious conspiracies abounded. He and the council submitted a report to Governor Clarke in May 1746, a report which demands scrutiny, for it summed up in high fashion the fear of public danger supposedly inherent in religious fanaticism, enthusiasm, and dissent. It epitomized the traditional, even historic, suspicion which orthodox and conventional societies conjured up regarding the nature of enthusiasm and sometimes just plain unorthodox religious beliefs. It recounted every possible way in which the activities of Whitefield and the Moravians could be considered subversive and a threat to the security of New York. It repeated with emphasis Horsmanden's charges during the Spanish War that the "stroling preachers" of the Awakening, who debauched colonists' minds with "Enthusiastic Notions," and the "Vilanous Practices" of popish "Emmysaries," who flooded the colonies disguised as schoolmasters and clergymen, were the principal causes of the slave mutiny which had so frightened the good burghers of New York in 1741.[62]

But this was not the end of these wicked activities, which had begun even earlier, the report went on. After Whitefield had traipsed from Georgia to Boston and back—"with what real Design he best knew"— he purchased several thousand acres of land at the Forks of the Delaware River in Pennsylvania, actually close to the borders of New York, where he laid plans for a "Seminary" to educate youths and Negroes "in his New-fangled principles or Tenents whatever they were." Once he had gulled enough money out of deluded colonists here and there, "under Colour of Charity" for both his orphanage in Georgia and the "Negro-Academy"—the real design being to "fill his own Pockets"—he sold his estate at the Forks to the Moravian bishop Count Zinzendorf, leader of a sect of fanatical Germans. "Professing themselves Protestants," Moravians also strolled up and down the countryside while they vented their "Unintelligible Doctrines" and attracted followers with the "same kind of Delusion."

Colonists had been suspicious of the Count and his Moravians, the report continued, ever since these foreign fanatics had begun sneaking into the colonies from Germany. Pennsylvania, because of its liberal charter and tolerant attitude, took no care about newcomers, and immigrants had been welcomed, Catholics as well as Protestants, without distinction. Moreover, these Germans had increased to such numbers that they could well take over the colony some day. Besides, they kept to themselves, refused to marry with the English, retained their language through their clergy and schoolteachers, even their own printers, and formed a "Distinct People," all of which might very likely have "Dangerous Consequences" for Pennsylvania and for all of His Majesty's colonies.

The council's report went out of its way to explain that Moravians, who would go anywhere to make converts, had done very well in Pennsylvania, New York, and other colonies. They kept their headquarters at the Forks of the Delaware as a kind of rendezvous, and they retained there Whitefield's scheme of a seminary for deluded "Votaries." From this place, Nazareth, they sent out teachers and preachers, "simple, illiterate persons" who in their own country were carpenters, bricklayers, tailors, wool combers, and "Such like Mechanical or handy-Craft" people, all of whom were infatuated with "Enthusiasm or Folly" and had become, perhaps unknown to themselves, mere tools to forward Count Zinzendorf's plans.

Not content to convert whites, who should have known better, the Moravians turned to the more difficult task of proselytizing among the Indians. By residing with them and intermarrying, they made progress, too, despite ignorance of the Indian languages. At Shekomeco their success aroused great suspicion among nearby colonists "lest they Seduce the Indians . . . from their Fidelity to his Majesty," during the war with France. The wary settlers complained to their government, which finally stepped in and put a stop to the whole business, finding that the Moravian missionaries made no pretension to being naturalized, besides having entered the colony without authority, and all the while refusing to take oaths of allegiance and in most cases bear arms.

This was the story. And what conclusions did Daniel Horsmanden and the council come to regarding the foreigners? These emissaries, these preachers and teachers, had artfully placed their missions in New York and neighboring colonies at convenient distances, forming a direct line of communication through the heart of the colonies, the better to dispatch intelligence from the extremities to the "Fountain head" at the Forks of the Delaware. The "audacious conduct" of these people, who sent countless messengers "backwards & forwards," was sufficiently suspicious in time of war so that the government of New York, the report concluded, found it absolutely necessary "to Guard against the Subtile Devices of Crafty men, Strangers & aliens, & to frustrate all wicked Practices of Designing Persons & Papists in Disguise under any Colour or Appearances whatsoever Calculated to delude the ignorant Savages, vailed under the Specious Shew of Care for their souls." These were the reasons, then, why the legislature reacted as it did, outlawed missionaries to the Indians, and named the Moravians in the law. And although the act would expire after a year, the committee added, it was a necessary and good law and ought to be continued.[63]

In New York, being German in the 1740s was bad enough, but being Moravian at the same time was even worse. Moravians were not only foreigners, they were enthusiasts, and no one could trust "that sort of people," particularly when they were intimate with the Indians, whom no one really trusted either, and at the very time Great Britain was at war with France, which traditionally utilized Indians in North America against its British enemies. In such hazardous times the fear of France, Catholicism, Moravians, Indians, revivalism, and enthusiasm were rolled into one and added up to subversion—or so many New Yorkers concluded, having had their share, they believed, of each. For these reasons the government drove Moravian missionaries out of the colony.[64]

Once the war was over the animus against Moravians diminished, at least in New York City. By 1751, after unsuccessfully trying to borrow or rent an empty church from some of the Lutherans, they felt sufficiently at home to build their own and solicited the "Fatherly Care and Protection" of the governor. Parliament played a role in changing attitudes; after scrutiny of its policy toward Moravians, it encouraged more of them to settle in the colonies and eased their lot by exempting them from taking oaths and bearing arms—the result of plenty of "*intrigue* and snaky crookedness," according to reports in Philadelphia.[65] The idea that they were sympathetic to France and the warring Indians faded during the early skirmishes of the Seven Years' War, when hostile Indians fell upon one of their Pennsylvania missions at Gnädenhut and killed most of the whites there.[66] Benjamin Franklin changed his mind, too, particularly after a visit to Bethlehem in 1755, where he found them well armed and where they entertained him splendidly with a capital sermon, "good musick, the organ being accompanied with violins, hautboys, flutes, clarinets, etc" and straightforward answers to his prying questions about religious practices, living arrangements, and marriage customs. They were all "very kind to me," he later recorded in the *Autobiography*. Although he was well aware that their use of firearms, if only for defensive purposes, was really a compromise of religious principles, he approved of it and later congratulated them for their helpful contributions during the war with France.[67] Times had changed. The Awakening had spent its momentum, and its enthusiasm dampened. Moravians were behaving more like ordinary colonists, arming and being warred upon, and winning the praise of Benjamin Franklin. No subversion there.

But New Yorkers had looked very differently upon revivalists and

Moravians in the 1740s. With Whitefield loose, behaving like Jesus, attracting thousands of crazy-acting converts, encouraging Negroes north and south, threatening to educate and convert them, and doing all these things on the eve of a Negro revolt which tore the city apart during a war with Catholic Spain, no wonder the government of New York became suspicious. And then this same government believed it was subject to similar subversion when the Moravians, already friendly with Whitefield and sharing his enthusiasm, took over his Negro academy, settled it and the neighborhood with several hundred fanatical foreigners like themselves, and then sent out their most zealous devotees to build missions where they taught Jesus and antinomianism and Christian unity to the Indians. In so doing they ignored established authorities, local churches, colonial boundaries, acts of naturalizaton, racial barriers, and colony laws, to say nothing of orthodox Protestantism. And all this just as Britain went to war with France and fought part of it in the New World very close to home.

Bad enough was these enthusiasts' foolishness about grace and conversion, about the immanent Spirit of Christ. But enthusiasm was explosive when it threatened to stir up black slaves to rebellion and made half-baked Christians out of Indians during a French war, besides instilling in both all manner of notions contrary to the settled order of things and their proper places within a white society. Enthusiasm was not just subversive; it courted revolution, and it ought to be suppressed wherever it emerged.

11

Enthusiasm and the
Cause of Mankind

*I*F ENTHUSIASM was subversive, sometimes revolutionary, what role
did it play, if any, in the American crisis of 1776? For a little perspective, let's go back for a minute or two and look at the nature of
Protestantism. After all, enthusiasm in America was directly related to
Protestantism, and colonists were Protestant almost to a fault. It was
their very Protestantism, some have argued, which intensified the revolutionary struggle on several fronts. Listen to Edmund Burke on the
subject. Religion has always been a "principle of energy," he told Parliament in his speech on conciliation in 1775, and among the "new people" in America it has not been the least impaired. They are Protestants
of a particular kind, a kind "most adverse to all implicit submission of
mind and opinion," a persuasion, he went on, altogether favorable to
liberty, in fact, "built upon it." All Protestantism is a kind of dissent, he
lectured the Commons, but that which is prevalent in the northern colonies is a "refinement on the principle of resistance; it is the dissidence
of dissent," said Burke, "and the Protestantism of the Protestant religion."
Colonists settled America when this spirit was high, and in those who
migrated it was highest of all. Since then a "stream of foreigners" has
joined them, mostly dissenters, too, from establishments abroad, and the
character and temper they brought with them readily mixed with what
already existed. It was this temper and character of dissident Protestantism which tolerated no interference with the spirit of liberty.[1]

Protestantism, then, was well accounted for in the years which preceded the turmoil of revolution. And Edmund Burke refined its meaning,
finding in it a special quality of protest which, he told Parliament, was
vital to the American rebellion. What Burke is really telling us is that it
was the evangelical character of American Protestantism which, he believed, gave it such a "strong claim to natural liberty." And several
historians lately, chiefly Alan Heimert, have elaborated this theme into
a full-scale, if controversial, thesis about Calvinist influence upon the

American mind and the effect of evangelical religion, mainly New Light revivalism, on the Revolutionary movement.[2]

The high point of evangelical Protestantism in eighteenth-century America was the Great Awakening of the 1740s. And, as we have seen, the Awakening was extremely vulnerable to charges of enthusiasm. Old Lights who thought deeply about these mischiefs warned of the dissolution of Church *and* State. Under the notion of liberty these fanatics had made a shambles of the solemn and sacred ties between ministers and their people. What was to prevent them from demanding the "same Liberty in other Relations"? With no plans to dampen the progress and growth of these extremists, wrote Charles Chauncy of Boston, there was no way of telling how far they would go or what the end might be.[3] Some of them even despised men's laws and "pretend Conscience to break them," added Massachusetts's Benjamin Doolittle.[4] In Connecticut there was talk of precisely how far they might go: as far as seizing the government and tyrannizing over any who opposed them. Some of the old guard hinted that besides the crackpots and fanatics, Separatists in Connecticut included the meaner sort, the soreheads, and others who would take advantage of the movement to defy authority.[5] At the same time revivalists insisted that their activities were a glorious manifestation of Christ's Spirit upon the land, which justified kicking over traditional restraints, even conventional guidelines.

There was, then, in the lives of American colonists a radical current, stemming from religion. It was an insidious strain, this enthusiasm, a kind of natural by-product of religion, an unconventional offspring which was offensive to many who, like old John Winthrop, believed it was above Scripture and reason and beyond control. It threatened change, and, according to its opponents, even some advocates, it barely missed fulfillment in the Great Awakening.

Baptists

During the Revolution, Baptists in Massachusetts and Virginia gave extraordinary expression to the enthusiasm inherent in evangelical Protestantism. They played an unexpected role in the colonial crisis by widening the conflict beyond government and politics and attempting to provoke a major social change in the two oldest British colonies in America. That Baptists, particularly Separate Baptists, were close legatees of the Great Awakening may have had something to do with how they regarded the revolutionary crisis, as well as how their opponents regarded them.

Few Congregationalists in the Bay Colony or Anglicans in Virginia doubted that Baptists were enthusiasts and had been since the days of

Münster. Moreover, there was first-hand evidence on their side, for Baptists carried on in such a way as to confirm a number of their antagonists' worst suspicions. Most recent evidence was their fanatical insistence that complete religious freedom was the order of the day, and that the American Revolution was the God-given means for its accomplishment.

Massachusetts had enjoyed an established Congregational Church since the 1630s. There was toleration, to be sure, but not actual freedom. Town tax money still paid ministers' salaries, and the law forced Anglicans, Quakers, and Baptists alike either to pay up and be quiet or to apply for exemptions, certifying they were bona fide dissenters who wished their tax money to support ministers and churches they had chosen. Certificates and red tape galled in particular the Baptists, and of these, chiefly the Separate Baptists, most of whom were New Light radicals of the Great Awakening and, therefore, suspect from the start as fraudulent dissenters. They had cut themselves off from the established churches in the 1740s, set up separate meetings, and then drifted into Baptists' practices, carrying strong doses of Calvinism with them, often a legacy of the Revival. Isaac Backus of Norwich, Connecticut, had come through all the stages, from Congregationalist to Separatist, to itinerant exhorter, then to Separate Baptist, and all in the years of turmoil during and following the Awakening. He eventually came to rest at Middleborough, Massachusetts, where he ministered to a Baptist congregation for over sixty years and spent almost a lifetime attacking what he believed was the illegal and discriminatory practices of government in behalf of the state Church.[6]

Baptists, whether in Massachusetts or Virginia, tended to be common and ordinary people, and Backus was no exception. Uneducated beyond simple schooling, unsophisticated, unordained, except by his own congregation, he represented that class of people who seem through time to be more susceptible to revivalism and motions of the Spirit than most. Soon after the Awakening he felt a direct call to preach and recorded that, as a result, he conversed with God as he never had before.[7] But a lack of education, sophistication, and official sanction blunted not at all a sharpness and stubbornness in defense of liberty as he saw it. And he saw it very clearly in the crucial years of the American Revolution. For Backus attacked the Massachusetts establishment at its weakest point and pushed home the glaring inconsistency between the patriot protest against Parliamentary taxation and royal tyranny, on the one hand, and Massachusetts's equally tyrannical discrimination against dissenters, particularly Baptists, on the other.

To Backus, then, the American Revolution was more—a good deal more—than a struggle against Parliament, King, and ministry for a separate and equal station among the nations of the earth. It was a struggle for religious liberty in America, and chiefly in Massachusetts. It was a struggle to force complete separation between Church and State. It was a struggle to expand a political and constitutional revolution to include a radical reform in one of Massachusetts's most cherished institutions.[8]

A confrontation between the two points of view occurred at Carpenters' Hall in Philadelphia in October 1774 during the early weeks of the First Continental Congress. Backus and a number of Baptists, supported by several weighty Philadelphia Quakers, arranged a meeting between themselves and the Massachusetts delegation to the Congress, which included John and Sam Adams. Once assembled the Baptists laid out the whole business boldly, particularly the notorious Ashfield case, which had left them bitterly resentful of the colony's establishment. The Massachusetts response was what one might expect from representatives of a colony which had supported a state Church for almost a century and a half. The delegates tried to explain away any hint of severity in the Church-State arrangement—that it was the mildest and most equitable establishment known to the world, if indeed, it could be called an establishment at all.[9] In their explanations, however, they let slip then and later what seems to be a key to the issue. Anyway, said Sam Adams, it was not the "*regular* Baptists" who kicked up the fuss, for they were "quite easy among us." Rather, the trouble and complaints "came from enthusiasts who made it a merit to suffer persecution."[10] Later he told James Warren that they had "hushed and abashed" the Baptists and Quakers at Carpenters' Hall, or, he added, at least the "reasonable Conscientious Part of them were convinced in one evening."[11] And John Adams confided to his diary that the delegation's explanation was so clear that every reasonable and impartial person must have been satisfied.[12] According to the Adamses, it was the enthusiasts, the fanatics, the revivalists, the unreasonable and partial people—that is, the Backuses and their followers—who were the subversives and who wished to tear apart the customs and traditions of Massachusetts Bay. Enthusiastic Baptists were a radical threat to patriotic Whigs; they were trying to kick over the traces of traditional society in New England and make of the Revolution something it had no business being.

A situation similar in some respects existed in Virginia. Although two-thirds of the people there already dissented from the Anglican Church, persecution of Baptists was more severe than in Massachusetts, where, Ezra Stiles said, it was "trifling" in comparison.[13] The Great Awakening had come later to Virginia than to New England. It began in the middle 1740s with the spectacular rise of the Separate Baptists, some from New England but most from Pennsylvania.[14] They, too, were an unlettered lot, yet full of enthusiasm and evangelical zeal. Henry Melchior Muhlenberg had heard one of these visiting New England Baptists preach in Philadelphia several years earlier. He found him "much too affected" and full of "strange gestures," the kind one often saw among uneducated exhorters who claimed they preached "by the immediate inspiration of the Spirit."[15] In Virginia these itinerants wandered about, exhorting and converting wherever they traveled, and with more success than most Virginians liked to admit.

Evangelical Baptists offended Virginians on several counts. First, their religious fervor and moral asceticism flew in the face of the free and easy, loose-living Virginia gentry. Christian fanaticism among the meaner sort was difficult for the ruling class to swallow. According to Rhys Isaac, these Baptist evangelicals presented a growing counterculture which by its very existence challenged the complacency of the gentry, "quite destroying pleasure," wrote Philip Vickers Fithian at Nomini Hall, for "they encourage ardent Pray'r; strong & constant faith, & an intire Banishment of *Gaming, Dancing* & Sabbath-Day Diversions."[16] Second, these religious carryings on and their popularity among the lesser folk were direct threats to the established and privileged Anglican Church. Their clergy openly ignored laws passed to regulate religious services and, maybe worse, severely attacked the Episcopal hierarchy and all that went with it. The Anglican clergy, with the help of the gentry and government, resorted to what James Madison called "that diabolical Hell[-]conceived principle of persecution," and Baptist ministers were repeatedly imprisoned until they knuckled under. Madison blamed chiefly the priesthood and what he called its "Pride, ignorance and Knavery," but he had some sharp words, too, for the "Vice and Wickedness among the Laity." Virginians suppressed the Baptists, he said, because the zealous dissenting ministers robbed the Anglican clergymen of the "people's good will" and in demanding religious equality impugned their security and livings.[17]

The establishment cracked down on the Baptists also because they had the nerve in time of crisis to work vigorously for separation of Church and State and a fair shake for all sects and denominations. Elisha Craig, jailed several times for illegal preaching, like Isaac Backus boldly represented their cause at Revolutionary meetings and general assemblies.[18] As in Massachusetts radical Baptists threatened unity and along with it the Revolutionary movement, said moderate patriots. And also as in Massachusetts, the establishment counterattacked with the same ammunition. The preachings and teachings of Baptist dissenters were "whimsical Fancies," said Fithian's vicar. At most theirs was a "Religion grown to Wildness & Enthusiasm!"[19] Despite his sympathy and his unselfish efforts to save Baptists from jail, Madison admitted that their "enthusiasm" helped to "render them obnoxious to sober public opin-ion." When the whole business of religious freedom came before the House of Burgesses in 1774, the dissenters lost much ground owing to "such incredible and extravagant stories," which quickly spread through-out the House, "of the monstrous effects of the Enthusiasm prevalent among" them. These stories were "greedily swallowed by their Ene-mies,"[20] by those who wanted to believe that the radical faction pro-moting religious freedom as well as disunion was really a sorry lot of enthusiasts bent on undermining Virginia's traditional society during a Revolution which was commenced for other reasons. But unlike the course of events in Massachusetts, the Revolution destroyed Virginia's establishment—not, however, without strong assists from the enlightened Madisons and Jeffersons and from other dissenters like the Presbyterians, who equated freedom from British tryanny with freedom from Virginia episcopacy.[21] Virginia emerged in the 1780s with religious freedom se-cure. Maybe the gentry were right; enthusiasm was subversive of an established complacent society and its church.

Complaints against Baptists continued throughout the war. Some pa-triots were certain that they had put liberty of conscience above patriotism and would adhere to the side which protected their freedom. Only an "enthusiastical bigot" and a "high-flier," reported a Boston newspaper, would complain in these critical times about the handling of State-Church affairs.[22] Ezra Stiles went so far as to claim that the ministry in London tried hard to persuade the religious sects in America to detach themselves from the "Cause of Liberty," and he feared it had succeeded only too well among Baptists and Quakers.[23]

The Whig campaign against the Baptists missed its mark, however, for by and large Baptists threw in their lot with the new nation. Their reasons, if Isaac Backus reflected them adequately, bear looking into, for they relate directly to a radical attempt to enlarge the Revolution beyond Whig dimensions. Admittedly, Baptists had suffered from the very be-ginning, he explained, and they would have suffered more severely at the hands of colonial governments had not the King intervened on their behalf. Why, then, were Baptists drawn to the Revolutionary party against the mother country? Backus made a case against the English because they were "episcopalians." Where Episcopalians ruled, they arbitrarily con-fined the liberty of those who were outside their church, taxing them to support the establishment and denying them civil offices. One had only to look at Virginia, where the government imprisoned Baptist clergymen for preaching without licenses to many starving souls. Joining the British, then, was no solution to vital questions of conscience and liberty. Sur-prisingly, Baptists in England offered Backus support, believing that liberty at home was tied to liberty in America, and if the colonists went under, Britain itself would not long be free.[24] Unfortunately, as Backus found through experience, the Congregationalists and their establishments in New England were hardly very different, and these were the people carrying on the war. Still, there was hope, and Backus based the Baptists' case on this hope. New Englanders at heart honored the compact idea in government, and so they opposed arbitrary demands from abroad which violated it, demands which denied "immutable rules of truth and equity." Had we accepted these illegal intrusions from the British, Backus argued, our guilt would have reduced us to a condition far worse than what we knew as colonists in Massachusetts.[25]

Baptists, like Quakers and other enthusiasts, gloried in the religious promise of America. But unlike Quakers they closely identified this promise with independence, still another cause for supporting the Revolution. And the "main ground" of their present hope, wrote Backus, was the marvelous quickening of religion which recently had spread throughout the land, largely among Baptists, and he pinpointed numerous towns in which "several thousands" were converted—and not just in New England, either, but in Virginia, the Carolinas, and Georgia, too. These "gracious visitations," as he called them, "bespoke a design of final deliverance" from the illegal restraints which then discriminated against them. The New World promise was double-barreled; it was linked to political independence, on the one hand, and to freedom of religion, on the other. And the struggle for each, wrote Backus, "kept a pretty even pace through the war." There were low times, he confessed in 1779, when the evils of the conflict "corrupted the morals of the people," but the "glorious work" of God, which opened hearts and increased the outpourings of divine grace upon the land, was promising evidence of America's rescue "from destruction."[26] The "final deliverance," Backus argued, would come through military victory and, as a necessary result, absolute freedom from religious constraint—the latter a radical goal in Congregational Massachusetts.

It was too radical as it turned out. The Revolution sharply disappointed many New England Baptists. They chose the winning side, to be sure, and for good reason, according to Backus; and like other erstwhile colonists they enjoyed the benefits of political independence, as well they should. But it is ironic that Baptists and Quakers and other sectaries in Virginia won complete religious freedom from "episcopalian" rulers and Tory priests as a result of the Revolution, while in Massachusetts, Connecticut, and New Hampshire, the overwhelming majority of patriotic Congregationalists kept a firm grip on the public worship of God through tax-supported churches well into the nineteenth century.[27] Some Old World institutions died hard in the New, if at all.

Despite their vigorous but unsuccessful attempts to enlarge its scope, Backus's Baptists looked better every day to most New Englanders once it was clear that they supported the Revolution. And then when copies of the new Federal Constitution circulated in the fall of 1787, Baptists endorsed it, winning high praise for their "love of order and government." "Call them no longer Enthusiasts," the *Connecticut Courant* announced, now that they had come to their senses and were firmly behind the new regime.[28]

From Religion to Politics

There will be no attempt to argue here that the enthusiasm of the Great Awakening was responsible for the American Revolution or that conceptions of a New Light in a New World midwifed the birth of a nation. What is suggested is that there was in the Revolutionary conflict a provocative strain of thinking, of discourse, even of action which a number of colonists at the time recognized and could only call enthusiasm—political enthusiasm—a radical and fanatical tendency in politics similar to what was already manifest in religion. We know that when enthusiasm was discovered in religion, as it was among the Baptists, it was promptly labeled subversive of both religion and society by a good many people. When some of these people detected in the resistance and rebellion of the 1760s and 70s an attempt to tear down governments, they became convinced that enthusiasm had spilled over into politics and that it was just as undermining of settled authority and the constitution as it was of orthodoxy and church order.

True as this translation from religion to politics may have been, it was less an innovation than a shift of emphasis. Enthusiasm traditionally had included a political dimension. To sixteenth- and seventeenth-century Englishmen dissent was always considered a kind of disloyalty, whether it was the enthusiasm of the Family of Love or the Separatism of the Pilgrim Fathers. Anne Hutchinson was a political risk, according to John Winthrop, for she "walked by such a rule as cannot stand with the peace of any State."[29] When Robert Baillie of Glasgow attacked enthusiasts during the English Civil War, he warned of people "loth to have their hands bound by the fetters of any humane Laws."[30] Enthusiasm led to antinomianism, which, owing to a fullness of grace, was a disregard not only of the laws of God but of governments, too. No one said this more forcefully, and bitterly, than the Royalist Gershom Bulkeley, when he blasted Connecticut's rebels for usurping the King's government at the time of the Glorious Revolution. "What, are Tho. Muncer and John of Leyden risen from the dead again?" Beware this independent, leveling, democratic spirit, he warned, which smacked of the Fifth Monarchy all over again.[31]

Shades of Münster hung over the Great Awakening of the 1740s as well. Enthusiasm, its opponents claimed, upset civil peace and private property and resisted lawful taxation. Most frightening of all, in South Carolina it threatened to stir up black slaves against their masters, as we have seen, while in New York, the government charged, it provoked the bloody slave revolt of 1741, which came within an eyelash of massacring whites and burning down the city.[32] Enthusiasm in religion was bad enough, but it had a way of spreading into other corners of society, and its enemies had only to look to their history, English and colonial, to prove it.

Patriots and Tories alike, in both colonies and mother country, early recognized the spill-over of enthusiasm from religion to politics. "It seems arbitrary to limit enthusiasm to one sentiment of the human mind," Jonathan Boucher concluded, as he looked back over his trying experiences as a Virginia Tory in the years before his exile.[33] John Adams agreed and explained to a friend that awakenings and revivals were "not peculiar to Religion," since "Philosophy and Policy at times" were vulnerable to the same kind of infection. Although religion "is among the most powerful causes of enthusiasm," wrote Edmund Burke, "there is no doctrine whatever, on which men can warm, that is not capable of the very same effect." A bitter Tory exile, Samuel Curwen of Salem, had learned the hard way that "political zeal, like religious, can steel the heart against the feelings of nature." Despite their earlier sympathy for America as the "favourite land of the Lord," John Wesley and his Methodists in England had somehow to rationalize a change of heart when a dozen or more years of colonial resistance burst into outright rebellion. It was "patriotic licentiousness," one of Wesley's supporters explained. "Political, as well as religious enthusiasm, is a fever of the mind." It "throws those who are attacked with it into temporary delirium" and "paroxysm." Burke found it hilarious that Thomas Mifflin, a grave and staunch and wealthy Quaker of Philadelphia, became aide-de-camp to General Washington. "What think you," he asked a friend, "of that political Enthusiasm, which is able to overpower so much religious Fanaticism?" What could one expect but violent protests, asked William Smith of New York; after all, America was settled by Englishmen, was it not, who were really "civil and religious Enthusiasts"?[34] Religious and political enthusiasm seemed very closely related in these exciting years. The first merged into the second and the second borrowed from the first to generate a radical tendency in the minds of many people which made revolution possible.

Strong evidence that enthusiasm was thought to play a vital role in the Revolutionary movement was the Tories' insistence upon it. They incessantly argued that revolutionaries were victims of a delusion in politics closely akin to enthusiasm in religion. After all, political enthusiasts were zealots, too, were they not, victims of false prophets, deceived by an ideological god?

Loyalists felt the need to discredit rebels in the most damning way possible, and the smear of enthusiasm, they believed, answered that need. Their attacks exploded on every corner of Revolutionary effort but landed most heavily on New England clergymen (perverters of Scripture), colonial troops (like the Anabaptists of Münster), members of the Continental Congress ("our mad freaks"), Tom Paine (a "Brain-sick enthusiast," a "crack-brained zealot"), and, of course, the Declaration of Independence (a radical example of civil antinomianism, so "absurd and visionary"). Enthusiasm was at the bottom of all these monstrous offenses.[35]

Even Whig extremists took a beating when their moderate compatriots discovered ungovernable strains of enthusiasm in Revolutionary ideas which might dangerously upset the kind of revolution they thought Americans were struggling to achieve. Enthusiasm provoked a "wanton abuse of liberty," Samuel Williams warned his Massachusetts colleagues; it provoked a leveling spirit with a blind and fierce zeal which destroyed "government, rulers, church, state, science and morals" and left them in ruins.[36] "The author of Common Sense is a political Enthusiast," wrote William Smith of New York, and what is more, "he has made others so." John Adams had his own opinion about Tom Paine's notorious contribution in 1776. He welcomed its boldness in advocating independence, but he shuddered at its visionary, equalitarian, and naive ideas about government. A "single assembly" was dangerously vulnerable, he charged, to "fits of humor, starts of passion, [and] flights of enthusiasm,"[37] and, therefore, irresponsible and beyond control.

Most Tories and even a number of moderate Whigs claimed that enthusiasm was an unpredictable and explosive ingredient in the Revolutionary mentality. It stemmed not from anything as noble as the rights of Englishmen or even Whig ideology but from an irrational and uncontrollable extremism similar to that already exposed in fanatical religion. Revolutionary radicals, they said, were political enthusiasts—that is, zealots unhinged from political convention, even civilized conduct. Like religious enthusiasts, they were subversive and conspiratorial and a menace to government and society and the accepted order of things.

The revivalists of the 1740s had identified their New Light with a New

World promise. They resisted stuffy establishments which suppressed their experimental relationship with God. For their boldness, for their presumption, they were dubbed enthusiasts by those who would retain the older legacies.[38] In 1776 American patriots, for a variety of reasons, rejected an imperial system of government, which, they argued, frustrated the realization of a political order the New World afforded them. They, too, were called enthusiasts, besides several other things.

Noble Enthusiasm

The meaning of enthusiasm broadened in the latter half of the eighteenth century, while attitudes toward it tended to shift. Edmund Morgan has told us that through indifference to religion after the Awakening, American colonists, when the Revolutionary crisis occurred, looked less to their clergy for direction than to politicians and statesmen. As leadership became secularized, so too did a number of ideas which heretofore had been confined pretty much to religion. Millennialism, always in the Protestant background but more intense among evangelicals, enjoyed a secular phase as enthusiasm assumed a political scope and a wave of nationalism swept over a former colonial people. While old ideas about natural right, liberty, and property expanded in meaning under the pressure of political crisis in the 1770s, so too did enthusiasm. This was particularly true as links between Church and State outside New England loosened or were severed altogether.[39] Secularized, enlarged, and idealized, enthusiasm took on more positive meaning when subjected to Revolutionary circumstances, particularly in the minds of radical patriots who sought in revolution "further truths" commensurate with New World promises and opportunities.

Provost William Smith of Philadelphia was no less Whig than John Adams, even though his political conscience forced him to tread a tortuous path toward loyal Whiggism. Still, in 1775 he fired the patriotism of Pennsylvanians in defense of their rights, charging them not to let difficult times discourage them. If God's mercies came in the shape of suffering, and so it seemed at the time, "let it animate you with a holy *fervor* . . . a divine enthusiasm" which will persuade you that the "cause of *virtue* and *Freedom* is the CAUSE OF GOD upon earth."[40] Provost Smith's namesake, jurist William Smith of New York, although eventually loyal, too, was a sound Whig in 1776. It was past all belief, he insisted, almost parroting Edmund Burke, that colonies "peopled by Enthusiasts from all Nations," democratically nurtured and prosperous, should peacefully knuckle under and give up their freedom to a Parliament in England.[41]

Samuel Adams called himself an enthusiast on more than one occasion, but never more so than when he contemplated the prospect of colonial union and attributed its good effects to the "Agency of the Supreme Being." Like Jonathan Edwards, he admired the fruits of enthusiasm, and he too concluded from experience that "mankind are governed more by their feelings than by reason." This psychological insight, which was the secret of Edwards's success as revivalist, served as well Sam Adams, politician extraordinaire and leader of patriots. The new nation, he boasted, arrived at perfection in the Declaration of Independence, and, what is more, fellow patriots promptly accepted it "as though it were a Decree promulgated from Heaven."[42]

Like that of the Great Awakening, Revolutionary enthusiasm had its millennial side and a vision of the future. As attitudes toward it tended to shift, and as the word itself expanded in meaning beyond religion to politics, so the millennial promise, rich in New World hope for the Kingdom of God, expanded too, and took on patriotic dress. It emerged in the 1760s and 70s as a kind of civil millennialism which Nathan O. Hatch has recently described.[43] It gave the Revolutionary movement a religious frame besides a strength and appeal which affected many. One of those affected was John Adams, who looked back upon the settlement of America as a providential design for the illumination of mankind, while Provost William Smith of Philadelphia confessed an "enthusiastic persuasion" that the new continent was in God's hands inviolate for "great and gracious purposes." Although Smith envisioned all this as part of the empire, he prayed for reconciliation in very patriotic language on behalf of America as *"a chosen seat of Freedom, Arts, and heavenly Knowledge."*[44]

For Ebenezer Baldwin, a Thanksgiving preacher in Connecticut, the calamities and afflictions of revolutionary war could only enhance the glory of God's New World plan. Besides America's becoming the heart of liberty and freedom, Christ would erect there his glorious Kingdom, and that was what the war was all about. Shocked at his own presumption, he almost suppressed his prophetic sermon "lest it should appear whimsical and Enthusiastical." But second thoughts gave him more courage and convinced him of its probability; such ideas, he argued, contributed to the political task ahead, lending vigor and strength and firmness to the rising "American Empire." Liberty, religion, and learning, like the sun and the seventeenth-century gospel, were moving westward, driven out of old Europe. It was not "chimerical" to imagine their rooting themselves in the new continent, where Christ's Kingdom would be established in the "last Ages of the World." Was not the present crisis, asked Baldwin, "remotely preparing the Way for it?"[45]

While some ardent patriots transcended the conflict and contemplated a visionary outcome, others prayed God to contribute right there and then to its immediate success rather than wait until the "latter days," however imminent. An outraged Ambrose Serle, secretary to Lord Howe, described what he called the "true Oliverian Style & Spirit" of dissenting ministers in America, who shamelessly called on God outright to destroy the King's troops and fleets—stinking corpses littering the beaches and all that. Serle fingered for particular scorn one of "these Worthies" who publicly begged God to take directly the patriots' side. If, however, God felt he could not play so active a role, the preacher pleaded, would he please "stand neuter" until the war was over.[46]

Enthusiasm and liberty revealed a strong patriotic connection. Londoners learned that colonists were wrought up to as high a pitch of enthusiasm by the word *liberty* as "could have been expected had religion been the cause." Don't discount this "enthusiasm of Liberty," an English traveler warned his fellows at home; it glows in the breasts of those who would be free and overrides armies and fleets and often prevails at last. The patriots' surprise victory over Gentleman Johnny Burgoyne at Saratoga was owing to the "courage that enthusiasm produces," whined a sour Tory, Samuel Curwen, once of Salem, then a restless exile.[47] Despite the prejudice against its traditional meaning and Tories' contempt for its political manifestation, the patriots' enthusiasm smacked of virtue, too, and noble deeds, and proved a welcome ingredient for revolution. It was this notion Tom Paine took with him to France a few years later. The glorious attack upon the Bastille displayed an "enthusiasm of heroism, such only as the highest animation of liberty could inspire."[48] Enthusiasm in revolutionary crises took on not only positive but heroic qualities.

Actually, a constructive meaning of enthusiasm had been around for some time, lurking in the philosophical and literary background, although not widely appreciated. It surfaced in the second half of the century in time to serve patriots' needs, having shed some of the pejorative sense attached to it for so long. Later it lent itself to the Romantic movement, and it may be that the two uses were not very far apart. In the colonists' time of crisis enthusiasm became idealistically linked with patriotism and liberty and the New World promise, besides a kind of secular millennialism which the Revolution stimulated. It contained a transcendent quality which went beyond traditional ideas of the century and encouraged a strengthening and ennobling of human endeavor among its adherents. This sounds very vague and romantic, and so it was; some colonists, in order to live with it, clothed it loosely in religious wraps.

Surprisingly, John Adams was one of the first of the Revolutionary generation to appreciate this novel and expansive meaning of enthusiasm and to put it and the colonies into a New World perspective. His "Dissertation on the Canon and Feudal Law" was published in 1765. Like Emerson's "American Scholar," which pleaded for intellectual independence several generations later, Adams's "Dissertation" looked forward to a similar disentanglement but in government, politics, and religion, a getting out from under European "systems," which centered around arbitrary institutions and historically tended toward tyranny. Like cousin Sam, John Adams had an understandable respect for his Massachusetts forebears, who had fled that tyranny and the "canon and feudal systems" in the early seventeenth century. In his own day and age, Adams explained, in these more sophisticated, perhaps cynical times, it was popular to look back upon the Puritans and ridicule them as "enthusiastical." Nonsense, Adams snorted. Their enthusiasm, given its principle and its end, was "far from being a reproach to them." And then in a remarkable outburst of what we might call eighteenth-century transcendentalism, a step beyond the rationalism of his age, Adams added: I believe "it will be found universally true, that no great enterprise for the honor or happiness of mankind was ever achieved without a large mixture of that noble infirmity."[49]

Intellectually, this was a historic moment. Adams here introduced to his generation a broad, positive understanding of enthusiasm, which heretofore had been regarded only as religious delusion. He was familiar, it seems, with the writings of Anthony Ashley Cooper, Third Earl of Shaftesbury, one of the few early eighteenth-century thinkers who had anything good to say about enthusiasm. Shaftesbury utilized for his philosophical purposes an imaginative, more secular meaning of the word and wrote admiringly of what he called "true enthusiasm," to distinguish it from out-and-out delusion among, say, French Prophets or fanatical sectaries. All great accomplishments, Shaftesbury wrote, whether by heroes, statesmen, poets, orators, even philosophers, were owing to a "noble ENTHUSIASM," described as an intuitive, an inspired sense, above reason but not contrary to it, which put creative human beings in touch with universal principles. True enthusiasm was not direct revelation but rose out of the minds of imaginative men and women and could be a common experience. It carried them beyond themselves and "raised the imagination to an opinion or conceit of something majestic and divine."[50] John Adams in 1765 identified this kind of enthusiasm with human endeavor in the New World; and America was one of those great enterprises "for the honor or happiness of mankind."

One would guess that Adams borrowed these ideas from Shaftesbury, as suggested here, rather than from John Shebbeare, for instance, a London essayist and government hack writer who had very similar things to say in 1755. The fact that Shebbeare expressed these sentiments attests to their currency in Adams's generation. Anyway, Shebbeare probably had read Shaftesbury, too, or at least was familiar with his ideas. He went a step farther, however, and in two philosophical volumes spread doubt among his contemporaries about the sufficiency of reason alone as a guide to noble pursuits and national prominence. "There has never yet been a nation," wrote Shebbeare, "who has greatly exalted itself by what is called superior reason; some kind of enthusiasm has been the source of all great actions."[51]

John Adams hardly said it differently in 1765, regardless of where he first became acquainted with the positive attributes of "that noble infirmity." Great enterprises, honor, happiness, heroism, statesmanship, large accomplishments, even poetry all were dependent upon enthusiasm, according to this erupting, expansive, and imaginative use of the concept, and the American Revolution was no exception. Several years later, reviewing events of the 1760s and 70s, Adams summed them up succinctly and in striking terms, although still, curiously, religious. The arbitrary treatment by the British after the French War provoked among Americans a "REVIVAL" and an "AWAKENING" in feelings and principles, along with an "enthusiasm which went on increasing, till in 1775 it burst out in open violence, hostility and fury" in pursuit of liberty and independence.[52] Enlightened John Adams found in Shaftesburian enthusiasm a vital component necessary to the progress of the human race. At the same time he continued to make sharp distinction between it—that is, "true enthusiasm"—on the one hand, and the nonsense he still found among religious extremists, such as Baptists and Quakers, or political fanatics like Tom Paine, on the other.

As early as 1755 John Shebbeare saluted enthusiasm in any people who attempted "great actions" and succeeded. He labeled this disposition "romantic."[53] Samuel Taylor Coleridge later elaborated Shaftesbury's, Shebbeare's, and John Adams's insights, as well as those of Tom Paine, in behalf of both America and France. History, Coleridge insisted, confirms unquestionably the ancient aphorism "that nothing great was ever achieved without enthusiasm," an assertion repeated word for word by Ralph Waldo Emerson in 1844.

Now, Coleridge's evidence from the early nineteenth century (1816), read back into the American Revolution, hardly carries much weight. But hear him out, for his argument epitomized the very nature of enthusiasm, religious or political, for those who were consciously or unconsciously its advocates, or perhaps even its victims. After all, "what is enthusiasm," Coleridge asked, "but the oblivion and swallowing-up of self in an object dearer than self, or in an idea more vivid." The "genuine enthusiasm of morals, religion, and patriotism, this enlargement and elevation of the soul above its mere self attest the presence, and accompany the intuition of ultimate PRINCIPLES alone."[54] Poet, critic, and philosopher, Coleridge not only prepared the way for Emerson and the American Transcendentalists; he also articulated a principal element of Romanticism which surprisingly Shaftesbury and John Adams, for all their enlightened thinking and rational understanding, already had identified and appreciated. This ingredient was a heightened, ennobled enthusiasm, no longer narrowly tied to religious extremism, no longer damned as delusion, but accepted at this juncture as a prerequisite to great and heroic purposes. It was an emerging conception whose driving force for a better world had gathered its strength sufficiently in 1776 to release patriots from parochial affairs and encourage them to embrace what Tom Paine and many others called the cause of mankind.

All revolutionaries appeal above the law or constitution to a higher law which they believe justifies their ideas and deeds. The Declaration of Independence was eloquent testimony to such a plea in 1776. But it was already a little old-fashioned, for it harked back for sanction to enlightened but hackneyed political ideas of the past, to John Locke and the Revolution of 1688. In the hearts and minds of imaginative Revolutionaries was another appeal, one which instead boldly looked ahead to a new romantic age. These patriots appealed above the century's assumptions, beyond natural law, to "further truths," to ultimate principles, not rationally but intuitively reached, which the New World helped to nurture. This, indeed, was a "noble enthusiasm."

Notes

Index

Abbreviations Used in the Notes

AAS   American Antiquarian Society, Worcester, Massachusetts

APC   *Acts of the Privy Council of England, Colonial Series,* 6 vols. (London, 1908–1912)

CSPC   *Calendar of State Papers, Colonial Series, America and the West Indies,* 44 vols. (London, 1860–1969)

CSPD   *Calendar of State Papers, Domestic Series,* 104 vols. (London, 1830–1924)

DAB   *Dictionary of American Biography,* ed. Dumas Malone (New York: Charles Scribner's Sons, 1934)

DNB   *Dictionary of National Biography,* ed. Sidney Lee (London: Smith, Elder, 1909)

MHS   Massachusetts Historical Society, Boston, Massachusetts

SPG   Society for the Propagation of the Gospel in Foreign Parts

Notes

1. The Finger of God

1. Edmund S. Morgan, *The Puritan Dilemma: The Story of John Winthrop* (Boston: Little, Brown, 1958), chap. 3.

2. Perry Miller, "Religion and Society in the Early Literature of Virginia," in *Errand into the Wilderness* (Cambridge, Mass.: Harvard University Press, 1956), pp. 99–140.

3. Howard Mumford Jones, *O Strange New World: American Culture, The Formative Years* (New York: Viking Press, 1967), pp. 192–193.

4. Thomas More, *Utopia: or the Happy Republic: A Philosophical Romance*, trans. Gilbert Burnet (Glasgow, 1743), pp. 117–133, 77–78; Francis Bacon, *The New Atlantis*, ed. A. B. Gough (Oxford: Oxford University Press, 1915), pp. 47 and xxxii–xxxiii; Jones, *O Strange New World*, pp. 34–36; William Shakespeare, *The Tempest*, act 2, sc. 1.

5. Roland Bainton, "The Present State of Servetus Studies," *Journal of Modern History*, 4 (Dec. 1932), 89. For Servetus's blasphemies while burning, see Frederick Spanhemius, *Englands Warning by Germanies Woe* (London, 1646), p. 20. For Calvin's missionaries to Brazil, see Jean de Léry, *Histoire d'un Voyage Faict en la Terre du Brésil*, new ed. with an introduction and notes by Paul Gaffarel (Paris, 1880), II, 104. Increase Mather, *Ichabod, or a Discourse* (Boston, 1702), p. 65.

6. D. B. Quinn, "The First Pilgrims," *William and Mary Quarterly*, 3d ser., 23, no. 3 (July 1966), 360–361.

7. Christopher Carleill, *A discourse upon the entended Voyage to the hethermoste parts of America* (London, 1583), p. iii; Quinn, "First Pilgrims," pp. 360–361.

8. Richard Hakluyt, *Discourse of Western Planting* (1584), in *The Original Writings and Correspondence of the Two Richard Hakluyts*, ed. E. G. R. Taylor (London: Hakluyt Society, 1935), II, 326.

9. Quinn, "First Pilgrims," pp. 359–360; Mattie Erma Edwards Parker, ed., *North Carolina Charters and Constitutions, 1578–1698* (Raleigh, N.C.: Carolina Charter Tercentenary Commission, 1963), p. 62; W. Noël Sainsbury, ed., *CSPC 1574–1660* (London, 1860), pp. 109–111.

10. R. A. Knox, *Enthusiasm: A Chapter in the History of Religion* (New

York: Oxford University Press, 1950), p. 206; Ruth Clark, *Strangers and Sojourners at Port Royal* (Cambridge: Cambridge University Press, 1932), p. 97, n. 4.

11. Thomas Paine, *Common Sense*, in M. D. Conway, ed., *The Writings of Thomas Paine* (New York, 1894), I, 89.

12. William Crashaw, *A Sermon Preached in London Before the Right Honorable the Lord Lawarre* (London, 1610), unpaginated.

13. Samuel Ward, *A Coale from the Altar, to Kindle the Holy Fire of Zeale* (London, 1615), pp. 83–84.

14. George Herbert, "The Church Militant" (ca. 1632), in A. B. Grosart, ed., *The Complete Works . . . of George Herbert* (n.p., 1874), II, 11 and xiv–xv.

15. William Hooke, *New-Englands Sence, of Old-England and Irelands Sorrowes* (London, 1645), pp. 25, 18–19; *New Englands Plantation, or A Short and True Description of the Commodities and Discommodities of that Country* (London, 1630), in Peter Force, ed., *Tracts and Other Papers Relating Principally to the Colonies in North America* (Washington, D.C., 1836), I, no. 12, p. 14.

16. Miller, "Religion and Society," pp. 99–140.

17. John White, *The Planters Plea* (London, 1630), p. 65.

18. Crashaw, *Sermon*, unpaginated.

19. *A New Life of Virginea* (London, 1612), in MHS *Collections*, 2d ser., vol. 8 (Boston, 1819), p. 214.

20. John Donne, *A Sermon . . . Preach'd to the Honourable Company of the Virginia Plantation* (London, 1622), pp. 13, 19–20, 24–25.

21. *The Complete Poetry and Selected Prose of John Donne and The Complete Poetry of William Blake* (New York: Random House, 1941), p. 85.

22. Herbert, "Church Militant," in *Works*, II, 12; Robert Gordon, *Encouragements, For such as shall have intention to bee Under-takers . . . of Cape Breton . . . by Mee Lochinvar* (Edinburgh, 1625), unpaginated; John Cotton, *Gods Promise to His Plantation* (London, 1630), p. 19.

23. White, *Planters Plea*, p. 3.

24. Christopher Levett, *A Voyage in New England Begun in 1623* (London, 1628), p. 36 (misprinted as 34); Cotton, *Gods Promise*, p. 9.

25. William Symonds, *A Sermon Preached at White-Chappel in the Presence of . . . the Adventurers and Planners for Virginia* (London, 1609), p. 9; Richard Eburne, *A Plain Pathway to Plantations* (1624), ed. Louis B. Wright (Ithaca, N.Y.: Cornell University Press, 1962), p. 13; Miller, "Religion and Society," pp. 119, 111.

26. White, *Planters Plea*, pp. 47–48.

27. Cotton, *Gods Promise*, pp. 4, 6, 11–12.

28. White, *Planters Plea*, pp. 8, 9–10, 14–15, 41–42. For Alexander Whitaker's use of "almost miraculous," see *Good Newes from Virginia* (London, 1613), in Conrad Cherry, ed., *God's New Israel: Religious Interpretations of American Destiny* (Englewood Cliffs, N.J.: Prentice-Hall, 1971), p. 32.

29. Hooke, *New-Englands Sence*, p. 21; Nathaniel Ward, *The Simple Cobler of Aggawam* (London, 1647), p. 23.

30. William M. Lamont, *Godly Rule: Politics and Religion, 1603–60* (London: Macmillan, 1969), passim.
31. Thomas Bastard, "The Marigold and the Sun," in *Twelve Sermons* (London, 1615), p. 40.
32. Donne, *Sermon . . . Preach'd*, pp. 39, 42–43.
33. Gordon, *Encouragements*, unpaginated; Cotton, *Gods Promise*, pp. 19–20; White, *Planters Plea*, p. 16.
34. Ibid., pp. 5–6, 12.
35. Bartholomew Keckermann, *Manuductio to Theologie*, trans. T. Vickers (n.p., 1621), pp. 93–95; Eburne, *Plain Pathway*, p. 29; Lawrence A. Cremin, *American Education: The Colonial Experience, 1607–1783* (New York: Harper and Row, 1970), pp. 103–104, 215.
36. Edward Johnson, *Wonder-working Providence of Sions Saviour* (London, 1654), pp. 14–16; White, *Planters Plea*, p. 25.
37. William Hooke, *The Privilege of the Saints on Earth, Beyond Those in Heaven* (London, 1673), p. 122.
38. Samuel Danforth, *An Astronomical Description of the Late Comet or Blazing Star* (Cambridge, 1665), p. 22. A wandering eccentric star was a frequent metaphor in the seventeenth century's catalogue of pejorative figures to describe an enthusiast. It reappeared during the 1740s to describe extremists of the Great Awakening. See Chapter 9.
39. Miller, "Religion and Society," p. 114. See Alexander Whitaker's use of the Devil in encouraging continued support of the Virginia Company's venture at Jamestown. Whitaker, *Good Newes*, pp. 32, 37.
40. These several statements are from the following: Gordon, *Encouragements*, unpaginated; Johnson, *Wonder-working Providence*, pp. 23, 112; Eburne, *Plain Pathway*, pp. 28–29; White, *Planters Plea*, pp. 14–15, 11; Richard Whitbourne, *A Discourse and Discovery of New-Found-Land* (London, 1620), pp. 14–15.
41. Hakluyt, *Discourse*, pp. 217–218; Quinn, "First Pilgrims," pp. 362–363.
42. Crashaw, *Sermon*, unpaginated. For John Rolfe, see Miller, "Religion and Society," p. 119. Donne, *Sermon . . . Preach'd*, pp. 44, 45; Gordon, *Encouragements*, unpaginated; White, *Planters Plea*, p. 22.
43. Johnson, *Wonder-working Providence*, p. 34.
44. Miller, "Religion and Society," p. 139.
45. Herbert, "Church Militant," in *Works*, II, 12, 13.

2. Whirligig Spirits

1. Thomas Scot, *Phylomythie: or Philomythologie* (London, 1616), unpaginated; Thomas Edwards, *Gangraena; or a Catalogue and Discovery of Many of the Errours, Heresies, Blasphemies . . . of the Sectaries*, pt. 1 (London, 1646), pp. 15–16.
2. John Ley, *A Discourse Concerning Puritans* (n.p., 1641), pp. 13–14.
3. Norman Cohn, *The Pursuit of the Millennium*, rev. ed. (New York: Oxford University Press, 1970), pp. 256–280; R. A. Knox, *Enthusiasm: A Chap-*

ter in the History of Religion (New York: Oxford University Press, 1950), pp. 139, 174–175, 581–582.

4. John Strype, *Annals of the Reformation* (London, 1709), pp. 519, 522.

5. *APC*, vol. 8, *1571–1575*, pp. 369, 389–390; *Harleian Miscellany* (London, 1809), II, 11; Knox, *Enthusiasm*, p. 139.

6. Edmund Jessop, *A Discovery of the Errors of the English Anabaptists* (London, 1623), "Dedicatory"; *Hell Broke Loose: or a Catalogue of many of the spreading Errors* (London, 1646).

7. Thomas Fuller, *The Holy State* (Cambridge, 1642), pp. 396–403; F. L. Cross, ed., *The Oxford Dictionary of the Christian Church* (London: Oxford University Press, 1957), pp. 415, 1370.

8. Robert Baillie, *Anabaptisme, the True Fountaine of Independency, Brownism, Antinomy, Familisme* (London, 1647), pp. 32–33, 54, 99–100, 102; John Sleidanus, *Mock-Majesty: or the Siege of Münster* (London, 1644), pp. 9–10, 24.

9. John Rogers, *The Displaying of an Horrible Secte* (London, 1578), unpaginated.

10. Knox, *Enthusiasm*, pp. 140–141; *The First Epistle of H. N.* [Amsterdam, 1574?]; John Knewstub, *A Confutation of Monstrous and Horrible Heresies* (London, 1579), pp. 71–72; William Wilkinson, *A Confutation of Certain Articles Delivered unto the Family of Love* (London, 1579), "Epistle Dedicatory" and ff.

11. Rogers, *Displaying*; Knewstub, *Confutation*, "Dedicatory"; Wilkinson, *Confutation*; I. B. Horst, *The Radical Brethren: Anabaptism and the English Reformation to 1558* (Nieuwkoop: De Graaf, 1972), pp. 152–154.

12. Rogers, *Displaying*; Horst, *Radical Brethren*, pp. 152–154.

13. *APC*, vol. 8, *1571–1575*, p. 398; vol. 10, *1577–1578*, p. 332; vol. 11 *1578–1580*, pp. 138–139, 444–445; vol. 12, *1580–1581*, pp. 231–233, 258, 269, 317–318; Felicity Heal, "The Family of Love and the Diocese of Ely," in Derek Baker, ed., *Schism, Heresy, and Religious Protest* (Cambridge: Cambridge University Press, 1972), pp. 213–222; Horst, *Radical Brethren*, p. 154; *DNB*, s.v. "Vitell, Christopher"; Wilkinson, *Confutation*, "Epistle Dedicatory," p. iii; "A Proclamation against the Sectaries of the Family of Love," in Proclamations by Queen Elizabeth, 18 Bodleian, p. 223.

14. *A Supplication of the Family of Love* (Cambridge, 1606), p. 57; Wilkinson, *Confutation*, "Epistle Dedicatory"; Heal, "The Family of Love," pp. 213–222; Eilert Ekwall, *The Concise Oxford Dictionary of English Place-Names*, 4th ed. (Oxford: Clarendon Press, 1960), p. 166. For a different source of the name Ely, see Thomas Thorowgood, *Jews in America* (London, 1660), p. 6. Charles Wilson, *England's Apprenticeship, 1603–1763* (London: Longmans, 1965; reprinted 1971), p. 30; John Bruce and W. D. Hamilton, eds. *CSPD, Charles I, 1638–1639* (London, 1871), no. 170, p. 343.

15. Heal, "The Family of Love," pp. 213–222; *APC*, vol. 12, *1580–1581*, pp. 232–233, 250.

16. *A Supplication of the Family*, p. 4; Stephen Denison, *The White Wolfe, or A Sermon Preached at Pauls Cross* (London, 1627); John Etherington, *The*

Deeds of Dr. Denison a Little More Manifested (London, 1642); John Etherington, *Brief Discovery of the Blasphemous Doctrine of Familisme* (London, 1645); Edwards, *Gangraena*, p. 84.

17. William Bray, ed., *The Diary of John Evelyn* (London: Bickers, 1906), III, 39–40; D. S. Lovejoy, *The Glorious Revolution in America* (New York: Harper and Row, 1972), pp. 195, 222–225.

18. Champlin Burrage, *Early English Dissenters* (Cambridge: Cambridge University Press, 1912), I, 41; B. R. White, *The English Separatist Tradition* (London: Oxford University Press, 1971), chaps. 1–2; Horst, *Radical Brethren*, pp. 150–151.

19. Thomas White, *A Discoverie of Brownisme: or, a briefe declaration of some of the errors and abhominations daily practised and increased among the English company of the separation . . . at Amsterdam* (London, 1605), p. 5.

20. Samuel Ward, *A Coale from the Altar, to Kindle the Holy Fire of Zeale* (London, 1615; reprinted 1627), p. 21; Walter Raleigh, *The History of the World, in Five Books*, 11th ed. (London, 1736), I, 167; Patricke Scot, *Vox Vera, or Observations from Amsterdam* (London, 1625), p. 41; D. B. Quinn, "The First Pilgrims," *William and Mary Quarterly*, 3d ser., 23, no. 3 (July 1966), 364–365.

21. White, *The English Separatist Tradition*, p. 30, but see also chap. 5, particularly pp. 165–166. Quinn, "The First Pilgrims," pp. 362, 367, 373–374; Cross, ed., *Oxford Dictionary of the Christian Church*, s.v. "Browne, Robert."

22. William Haller claimed that a succession of "enthusiasts" followed Browne and Robinson. *The Rise of Puritanism* (New York: Columbia University Press, 1938), p. 191; Raleigh, *History*, I, 167. This was a change of mind for Raleigh. In 1593 he spoke in Parliament against religious persecution. *DNB*, s.v. "Raleigh, Walter"; Jessop, *Discovery of the Errors*, "Dedicatory."

23. White, *Discoverie of Brownisme*, Preface and pp. 2–11, 16.

24. See Perry Miller's discussion of Arminianism and antinomianism in *The New England Mind: The Seventeenth Century* (Cambridge, Mass.: Harvard University Press, 1939; reprinted 1954), p. 373.

25. Ward, *A Coale from the Altar*, pp. 23, 26, 21; Patricke Scot, *Vox Vera*, p. 40.

26. Burrage, *Early English Dissenters*, I, 41; *The Anatomy of Separatists* (London, 1642), pp. 1, 3, 5.

27. For examples of these dangerous irregularities, see William Clever, *Foure Profitable Bookes* (London, 1597), "Dedicatorie"; *Supplication of the Family*, pp. 1–20, 25; Edwards, *Gangraena*, pp. 30, 33, 79–80, 84, 85, 66, 104, 123; Baillie, *Anabaptisme*, p. 54; Jeremy Taylor, Sermon XI, "The Minister's Duty in Life and Doctrine," in *The Whole Works of the Right Rev. Jeremy Taylor, D. D.* (London, 1850), VIII, 525; Denison, *White Wolfe*, pp. 19, 23, 33.

28. Clever, *Foure Profitable Bookes*, "Dedicatorie"; Thomas Scot, *Philomythie*, unpaginated; Rufus M. Jones, *Studies in Mystical Religion* (London: Macmillan, 1909), pp. 436–447; *Supplication of the Family*, pp. 4, 19; Knewstub, *Confutation*, "Dedicatory"; Patricke Scot, *Vox Vera*, p. 41; *Anatomy of the Separatists*, p. 5; Baillie, *Anabaptisme*, Preface and p. 62.

29. *Supplication of the Family,* p. 19; William Walwyn, *The Power of Love* (London, 1643), "To every Reader"; Ephraim Pagitt, *Heresiography* (London, 1661), p. 157; Edwards, *Gangraena,* p. 34; D. B. Quinn, "The First Pilgrims," pp. 363–365; Michael R. Watts, *The Dissenters: From the Reformation to the French Revolution* (Oxford: Clarendon Press, 1978), pp. 81–82.

30. Knox, *Enthusiasm,* p. 136. For Quaker nudity, see Chapter 6. *A Short History of the Anabaptists of High and Low Germany* (London, 1642), p. 53.

31. According to *The Oxford English Dictionary, antinomian* and *antinomianism,* meaning "rejection of the moral law," came into use in the 1640s. There is an example of *antinomist* from 1632 (Oxford: Clarendon Press, 1961), s.v. "antinomian." See use of the word in William Walwyn, *Walwyns Just Defence against the Aspersions Cast upon Him* (London, 1649), p. 8; John Sedgwick, *Antinomianisme Anatomized* (London, 1643), pp. 29–30.

32. Cross, ed., *The Oxford Dictionary of the Christian Church,* s.v. "antinomianism"; Knox, *Enthusiasm,* p. 136; Watts, *Dissenters,* p. 181.

33. Norman Cohn, "The Ranters: the 'Underground' in the England of 1650," *Encounter,* 34, no. 4 (April 1970), 15–25.

34. Heal, "The Family of Love," pp. 213–222; Baillie, *Anabaptisme,* passim; Jones, *Mystical Religion,* p. 436.

35. Walwyn, *Just Defence,* p. 8; Walwyn, *The Power of Love,* pp. 20, 30, 38–41; Christopher Hill, *The World Turned Upside Down* (London: Temple Smith, 1972), pp. 133, 271; A. L. Morton, *The World of the Ranters* (London: Lawrence and Wishart, 1970), p. 146.

36. Thomas Bakewell, *A Short View of the Antinomian Errours* (London, 1643), p. 21; Sedgwick, *Antinomianism Anatomized,* p. 30.

37. *The Arraignment and Tryall with a Declaration of the Ranters* (n.p., 1650), p. 4; *A Description of the Sect called the Family of Love* (London, 1641). For Anne Hutchinson's trial, see Chapter 4.

38. Thomas Middleton, *The Famelie of Love. Acted by the Children of his Majesties Revells* (London, 1608), "To the Reader." Richard Hindry Barker has claimed that the play "can scarcely be dated much later than 1602"; see his *Thomas Middleton* (New York: Columbia University Press, 1958), p. 10.

39. Act 5, sc. 1; act 3, sc. 1.

40. Act 2, sc. 1; act 3, sc. 1.

41. White, *Discoverie of Brownisme,* pp. 2–3, 7, 10, 11, 16, 26.

42. *Anatomy of the Separatists,* p. 1; Watts, *Dissenters,* pp. 81–82.

43. *The Nest of Serpents* (n.p., n.d. [1640s?]), pp. 1–2, 6; *Short History of the Anabaptists,* pp. 42–43, 56.

44. Henry More, *Enthusiasmus Triumphatus; or a Brief Discourse of the Nature, Causes, Kinds, and Cure of Enthusiasm* (London, 1662; reprinted Los Angeles: W. A. Clark Library, 1966), p. 37; Thomas Long, *The Character of a Separatist* (London, 1677), p. 70; Richard Sibbes, *The Soules Conflict with It Selfe* (London, 1635), p. 236.

45. Wilkinson, *A Confutation of Certain Articles,* unpaginated.

46. Etherington, *Brief Discovery,* p. 12.

47. *Supplication of the Family,* p. 25; Denison, *White Wolfe,* p. 19; [John

Taylor], *New Preachers, New, Greene the Feltmaker* ([London], 1641), unpaginated; Thomas Fuller, *The Holy State,* p. 402; *Anatomy of the Separatists,* p. 3.
48. Edwards, *Gangraena,* p. 30; Baillie, *Anabaptisme,* p. 54; George Whitefield, *A Letter to the Rev. The President . . . of Harvard College* (Boston, 1745), pp. 14–15.
49. N.p., 1644. See also *Remarkable Passages in the Life of William Kiffin,* ed. William Orme (London, 1823), p. 130.
50. Walwyn, *The Power of Love,* pp. 43–45, 47–50.
51. Edwards, *Gangraena,* A3 and p. 179.

3. Separatists and the New World

1. Quoted in D. B. Quinn, "The First Pilgrims," *William and Mary Quarterly,* 3d ser., 23, no. 3 (July 1966), 368, 387.
2. Ibid., passim, particularly pp. 388–390; D. B. Quinn, *Raleigh and the British Empire,* rev. ed. (New York: Collier Books, 1962), pp. 166–167.
3. Joseph Hall, *The Discovery of a New World, or a Description of the South Indies, Hetherto Unknown* (London, 1609), p. 215, first published as *Mundus Alter et Idem,* supposedly at Frankfurt, 1605. See a recent edition, trans. and ed. John Millar Wands, *Another World and Yet the Same* (New Haven: Yale University Press, 1981), pp. 104, 188. Quinn, "First Pilgrims," pp. 365–366, 385–387.
4. William Crashaw, *A Sermon Preached in London Before the Right Honorable the Lord Lawarre* (London, 1610), unpaginated.
5. Alexander Young, *Chronicles of the Pilgrim Fathers of the Colony of Plymouth* (Boston, 1841), p. 68, n. 2; Sydney V. James, Jr., ed., *Three Visitors to Early Plymouth* (Plymouth, Mass.: Plimoth Plantation, 1963), p. 5, n. 3; Edwin Sandys to John Robinson and William Brewster, Nov. 12, 1617, in William Bradford, *Of Plymouth Plantation, 1620–1647,* ed. S. E. Morison (New York: Modern Library, 1967), p. 32.
6. Ibid., p. 29 n.; Edward Winslow, "Brief Narration of the True Grounds or Cause of the First Planting in New England," in Young, *Chronicles,* p. 382; Ruth A. McIntyre, *Debts Hopeful and Desperate* (Plymouth, Mass.: Plimoth Plantation, 1963), p. 69, n. 3; *DNB,* s.v. "Sandys, Sir Edwin."
7. "The Ten Counterdemaunds in reaction to the Seven Demands of Francis Johnson," in Champlin Burrage, *The Early English Dissenters* (Cambridge: Cambridge University Press, 1912), II, 145; ibid., I, 171; B. R. White, *The English Separatist Tradition* (London: Oxford University Press, 1971), p. 155; Babette M. Levy, *Early Puritanism in the Southern and Island Colonies* (Worcester, Mass.: AAS, 1960), pp. 104–105.
8. S. M. Kingsbury, ed., *The Records of the Virginia Company of London* (Washington, D.C.: Government Printing Office, 1935), IV, 194–195, 413. But see, too, W. F. Craven, *The Dissolution of the Virginia Company: The Failure of a Colonial Experiment* (New York: Oxford University Press, 1932), pp. 282–283.
9. Robert Barclay, *The Inner Life of the Religious Societies of the Com-*

monwealth (London, 1876), pp. 43, 65; "Biographical Memoir of Rev. John Lothropp by Rev. John Lothrop, D. D.," in MHS *Collections,* 2d ser. (Boston, 1838), I, 164–167; Henry Jacob, *Reasons Taken out of Gods Word and the Best Humane Testimonies Proving a Necessitie of Reforming our Churches in England* ([Middleburgh], 1604), unpaginated; Henry Jacob, *To the right High and mightie Prince James . . . An humble Supplication for Toleration* (Middleburgh, 1609), pp. 20, 41, 45; [Henry Jacob], *An Attestation of Many Learned, Godly, and famous Divines* (n.p., 1613), pp. 307–308; White, *Separatist Tradition,* pp. 165–166.

10. Daniel Neal, *History of the Puritans* (London, 1822), II, 92; Barclay, *Inner Life,* p. 98; "Biographical Memoir of Rev. Lothropp," pp. 164–167; White, *Separatist Tradition,* pp. 165–166; Rufus Jones, *Studies in Mystical Religion* (London: Macmillan, 1909), pp. 415–416; *DNB,* s.v. "Jacob, Henry."

11. "Biographical Memoir of Rev. Lothropp," p. 167; "So-called Jessey Records or Memoranda," in Burrage, *English Dissenters,* II, 195, and I, 319–320; *Virginia Magazine of History and Biography,* 9 (1901–1902), 221; ibid., 29 (1921), 47, 294. See again *DNB,* s.v. "Jacob, Henry."

12. "Reports Relating to the Appearance of Certain Separatists Before the High Commission Between April 19 and June 21, 1632," in Burrage, *English Dissenters,* II, 313, 319; "Biographical Memoir of Rev. Lothropp," pp. 163–178; Jones, *Mystical Religion,* pp. 416–417; Neal, *Puritans,* II, 340.

13. Ibid., II, 340–341; "The Examination of Mrs. Anne Hutchinson," in David D. Hall, ed., *The Antinomian Controversy, 1636–1638: A Documentary History* (Middletown, Conn.: Wesleyan University Press, 1968), pp. 322–323; Edmund S. Morgan, *Visible Saints: The History of a Puritan Idea* (New York: New York University Press, 1963), p. 86.

14. Jones, *Mystical Religion,* pp. 416–417; Neal, *Puritans,* II, 341; White, *Separatist Tradition,* pp. 167–168.

15. *John Pory's Lost Description of Plymouth Colony in the Earliest Days of the Pilgrim Fathers,* ed. Champlin Burrage (Boston: Houghton Mifflin, 1918), pp. 35–36; James, ed., *Three Visitors,* p. 5, n. 3.

16. John Robinson to departing Pilgrims, in Cotton Mather, *Magnalia Christi Americana,* bks. 1 and 2, ed. K. B. Murdock (Cambridge, Mass.: Harvard University Press, 1977), pp. 144–145; White, *Separatist Tradition,* chap. 7; Michael R. Watts, *The Dissenters: From the Reformation to the French Revolution* (Oxford: Oxford University Press, 1978), pp. 62–66.

17. Ibid., pp. 72–77; David D. Hall, *The Faithful Shepherd: A History of the New England Ministry in the Seventeenth Century* (Chapel Hill: University of North Carolina Press, 1972), pp. 30, 39; Edmund S. Morgan, *Roger Williams: The Church and the State* (New York: Harcourt, Brace and World, 1967), p. 21; A. S. P. Woodhouse, ed., *Puritanism and Liberty, Being the Army Debates (1647–9)* (Chicago: University of Chicago Press, 1951), Introduction, p. 46.

18. John Robinson, "A Justification of Separation from the Church of England," in Robert Ashton, ed., *The Works of John Robinson* (London, 1851), I, 246–251; ibid., pp. xliv–xlv; Robinson to John Carver, July 1620, in Bradford, *Plymouth Plantation,* p. 367; Mather, *Magnalia,* pp. 144–145.

19. 1 Cor. 14; John Goodwin, *Imputatio Fidei* (London, 1642), Preface.

20. Woodhouse, ed., *Puritanism and Liberty,* Introduction, pp. 45–46.

21. *Oxford English Dictionary,* J. A. H. Murray, ed. (Oxford: Clarendon Press, 1909), VII, pt. 2, s.v. "prophesying"; Michael Walzer, *The Revolution of the Saints* (Cambridge, Mass.: Harvard University Press, 1965), pp. 127–128; Robinson, *Works,* I, 246–247; Jacob, *An Attestation,* p. 119; Watts, *Dissenters,* p. 55; Goodwin, *Imputatio,* Preface.

22. Robinson, *Works,* III, 58; Hanserd Knollys, *Christ Exalted* (London, 1646), pp. 13–14. See also Thomas Goodwin, *A Glimpse of Syons Glory: or the Churches Beauty Specified* (London, 1641), pp. 4, 8.

23. Goodwin, *Imputatio,* Preface; Morgan, *Roger Williams,* p. 21.

24. *A Short History of the Anabaptists in High and Low Germany* (London, 1642), pp. 55–56; Ephraim Pagitt, *Heresiography, or a Discription of the Her- etickes and Sectaries,* 4th ed. (London, 1648), p. 70; Thomas Edwards, *Gan- graena; or a Catalogue and Discovery of Many of the Errours, Heresies, Blasphemies . . . of the Sectaries,* 2d ed. (London, 1646), pp. 30–31; Watts, *Dissenters,* p. 306.

25. William Penn, *The Rise and Progress of the People Called Quakers* (1694), in *The Witness of William Penn,* ed. F. B. Tolles and E. G. Alderfer (New York: Macmillan, 1957), p. 14; Morgan, *Visible Saints,* pp. 82, 99.

26. John Milton, *Areopagitica; a Speech of Mr. John Milton for the Liberty of Unlicenc'd Printing, To the Parliament of England* (London, 1644), pp. 29– 30, 31–32, 38–39, 26.

27. *Winthrop's Journal,* ed. J. K. Hosmer (New York: Charles Scribner's Sons, 1908), I, 93–94; Thomas Prince, *Annals of New England,* in MHS *Col- lections,* 2d ser. (Boston, Mass., 1801; reprinted 1846), VII, 70–71.

28. Mather, *Magnalia,* pp. 225, 445, 72–73.

29. Ibid., 140, 400, 402 n.; *Winthrop's Journal,* I, 167.

30. Ibid., pp. 93–94; George D. Langdon, Jr., *Pilgrim Colony: A History of New Plymouth, 1620–1691* (New Haven: Yale University Press, 1966), p. 116.

31. Mather, *Magnalia,* p. 402 n.; Bradford, *Plymouth Plantation,* pp. 327, 328; *An Account of the Church . . . in Plymouth by John Cotton* (1760), in MHS *Collections,* 1st ser. (Boston, 1795; reprinted 1835), IV, 107–117, 136. See also Isaac Backus, *A History of New England* (Newton, Mass., 1871; reprinted 1969), I, 451–452.

32. Thomas Morton, *The New English Canaan* (1637), Prince Society Pub- lications (Boston, 1883), pp. 322–323; Bradford, *Plymouth Plantation,* pp. 204– 210.

33. Ibid., p. 274 and note; MHS *Collections,* 1st ser., IV, 120 n.; *Winthrop's Journal,* I, 163–164.

34. William Rathband, *A Brief Narration of Some Church Courses . . . in New England* (London, 1644), pp. 46–47.

35. Robert Cushman, *A Sermon Preached at Plimmoth in New-England De- cember 9, 1621* (London, 1622).

36. *Winthrop's Journal,* I, 60, 116, 123; Morgan, *Visible Saints,* pp. 82, 99; Hall, *Shepherd,* 93.

37. *Winthrop's Journal,* I, 205, 209; Hall, *Shepherd,* p. 161; *Church-Government and Church-Covenant Discussed* (London, 1643), reprinted in J. B. Felt, *The Ecclesiastical History of New England* (Boston, 1862), I, 385. Robert Baillie, a Scottish Presbyterian, described nothing but "unhappy" results in Boston from both prophesying and the habit of questioning ministers after sermons. These unfortunate experiences, wrote Baillie, persuaded the Massachusetts Congregationalists gladly to quit both. *A Dissuasive from the Errours of the Time* (London, 1646), p. 118.

38. Felt, *Ecclesiastical History,* I, 281, 282, 385; *Winthrop's Journal,* I, 234; Hall, *Shepherd,* p. 111; Williston Walker, *The Creeds and Platforms of Congregationalism* (New York, 1893; reprinted Boston, 1960), pp. 134 n., 135 and note.

39. Felt, *Ecclesiastical History,* I, 282, 385.

40. Ibid., pp. 432, 431; *A Coppy of a Letter of Mr. Cotton . . . in Answer of Certain Objections* (n.p., 1641), p. 4; John Cotton, *The Doctrine of the Church, to which is committed the Keyes of the Kingdome of Heaven* (London, 1642), p. 6.

41. See Robert E. Wall, Jr., *Massachusetts Bay: The Crucial Decade* (New Haven: Yale University Press, 1972), esp. chap. 4.

42. *Winthrop's Journal,* II, 324. For Hanserd Knollys's free use of pulpits in England, see Barclay, *Inner Life,* pp. 289–290.

43. M. H. Thomas, ed., *Diary of Samuel Sewall, 1674–1729* (New York: Farrar, Straus and Giroux, 1973), II, 1073; Joshua Coffin, *A Sketch of the History of Newbury, Newburyport, and West Newbury* (Boston, 1845), p. 61; T. B. Strandness, *Samuel Sewall: A Puritan Portrait* (East Lansing: Michigan State University Press, 1967), p. 4; Ezekiel Rogers to John Winthrop, in *The Winthrop Papers* (Boston, Mass.: MHS, 1944), IV, 160.

44. *The Cambridge Platform,* in Walker, *Creeds,* pp. 212–214; Cotton Mather, *Magnalia Christi Americana* (London, 1702), bk. 7, p. 18; Cotton Mather, *Magnalia Christi Americana* (Hartford, Conn., 1820), II, 451; Hall, *Shepherd,* pp. 129 and note, 184 and note.

45. For Baptists' troubles in Massachusetts, see *Diary of John Hull,* in AAS *Transactions and Collections* (Boston, Mass., 1857), III, 219, 226, 227, 238; *Winthrop's Journal,* II, 177; Mather, *Magnalia* (1820), II, 460; William G. McLoughlin, *New England Dissent, 1630–1833: The Baptists and the Separation of Church and State* (Cambridge, Mass.: Harvard University Press, 1971), I, 56 and note, 67.

46. R. A. Knox, *Enthusiasm: A Chapter in the History of Religion* (New York: Oxford University Press, 1950), pp. 134–135; McLoughlin, *New England Dissent,* I, 56–57.

47. John Clarke, *Ill Newes from New-England* (London, 1652), reprinted in MHS *Collections,* 4th ser. (Boston, 1854), II, 15, 96; McLoughlin, *New England Dissent,* I, 56–57 and note.

48. Roger Williams, *The Hireling Ministry None of Christs* (1652), in Perry Miller, ed., *The Complete Writings* (New York: Russell and Russell, 1963), VII, 160–161, 166–167, 176.

49. *An Account of the Church . . . in Plymouth*, p. 118; Bradford, *Plymouth Plantation*, pp. 324, 346, 347 n.; Mather, *Magnalia* (1977), p. 207.

50. Ibid., pp. 209–210, 143, 402, 438. For the conflict over liberty of conscience in Plymouth, see *Winthrop Papers*, V, 55–56. Backus, *History of New England*, I, 433–434; Walker, *Creeds*, p. 164 and note; Colonel Aspinwall, "William Vassal no Factionist," MHS *Proceedings*, vol. 6, *1862–1863* (Boston, 1863), pp. 476–478.

51. Quakers argued that they suffered unduly in Plymouth because the Old Colony's leaders aped Boston and its harsh punishments, or as several expressed it, "Now Plymouth-Saddle is upon the Bay-Horse." John Rous et al., *New-England a Degenerate Plant* (London, 1659), p. 16.

52. William Haller, *The Rise of Puritanism* (New York: Columbia University Press, 1938), p. 191; McLoughlin, *New England Dissent*, I, 56–57.

53. Prince, *Annals of New England*, pp. 70–71.

4. Anne Hutchinson and the Naked Christ

1. Jonathan Mitchell, "To the Reader," in Thomas Shepard, *The Parable of the Ten Virgins Opened & Applied* (London, 1660); Seymour Van Dyken, *Samuel Willard, 1640–1707: Preacher of Orthodoxy in an Era of Change* (Grand Rapids, Mich.: Wm. B. Eerdmans, 1972), p. 122. Michael Kammen has some striking things to say about the tensions within Puritanism in *People of Paradox: An Inquiry Concerning the Origins of American Civilization* (New York: Alfred A. Knopf, 1972), pp. 143–144.

2. William Stoughton, *New-Englands True Interest* (Cambridge, 1670), excerpted in Perry Miller and T. H. Johnson, eds., *The Puritans* (New York: American Book Co., 1938), p. 246; David D. Hall, *The Faithful Shepherd: A History of the New England Ministry in the Seventeenth Century* (Chapel Hill: University of North Carolina Press, 1972), p. 89.

3. "Reports Relating to the Appearance of Certain Separatists Before the Court of High Commission . . . 1632," reprinted in Champlin Burrage, *The Early English Dissenters* (Cambridge: Cambridge University Press, 1912), II, 313.

4. Thomas Shepard, *God's Plot: The Paradoxes of Puritan Piety, Being the Autobiography & Journal of Thomas Shepard*, ed. Michael McGiffert (Amherst: University of Massachusetts Press, 1972), p. 28; Thomas Shepard, *The Saints Refuge, A Sermon Preached by a Reverend Divine* (Rotterdam, 1641), pp. 28, 29, 34.

5. Thomas Hooker, *The Danger of Desertion*, in G. H. Williams et al., eds., *Writings in England and Holland, 1626–1633* (Cambridge, Mass.: Harvard University Press, 1975), p. 244; Charles Severn, ed., *The Diary of the Rev. John Ward, 1648–1679* (London, 1839), p. 131.

6. Samuel Ward, *A Coale from the Altar, to Kindle the Holy Fire of Zeale* (London, 1616); John Bruce, ed., *CSPD 1633–1634* (London, 1863), p. 450, no. 17.

7. Robert Baillie, *The Unlawfulnesse and Danger of Limited Episcopacie* (London, 1641), pp. 22–23.

8. "A proper newe Ballet called The Summons to Newe England to the Tune of the Townsman Capp," Tanner Mss, 306 (fols. 286, 287), Bodleian Library, Oxford, printed in C. H. Firth, ed., *An American Garland, being a Collection of Ballads Relating to America, 1563–1759* (Oxford: B. H. Blackwell, 1915), pp. 29–30.

9. Kammen, *People of Paradox*, p. 140; Van Dyken, *Willard*, p. 123.

10. Larzer Ziff, *The Career of John Cotton: Puritanism and the American Experience* (Princeton, N.J.: Princeton University Press, 1962), chaps. 2 and 3; Perry Miller, " 'Preparation for Salvation' in Seventeenth-Century New England" (1943), reprinted in his *Nature's Nation* (Cambridge, Mass.: Harvard University Press, 1967), pp. 50–77; David D. Hall, ed., *The Antinomian Controversy, 1636–1638: A Documentary History* (Middletown, Conn.: Wesleyan University Press, 1968), Introduction, and John Cotton's correspondence with the elders, pp. 24–149; Norman Pettit, *The Heart Prepared: Grace and Conversion in Spiritual Life* (New Haven: Yale University Press, 1966), chap. 5, and see pp. 131–133; Everett H. Emerson, *John Cotton* (New York: Twayne Publishers, 1965), chaps. 3 and 5.

11. Hall, ed., *Antinomian Controversy*, p. 85.

12. Ibid., p. 88; Robert Baillie, *A Dissuasive Against the Errours of the Time* (London, 1645), pp. 55, 56.

13. See Chapter 1, and John Cotton, *Gods Promise to His Plantation* (London, 1630).

14. Edward Johnson, *Good News from New-England* (London, 1648), p. 17; William Hubbard, *A General History of New England from the Discovery to MDCLXXX*, in MHS *Collections*, 2d ser. (1815), V, pt. 1, p. 180; Hall, ed., *Antinomian Controversy*, pp. 13–16.

15. Shepard, *God's Plot*, p. 65.

16. Emery Battis, *Saints and Sectaries: Anne Hutchinson and the Antinomian Controversy in the Massachusetts Bay Colony* (Chapel Hill: University of North Carolina Press, 1962), pp. 44–45 and passim.

17. Shepard, *God's Plot*, p. 42, n. 14; Stephen Denison, *The White Wolfe, or a Sermon Preached at Pauls Crosse* (London, 1627), p. 39; Edmund S. Morgan, *The Puritan Dilemma: The Story of John Winthrop* (Boston, Mass.: Little, Brown, 1958), p. 146; *Winthrop's Journal, 1630–1649*, ed. J. K. Hosmer (New York: Charles Scribner's Sons, 1908), I, 219.

18. John Winthrop, *A Short Story of the Rise, reign, and ruine of the Antinomians* (London, 1645), in Hall, ed., *Antinomian Controversy*, pp. 201–310. See Hall's headnote, ibid., pp. 199–200. For the above material, see ibid., pp. 271–273. "The Examination of Mrs. Anne Hutchinson at the Court at Newtowne," ibid., pp. 336–337.

19. Ibid., pp. 322–323, 338–339; Winthrop, *Short Story*, pp. 263–264.

20. *Winthrop's Journal*, I, 195; Winthrop, *Short Story*, pp. 263, 273–274; *Johnson's Wonder-Working Providence, 1628–1651*, ed. J. F. Jameson (New York: Charles Scribner's Sons, 1910), p. 124; Ephraim Pagitt, *Heresiography*,

or a Description of the Heretickes and Sectaries Sprang up in these Latter Times (London, 1661), p. 124; Samuel Rutherford, *A Survey of the Spirituall Antichrist* (London, 1648), pt. 1, pp. 171, 176.

21. Battis, *Saints and Sectaries*, chap. 6; Morgan, *Puritan Dilemma*, p. 138; Ziff, *Cotton*, pp. 116–117.

22. John Cotton, *The Way of Congregational Churches Cleared* (London, 1648), in Hall, ed., *Antinomian Controversy*, pp. 412–413.

23. Ibid., p. 413; Shepard, *God's Plot*, p. 65; Winthrop, *Short Story*, pp. 274, 205, 263, 264; *Winthrop's Journal*, I, 195, 206.

24. For Edward Johnson's impressions of a "naked Christ," see *Wonder-Working Providence*, pp. 134–135; "Mr. Cottons Rejoynder," in Hall, ed., *Antinomian Controversy*, p. 85; William Walwyn, *The Power of Love* (London,1643), p. 20.

25. No. 5 of the "Unsavoury speeches confuted," in Winthrop, *Short Story*, p. 246.

26. Shepard, *God's Plot*, p. 65; Battis, *Saints and Sectaries*, pp. 154, 156; [?] to John Winthrop, ca. May 1637, in *Winthrop Papers*, (Boston, Mass.: MHS, 1943), III, 403.

27. Battis, *Saints and Sectaries*, pp. 113–114; *Winthrop's Journal*, I, 196–197 n.; Bernard Nutter, *The Story of the Cambridge Baptists* (Cambridge: W. Heffer and Sons, 1912), p. 25; Robert Barclay, *The Inner Life of the Religious Societies of the Commonwealth* (London, 1876), p. 219 and note.

28. Battis, *Saints and Sectaries*, p. 57; *Winthrop's Journal*, I, 196–197 n.; John Wheelwright, *His Writings . . . and a Memoir by Charles H. Bell* (Boston, 1876), pp. 6–7.

29. Battis, *Saints and Sectaries*, pp. 122–124; Darrett B. Rutman, *Winthrop's Boston: A Portrait of a Puritan Town, 1630–1649* (Chapel Hill: University of North Carolina Press, 1965), p. 119.

30. Battis, *Saints and Sectaries*, pp. 141–142.

31. John Wheelwright, *A Fast-Day Sermon*, in Hall, ed., *Antinomian Controversy*, pp. 152–172, passim, but esp. pp. 158–160, 163–165.

32. Winthrop, *Short Story*, pp. 210–211, 248, 252–254; Shepard, *God's Plot*, p. 66; Wheelwright, *Writings*, "Memoir," p. 28; Ziff, *Cotton*, p. 125; Hall, *Faithful Shepherd*, pp. 161–162.

33. *Winthrop's Journal*, I, 211, 215; *The Hutchinson Papers*, Prince Society Publications (Albany, N.Y., 1865), I, 72–78; Winthrop, *Short Story*, pp. 249–250, 277–278.

34. *Hutchinson Papers*, I, 79, n. 78, 79–83, 96–113; *Winthrop Papers*, III, 460–461, 506; Winthrop, *Short Story*, pp. 250–251; *Winthrop's Journal*, I, 219, 229.

35. Shepard, *God's Plot*, p. 66; *Winthrop Papers*, III, 499 n.; Ziff, *Cotton*, p. 134.

36. Winthrop, *Short Story*, p. 251; *Winthrop Papers*, III, 506; *Winthrop's Journal*, I, 197 n.; Battis, *Saints and Sectaries*, p. 261.

37. "Examination," in Hall, ed., *Antinomian Controversy*, pp. 336–337; Winthrop, *Short Story*, p. 275.

38. "Examination," in Hall, ed., *Antinomian Controversy,* p. 337.

39. Winthrop, *Short Story,* pp. 230, 274; "Examination," in Hall, ed., *Antinomian Controversy,* p. 341.

40. Ibid., pp. 342, 344.

41. Winthrop, *Short Story,* p. 274.

42. N. B. Shurtleff, ed., *Records of the Governor and Company of the Massachusetts Bay Colony* (Boston, Mass., 1853), I, 207, 211; *Winthrop's Journal,* I, 241 n.

43. Winthrop, *Short Story,* p. 279; *Winthrop Papers,* IV, 121–122; Shepard, *Parable of the Ten Virgins,* p. 167.

44. *Winthrop's Journal,* I, 205.

45. Bernard Bailyn, *The New England Merchants in the Seventeenth Century* (Cambridge, Mass.: Harvard University Press, 1955), p. 40; Battis, *Saints and Sectaries,* pp. 268–269, 274.

46. "A Report of the Trial of Mrs. Hutchinson before the Church in Boston," in Hall, ed., *Antinomian Controversy,* pp. 380, 362.

47. *Johnson's Wonder-Working Providence,* pp. 128, 127.

48. Ibid., pp. 127–128; Winthrop, *Short Story,* p. 208; *Winthrop Papers,* IV, 10–11.

49. Winthrop, *Short Story,* p. 279.

50. For a defense of Winthrop along these lines, see Morgan, *Puritan Dilemma,* chap. 10.

51. *Winthrop Papers,* IV, 414–415, 449–450.

52. Ibid., pp. 449–450.

53. Quoted in Hall, ed., *Antinomian Controversy,* p. 423 n.

54. Winthrop, *Short Story,* pp. 201–310.

55. *Mercurius Americanus, Mr. Welds his Antitype, or, Massachusetts great Apologie examined* (London, 1645), p. 3. The Prince Society has reprinted *Mercurius Americanus* in Wheelwright, *Writings,* pp. 181–228.

56. Ibid., p. 221.

57. *Mercurius Americanus* (1645), pp. 19–23.

58. Ibid., pp. 7–8, 4–5.

59. Ibid., p. 8.

60. "The Answer of me John Pratt," in MHS *Collections,* 2d ser. (Boston, 1818), VII, 123; "A Brief Answer to a Certain Declaration," in *Hutchinson Papers,* I, 93–94; *Winthrop's Journal,* I, 220 n.

61. Ziff, *Cotton,* pp. 118–119; Cotton, *The Way of Congregational Churches Cleared,* in Hall, ed., *Antinomian Controversy,* pp. 414–415. Robert Baillie, staunch Scottish Puritan and enemy of Independency, claimed that Cotton had asked Roger Williams to secure for him and Henry Vane a piece of land outside Massachusetts's jurisdiction where they and their people might "retire and live according to their own mind." Baillie, *A Dissuasive against the Errours,* p. 63.

62. Winthrop, *Short Story,* pp. 278–279; Cotton, *The Way,* pp. 400, 422–423.

5. *New England Enthusiasts and the English Civil War*

1. John Winthrop, *A Short Story of the Rise, reign, and ruine of the Anti-nomians* (London, 1645), in D. D. Hall, ed., *The Antinomian Controversy, 1636–1638: A Documentary History* (Middletown, Conn.: Wesleyan University Press, 1968), pp. 214–217, 279–280; *Winthrop's Journal, 1630–1649*, ed. J. K. Hosmer (New York: Charles Scribner's Sons, 1908), I, 266–268.

2. Thomas Weld, Preface to Winthrop's *Short Story*, in Hall, ed., *Antinomian Controversy*, p. 218; Emery Battis, *Saints and Sectaries: Anne Hutchinson and the Antinomian Controversy in the Massachusetts Bay Colony* (Chapel Hill: University of North Carolina Press, 1962), p. 271.

3. *Winthrop's Journal*, I, 284, 297; ibid., II, 41; Robert Baillie, *A Dissuasive from the Errours of the Time* (London, 1645), quoted in H. M. Chapin, ed., *Documentary History of Rhode Island* (Providence, R.I.: Preston and Rounds Co., 1919), II, p. 60; Thomas Lechford, *Plain Dealing: or Newes from New-England* (London, 1642), p. 41.

4. Weld, "Preface," p. 218; Battis, *Saints and Sectaries*, p. 248.

5. Nathaniel Ward, *The Simple Cobler of Aggawam* (London, 1647), p. 3.

6. Cotton Mather, *Magnalia Christi Americana* (London, 1702), bk. 7, pp. 20–21; Ward, *Cobler*, p. 3; Berkeley to Tom Prior, Newport, R.I., April 24, 1729, in A. A. Luce and T. E. Jessop, eds., *The Works of George Berkeley* (London: Thomas Nelson and Sons, 1956), VIII, 196.

7. Quoted in C. F. Pascoe, *Two Hundred Years of the S.P.G. . . . 1701–1900* (London: SPG, 1901), p. 45.

8. T. H. Breen, ed., "George Donne's 'Virginia Reviewed': A 1638 Plan to Reform Colonial Society," *William and Mary Quarterly*, 3d ser., 30, no. 3 (July 1973), 464–465, 463.

9. For English use of the Antinomian Controversy and Winthrop's *Short Story*, see Robert Baillie, *The Unlawfulnesse and Danger of Limited Episcopacie* (London, 1641), p. 28; Baillie, *A Dissuasive*, passim; *A Brief Narration of the Practices of the Churches of New-England* (London, 1645), p. 18; Thomas Edwards, *Gangraena; or a Catalogue and Discovery of Many of the Errours, Heresies, Blasphemies . . . of the Sectaries* (London, 1646), pp. 3, 11, 147–148; Ephraim Pagitt, *Heresiography, or a Description of the Heretickes and Sectaries Sprang up in these Latter Times* (London, 1661), pp. 124–126, 131, 133–135, 99–100; Samuel Rutherford, *A Survey of the Spirituall Antichrist* (London, 1648), pt. 2, pp. 171–193, 209, 220; William Rathband, *A Briefe Narration of Some Church Courses . . . in New England* (London, 1644), pp. 51–54, 24 n., 40 n.; Thomas Weld, *An Answer to W. R. His Narration* (London, 1644), pp. 4, 12, 60–63, 66, 67.

10. Perry Miller, *Orthodoxy in Massachusetts, 1630–1650* (Cambridge, Mass.: Harvard University Press, 1933), chap. 4.

11. *The Anatomy of the Separatists, alias Brownists* (London, 1642), pp. 1, 3; Edwards, *Gangraena*, pp. 147–148.

12. For Samuel Eaton, see *The Brownists Conventicle: Or an Assemble of Brownists, Separatists, and Non-conformists* (n.p., 1641), pp. 3–4, 5–6.

13. *Winthrop's Journal*, I, 160 and note, 203–204.

14. Hall, ed., *Antinomian Controversy*, pp. 380, 382–383.

15. *Winthrop's Journal*, II, 23–24, 168–169, 178.

16. Ibid., pp. 25, 31–32.

17. See Chapter 4. *Somers Tracts*, ed. Walter Scott, 2nd ed. (London, 1812), VII, 110 n.

18. Clement Walker, *Anarchia Anglicana: or The History of Independencie*, pt. 2 (London, 1649), p. 26. For Vane's political career, see Violet A. Rowe, *Sir Henry Vane the Younger: A Study in Political and Administrative History* (London: University of London Press, 1970), and J. H. Adamson and H. F. Folland, *Sir Harry Vane: His Life and Times (1613–1662)* (Boston, Mass.: Gambit, Inc., 1973).

19. N. H. Keeble, ed., *Autobiography of Richard Baxter*, abridged by J. M. Lloyd Thomas (London: J. M. Dent and Son, 1974), p. 73. Clarendon's comments are quoted in Susie I. Tucker, *Enthusiasm: A Study in Semantic Change* (Cambridge: Cambridge University Press, 1972), pp. 22–23; *Bishop Burnet's History of His Own Time* (London, 1857), p. 108; Rowe, *Vane*, p. 202; Battis, *Saints and Sectaries*, p. 269.

20. For Aspinwall's early years in Boston, see the Introduction to *Aspinwall Notorial Records* (Boston, Mass.: Boston Records Commission, 1903), V, 32.

21. Winthrop, *Short Story*, pp. 259–261.

22. Aspinwall, Introduction; Chapin, ed., *Documentary History*, II, 50, 51, 56; J. R. Bartlett, ed., *Rhode Island Colony Records* (Providence, R.I., 1856), I, 66.

23. William Aspinwall, *Certaine Queries of the Ordination of Ministers* (London, 1647), pp. 42, 21, 23, 26–27, 34, 36.

24. Samuel Gorton, *Simplicities Defence against Seven-Headed Policy* (London, 1646), reprinted in Rhode Island Historical Society *Collections* (1835), II, 46.

25. Nathaniel Morton, *New Englands Memoriall* (Cambridge, 1669), pp. 108–109.

26. W. Noël Sainsbury, ed., *CSPC 1574–1660* (London, 1860), p. 112; American Antiquarian Society (AAS) *Transactions and Collections* (1857), III, cxv–cxvi; William Coddington to John Winthrop, Dec. 9, 1639, in *Winthrop Papers* (Boston, Mass.: MHS, 1944), IV, 161; Edward Winslow, *Hypocrisie Unmasked: Being a True Relation of the Proceedings of the Governour and Company of the Massachusetts Against Samuel Gorton of Rhode Island* (London, 1646; reprinted New York, 1968), p. viii.

27. Ibid.; *Rhode Island Records*, I, 112.

28. Lechford, *Plain Dealing*, p. 41; Morton, *Memoriall*, pp. 108–109. For comment at the whipping post, see Charles Dean, *Some Notices of Samuel Gorton* (Boston, Mass., 1850), p. 39.

29. Thomas Hutchinson, *History of the Colony and Province of Massachusetts-Bay*, ed. L. S. Mayo (Cambridge, Mass.: Harvard University Press, 1936), I, 102.

30. Roger Williams to John Winthrop (1640), in Edward Winslow, *The Danger of Tolerating Levellers in a Civil State* (London, 1649), pp. 55–56, 59–61; *Winthrop's Journal*, II, 53–54, 81.

31. *CSPC 1574–1660*, p. 326; Winslow, *Hypocrisie Unmasked*, p. viii.

32. *Winthrop's Journal*, II, 53–54, 81; Edward Johnson, *Good News from New-England* (London, 1648), p. 13.

33. N. B. Shurtleff, ed., *Records of the Governor and Company of the Massachusetts Bay* (Boston, 1853), II, 41, 46; *Rhode Island Records*, II, 128–129.

34. *Winthrop's Journal*, II, 81.

35. Ibid., pp. 144–145, 147.

36. Winslow, *The Danger*, p. 78; Morton, *Memoriall*, p. 110; Mather, *Magnalia*, bk. 7, p. 12.

37. *Winthrop's Journal*, II, 149; Winslow, *The Danger*, p. 50; *Johnson's Wonder-Working Providence, 1628–1651*, ed. J. F. Jameson (New York: Charles Scribner's Sons, 1910), p. 224; Morton, *Memoriall*, pp. 109–110.

38. Ibid., p. 110; *Winthrop's Journal*, II, 147; *Hutchinson Papers*, in MHS *Collections*, 3d ser. (Boston, 1825; reprinted 1846), I, 12.

39. *Winthrop's Journal*, II, 146, 147; *Ecclesiastical History of Massachusetts*, in MHS *Collections*, 1st ser. (Boston, 1804), IX, 37.

40. *Winthrop's Journal*, II, 149; Shurtleff, ed., *Records of Massachusetts Bay*, II, 51–52. For a detailed account of Gorton's trial and punishment, see Robert Emmet Wall, Jr., *Massachusetts Bay: The Crucial Decade, 1640–1650* (New Haven: Yale University Press, 1972), pp. 134–145.

41. *Winthrop's Journal*, II, 160; *Winthrop Papers*, IV, 439.

42. Battis, *Saints and Sectaries*, pp. 113–114; James Culross, *Hanserd Knollys* (London, 1895), pp. 28–29; *Winthrop's Journal*, I, 295–296, 328.

43. Ibid., p. 309; Culross, *Knollys*, p. 29; Hugh Peter to John Winthrop, Sept. 6, 1639, in *Winthrop Papers*, IV, 140; John Underhill to John Winthrop, Oct. 12, 1639, ibid., pp. 143–144, 179, 229; Knollys to Winthrop, Feb. 21, 1640, ibid., p. 177.

44. *Winthrop's Journal*, I, 275.

45. Ibid., p. 328; ibid., II, 27–28; *Winthrop Papers*, IV, 317–319; Hutchinson, *History*, I, 94–95.

46. *Winthrop's Journal*, I, 276, 277; ibid., II, 28, 88–89.

47. Gorton, *Simplicities Defence*, passim; Edward Winslow, *New-Englands Salamander Discovered By an Irreligious and Scornful Pamphlet* (London, 1643), p. 22; William Bradford, *Of Plymouth Plantation, 1620–1647*, ed. S. E. Morison (New York: Modern Library, 1967), pp. 346–347; *Winthrop Papers*, V, 87; Winslow, *Hypocrisie Unmasked*.

48. John Winthrop, *The History of New England from 1630 to 1649*, ed. James Savage (Boston, 1826; reprinted New York, 1972), II, 58; Samuel Gorton, *An Incorruptible Key, Composed of the CX Psalme* (London, 1647), "To the Reader"; Lewis G. Janes, *Samuel Gorton* (Providence, R.I., 1896), p. 94.

49. Ibid.; Gorton, *Simplicities Defence*, "Epistle."

50. *Winthrop's Journal*, II, 282–283, 292–293.

51. See Gorton's answer to Nathaniel Morton's *Memoriall* in Peter Force,

ed., *Tracts and Other Papers Relating Principally to the Colonies in North America* (Washington, D.C., 1846), IV, 14–15; Hutchinson, *History*, I, 456–457. For Gorton's career in England, see Wall, *Crucial Decade*, pp. 154–155, 210, and esp. Philip F. Gura, "The Radical Ideology of Samuel Gorton: New Light on the Relation of English to American Puritanism," *William and Mary Quarterly*, 3d ser., 36 (Jan. 1979), 78–100.

52. Samuel Gorton, *An Antidote against the Common Plague of the World* (London, 1657), pp. 284, 273–276.

53. *A Journal of the Life, Travels . . . of William Edmundson* (Dublin, 1715), p. 66; *The Truth Exalted in the Writings of John Burnyeat* (London, 1691), p. 53.

54. Gorton, *Antidote*, p. 284.

55. Gorton, *Simplicities Defence*, p. 100; Samuel Gorton, *Saltmarsh Returned from the Dead* (London, 1655), p. 198.

56. Hanserd Knollys, *Christ Exalted: A Lost Sinner Sought, and Saved by Christ* (London, 1646), pp. 6, 12, 13–14; William Haller, *Liberty and Reformation in the Puritan Revolution* (New York: Columbia University Press, 1955), p. 204; Thomas Goodwin, *A Glimpse of Syons Glory* (London, 1641), pp. 4, 8. See also A. S. P. Woodhouse, ed., *Puritanism and Liberty, Being the Army Debates (1647–9)* (Chicago: University of Chicago Press, 1951), p. 234.

57. Edwards, *Gangraena*, pt. 1, pp. 97–98, 184; Robert Barclay, *The Inner Life of the Religious Societies of the Commonwealth* (London, 1876), pp. 289–290.

58. *For the Son of Man is Come to Seek and to Save* (1646), published with *Christ Exalted*, p. 23.

59. Rufus Jones, *Studies in Mystical Religion* (London: Macmillan, 1909), pp. 423–425.

60. *Gangraena*, pt. 1, pp. 95, 98. Knollys's statement about anointing the sick is in Barclay, *Inner Life*, p. 219 and note. Culross, *Knollys*, pp. 30–31; Haller, *Liberty and Reformation*, p. 204; William G. McLoughlin, *New England Dissent, 1630–1833: The Baptists and the Separation of Church and State* (Cambridge, Mass.: Harvard University Press, 1971), I, 5.

61. See B. S. Capp, *The Fifth Monarchy Men* (London: Faber and Faber, 1972), for an excellent description of Fifth Monarchists' ideas and activities.

62. William Aspinwall, *An Explication and Application of the Seventh Chapter of Daniel* (London, 1654), title page and pp. 32–33, 36.

63. William Aspinwall, *The Work of the Age: Or The sealed Prophecies of Daniel opened and applied* (London, 1655), pp. 46–47.

64. Aspinwall, *An Explication*, p. 29.

65. Capp, *Fifth Monarchy*, p. 185; P. M. Rattansi, "Paracelsus and the Puritan Revolution," *Ambix*, 11 (Feb. 1963), 25–26; Wayne Shumaker, *The Occult Sciences in the Renaissance* (Berkeley: University of California Press, 1972), p. 182. For Jacob Boehme, see *The Way to Christ*, trans. with an introduction by Peter Erb (New York: The Paulist Press, 1978), p. 8; Christopher Hill, *The World Turned Upside Down* (London: Temple Smith, 1972), p. 141; Keith Thomas, *Religion and the Decline of Magic* (London: Weidenfeld and Nicolson, 1971), pp. 375–376.

66. William Aspinwall, *A Premonition of Sundry Sad Calamities Yet to Come* (London, 1655), pp. 8, 23, 37–39.

67. *Winthrop's Journal,* I, 323; George Lee Haskins, *Law and Authority in Early Massachusetts* (New York: Macmillan, 1960), pp. 125–126; Isabel M. Calder, *The New Haven Colony* (New Haven: Yale University Press, 1934), p. 106.

68. *Hutchinson Papers,* I, 181–182; Haskins, *Law and Authority,* p. 265, n. 63; Capp, *Fifth Monarchy,* p. 170.

69. William Aspinwall, *An Abstract of Laws and Government,* MHS *Collections,* 1st ser. (1798; reprinted 1835), V, 187–188; Aspinwall, *Premonition,* p. 39.

70. London, 1656.

71. MHS *Collections,* 1st ser., V, 188–192; Capp, *Fifth Monarchy,* pp. 157, 162–164; Haskins, *Law and Authority,* p. 125.

72. Capp, *Fifth Monarchy,* p. 170.

73. William Aspinwall, *The Legislative Power is Christ's Peculiar Prerogative* (London, 1656), sig. A2.

74. Thomas Venner's activities in Salem and Boston are traceable from the following: *Historical Collections of the Essex Institute,* (Salem, Mass., 1859–1869), IX, 51, 121; ibid. (1859), I, 39; ibid. (1865), VII, 18, 185, 186, 274; ibid. (1863), V, 266; James Savage, *A Genealogical Dictionary of the First Settlers of New England* (Boston, 1860–1862; reprinted 1965), IV, 369; Joseph Felt, *Annals of Salem* (Salem, Mass., 1849), II, 577; Zachariah G. Whitman, *Historical Sketch of the Ancient and Honourable Artillery Company* (Boston, 1820), p. 155; Shurtleff, ed., *Records of Massachusetts Bay,* II, 250–251; ibid., III, 252; *Ninth Report of Record Commissioners* (Boston, 1883), pp. 18–19, 31. See also Charles Edward Banks, "Thomas Venner, the Boston Wine-Cooper and Fifth Monarchy Man," *New England Historical and Genealogical Register, 1893* (Boston, 1893), XLVII, 439.

75. [White Kennett], *A Register and Chronicle* (London, 1728), I, 355–356.

76. Cotton Mather, *Magnalia Christi Americana,* bks. 1 and 2, ed. K. B. Murdock (Cambridge, Mass.: Harvard University Press, 1977), p. 409 n.; Williams to John Cotton of Plymouth, Providence, R.I., March 25, 1671, in Perry Miller, *Roger Williams* (Indianapolis: Bobbs–Merrill, 1953), pp. 238–239.

77. See the excellent biography by Raymond P. Stearns, *The Strenuous Puritan: Hugh Peter, 1598–1660* (Urbana: University of Illinois Press, 1954).

78. Giles Fermin to John Winthrop, Colchester, July 1, 1646, in *Winthrop Papers,* V, 89. See also Peter's letters to John Winthrop and John Winthrop, Jr., ibid., pp. 146–147, 102. Edwards, *Gangraena,* p. 98.

79. Ibid., p. 183; Haller, *Liberty and Reformation,* p. 210.

80. Quoted in R. P. Stearns, "The Weld-Peter Mission to England," in Colonial Society of Massachusetts *Publications* (Boston, 1937), XXXII, 213.

81. *Burnet's History,* p. 106; Edwards, *Gangraena,* pp. 98–100, 182–183; John Lilburne, *Legal Fundamental Liberties* (1649), in Woodhouse, ed., *Puritanism and Liberty,* p. 344.

82. *Burnet's History,* p. 106; quotations from Stearns, *Strenuous Puritan,* p. 330.

83. Capp, *Fifth Monarchy,* p. 93; Edwards, *Gangraena,* pp. 98–99.

84. *Burnet's History,* p. 108 n.; Rowe, *Henry Vane,* p. 202.

85. Ibid., pp. 206–207, 223–224; Geoffrey F. Nuttall, "James Nayler: A Fresh Approach," *Journal of the Friends Historical Society,* supplement 26 (Spring 1954), 11–12.

86. *Diary of the Rev. John Ward, 1648–1679,* ed. Charles Severn (London, 1839), p. 151; Rowe, *Henry Vane,* p. 202; Nuttall, "Nayler," pp. 11–12; Battis, *Saints and Sectaries,* p. 269.

87. Kennett, *Register,* I, 384; Capp, *Fifth Monarchy,* p. 119.

88. *Collection of State Papers of Thomas Thurloe* (London, 1742), V, 197, 220.

89. William Hooke to John Winthrop, Jr., April 13, 1657, MHS *Collections,* 3d ser. (1825; reprinted 1846), I, 184; Capp, *Fifth Monarchy,* pp. 117–119; Michael R. Watts, *The Dissenters: From the Reformation to the French Revolution* (Oxford: Oxford University Press, 1978), pp. 222–223.

90. Ephraim Pagitt, *Heresiography* (London, 1662), pp. 282–288; Kennett, *Register,* I, 354–356.

91. Clement Walker, *Anarchia Anglicana,* pt. 4 (London, 1660), pp. 115–116; Felt, *Ecclesiastical History,* I, 434; Stearns, "Weld-Peter Mission," p. 213; *Burnet's History,* p. 106.

92. Adamson and Folland, *Harry Vane,* p. 424; *Burnet's History,* pp. 106, 107, and note; Stearns, *Strenuous Puritan,* p. 425.

93. Edwards, *Gangraena,* pp. 288–290; Kennett, *Register,* I, 355–356, 362, 384, 711; *The Last Speech and Prayer with other Passages of Thomas Venner* (London, 1660), pp. 1–8; *Somers Tracts,* VII, 47, 469–472; Rowe, *Henry Vane,* p. 239.

94. Venner, *Last Speech,* p. 8; Edwards, *Gangraena,* pp. 288, 290–291; Kennett, *Register,* I, 362, 363; *Somers Tracts,* VII, 636; "Diary of John Hull," in AAS *Trans. and Coll.* (1857), III, 200–201.

95. Kennett, *Register,* I, 363; *Somers Tracts,* VII, 47.

96. Quoted in John G. Palfrey, *History of New England* (Boston, 1875), IV, 65.

97. Mary A. E. Green, ed., *CSPD 1660–1661* (London, 1860), pp. 470–471; Champlin Burrage, *The Early English Dissenters* (Cambridge: Cambridge University Press, 1912), I, 353; MHS *Collections,* 3d ser. (1830), II, 354–355.

98. John Eliot, *The Christian Commonwealth* (London, [1659]), Preface and pp. 3–4 5–6, 35; Capp, *Fifth Monarchy,* pp. 51, 140, 170.

99. "Diary of John Hull," pp. 200–201; Palfrey, *History,* II, 511; Ola Elizabeth Winslow, *John Eliot, "Apostle to the Indians"* (Boston: Houghton Mifflin, 1968), p. 197.

100. Kennett, *Register,* I, 356, 711, 709; *Burnet's History,* p. 108 and note; *Diary of John Ward,* pp. 173–174.

6. Quakers of the First Generation

1. For the origins of Quakerism, see Hugh Barbour, *The Quakers in Puritan England* (New Haven: Yale University Press, 1964), passim, esp. p. 28 and note; Richard Baxter, *The Quaker Catechism, or the Quakers Questioned* (London, 1655); *The Truth Exalted in the Writings . . . of John Burnyeat* (London, 1691), pp. 202, 203; Charles Severn, ed., *Diary of the Rev. John Ward, 1648–1679* (London, 1839), p. 141; Kenneth L. Carroll, "Early Quakers and 'Going Naked as a Sign,' " *Quaker History*, 67, no. 2 (Autumn 1978), 69, 72; Rufus M. Jones, *Studies in Mystical Religion* (London: Macmillan, 1909), p. 465; R. A. Knox, *Enthusiasm: A Chapter in the History of Religion* (New York: Oxford University Press, 1950), pp. 174, 175; Christopher Hill, *Milton and the English Revolution* (London: Faber and Faber, 1977), p. 95.

2. There are several editions of Fox's journal: George Fox, *Journal* (London, 1694), p. 220; Norman Penney, ed., *The Journal of George Fox* (Cambridge: Cambridge University Press, 1911); J. L. Nickalls, ed., *The Journal of George Fox* (Cambridge: Cambridge University Press, 1952), p. 7; *The Journal of George Fox* (London, 1852), I, 55–56; Rufus M. Jones, ed., *The Journal of George Fox* (New York: Capricorn Books, 1963), pp. 101–102, 103. See, too, Geoffrey F. Nuttall, *The Holy Spirit in Puritan Faith and Experience* (Oxford: B. Blackwell, 1946), p. 52.

3. Thomas Weld et al., *The Perfect Pharise . . . in the Generation of Men called Quakers* (London, 1654), unpaginated; Jones, ed., *Journal of George Fox,* pp. 88–89; Richard Blome, "Questions Propounded to George Whitehead and George Fox &c.," in *The Quaker Disarm'd or a True Relation of a Late Publick Dispute held at Cambridge* (London, 1659), unpaginated. See nos. 34, 45.

4. Roger Williams, *George Fox Digg'd out of his Burrowes* (Boston, 1676), pp. 3, 19; Ephraim Pagitt, *Heresiography, Or a Description of the Heretickes and Sectaries* (London, 1661), p. 259; John Norton, *The Heart of N—— England Rent at the Blasphemies of the Present Generation* (Cambridge [New England], 1659), pp. 1–2.

5. Quoted in Geoffrey F. Nuttall, *Studies in Christian Enthusiasm: Illustrated in Early Quakerism* (Wallingford, Pa.: Pendle Hill, 1948), pp. 53, 59–61. See, too, Weld et al., *Perfect Pharise,* under "Their practises."

6. Fox, *Journal* (1694), p. 220; Nuttall, *Christian Enthusiasm,* pp. 86–87.

7. N. H. Keeble, ed., *The Autobiography of Richard Baxter,* abridged by J. M. Lloyd Thomas (London: J. M. Dent and Sons, 1974), p. 73; Jones, *Mystical Religion,* pp. 466–467, 475, 479–480; Nuttall, *Christian Enthusiasm,* pp. 85–87; Michael R. Watts, *The Dissenters: From the Reformation to the French Revolution* (Oxford: Clarendon Press, 1978), pp. 181–183.

8. For Fox's difficulties with Ranters, see *Journal* (1694), pp. 29–30, 57–58, 130, 131, 152, 320.

9. Ibid., p. 320; Norman Cohn, "The Ranters: The 'Underground' in the England of 1650," *Encounter,* 34, no. 4 (April 1970), 7.

10. Fox, *Journal* (1694), pp. 211, 247–248, 229–230, 231; Jones, ed., *Journal of George Fox*, pp. 368–369.

11. Fox, *Journal* (1694), pp. 247–248.

12. For Ranters in America and the fear of Fifth Monarchists, see Chapter 7.

13. George Fox and William Loddington, *Plantation Work, the Work of this Generation* (London, 1682), unpaginated; William Dewsbury, *The Work of the Lord to Sion in the New Jerusalem* (London, 1664), pp. 5–7; Rufus M. Jones, *Quakers in the American Colonies* (London: Macmillan, 1911), pp. xiv, 444.

14. Ibid.; Josiah Coale, "The First Epistle to Friends in New England," in *The Books and Divers Epistles . . . of Josiah Coale* (n.p., 1671), p. 51; Fox and Loddington, *Plantation Work*.

15. "To the Parliament of the Commonwealth of England," in John Rous et al., *New-England a Degenerate Plant* (London, 1659), p. 2.

16. George Bishop, *New-England Judged, Not by Man's, but the Spirit of the Lord* (London, 1661), pp. 8, 12, 26–27, 35.

17. Cotton Mather, *Magnalia Christi Americana*, bks. 1 and 2, ed. K. B. Murdock (Cambridge, Mass.: Harvard University Press, 1977), p. 143; William Bray, ed., *Diary of John Evelyn* (London: G. Routledge [1906?]), II, 86; *The Fanatick History: or an Exact Relation and Account of the Old Anabaptists and New Quakers* (London, 1660), pp. 66–67, 198.

18. Blome, "Questions Propounded"; Fox, *Journal* (1694), pp. 218, 220.

19. Norton, N—— *England Rent*, pp. 5, 41–43. For the Antinomian Controversy, see Chapter 4; for harassment of Baptists, see Chapter 3.

20. Francis Howgill, *The Popish Inquisition Newly Erected in New-England* (1659), in *The Dawnings of the Gospel-Day* ([London], 1676), p. 257; "Resolve of the Commissioners of the United Colonies of New England Concerning the Quakers," in W. K. Kavenagh, ed., *Foundations of the American Colonies: A Documentary History* (New York: Chelsea House, 1973), I, 502; Merrill Jensen, ed., *English Historical Documents*, vol. 9, *American Colonial Documents to 1776* (London: Eyre and Spottiswoode, 1955), pp. 527–528; "Petition from Massachusetts General Court," Feb. 11, 1661, in W. Noël Sainsbury, ed., *CSPC 1661–1668* (London, 1880), no. 26, pp. 8–10.

21. David Pulsiver, ed., *Records of Plymouth Colony* (Boston, 1855), III, 130; J. R. Bartlett, ed., *Rhode Island Colony Records* (Providence, R.I., 1856), I, 377; C. J. Hoadly, ed., *Records of the Colony . . . of New Haven*, vol. 2, *1653–1665* (Hartford, Conn., 1858), p. 292.

22. Williams, *George Fox Digg'd*, pp. 73, 163–164.

23. Isaac Backus, *A History of New England* (Newton, Mass., 1871; reprinted New York, 1969), I, 370. For Fox's rejoinder, see note 67.

24. *The Danger of Enthusiasm Discovered, in an Epistle to the Quakers* (London, 1674), p. 97; Blome, "Questions Propounded," in *Quaker Disarm'd*, nos. 16, 42, 50, 26, 27, 29, 30, 53; W. Noël Sainsbury, ed., *CSPC 1574–1660* (London, 1860), p. 495.

25. *New-England a Degenerate Plant*, p. 16; Cotton Mather, *Magnalia* (Hartford, Conn., 1820), II, 452.

26. *New-England a Degenerate Plant,* p. 16; Nathaniel Morton, *New Englands Memoriall* (Cambridge, 1669), pp. 157–158; "Act for Suppressing the Quakers in Virginia," March 1660, in Kavenagh, ed., *Foundations,* III, 2272.

27. N. B. Shurtleff, ed., *Records of the Governor and Company of the Massachusetts Bay* (Boston, 1853), IV, pt. 2, pp. 2–4, 8, 19–20; *Records of Plymouth Colony,* x, 156–158, 181–182, 212; Jensen, ed., *English Historical Documents,* IX, 527–528; *New-England a Degenerate Plant,* p. 2.

28. "Act for Suppressing Quakers in Virginia," p. 2272; Thomas Jefferson, *Notes on the State of Virginia,* ed. William Peden (Chapel Hill: University of North Carolina Press, 1955), p. 157; *CSPC 1661–1668,* no. 402, p. 118.

29. Francis Howgill, *The Deceiver of the Nations Discovered* (1660), in *Dawnings of the Gospel-Day,* p. 378; Babette M. Levy, *Early Puritanism in the Southern and Island Colonies* (Worcester, Mass.: AAS, 1960), pp. 231–232.

30. *The American Historical Record,* ed. B. J. Lossing (Philadelphia, 1872), I, no. 1, pp. 4–8, 117–118; no. 2, p. 49; no. 7, pp. 289–290; no. 6, pp. 257–258. *Ecclesiastical Records of the State of New York* (Albany, N.Y., 1901), I, 409–410, 433; E. B. O'Callaghan, ed., *Documentary History of the State of New-York* (Albany, N.Y., 1850), III, 344, 1001–1003, 1007–1012; Michael Kammen, *Colonial New York, A History* (New York: Charles Scribner's Sons, 1975), p. 62.

31. J. H. Trumbull, ed., *Public Records of the Colony of Connecticut* (Hartford, Conn., 1850), I, 283, 284, 303, 308, 324; II, 87, 88; III, 280.

32. *Records of New Haven,* II, 217, 276, 363, 238–241; Isabel B. Calder, *The New Haven Colony* (New Haven: Yale University Press, 1934), pp. 95, 97.

33. Norton, *N—— England Rent,* pp. 25–26.

34. John Yeo to Most Reverend Father, Patuxant River in Maryland, May 25, 1676, in Tanner Mss, 114, f.79, Bodleian Library, Oxford. Yeo's letter is reprinted in W. H. Browne, ed., *Archives of Maryland* (Baltimore, 1887), V, 130–132.

35. Mather, *Magnalia* (1820), II, 451; Jones, *Quakers in the American Colonies,* pp. xix, xxxi.

36. Morton, *Memoriall,* p. 151; Barbour, *Quakers in Puritan England,* p. 60.

37. The Reverends Megapolensis and Dirsius to the Classis of Amsterdam, *Ecclesiastical Records of New York,* I, 409–410, 433.

38. *Rhode Island Records,* I, 375–377.

39. Ibid., pp. 376–381.

40. "The Diary of John Hull," in AAS *Transactions and Collections* (n.p., 1857), III, 182.

41. *New-England a Degenerate Plant,* p. 15; Nathaniel Bouton et al., eds., *Provincial and State Papers of New Hampshire* (Concord, N.H., 1867), I, 243–244; Philip A. Bruce, *Social Life in Old Virginia* (New York: Capricorn Books, 1965), p. 251.

42. Nuttall, *Christian Enthusiasm,* pp. 34, 35; Carroll, "Early Quakers and 'Going Naked as a Sign,'" p. 76.

43. For the Adamites, see *The Nest of Serpents* (n.p., n.d. [1640s?]), pp. 1–

6; Pagitt, *Heresiography*, 6th ed. (London, 1661), pp. 37, 117–120; *Religions Lotterie, or the Churches Amazement* (London, 1642), unpaginated; *A Short History of the Anabaptists in High and Low Germany* (London, 1642), pp. 42–43, 54; F. L. Cross, *The Oxford Dictionary of the Christian Church* (London: Oxford University Press, 1957), p. 16; *The New Schaff-Herzog Encyclopedia of Religious Knowledge* (New York: Funk and Wagnalls, 1908), s.v. "Adamites."

44. See Thomas Brown's accusations and evidence in John Symonds, *Thomas Brown and the Angels: A Study in Enthusiasm* (London: Hutchinson and Co., 1961), pp. 69, 114–117; *DNB*, s.v. "Lee, Mother Ann."

45. Edwin S. Gaustad, ed., *Baptist Piety: The Last Will and Testimony of Obadiah Holmes* (Grand Rapids, Mich.: Christian University Press, 1978), pp. 32, 143, n. 23.

46. Hill, *Milton*, p. 495.

47. Williams, *George Fox Digg'd*, p. 160.

48. Is. 20:2–5; Penney, ed., *Journal of George Fox*, II, 1–2, 373; William Simpson, *Going Naked, a Sign*, appended to *A Discovery of the Priests and Professors; and of Their Nakedness and Shame* (London, 1660), pp. 4, 7–8; Carroll, "Early Quakers and 'Going Naked as a Sign,'" p. 79.

49. Penney, ed., *Journal of George Fox*, II, 1–2, 428, n. 5; Barbour, *Quakers of Puritan England*, pp. 87, 234.

50. Penney, ed., *Journal of George Fox*, II, 90. For Fox's other comments on Quaker nudity, see ibid., I, 89, 355, 462; II, 373. M. A. E. Green, ed., *CSPD 1660–61* (London, 1860), p. 472.

51. Nuttall, *Christian Enthusiasm*, pp. 63–64.

52. Blome, "Questions Propounded."

53. Willem Sewel, *History of the Rise . . . of the Christian People Called Quakers* (London, 1722), excerpted in Jessamyn West, ed., *The Quaker Reader* (New York: Viking Press, 1969), p. 124.

54. Fox's *Journal*, ibid., p. 98; Nuttall, *Christian Enthusiasm*, p. 65.

55. George Bishop, *New-England Judged* (London, 1703), pp. 131–133; Marmaduke Stevenson, *A Call from Death to Life* (London, 1660; reprinted Edinburgh, 1888), p. 42; William Robinson, *Several Epistles Given forth by Two of the Lords Faithful Servants Whom he sent to New-England* (London, 1669), pp. 3, 4; Jensen, ed., *English Historical Documents*, IX, 529–531.

56. Stevenson, *Call from Death*, Introductory by "E. G.," p. 5.

57. Mary Dyer, Quaker, *Two Letters of William Dyer of Rhode Island, 1659–1660* (Cambridge, Mass., n.d.).

58. "Diary of John Hull," p. 189; *John Josselyn's Chronological Observations of America*, MHS Collections, 3d ser. (Boston, Mass., 1833), III, 389; Peter Pearson's description of the execution is in Stevenson, *Call from Death*, pp. 46–55.

59. Mary Dyer, Quaker, *Two Letters*.

60. Edward Burrough, *A Declaration of the Sad and Great Persecution and Martyrdom of the People of God called Quakers, in New-England* (London [1660]; reprinted San Francisco, 1939), pp. 22, 23; "Diary of John Hull," p. 193.

61. Jensen, ed., *English Historical Documents*, IX, 533; *CSPC 1661–1668*, nos. 89, 90, 92, pp. 31–33; Burrough, *Declaration*, pp. 8, 9–10.

62. Ibid., p. 30.

63. *CSPC 1661–1668*, nos. 89, 90, 92, pp. 31–33; no. 314, p. 94; no. 1103, p. 345. Kavenagh, ed., *Foundations*, I, 138, 480; *Records of Massachusetts Bay*, IV, pt. 2, pp. 2–4. For Alice Ambrose's persecution, see Bishop, *New-England Judged* (1703), pp. 361–364, 370, 373, 374, 400, 402, 422, 440, 459, 467; Bouton, ed., *New Hampshire State Papers*, I, 243–244. It was probably Alice Ambrose whom Jasper Danckaerts met in Maryland, where she lived in 1679. Colonists there called her the "great prophetess," and she traveled throughout the country, forsaking "husband and children, plantation and all," "in order to quake." *Journal of Jasper Danckaerts*, ed. B. B. James and J. Franklin Jameson (New York: Charles Scribner's Sons, 1913), p. 104.

64. Bishop, *New-England Judged*, pp. 376–377, 383–384; Carroll, "Early Quakers and 'Going Naked as a Sign,' " p. 82.

65. M. H. Thomas, ed., *Diary of Samuel Sewall, 1674–1729* (New York: Farrar, Straus and Giroux, 1973), I, 44; George Fox, *Something in Answer to a Letter . . . of John Leverat . . . to William Coddington . . . Dated 1677* (n.p., n.d.), pp. 2–3; Bishop, *New-England Judged*, pt. 2, pp. 102–103.

66. Jones, *Quakers in the American Colonies*, p. 110; *Bishop Burnet's History of His Own Time* (London, 1857), pp. 183–184.

67. Williams, *George Fox Digg'd*, pp. 9, 18, 202–203, but see also pp. 38–40, 159–160 (where he calls Quakers "our Adamites"), and p. 181. George Fox and John Burnyeat answered Williams and defended the practice, only, of course, when Quakers "were called unto it by the Lord, as a Sign of Nakedness of the Professors of Our Age, who want the Covering of the Spirit." *A New-England Fire-Brand Quenched* (London, 1679), pp. 28–29, 32, 174, 196–197, 224.

68. George Alsop, *A Character of the Province of Mary-land* (1666), in C. C. Hall, ed., *Narratives of Early Maryland, 1633–1684* (New York: Charles Scribner's Sons, 1910), pp. 349–350, 353.

69. Rufus Jones, ed., *Journal of George Fox*, pp. 74–76; Edward Burrough, *A Vindication of the People of God Called Quakers* (London, n.d.; reprinted San Francisco, 1939), pp. 46–47.

70. *A Relation of the Labour, Travail and Suffering . . . of Alice Curwen* (n.p., 1680), pp. 16–17; Williams, *George Fox Digg'd*, pp. 159, 194.

71. William Penn, *The Rise and Progress of the People Called Quakers* (1694), in *The Witness of William Penn*, ed. F. B. Tolles and E. G. Alderfer (New York: Macmillan, 1957), pp. 37, 30.

72. George Fox, *Journal* (1694), pp. 366, 368; Nickalls, ed., *Journal of George Fox*, p. 624.

73. William Penn, *A Testimony to the Truth of God, As held by the People called Quakers* (1698), in *A Collection of the Works of William Penn* (London, 1726), II, 879; Bliss Perry, ed., *The Heart of Emerson's Journals* (Boston: Houghton Mifflin, 1926), p. 281.

74. Penn, *Rise and Progress*, p. 32.

75. Caroline Hazard, *The Narragansett Friends' Meeting in the XVIIIth Century* (Boston, 1899), pp. 120–123.

76. R. W. Emerson, "Self-Reliance," in Frederic I. Carpenter, ed., *Ralph Waldo Emerson: Representative Selections* (New York: American Book Co., 1934), p. 93.

7. Quakers from William Penn to John Woolman

1. William C. Braithwaite, *The Second Period of Quakerism* (London: Macmillan and Son, 1919), pp. 247–248; Kenneth L. Carroll, "Early Quakers and 'Going Naked as a Sign,' " *Quaker History*, 67 (Autumn 1978), p. 86; Hugh Barbour, *The Quakers in Puritan England* (New Haven: Yale University Press, 1964), pp. 234–235.

2. For the 1660s as a turning point, see Richard S. Westfall, *Science and Religion in Seventeenth-Century England* (New Haven: Yale University Press, 1958), chap. 1; C. M. Andrews, *The Colonial Period of American History* (New Haven: Yale University Press, 1937), III, ix–xiii. For a reaction in religion, see Charles Severn, ed., *Diary of the Rev. John Ward* (London, 1839), p. 198.

3. Michael R. Watts, *The Dissenters: From the Reformation to the French Revolution* (Oxford: Clarendon Press, 1978), p. 387; Henry J. Cadbury, ed., *George Fox's "Book of Miracles"* (Cambridge: Cambridge University Press, 1948). For Cotton Mather's opinion of Fox's "miracles," along with several other thoughts about "that proud fool," see *Magnalia Christi Americana* (Hartford, Conn., 1820), II, 455.

4. N. H. Keeble, ed., *The Autobiography of Richard Baxter*, abridged by J. M. Lloyd Thomas (London: J. M. Dent and Sons, 1974), p. 74; Mather, *Magnalia*, II, 452, 455; Cotton Mather, *Three Letters from New-England, Relating to the Controversy of the Present Time* (London, 1721), p. 16; *Diary of Cotton Mather, 1681–1709* (New York: Frederick Unger, 1957), I, 571–572.

5. *An Abstract of a Letter from Thomas Paskell of Pennsylvania to his Friend J. J. Chippenham* (London, 1683), pp. 1–2.

6. Braithwaite, *Second Period*, p. 248; Carroll, "Early Quakers and 'Going Naked as a Sign,' " p. 86; Michael Kammen, *People of Paradox: An Inquiry Concerning the Origins of American Civilization* (New York: Alfred A. Knopf, 1972), p. 147.

7. William Penn, *Primitive Christianity Revived, in the Faith and Practice of the People called Quakers* (1696), in *A Collection of the Works of William Penn* (London, 1726), II, 855.

8. William Penn, *A Testimony to the Truth of God, As held by the People called Quakers* (1698), ibid., pp. 879–881; William Penn, *From Fruits of a Father's Love* (1726), in F. B. Tolles and E. G. Alderfer, eds., *The Witness of William Penn* (New York: Macmillan, 1957), pp. 195–196. For a broad discussion of Quaker principles, see William Penn, *The Rise and Progress of the People Called Quakers*, ibid., pp. 21–29.

9. William Penn, *A Serious Apology for the Principles and Practices of the People call'd Quakers, The Second Part* (1671), in *Works*, II, 38.

10. *Journal of the Life and Travels of James Dickinson*, in *The Friends' Library* (Philadelphia, 1848), XII, 389. See Prov. 29:18.

11. Samuel Bownas, *An Account of the Life, Travels* . . . (London, 1756), p. 159.

12. Penn, *Rise and Progress*, p. 14. In the 1750s Gottlieb Mittelberger described the open, democratic nature of prophesying among Quakers in Philadelphia. See *Journey to Pennsylvania*, ed. and trans. Oscar Handlin and John Clive (Cambridge, Mass.: Harvard University Press, 1960), p. 38.

13. William Penn, *From Some Fruits of Solitude* (1693), in Tolles and Alderfer, eds., *Witness*, p. 187.

14. Penn, *Rise and Progress*, pp. 29–30.

15. *George Whitefield's Journals* (London: Banner of Truth Trust, 1960), p. 406. Whitefield frequently associated and worshipped with Quakers. See *Journals*, passim, and *Hannah Logan's Courtship*, ed. A. C. Myers (Philadelphia: Ferris and Leach, 1904), pp. 76, 98.

16. Penn, *Father's Love*, pp. 199, 197; William Walwyn, *Walwyns Just Defence against the Aspersions Cast upon Him* (London, 1649); Samuel How, *Sufficiency of the Spirit's Teaching, without Humane Learning* (London, 1644; reprinted Wilmington, Delaware, 1763).

17. *A Journal of the Life of Thomas Story* (Newcastle-upon-Tyne, 1747), pp. 340–342. From the *Journal of John Woolman*, in Jessamyn West, ed., *The Quaker Reader* (New York: Viking Press, 1962), p. 255.

18. *Journal of Thomas Story*, p. 340; R. W. Emerson, "The American Scholar," in F. I. Carpenter, ed., *Ralph Waldo Emerson: Representative Selections* (New York: American Book Co., 1934), p. 56.

19. *The Brief Journal of the Life, Travels, and Labors of Love of Thomas Wilson* (London, 1784), pp. 29–30.

20. *Journal of James Dickinson*, pp. 383–384. Thomas Wilson also recorded the incident, *Journal*, pp. 39–41.

21. W. Noël Sainsbury and J. W. Fortescue, eds., *CSPC 1677–1680* (London, 1896), no. 1360, pp. 528–530; M. H. Thomas, ed., *The Diary of Samuel Sewall* (New York: Farrar, Straus and Giroux, 1973), I, 29–30, 61 and note, 62 n.; D. S. Lovejoy, *The Glorious Revolution in America* (New York: Harper and Row, 1972), p. 133.

22. *Journal of James Dickinson*, p. 382; Samuel Bownas, *Account of the Life*, pp. 99, 107, 143–145; Joshua Coffin, *A Sketch of the History of Newbury, Newburyport, and West Newbury* (Boston, 1845), p. 187.

23. *Journal of Thomas Story*, p. 342.

24. Sewall, *Diary*, I, 600.

25. *A Journal of the Life, Travels* . . . of *William Edmundson* (Dublin, 1715), p. 65.

26. For Quaker leaders' encounters with Ranters in the colonies, see ibid., pp. 91–92; *A Journal or Historical Account of the Life, Travels* . . . of . . . *George Fox* (London, 1694), pp. 367–368; *The Journal of George Fox*, ed. Rufus M. Jones (New York: Capricorn Books, 1963), p. 507; *The Truth Exalted in the Writings* . . . of *John Burnyeat* (London, 1691), pp. 41–42, 45–46; *Journal of*

Thomas Story, pp. 192–193, 220; "Friends' Meeting-House at Oyster Bay, L.I.," in B. J. Lossing, ed., *American Historical Record* (Philadelphia, 1872), I, no. 4, pp. 219, 258–259; no. 7, pp. 290, 291.

27. *A Relation of the Labour, Travail and Suffering . . . of Alice Curwen* (n.p., 1680), pp. 19–20, 40.

28. Mather, *Magnalia*, II, 456; "Friends' Meeting-House," I, 219–220.

29. Charles Leslie, *The Snake in the Grass, or Satan Transform'd into an Angel of Light* (London, 1698), pp. 75–79; George Keith, *A Journal of Travels from New-Hampshire to Caratuck, on the Continent of North-America* (London, 1706); reprinted in *Historical Magazine of the Protestant Episcopal Church*, 20 (Dec., 1951), 425–426.

30. Leslie, *Snake in the Grass*, pp. 75–79.

31. Mather, *Magnalia*, II, 457–458.

32. "Friends' Meeting-House at Matinecook, *American Historical Record*, I, no. 4, pp. 258–259.

33. For widespread Ranter activity, see *Notes on the Travels of Aaron Atkinson in America, 1698, 1699*, in Norman Penney, ed., *The Journal of the Friends Historical Society*, 14 (1917), 31–32; *Journal of William Edmundson*, p. 92; *Journal of Thomas Story*, pp. 192–193, 220; Bownas, *An Account of the Life, Travels*, p. 99.

34. *Journal of James Dickinson*, p. 394; *Journal of William Edmundson*, p. 95; *Journal of Thomas Story*, p. 158; *The Journal of Madam Knight*, excerpted in P. Miller and T. H. Johnson, eds., *The Puritans* (New York: American Book Co., 1938), p. 445.

35. *Journal of Thomas Story*, pp. 192–193.

36. Ethyn Williams Kirby, *George Keith (1638–1716)* (New York: Appleton-Century, 1942), chap. 1 and pp. 27–28, 29, 36–39, 44–45; *Bishop Burnet's History of His Own Time* (London, 1857), p. 670.

37. George Keith, *Immediate Revelation, or Jesus Christ . . . revealed in man . . . immediately* (n.p., 1668), pp. 1–6, 136.

38. George Keith, *The Woman-Preacher of Samaria* (London, 1674), pp. 6, 11–13.

39. Kirby, *Keith*, chap. 4 and pp. 46–47; *Burnet's History*, p. 670.

40. George Keith, *The Plea of the Innocent* (Philadelphia, 1692), passim and p. 10; George Keith, *A Testimony against that false & absurd opinion* (Philadelphia, 1692; reprinted London, 1693, as *The Christian Quaker, or George Keith's eyes opened*); J. William Frost, "Unlikely Controversialists: Caleb Pusey and George Keith," *Quaker History*, 64, no. 1 (Spring, 1975), 16–36.

41. *Burnet's History*, p. 670; Keith, *Plea of the Innocent*, passim, esp. p. 15.

42. Ibid., pp. 4–6, 8.

43. Ibid., p. 9; Gabriel Thomas, *An Historical and Geographical Account of . . . Pensilvania* (London, 1698), in A. C. Myers, ed., *Narratives of Early Pennsylvania, West New Jersey, and Delaware, 1630–1707* (New York: Charles Scribner's Sons, 1912), pp. 335–336; Francis Daniel Pastorius, *Circumstantial Geographical Description of . . . Pennsylvania* (Frankfort, 1700), in ibid., pp. 417–418; *Journal of Thomas Wilson*, pp. 32–35.

44. George Keith, *New-Englands Spirit of Persecution* (New York, 1693); Kirby, *Keith*, pp. 80–92.

45. *Burnet's History*, p. 670.

46. See again Keith, *Plea of the Innocent*, p. 8.

47. The London Yearly Meeting's repudiation of Keith is quoted in Rufus M. Jones, *Quakers in the American Colonies* (London: Macmillan, 1911), p. 454; *Burnet's History*, p. 670; Thomas, *Historical Account of Pensilvania*, pp. 336–337.

48. *Mr. George Keith's Reasons for Renouncing Quakerism, And Entring into Communion with the Church of England* (London, 1700), p. 9; *Burnet's History*, p. 670.

49. For Penn's attack on Keith, see Braithwaite, *Second Period*, pp. 485–486; Jones, *Quakers in the American Colonies*, p. 454, n. 1.

50. George Keith, *The Deism of William Penn, And his Brethren, Destructive to the Christian Religion* (London, 1699), p. 152.

51. Sewall, *Diary*, I, 469.

52. Keith, *Journal*, pp. 379–380, 383–385, 393.

53. Ibid., pp. 404, 415; E. B. O'Callaghan, ed., *Documentary History of the State of New-York* (Albany, N.Y., 1850), III, 414; C. F. Pascoe, ed., *Two Hundred Years of the S.P.G. . . . 1701–1900* (London: SPG, 1901), p. 31.

54. Kirby, *Keith*, pp. 92–94, 149–150; Keith, *Journal*, p. 421; Bownas, *An Account of the Life, Travels*, p. 56.

55. George Keith, *The Magick of Quakerism* (London, 1707), Preface and pp. 34, 53, 83, 86–91.

56. *Whitefield's Journals*, pp. 335, 341, 237; Jonathan Edwards, *The Distinguishing Marks of a Work of the Spirit of God,* in *Works*, vol. 4, *The Great Awakening*, ed. C. C. Goen (New Haven: Yale University Press, 1972), p. 250.

57. *The Journals of Henry Melchior Muhlenberg*, trans. T. G. Tappert and J. W. Doberstein (Philadelphia: Muhlenberg Press, 1942), I, 85, 143, 145, 147, 213, 234–235, and 3–4.

58. Samuel Seabury's letters to the SPG are in O'Callaghan, ed., *Documentary History of New-York*, III, 321–322, 327, 329; Richard J. Hooker, ed., *The Carolina Backcountry on the Eve of the Revolution: The Journal and Other Writings of Charles Woodmason, Anglican Itinerant* (Chapel Hill: University of North Carolina Press, 1953), p. 46.

59. *Some Considerations on the Keeping of Negroes* (1754), in P. P. Moulton, ed., *The Journal and Major Essays of John Woolman* (New York: Oxford University Press, 1971), p. 200; Benjamin Lay, *All Slave-Keepers That keep the Innocent in Bondage, Apostates* (Philadelphia, 1737), p. 61; William Penn, *Primitive Christianity*, p. 874.

60. William Penn, *Rise and Progress*, p. 23; *Journal of William Edmundson*, pp. 97–98.

61. Woolman, *Some Considerations*, passim and esp. Introduction. See David Brion Davis's appraisal of Woolman in *The Problem of Slavery in Western Culture* (Ithaca, N.Y.: Cornell University Press, 1966), pp. 483–493, esp. p. 489.

62. Woolman, *Some Considerations*, pt. 2, pp. 236–237; Anthony Benezet,

A Short Account of that Part of Africa Inhabited by Negroes, 2nd ed. (1762), in *Views of American Slavery, Anthony Benezet and John Wesley* (Philadelphia, 1858; reprinted New York, 1969), p. 65.

63. Woolman, *Some Considerations,* pt. 2, pp. 225, 232–233, 237, 63; Woolman, *A Plea for the Poor,* in Moulton, ed., *Journal,* p. 255.

64. Anthony Benezet, *Serious Considerations on Several Important Subjects* (Philadelphia, 1778), p. 27; John Woolman, *A Word of Remembrance and Caution to the Rich* (Dublin, 1793), pp. 24, 36–37, 62, 67–68, 81, 90, 91.

65. Woolman, *Journal,* in Moulton, ed., pp. 38, 93, 129; Benezet, *Short Account,* pp. 51–55, 57, 63.

8. Continental Strains

1. *Common Sense,* M. D. Conway, ed., *The Writings of Thomas Paine* (New York, 1894), I, 89.

2. R. A. Knox, *Enthusiasm: A Chapter in the History of Religion* (New York: Oxford University Press, 1950), pp. 389, 392.

3. Rufus M. Jones, *Spiritual Reformers in the 16th and 17th Centuries* (New York: Macmillan, 1914), pp. 114–116, 117; George L. Smith, *Religion and Trade in New Netherland* (Ithaca, N.Y.: Cornell University Press, 1973), p. 231.

4. Pieter Cornelius Plockhoy, *The Way to the Peace and Settlement of these Nations fully Discovered* (1659), in Walter Scott, ed., *Somers Tracts,* 2d ed. (London, 1811), pp. 487–493. Plockhoy's tracts are reprinted in Leland Harder and Marvin Harder, *Plockhoy from Zurik-Zee: The Study of a Dutch Reformer in Puritan England and Colonial America* (Newton, Kansas: General Conference Mennonite Church, 1952).

5. Smith, *Religion and Trade,* p. 232; Arthur Bestor, *Backwoods Utopias . . . 1663–1829* (Philadelphia: University of Pennsylvania Press, 1950; 2d ed., 1970), p. 27.

6. Harder and Harder, *Plockhoy,* pp. 189–205, 174–188; E. B. O'Callaghan, ed., *Documents Relative to the Colonial History of the State of New-York* (Albany, N.Y., 1858), II, 176–177.

7. B. B. James, "The Labadist Colony in Maryland," Johns Hopkins University, *Studies in History and Political Science,* ser. 17, no. 6 (June 1899), 1–27; Catherine P. Owen, *William Penn* (Philadelphia: J. B. Lippincott, 1956), pp. 141, 142; Penn to John de Labadie's Company, Oct. 1671, in Mary Maples Dunn and Richard S. Dunn, eds., *The Papers of William Penn,* vol. 1, *1644–1679* (Philadelphia: University of Pennsylvania Press, 1981), pp. 215–219; Bestor, *Backwoods Utopias,* p. 28; *The New Schaff-Herzog Encyclopedia of Religious Knowledge* (Grand Rapids, Mich., 1949–1950), s.v. "Labadie, Jean de; Labadists."

8. B. B. James and J. F. Jameson, eds., *The Journal of Jasper Danckaerts, 1679–1680* (New York: Charles Scribner's Sons, 1913; reprinted 1969), Introduction and pp. 141, n. 2, 249–250; Babette M. Levy, *Early Puritanism in the Southern and Island Colonies,* AAS, *Proceedings,* 70 (1961), 223–226.

9. James, "Labadist Colony," pp. 28–40; Levy, *Early Puritanism,* pp. 223–

226; A. C. Myers, ed., *Narratives of Early Pennsylvania, West New Jersey, and Delaware* (New York: Charles Scribner's Sons, 1912), p. 286 n.

10. J. F. Sachse, *The German Pietists in Provincial Pennsylvania, 1694–1708* (Philadelphia, 1895), pp. 15–16, 39, 43–47; Donald F. Durnbaugh, "Work and Hope: The Spirituality of the Radical Pietists Communities," in *Church History,* 39, no. 1 (March 1970), 74; *The Principles of a People Stiling themselves Philadelphians* (London, 1697), p. 2.

11. Sachse, *German Pietists,* pp. 27–31, 34–39, 48 n.

12. Charles H. Maxson, *The Great Awakening in the Middle Colonies* (Chicago: University of Chicago Press, 1920; reprinted 1958), pp. 6–9; Keith Thomas, *Religion and the Decline of Magic* (London: Weidenfeld and Nicolson, 1971), p. 269; "Report from Justus Faulckner to Heinrich Muhlen," August 1, 1701, *Pennsylvania Magazine of History and Biography,* 21 (1897), 218–220, 222.

13. O'Callaghan, ed., *Documents of New-York,* III, 346; Smith, *Religion and Trade,* pp. 231, 233–234; Bestor, *Backwoods Utopias,* p. 27.

14. *Danckaerts Journal,* p. 141, n. 2; James, "Labadist Colony," pp. 39–40; George A. Leakin, "The Labadists of Bohemia Manor," *Maryland Historical Magazine,* 1, no. 4 (Dec. 1906).

15. *An Account of the Life, Travels, and Christian Experiences . . . of Samuel Bownas* (London, 1756), pp. 58–59.

16. *Danckaerts Journal,* passim.

17. Bestor, *Backwoods Utopias,* pp. 28–29; *American Historical Record,* 2 (1896–97), 358–360.

18. Bestor, *Backwoods Utopias,* p. 29; Durnbaugh, "Work and Hope," pp. 76–77; Felix Reichman and Eugene E. Doll, eds., *Ephrata as Seen by Contemporaries* (Allentown, Pa.: German Folklore Society, 1952), pp. 116–117.

19. George Whitefield to Mrs. Elizabeth D——, Savannah, Feb. 1, 1740, in *The Works of the Reverend George Whitefield* (London, 1771), I, 148; *George Whitefield's Journals* (London: Banner of Truth Trust, 1960), pp. 287, 358; Maxson, *Great Awakening,* p. 9; A. C. Myers, ed., *Hannah Logan's Courtship* (Philadelphia: Ferris and Leach, 1904), pp. 225–226.

20. W. C. Reichel, ed., *Memorials of the Moravian Church* (Philadelphia, 1870), I, 169.

21. Knox, *Enthusiasm,* pp. 390–391, 398, 401–402; Edwin S. Gaustad, *A Religious History of America* (New York: Harper and Row, 1966), p. 107 n.; Sydney Ahlstrom, *A Religious History of the American People* (New Haven: Yale University Press, 1972), p. 241; Maxson, *Great Awakening,* p. 5.

22. Knox, *Enthusiasm,* pp. 403, 405–408, 419; James Logan to Governor Clarke of New York, March 30, 1742, in Reichel, ed., Memorials of the Moravian Church, pp. 14–15 n.

23. Knox, *Enthusiasm,* pp. 402–403, 409, 411–412, 419, 421.

24. *An Extract of the Rev. Mr. John Wesley's Journal,* 3d ed. (Bristol, 1765), p. ix; Elie Halévy, *The Birth of Methodism in England,* trans. and with an introduction by Bernard Semmel (Chicago: University of Chicago Press, 1971), pp. 57–58; *Whitefield's Journals,* pp. 194, 196 and n., 197, 206; Knox, *Enthusiasm,* p. 478.

25. Ibid., pp. 470–478. See Whitefield's letters in *Works*, I, generally pp. 210–225, and specifically pp. 211–212, 228–229; [George Lavington], *The Moravians Compared and Detected* (London, 1755), pp. v–vi, 72–73; Halévy, *Birth of Methodism*, p. 57.

26. See again Whitefield's letters to Wesley, in *Works*, I, 205, 211–212, 219, 225; *Whitefield's Journals*, p. 587.

27. Whitefield to Mr. J—— H——, March 25, 1741, in *Works*, I, 256; H. E. Davis, *The Fledgling Province: Social and Cultural Life in Colonial Georgia, 1733–1776* (Chapel Hill: University of North Carolina Press, 1976), p. 214; Jonathan Edwards, *Some Thoughts Concerning the Present Revival of Religion in New England* (Boston, 1742), in *The Works of Jonathan Edwards*, vol. 4, *The Great Awakening*, ed. C. C. Goen (New Haven: Yale University Press, 1972), p. 341.

28. Leo F. Stock, ed., *Proceedings and Debates of the British Parliaments Respecting North America* (Washington, D.C.: Carnegie Institution of Washington, 1941), V, xv, 301–302; Reichel, ed., *Memorials of the Moravian Church*, I, 162–163.

29. *Whitefield's Journals*, p. 412; Carl Bridenbaugh, ed., *Gentleman's Progress: The Itinerarium of Dr. Alexander Hamilton, 1744* (Chapel Hill: University of North Carolina Press, 1948), p. 58; Maxson, *Great Awakening*, p. 59.

30. *Whitefield's Journals*, pp. 410–412, 420; Reichel, ed., *Memorials of the Moravian Church*, I, 162–164, 14–15 n.

31. Whitefield to Wesley, Dec. 24, 1740, in *Whitefield's Journals*, p. 587; Whitefield to Mr. G—— C——, Dec. 11, 1740, in *Works*, I, 228–229; Whitefield to Wesley, Nov. 24, 1740, ibid., p. 225; Reichel, ed., *Memorials of the Moravian Church*, I, 164.

32. Richard Peters to Thomas Penn, Dec. 15, 1741, July 9 and Nov. 21, 1742, in Reichel, ed., *Memorials of the Moravian Church*, I, 15–16 and notes. For arrival of the "Sea-Congregation," see ibid., p. 185 and note. For a breakdown of Moravians at Bethlehem, see Leonard Ellinwood, "Religious Music in America," in J. W. Smith and A. L. Jamison, eds., *Religious Perspectives in American Culture*, vol. 2 of *Religion in American Life* (Princeton, N.J.: Princeton University Press, 1961), p. 345; Glenn Weaver, "Benjamin Franklin and the Pennsylvania Germans," *William and Mary Quarterly*, 3d ser., 14, no. 4 (Oct. 1957), 545; Stock, ed., *Proceedings and Debates*, V, 301–302.

33. Reichel, ed., *Memorials of the Moravian Church*, I, 169, 178, and note, 180, 181.

34. Stock, ed., *Proceedings and Debates*, V, 249 and note, 302–303; "Moravian Indians in Philadelphia," *American Historical Record* (Philadelphia, 1872), I, no. 5, 216–217; Wilcomb E. Washburn, *The Indian in America* (New York: Harper and Row, 1975), p. 114.

35. Knox, *Enthusiasm*, p. 401.

36. Ibid., chap. 15. For a contemporary account of the French Prophets, or les Camisards, see *Bishop Burnet's History of His Own Time* (London, 1857), pp. 716, 733–734, 759. *Encyclopaedia Britannica*, 11th ed. (Cambridge: Cambridge University Press, 1911), s.v. "Camisards"; *Webster's New Geographical*

Dictionary (Springfield, Mass.: G. and C. Merriam, 1972), p. 646.

37. William Bray, ed., *Diary of John Evelyn* (London: G. Routledge, 1906), III, 36–37; D. S. Lovejoy, *The Glorious Revolution in America* (New York: Harper and Row, 1972), p. 30.

38. Charles Tylor, *The Camisards: A Sequel to "The Huguenots of the Seventeenth Century"* (London, 1893), pp. 209–210.

39. John Lacy, in Preface to *Cry from the Desart: Or, Testimonials of the Miraculous Things Lately Come to Pass in the Cévennes*, by F. M. Misson (London, 1707), trans. John Lacy, pp. v–vii, x–xviii, xxi, xxiii–xxiv, 86.

40. *The Prophetical Warnings of John Lacy, Esq.* (London, 1707), pp. iii–xiv, 7, 57–58; Knox, *Enthusiasm*, p. 553.

41. Ofspring Blackall [sic], *The Way of Trying Prophets* (London, 1707); *The Shortest Way with the French Prophets* (London, 1708); *A Dissuasive against Enthusiasm* (London, 1708). For a brief comparison with the "jugglings" of George Fox, see pp. 65 and 75. John Humphry, *A Further Account of our Late Prophets in Two Letters to Sir Richard Buckley* (London, 1708), contains a serious discussion of enthusiasm.

42. Anthony Ashley Cooper, Third Earl of Shaftesbury, *A Letter Concerning Enthusiasm* (London, 1708), see chiefly pp. 21, 35, 41–42, 77, 80–82. *Remarks Upon the Letter to a Lord Concerning Enthusiasm* (London, 1708); Edward Fowler, *Reflections upon a Letter Concerning Enthusiasm* (London, 1709). Fowler chided Shaftesbury for being an enthusiast for deism. According to Charles Tylor, there was a remnant of the French Prophets in London as late as the 1740s; *Camisards*, p. 329.

43. For Keimer's early years in England, see his *Brand Pluck'd from the Burning: Exemplify'd in the Unparallel'd Case of Samuel Keimer* (London, 1718). This is chiefly an autobiography and exposé of the Prophets. I am indebted to Daniel Kastenholz of the University of Wisconsin, Madison, who lent me his Xerox copy of Keimer's *Brand*, taken from the 1718 edition in the Library of Haverford College, Haverford, Pa.

See, too, *The Journal of the Friends Historical Society*, 22, nos. 1–4 (1925), 5–7.

44. Keimer, *Brand*, pp. 103, 70.

45. Ibid., p. 124; *Journal of the Friends Historical Society*, pp. 6–7.

46. Carl Van Doren, ed., *Benjamin Franklin's Autobiographical Writings* (New York: Viking Press, 1945), pp. 235, 241.

47. Isaiah Thomas, *The History of Printing in America* (1810), ed. M. A. McCorison (New York: Weathervane Books, 1970), p. 364; Van Doren, ed., *Franklin's Autobiographical Writings*, pp. 241–242, 255.

48. Ibid., pp. 235, 265; Joseph Smith, *Short Biographical Notices of William Bradford, Reiner Jansen, Andrew Bradford, and Samuel Keimer, Early Printers in Pennsylvania* (London, 1891), pp. 20–21; Thomas, *History of Printing*, pp. 604–606.

49. Stock, ed., *Proceedings and Debates*, II, 57–58 and note; M. H. Thomas, ed., *Diary of Samuel Sewall, 1674–1729* (New York: Farrar, Straus and Giroux, 1973), I, 102 and note; A. S. Salley, ed., *Narratives of Early Carolina, 1650–*

1708 (New York: Charles Scribner's Sons, 1911), pp. 208–209 n., 238 n., 246 and note; William J. Rivers, *A Sketch of the History of South Carolina* (Charleston, 1856), p. 392; Bray, ed., *Diary of John Evelyn*, III, 8, 9, 11, 16, 18, 20–23, 41, 43, 44, 46; Robert M. Kingdon, "Pourquoi les Réfugiés huguenots aux colonies américaines, sont-ils devenus épiscopaliens?" *Bulletin de la Société de l'Histoire du Protestantisme Français* (Oct.–Dec. 1969), 487–509; Wesley Frank Craven, *The Southern Colonies in the Seventeenth Century, 1607–1689* (n.p.: Louisiana State University Press, 1949), p. 9.

50. Virginia Historical Society *Collections,* n. s., vol. 6, *Miscellaneous Papers, 1672–1865* (Richmond, Va., 1886), pp. 61–67.

51. Sept. 20, 1708, in F. J. Klingberg, ed., *Carolina Chronicle: The Papers of Commissary Gideon Johnston, 1707–1716* (Berkeley, Calif.: University of California Press, 1946), p. 22; "The Present State of the Clergy in South Carolina," [1713], Rawlinson Mss, C. 943, pp. 3–4, final two pages and article 4, Bodleian Library, Oxford.

52. David Duncan Wallace, *The History of South Carolina* (New York: American Historical Society, 1934), I, 415.

53. The best account is Alexander Garden, *A Brief Account of the Deluded Dutartres* (New Haven, Conn., 1762). See also Alexander Garden, *The Case of the Dutartres,* Appendix to *A Serious Address to Lay-Methodists* (London, 1745). See again Wallace, *History of South Carolina,* I, 415–416; Cecil Headlam, ed., *CSPC 1724–1725* (London, 1936), no. 388v, p. 246.

54. Keimer, *Brand,* pp. 110, 70; George Lavington, *The Enthusiasm of the Methodists and the Papists Compared* (London, 1749), pt. 2, 161.

55. Garden, *Brief Account,* passim; Garden, *Case of the Dutartres,* pp. 27, 29.

56. Edward Wigglesworth, *A Seasonable Caveat against believing every Spirit* (Boston, 1735), esp. pp. 13–14; Perry Miller, *Jonathan Edwards* (n.p.: William Sloane Associates, 1949), p. 129.

57. For the Benezet saga, see Tylor, *Camisards,* pp. 431–434; George S. Brookes, *Friend Anthony Benezet* (Philadelphia: University of Pennsylvania Press, 1937), pp. 15–22, 96; *Whitefield's Journals,* p. 419 and note; Reichel, ed., *Memorials of the Moravian Church,* I, 171 and note, 173, 138–139 n.

58. Myers, ed., *Hannah Logan's Courtship,* p. 305.

9. The Great Awakening as Enthusiasm

1. Perry Miller, "Jonathan Edwards and the Great Awakening," in *Errand into the Wilderness* (Cambridge, Mass.: Harvard University Press, 1956), pp. 156–157.

2. See Alexander Pope, *Essay on Man,* Epistle IV, l. 394.

3. Voltaire, *Candide* (New York: Bantam Books, 1959), p. 18.

4. Perry Miller, "The Rhetoric of Sensation," in *Errand into the Wilderness,*" chap. 7. Whitefield was well aware that what severe critics called "his enthusiastic ravings" were effective. "I know this foolishness of preaching," he

wrote in 1739, "is made instrumental to the conversion and edification of numbers." *George Whitefield's Journals* (London: Banner of Truth Trust, 1960), p. 265.

5. William G. McLoughlin discusses a changing conception of God in "Free Love, Immortalism, and Perfectionism in Cumberland, Rhode Island, 1748–1768," *Rhode Island History*, 33, nos. 3 and 4 (August and Nov. 1974), 80. See, too, William G. McLoughlin, *Revivals, Awakenings, and Reform* (Chicago: University of Chicago Press, 1978), pp. 215–216. For Gilbert Tennent's defense of exceptional methods during exceptional times, see William Nelson, ed., *Documents Relating to the Colonial History of the State of New Jersey* (Paterson, N.J., 1895), II, 67–68.

6. Josiah Smith, *A Sermon, on the Character, Preaching &c. of the Rev. Mr. Whitefield* (1740), in Alan Heimert and Perry Miller, eds., *The Great Awakening: Documents Illustrating the Crisis and Its Consequences* (Indianapolis: Bobbs-Merrill, 1967), p. 69.

7. *Whitefield's Journals*, pp. 165, 486, 363; *The Works of the Reverend George Whitefield* (London, 1771), I, 45, 220, 217.

8. Thomas Prince, ed., *The Christian History, Containing Accounts of the Revival . . . of Religion in Great Britain & America . . . 1743* (Boston, Mass., 1744), I, 335, 262. For other discussions of terror, see ibid., II, 384–390, and Jonathan Edwards, *Distinguishing Marks, of a Work of the Spirit of God* (Boston, 1741), in *The Works of Jonathan Edwards*, vol. 4, *The Great Awakening*, ed. C. C. Goen (New Haven: Yale University Press, 1972), pp. 246–248. Gilbert Tennent, *Remarks upon a Protestation Presented to the Synod of Philadelphia* (Philadelphia, 1741), pp. 23–24.

9. *Whitefield's Journals*, p. 348.

10. Perry Miller, "The Rhetoric of Sensation."

11. Prince, *Christian History*, I, 391.

12. Rom. 2:29.

13. Patrick Henry, Sr., covers each of these points in his letter to Commissary William Dawson, Hanover, Va., Feb. 13, 1745, in D. S. Lovejoy, ed., *Religious Enthusiasm and the Great Awakening* (Englewood Cliffs, N.J.: Prentice-Hall, 1969), pp. 56–57. See also Tennent, *Remarks upon a Protestation*, in Heimert and Miller, eds., *Great Awakening*, pp. 172–173.

14. Lovejoy, ed., *Religious Enthusiasm*, pp. 55–56.

15. C. C. Goen, *Revivalism and Separatism in New England, 1740–1800* (New Haven: Yale University Press, 1962), pp. 62–63, 175–176; Charles Maxson, *The Great Awakening in the Middle Colonies* (Chicago: University of Chicago Press, 1920), chap. 3.

16. "Isaac Backus his writeing Containing Some Particular account of my Conversion"; "An Account of the Life of Isaac Backus," pp. 31–39. Both manuscripts are in the Andover-Newton Theological School Library, Newton Center, Massachusetts. For a full treatment of Backus, see William G. McLoughlin, *Isaac Backus and the American Pietistic Tradition* (Boston: Little, Brown, 1967).

17. Carl Bridenbaugh, ed., *Gentleman's Progress: The Itinerarium of Dr.*

Alexander Hamilton, 1744 (Chapel Hill: University of North Carolina Press, 1948), p. 161; Charles Chauncy, *Seasonable Thoughts on the State of Religion in New-England* (Boston, 1743), pp. 220–223 n.

18. Richard Warch, "The Shepherd's Tent: Education and Enthusiasm in the Great Awakening," *American Quarterly*, 30, no. 2 (Summer 1978), 177–198; Goen, *Revivalism and Separatism*, pp. 62–63.

19. Isaac Backus, *A Fish Caught in his Own Net* (Boston, 1768), in William G. McLoughlin, ed., *Isaac Backus on Church, State, and Calvinism: Pamphlets, 1754–1789* (Cambridge, Mass.: Harvard University Press, 1968), p. 235.

20. *Whitefield's Journals*, p. 144. For Whitefield's comments on Jacob Boehme and William Law, see ibid., pp. 45, 79, 105, 144, 287, and *Works*, I, 148.

21. George Whitefield, *A Letter to the Rev. The President . . . of Harvard College* (Boston, 1745), pp. 14–15.

22. Letter to Dr. William Douglass, reprinted in *Documentary History of New Jersey*, II, 550–551.

23. *Whitefield's Journals*, pp. 482–483; Whitefield to Mr. M____, Reedy Island, May 19, 1740, in *Works*, I, 171; Whitefield to Mr. P____, Boston, Sept. 19, 1740, ibid., p. 207. For criticism of Whitefield's method of preaching, see *The Testimony of the President, Professors, Tutors . . . of Harvard College, against George Whitefield* (Boston, 1744), pp. 12–13.

24. Prince, *Christian History*, Jan. 12, 1744, no. 98; Sarah Edwards to James Pierrepont, Oct. 24, 1740, in Luke Tyerman, *The Life of the Rev. George Whitefield* (New York, 1877), I, 428–429; W. C. Ford, ed., *Statesman and Friend: Correspondence of John Adams with Benjamin Waterhouse, 1784–1822* (Boston: Little, Brown, 1927), p. 118.

25. W. S. Perry, ed., *Historical Collections Relating to the American Colonial Church*, vol. 2, *Pennsylvania* (Hartford, Conn., 1871), pp. 208–209; Alexander Garden, *Regeneration, and the Testimony of the Spirit* (Charleston, S.C., 1740), in Heimert and Miller, eds., *Great Awakening*, p. 61.

26. *Journals of H. M. Muhlenberg*, trans. T. G. Tappert and J. W. Duberstein (Philadelphia: Muhlenberg Press, 1942), II, 696; ibid., p. 231.

27. Ibid., p. 545.

28. Prince, *Christian History*, Jan. 26 and Feb. 2, 1745, nos. 100, 101.

29. Perry, ed., *Historical Collections*, II, 208–209; Bridenbaugh, ed., *Gentleman's Progress*, p. 22.

30. Opponents of the Awakening published voluminously and vigorously. See, for example, Chauncy, *Seasonable Thoughts;* Garden, *Regeneration, and the Testimony of the Spirit;* John Thomson, *Doctrine of Convictions* (Philadelphia, 1741); "The Wandering Spirit," in *The General Magazine and Historical Chronicle*, 1, no. 4 (Feb. 1741); Isaac Stiles, *The Declaration of the Association of the County of New-Haven, Connecticut . . . Concerning the Reverend Mr. George Whitefield* (Boston, 1745).

31. William Rand, *The Late Religious Commotions in New-England Considered* (Boston, 1743), esp. p. 18.

32. *Whitefield's Journals*, p. 347.

33. C. J. Hoadly, ed., *The Public Records of the Colony of Connecticut*, vol.

8, *1735–1743* (Hartford, Conn., 1874), pp. 454–457. For a similar law restricting unlicensed schools and colleges, such as the Shepherd's Tent, see ibid., pp. 500–502.

34. Davies to Bishop of London, in W. H. Foote, *Sketches of Virginia, Historical and Biographical* (Philadelphia, 1850), p. 195.

35. *Boston Weekly News-Letter,* Sept. 2, 1742; Chauncy, *Seasonable Thoughts,* pp. 151, 153–157; Chauncy to G. Wishart, Boston, August 4, 1742, in Lovejoy, ed., *Religious Enthusiasm,* pp. 79–80; Edwin S. Gaustad, *The Great Awakening in New England* (New York: Harper and Brothers, 1957), pp. 40–41; Goen, *Revivalism and Separatism,* pp. 23–27.

36. Jonathan Mayhew, *Seven Sermons upon the Following Subjects* (Boston, 1749), quoted in Perry Miller, *Jonathan Edwards* (n.p.: William Sloane Associates, 1949), p. 322; Alan Heimert, *Religion and the American Mind* (Cambridge, Mass.: Harvard University Press, 1966), p. 177.

37. *Whitefield's Journals,* p. 442.

38. "The Wandering Spirit," in *General Magazine* (Feb. 1741), 122.

39. Charles Brockwell to Secretary, SPG, Salem, Mass., Feb. 18, 1742, in Perry, ed., *Historical Collections,* III, 453–454.

40. Chauncy, *Seasonable Thoughts,* pp. 374–375. Chauncy's Preface is a commentary on the Antinomian Controversy in Boston a hundred years earlier. He found a "surprising Agreement" between it and the revivals of the 1740s. See p. iii.

41. *The Wonderful Narrative, or a Faithful Account of the French Prophets* (Boston, 1742), Appendix, pp. 97–104, often attributed to Charles Chauncy but recently questioned. See Gaustad, *Great Awakening,* p. 89.

42. Chauncy, *Seasonable Thoughts,* p. 422.

43. Edwards, *Distinguishing Marks,* p. 228.

44. Gilbert Tennent, *The Examiner, Examined or Gilbert Tennent, Harmonious* (Philadelphia, 1743), pp. 4–7, 31–32; Gilbert Tennent, "Paper Read at the Synod," in Charles Hodge, *The Constitutional History of the Presbyterian Church* (Philadelphia, 1851), pp. 120–124; Gilbert Tennent, *The Danger of an Unconverted Ministry* (Philadelphia, 1740), passim.

45. George Whitefield, *A Vindication and Confirmation of the Remarkable Work of God in New-England* (Glasgow, n.d.; reprinted London, 1742), p. 27.

46. "Extract from a Letter from Mr. Gilbert Tennent to Mr. Prince at Boston, August 24, 1744," in John Gillies, *Historical Collections Relating to . . . the Success of the Gospel* (Glasgow, 1754), II, 322–323.

47. *Testimony against George Whitefield,* in Heimert and Miller, eds., *Great Awakening,* p. 346; Whitefield, *A Letter to the President,* in Lovejoy, ed., *Religious Enthusiasm,* p. 106.

48. Edwards, *Distinguishing Marks,* pp. 229, 230, 232, 244.

49. Gillies, *Historical Collections,* II, 318.

50. The *Boston Evening-Post,* July 26, 1742; *The Reverend Mr. James Davenport's Confession & Retractions* (Boston, 1744), in Heimert and Miller, eds., *Great Awakening,* pp. 257–262.

51. George Whitefield, *Some Remarks on a Pamphlet Intitled The Enthusiasm*

of Methodists and Papists Compar'd (Boston [New England], 1749), pp. 24–25.

52. Jonathan Edwards, "Reflections and Observations on the Preceding Memoirs of Mr. Brainerd," in *The Works of President Edwards* (New York, 1851), I, 662–663.

53. Garden, *Regeneration,* in Heimert and Miller, eds., *Great Awakening,* p. 49.

54. Jonathan Edwards, *Some Thoughts Concerning the Revival of Religion in New-England* (Boston, 1742), in Goen, ed., *Works,* IV, 334, 339, 341.

55. Whitefield, *Vindication and Confirmation,* p. 27.

56. Edwards, *Distinguishing Marks,* pp. 229, 233.

57. Edwards, *Some Thoughts Concerning the Revival,* p. 358.

58. See Chapter 1.

59. Edwards, *Some Thoughts Concerning the Revival,* p. 357.

60. *John Wesley's Journal . . . Covering His Visit to America* (New Orleans: The *New Orleans Picayune,* 1901), pp. 5, 13–14.

61. *Whitefield's Journals,* pp. 419 and note, and p. 428; Whitefield to the Allegany Indians, Reedy Island, May 21, 1740, in *Works,* I, 174.

62. Edwards, *Some Thoughts Concerning the Revival,* p. 346; Jonathan Edwards, *A History of the Work of Redemption* (1774), in Heimert and Miller, eds., *Great Awakening,* pp. 27–28; Ola Elizabeth Winslow, *Jonathan Edwards, 1703–1758* (New York: Macmillan, 1940), chap. 13.

63. "Biography of the late rev. Daniel Marshall . . . by the rev. Abraham Marshall," in Henry Holcombe, *Georgia Analytical Repository,* 1, no. 1, 2d ed. (Savannah, Ga., 1802), 23–31.

64. "From the Abridgement of Brainerd's Journal printed in 1748," in Gillies, *Historical Collections,* II, 424.

10. The Great Awakening as Subversion and Conspiracy

1. H. A. Brockwell to Secretary, SPG, quoted in L. J. Greene, *The Negro in Colonial New England* (New York: Columbia University Press, 1942), p. 276; D. S. Lovejoy, ed., *Religious Enthusiasm and the Great Awakening* (Englewood Cliffs, N.J.: Prentice-Hall, 1969), p. 15; Charles Chauncy, *Seasonable Thoughts on the State of Religion in New England* (Boston, 1743), pp. 304–305.

2. Samuel Davies to Bishop of London, Jan. 10, 1752, in W. H. Foote, *Sketches of Virginia, Historical and Biographical* (Philadelphia, 1850), pp. 197–198. For Virginia proclamation (1747), see G. W. Pilcher, *Samuel Davies: Apostle of Dissent in Colonial Virginia* (Knoxville: University of Tennessee Press, 1971), p. 33 n.

3. C. H. Hoadly, ed., *The Public Records of the Colony of Connecticut,* vol. 8, *1735–1743* (Hartford, Conn., 1874), pp. 483–484 and 454–457. For Governor John Law's description of social disruption in Connecticut provoked by the ministers' "Enthusiastic Principles," see his letter of November 1743 to Dr. Avery in London, in Bernard Lord Manning, *The Protestant Dissenting Deputies,* ed. Omerod Greenwood (Cambridge: Cambridge University Press, 1952), pp. 411–413.

4. Samuel Niles, *Tristitiae Ecclesiarum, or a brief and sorrowful Account*

of the *Present State of the Churches in New-England* (Boston, 1754), p. 4; Chauncy, *Seasonable Thoughts*, p. 51.

5. Sarah Edwards to James Pierrepont, Oct. 24, 1740, in Luke Tyerman, *Life of . . . George Whitefield* (New York, 1877), I, 428–429; Josiah Smith, *A Sermon on the Character, Preaching, &c. of the Rev. Mr. Whitefield* (1740), in Alan Heimert and Perry Miller, eds., *The Great Awakening: Documents Illustrating the Crisis and Its Consequences* (Indianapolis: Bobbs-Merrill, 1967), pp. 67–68; Chauncy, *Seasonable Thoughts*, p. 51; William Nelson, ed., *Documents Relating to the Colonial History of the State of New Jersey* (Paterson, N.J., 1895), II, 211–212; George Whitefield, *A Vindication and Confirmation of the Remarkable Work of God in New-England* (London, 1742), p. 12.

6. Charles Chauncy, *Enthusiasm described and caution'd against* (Boston, 1742), in Heimert and Miller, eds., *Great Awakening*, p. 243; William G. McLoughlin, "Free Love, Immortalism, and Perfectionism in Cumberland, Rhode Island, 1748–1768," in *Rhode Island History*, 33, nos. 3 and 4 (August and Nov. 1974), 70.

7. Jonathan Edwards, *The Distinguishing Marks of a Work of the Spirit of God* (Boston, 1741), *The Works of Jonathan Edwards*, vol. 4, *The Great Awakening*, ed. C. C. Goen (New Haven: Yale University Press, 1972), pp. 256–257; Jonathan Edwards, *Some Thoughts Concerning the present Revival of Religion in New-England* (Boston, 1742), ibid., pp. 468–469.

8. Isaac Backus, *A History of New England with Particular Reference to the Baptists* (Newton, Mass., 1871; reprinted 1969), II, 88–89; Niles, *Tristitiae Ecclesiarum*, p. 4; C. C. Goen, *Revivalism and Separatism in New England, 1740–1800* (New Haven: Yale University Press, 1962), pp. 200–203; McLoughlin, "Free Love," p. 70.

9. A discussion of these difficulties is in "A True Copy of the Clergy of South Carolina's Instructions to Mr. Johnston" (1713), art. 2, Rawlinson Mss, C. 943, Bodleian Library, Oxford; *Carolina Chronicle: The Papers of Gideon Johnston, 1707–1716*, ed. F. J. Klingberg (Berkeley: University of California Press, 1946), p. 123. See also F. J. Klingberg, *An Appraisal of the Negro in South Carolina* (Washington, D.C.: Associated Publishers, 1944), pp. 5–6.

10. E. S. DeBeer, ed., *The Diary of John Evelyn* (London: Oxford University Press, 1959), p. 824.

11. Philip Alexander Bruce, *Social Life in Old Virginia* (New York: Capricorn Books, 1965), pp. 236–237.

12. *A Journal of the Life, Travels . . . of William Edmundson* (Dublin, 1715), pp. 74–75.

13. *A Relation of the Labour, Travail and Suffering . . . of Alice Curwen* (n.p., 1680), p. 8.

14. See note 9 above. M. Eugene Sirmans, *Colonial South Carolina: A Political History* (Chapel Hill: University of North Carolina Press, 1966), p. 99. Several colonies enacted laws—Virginia as early as 1668—making it clear that conversion and baptism had no bearing whatever on slavery. See Virginia's, South Carolina's, and New York's acts in W. K. Kavenagh, ed., *Foundations of Colonial America: A Documentary History* (New York: Chelsea House, 1973), III, 2076,

2092; II, 1198. Parliament came to the aid of the slaveowner in 1712 and in a "Bill for Settling the Trade to Africa" explicitly stated that no planter would lose his property as a result of his slaves' "professing the Christian religion, or being baptized into the same." Leo F. Stock, ed., *Proceedings and Debates of the British Parliaments Respecting North America* (Washington, D.C.: Carnegie Institution of Washington, 1941), III, 295, 296.

15. *Letters from the Rev. Samuel Davies* (London, 1757), pp. 8–9, 10–11, 17–18.

16. Stock, ed., *Proceedings and Debates*, V, 105–106 and note; Whitefield to Mr. B____, Bristol, March 22, 1751, in *A Select Collection of Letters of . . . George Whitefield* (London, 1772), II, 404–405.

17. *Whitefield's Journals* (London: Banner of Truth Trust, 1960), pp. 419–420; *To the Inhabitants of Maryland, Virginia, North and South Carolina, concerning their Negroes, in Three Letters from the Reverend George Whitefield* (Philadelphia, 1740); *Pennsylvania Gazette*, April 17, 1740; Whitefield to Mr. B____, Cambusland, August 18, 1742, in *The Works of the Reverend George Whitefield* (London, 1771), I, 425.

18. *Whitefield's Journals*, pp. 400–401, 442, 444. See also Alexander Garden, *Regeneration, and the Testimony of the Spirit* (Charlestown, S.C., 1740), in Heimert and Miller, eds., *Great Awakening*, p. 47, and David T. Morgan, "The Great Awakening in South Carolina, 1740–1775," *The South Atlantic Quarterly*, 70, no. 4 (Autumn 1971), 596–600. C. H. Maxson, *The Great Awakening in the Middle Colonies* (Chicago: University of Chicago Press, 1920), pp. 57–58.

19. Richard J. Hooker, ed., *The Carolina Backcountry on the Eve of the Revolution: The Journal and Other Writings of Charles Woodmason, Anglican Itinerant* (Chapel Hill: University of North Carolina Press, 1953), p. 64.

20. *Whitefield's Journals*, pp. 361, 401, 450.

21. *South Carolina Gazette*, Jan. 8, 1741; Whitefield to Mr. C____, Charles-Town, Jan. 12, Jan. 16, 1741, in *Works*, I, 231–232; Isaiah Thomas, *The History of Printing in America* (1810), ed. M. A. McCorison (New York: Weathervane Books, 1970), p. 568; *Whitefield's Journals*, pp. 502–504.

22. Ibid., pp. 501–502; Whitefield to Mr. C____, Good-Hope, S.C., Jan. 1, 1741, in *Works*, I, 230.

23. The story of Hugh Bryan's fanaticism can be pieced together from the following: J. H. Easterby and Ruth S. Green, eds., *The Colonial Records of South Carolina*, ser. 1, *The Journal of the Commons House of the Assembly, 1736–1750* (Columbia: Historical Commission of South Carolina, 1952), II, 406–407; ibid., IV, 72; *South Carolina Gazette*, March 3, 1742; *Boston Post-Boy*, May 3, 1742; Elise Pinckney, ed., *The Letterbook of Eliza Lucas Pinckney, 1739–1762* (Chapel Hill: University of North Carolina Press, 1972), pp. 27–28, 29, 30–31; Joseph Tracy, *The Great Awakening* (Boston, 1841), pp. 240 n., 241 n.

24. *South Carolina Gazette*, June 21, 1742; Pinckney, ed., *Letterbook of Eliza Lucas Pinckney*, p. 42 and note.

25. *Whitefield's Journals*, pp. 386–387, 411, 420; James Logan to Governor Clarke of New York, March 30, 1742, in William C. Reichel, ed., *Memorials of*

the Moravian Church (Philadelphia, 1870), I, 14–15 n.; Maxson, *Great Awakening*, p. 58.

26. *Whitefield's Journals,* pp. 347–348, 360, 388, 483–485; Whitefield to Mr. M____, Philadelphia, Nov. 10, 1740, in *Works,* I, 222.

27. Two recent discussions of the "Negro Conspiracy" in New York (1741) are by Thomas J. Davis in an introduction to his edition of Daniel Horsmanden, *The New York Conspiracy* (Boston: Beacon Press, 1971)—this is a scholarly reprint of *The New-York Conspiracy, or a History of the Negro Plot . . . 1741– 42* (New York, 1810)—and Edgar J. McManus, *Black Bondage in the North* (Syracuse, N.Y.: Syracuse University Press, 1973), pp. 133–139. See also Joel Tyler Headley, *The Great Riots of New York, 1712 to 1873* (New York, 1873; facsimile ed., Indianapolis: Bobbs-Merrill, 1970), chap. 2.

28. McManus, *Black Bondage,* pp. 127–131.

29. E. B. O'Callaghan, ed., *The Documentary History of the State of New-York* (Albany, N.Y., 1850), III, 125–126, 129; McManus, *Black Bondage,* pp. 130–131.

30. Quoted in Winthrop D. Jordan, *White Over Black: American Attitudes Toward the Negro, 1550–1812* (Chapel Hill: University of North Carolina Press, 1968), pp. 181, 120.

31. Horsmanden, *New York Conspiracy,* pp. 360–361, 334; *Whitefield's Journals,* pp. 360–361.

32. For Oglethorpe's campaigns, see Howard H. Peckham, *The Colonial Wars, 1689–1762* (Chicago: University of Chicago Press, 1964), pp. 87–95, 223.

33. Daniel Horsmanden to Cadwallader Colden, August 7, 1741, in *The Letters and Papers of Cadwallader Colden,* New York Historical Society *Collections, 1918* (New York, 1919), II, 225.

34. Horsmanden, *New York Conspiracy,* p. 351.

35. O'Callaghan, ed., *Documentary History of New-York,* III, 1023; Horsmanden, *New York Conspiracy,* pp. 308–310, 353 n., 364, 370–371; ibid., pp. 14, 15, 103, 158; N.Y. Hist. Soc. *Collections, 1918,* II, 225; E. B. O'Callaghan, ed., *Documents Relative to the Colonial History of the State of New-York* (Albany, 1853), VI, 196, 198, 201–203.

36. O'Callaghan, ed., *Documentary History of New-York,* III, 1022–1024; Horsmanden, *New York Conspiracy,* pp. 360–361.

37. *South Carolina Gazette,* Oct. 16, 1740.

38. *The General Magazine and Historical Chronicle,* Philadelphia, Feb. 1741, p. 122.

39. *A Short Reply to Mr. Whitefield's Letter Which He Wrote in Answer to the Querists* (Philadelphia, 1741), in Heimert and Miller, eds., *Great Awakening,* p. 140.

40. Patrick Henry, Sr., to William Dawson, *William and Mary Quarterly,* 2d ser., 1 (1921), 266.

41. London, 1749. For other insinuations of Catholicism, see Alexander Garden, *Regeneration, and the Testimony of the Spirit,* in Heimert and Miller, eds., *Great Awakening,* pp. 58, 60–61; David McGregor, *The Spirits of the Present*

Day Tried (Boston, 1742), ibid., p. 224; A Short Reply to Mr. Whitefield's Letter, ibid., p. 138.

42. Whitefield sailed from Charleston in late January 1741; Whitefield's Journals, p. 505. Headley, The Great Riots of New York, pp. 41, 42–43; McManus, Black Bondage, p. 138.

43. Revd Mr. Colgan to the Secretary (SPG), Jamaica, N.Y., Nov. 22, 1740, Dec. 15, 1741, in O'Callaghan, ed., Documentary History of New-York, III, 316–317; ibid., 1022–1023.

44. Reichel, ed., Memorials of the Moravian Church, I, 15–16 n., 162–165; Sydney E. Ahlstrom, A Religious History of the American People (New Haven: Yale University Press, 1972), p. 242; Maxson, Great Awakening, p. 5; R. A. Knox, Enthusiasm: A Chapter in the History of Religion (New York: Oxford University Press, 1950), p. 403.

45. O'Callaghan, ed., Documentary History of New-York, III, 1025.

46. Reichel, ed., Memorials of the Moravian Church, I, 164, 169; Count Zinzendorf, Narrative of a Journey to Shecomeco ... 1742, ibid., pp. 53 and note, 54–55; "Moravian Indians in Philadelphia," in B. J. Lossing, ed., American Historical Record (Philadelphia, 1872), I, no. 5, pp. 216–217.

47. Reichel, ed., Memorials, I, 180; Lossing, ed., American Historical Record, I, no. 1, p. 11; [William C. Reichel, ed.], A Memorial of the Dedication of Monuments Erected by the Moravian Historical Society (New York, 1860), pp. 41–42.

48. Reichel, ed., Memorials, I, 169, 170, 171; Zinzendorf, Narrative, ibid., 59 n.

49. Leonard Ellinwood, "Religious Music in America," in J. W. Smith and A. L. Jamison, eds., Religious Perspectives in American Culture (Princeton, N.J.: Princeton University Press, 1961), p. 345. Glenn Weaver gives a slightly lower total figure, in "Benjamin Franklin and the Pennsylvania Germans," William and Mary Quarterly, 3d ser., 14, no. 4 (Oct. 1957), 545. O'Callaghan, ed., Documentary History of New-York, III, 1016.

50. Reichel, ed., Memorials, I, 185–186 n.; Memoirs of James Logan by Wilson Armistead (London, 1851), pp. 96–97; Weaver, "Franklin and the Pennsylvania Germans," pp. 538–542.

51. Gentleman's Progress: The Itinerarium of Dr. Alexander Hamilton, 1744, ed. Carl Bridenbaugh (Chapel Hill: University of North Carolina Press, 1948), p. 58.

52. See Chapter 9.

53. Gilbert Tennent, Some Account of the Principles of the Moravians (London, 1743), passim; "Extract of a Letter from the Rev. Mr. G. Tennent, to the Rev. Mr. Dickinson," New Brunswick, N.J., Feb. 12, 1742, in the Boston Evening-Post, July 26, 1742.

54. George Whitefield to ?, Edinburgh, Sept. 13, 1742, in Tyerman, Life of Whitefield, I, 31.

55. Tennent, Some Account, pp. iv–vii, 14, 18, 28, 29, 31, 33, 38, 41, 45.

56. Charles Chauncy, to G. Wishart, August 4, 1742, in Lovejoy, ed., Religious Enthusiasm, pp. 79–80.

57. Tennent, *Some Account*, p. 41.

58. O'Callaghan, ed., *Documentary History of New-York*, III, 1016–1022; Lossing, ed., *American Historical Record*, I, no. 1, pp. 11–12; John Heckewelder, *A Narrative of the Mission of the United Brethren* (Philadelphia, 1820), pp. 22–31.

59. O'Callaghan, ed., *Documentary History of New-York*, III, 1019–1020; [Reichel, ed.], *Memorial of the Dedication of Monuments*, pp. 41–42, 45–53; Lossing, ed., *American Historical Record*, I, 11–12, 216–217; Heckewelder, *Narrative*, pp. 22–31; William M. Beauchamp, ed., *Moravian Journals Relating to Central New York, 1745–66* (Syracuse, N.Y.: Dehler Press, 1916), p. 17.

60. John Sergeant to Capt. Thomas Coran, in Samuel Hopkins, *Historical Memoirs Relating to the Housatonic Indians . . .* (*1693–1755*) (Boston, 1753), reprinted in *The Magazine of History*, extra number no. 17 (New York: W. Abbatt, 1911), p. 137; Stock, ed., *Proceedings and Debates*, V, 304 n.

61. O'Callaghan, ed., *Documentary History of New-York*, III, 1020–1022; Stock, ed., *Proceedings and Debates*, V, xiv, 301.

62. The council's report is in O'Callaghan, ed., *Documentary History of New-York*, III, 1022–1027.

63. Ibid., pp. 1023–1027.

64. Hopkins, *Historical Memoirs*, p. 137; Lossing, ed., *American Historical Record*, I, 11–12.

65. O'Callaghan, ed., *Documentary History of New-York*, III, 1027; Stock ed., *Proceedings and Debates*, V, xv, 301, 302–303; *The Journals of Henry Melchior Muhlenberg*, trans. T. G. Tappert and J. W. Doberstein (Philadelphia: The Muhlenberg Press, 1942), I, 257; *A Brief History of the Episcopal Church of the Moravian Brethren* (London, 1750), pp. 10–11, 14–20, 31–32.

66. Weaver, "Franklin and the Pennsylvania Germans," p. 546.

67. Ibid., p. 554; Carl Van Doren, ed., *Benjamin Franklin's Autobiographical Writings* (New York: Viking Press, 1945), p. 747.

11. Enthusiasm and the Cause of Mankind

1. Edmund Burke, *Works* (London, 1886), I, 466, 474.

2. Alan Heimert, *Religion and the American Mind: From the Great Awakening to the Revolution* (Cambridge, Mass.: Harvard University Press, 1966). See also William G. McLoughlin, "The Role of Religion in the Revolution," in S. G. Kurtz and J. H. Hutson, eds., *Essays on the American Revolution* (Chapel Hill: University of North Carolina Press, 1973), pp. 197–255; W. G. Mc-Loughlin, " 'Enthusiasm for Liberty': The Great Awakening as the Key to the Revolution," AAS, *Proceedings*, 87 (1977), 69–95.

3. *A Short Reply to Mr. Whitefield's Letter Which He Wrote in Answer to the Querists* (Philadelphia, 1741), in Alan Heimert and Perry Miller, eds., *The Great Awakening: Documents Illustrating the Crisis and Its Consequences* (Indianapolis: Bobbs-Merrill, 1967), p. 141; Charles Chauncy, *Enthusiasm described and caution'd against* (Boston, 1742), ibid., p. 256; *The Wonderful Narrative . . . of the French Prophets*, in D. S. Lovejoy, ed., *Religious Enthusiasm*

and the Great Awakening (Englewood Cliffs, N.J.: Prentice-Hall, 1969), p. 64.

4. Benjamin Doolittle, *An Inquiry into Enthusiasm, Being an Account of what it is* (Boston, 1743), pp. 16–17.

5. Samuel Johnson to SPG, March 25, 1742, quoted in Heimert, *Religion and the American Mind*, p. 12; Ellen Larned, *Historic Gleanings in Windham County, Connecticut* (Providence, R.I., 1899), pp. 38–39.

6. The best scholarly volumes on the Baptists are William G. McLoughlin, *New England Dissent, 1630–1833: The Baptists and the Separation of Church and State*, 2 vols. (Cambridge, Mass.: Harvard University Press, 1971), and by the same author, *Isaac Backus and the American Pietistic Tradition* (Boston: Little, Brown, 1967).

7. "An Account of the Life of Isaac Backus," Isaac Backus Papers, Andover-Newton Theological School Library, Newton Center, Massachusetts, pp. 31–39, 43, excerpted in Lovejoy, ed., *Religious Enthusiasm*, p. 46.

8. Backus's pamphlets have been reprinted in W. G. McLoughlin, ed., *Isaac Backus on Church, State, and Calvinism* (Cambridge, Mass.: Harvard University Press, 1968).

9. For descriptions of this meeting from several points of view, see W. G. McLoughlin, ed., *The Diary of Isaac Backus* (Providence, R.I.: Brown University Press, 1979), II, 917; Isaac Backus, *A History of New England* (Newton, Mass., 1871; reprinted 1969), II, 201–202; *Diary and Autobiography of John Adams*, L. H. Butterfield et al., eds. (Cambridge, Mass.: Harvard University Press, 1961), II, 152–154; III, 311–313. *Literary Diary of Ezra Stiles*, F. B. Dexter, ed. (New York: Charles Scribner's Sons, 1901), I, 472–474. For opposing views of the Ashfield case, see Backus, *An Appeal to the Public for Religious Liberty* (Boston, 1773), in McLoughlin, ed., *Backus on Church, State*, p. 328 and note; Stiles, *Diary*, I, 472–473 n.

10. Backus, *History*, II, 202 n.; McLoughlin, ed., *Backus Diary*, II, 917.

11. W. C. Ford, ed., *The Warren-Adams Letters* (Boston: MHS, 1917), I, 168.

12. *Diary and Autobiography*, Butterfield, ed., III, 312.

13. Thomas Jefferson, *Notes on the State of Virginia*, William Peden, ed. (Chapel Hill: University of North Carolina Press, 1955), pp. 157–158; Stiles, *Diary*, I, 474–475.

14. Wesley M. Gewehr, *The Great Awakening in Virginia, 1740–1790* (Durham, N.C.: Duke University Press, 1930); George W. Pilcher, *Samuel Davies: Apostle of Dissent in Colonial Virginia* (Knoxville: University of Tennessee Press, 1971).

15. *Journals of Henry Melchior Muhlenberg*, trans. T. G. Tappert and J. W. Doberstein (Philadelphia: Muhlenberg Press, 1942), I, 277.

16. Rhys Isaac, "Evangelical Revolt: The Nature of the Baptists' Challenge to the Traditional Order in Virginia, 1765 to 1775," *William and Mary Quarterly*, 3d ser., 31 (July 1974), 345–368; Rhys Isaac, "Preachers and Patriots: Popular Culture and the Revolution in Virginia," in Alfred F. Young, ed., *The American Revolution: Explorations in the History of American Radicalism* (DeKalb, Ill.: Northern Illinois University Press, 1976), pp. 125–156; H. D. Farish, ed., *Journal*

and Letters of Philip Vickers Fithian, 1773–1774: A Plantation Tutor of the Old Dominion (Williamsburg, Va.: Colonial Williamsburg, 1943), p. 96.

17. W. T. Hutchinson and W. M. E. Rachal, eds., *The Papers of James Madison* (Chicago: University of Chicago Press, 1962), I, 170.

18. Backus, *History*, II, 333–334; *Madison Papers*, I, 106, 112, 183, n. 7.

19. Farish, ed., *Fithian Journal*, p. 97.

20. *Madison Papers*, I, 107, n. 9, and p. 112.

21. "Memorial from the Presbytery of Hanover County, Virginia," in Merrill Jensen, ed., *English Historical Documents*, vol. 9, *American Colonial Documents to 1776* (London: Eyre and Spottiswoode, 1955), pp. 549–551. For Virginia's "Act for Establishing Religious Freedom," see S. E. Morison, ed., *Sources and Documents Illustrating the American Revolution, 1764–1788* (Oxford: Clarendon Press, 1929), pp. 206–208.

22. Backus, *Appeal*, in McLoughlin, ed., *Backus on Church, State*, p. 328.

23. Stiles, *Diary*, I, 490–491, 528. For other accusations against the sects, see ibid., pp. 474–475, 492–496; Muhlenberg, *Journals*, III, 158; *Rivington's Gazette*, March 2, 1775, quoted in Frank Moore, *Diary of the American Revolution* (New York, 1860; reprinted 1969), I, 30.

24. Backus, *History*, II, 197–198 and note.

25. Ibid., p. 198.

26. Ibid., pp. 198–199, 278–283, 459.

27. For the struggle against establishments, see McLoughlin, *New England Dissent*, vol. 2, passim.

28. John P. Kaminski and Gaspare J. Saladino, eds., *The Documentary History of the Ratification of the Constitution*, vol. 13, *Commentaries on the Constitution, Public and Private* (Madison: State Historical Society of Wisconsin, 1981), I, 374–375 and note.

29. David D. Hall, ed., *The Antinomian Controversy, 1636–1638: A Documentary History* (Middletown, Conn.: Wesleyan University Press, 1968), p. 274.

30. Robert Baillie, *Anabaptisme, the True Fountaine of Independency, Brownism, Antinomy, Familisme* (London, 1647), p. 62.

31. Gershom Bulkeley, *Will and Doom, or the Miseries of Connecticut* (1692), in Connecticut Historical Society, *Collections* (Hartford, Conn., 1895), III, 90, 236.

32. For these troubles in South Carolina and New York, see Chapter 10.

33. Quoted in Heimert, *Religion and the American Mind*, p. 354.

34. These statements and quotations are taken in order from the following: W. C. Ford, ed., *Statesman and Friend: Correspondence of John Adams with Benjamin Waterhouse, 1784–1822* (Boston: Little, Brown, 1927), p. 120; Burke, *Works*, V, 245; Samuel Curwen, *Journal and Letters*, G. A. Ward, ed. (New York, 1845), p. 225; *An Old Fox Tarr'd and Feathered* (London, n.d. [1775], p. 13; John Fletcher, *American Patriotism Further Confronted with Reason, Scripture and the Constitution* (Shrewsbury, 1776), pp. 120–121; Edmund Burke to Charles O'Hare, August 17, 1775, in *The Correspondence of Edmund Burke*, G. H. Guttridge, ed. (Cambridge: Cambridge University Press, 1961), III, 187;

278 Notes to Pages 224-227

Historical Memoirs . . . of William Smith, W. H. W. Sabine, ed. (New York: Arno Press, 1969), I, 247.

35. [Charles Inglis], *The True Interest of America* (Philadelphia, 1776), p. 33; Thomas B. Chandler, *A Friendly Address to all Reasonable Americans* (New York, 1774), pp. 18, 29, 44, 47; [Samuel Seabury], *A View of the Controversy Between Great Britain and her Colonies* (New York, 1774), pp. 17, 26. Two of the most virulent attacks on Paine's *Common Sense* were [Inglis], *The True Interest of America*, and "Candidus" [James Chalmers], *Plain Truth Addressed to the Inhabitants of America* (Philadelphia, 1776). For the charge of antinomianism against the Declaration of Independence, see [John Lind], *An Answer to the Declaration of the American Congress* (London, 1776), pp. 119, 121–122.

36. Samuel Williams, *A Discourse on the Love of our Country* (Salem, Mass., 1775), p. 14.

37. *Historical Memoirs . . . of William Smith*, Sabine, ed., II, 44; John Adams, *Thoughts on Government* (Philadelphia, 1776), in C. F. Adams, ed., *Works* (Boston, 1851), IV, 195.

38. Lovejoy, ed., *Religious Enthusiasm*, pp. 4–17.

39. Edmund S. Morgan, "The American Revolution Considered as an Intellectual Movement," in A. M. Schlesinger, Jr., and Morton White, eds., *Paths of American Thought* (Boston: Houghton Mifflin, 1963), p. 11; Nathan O. Hatch, "The Origins of Civil Millennialism in America: New England Clergymen, War with France, and the Revolution," *William and Mary Quarterly*, 3d ser., 31 (July 1974), 407–430. See also the same author's *Sacred Cause of Liberty: Republican Thought and the Millennium in Revolutionary New England* (New Haven: Yale University Press, 1977); Susie I. Tucker, *Enthusiasm: A Study in Semantic Change* (Cambridge: Cambridge University Press, 1972), p. 100.

40. William Smith, *A Sermon on the Present Situation of American Affairs* (Philadelphia, 1775), p. 26.

41. *Historical Memoirs . . . of William Smith*, II, 7.

42. H. A. Cushing, ed., *The Writings of Samuel Adams* (New York: G. P. Putnam's Sons, 1907), III, 21, 199, 284, 304. Stephen E. Patterson describes Adams's understanding of "crowd psychology" in *Political Parties in Revolutionary Massachusetts* (Madison: University of Wisconsin Press, 1973), p. 89.

43. Hatch, *Sacred Cause of Liberty*, passim.

44. John Adams, "A Dissertation on the Canon and the Feudal Law," in C. F. Adams, ed., *Works*, III, 452 n.; William Smith, *A Sermon*, p. 28.

45. Ebenezer Baldwin, *The Duty of Rejoicing Under Calamities and Afflictions* (New York, 1775), pp. 30–31, 38–39 and note, 40 n.; James W. Davidson, *The Logic of Millennial Thought: Eighteenth-Century New England* (New Haven: Yale University Press, 1977), pp. 248–249.

46. Edward H. Tatum, Jr., ed., *The American Journal of Ambrose Serle, 1776–1778* (San Marino, Calif.: Huntington Library, 1940), pp. 89–90.

47. William Gilchrist to SPG, Dec. 7, 1770, in W. S. Perry, ed., *Historical Collections Relating to the American Colonial Church*, vol. 3, *Massachusetts* (Hartford, Conn., 1873), p. 555; *The Thoughts of a Traveller upon our American Disputes* (London, 1774), p. 15; Curwen, *Journal and Letters*, p. 168.

48. Thomas Paine, *The Rights of Man,* in M. D. Conway, ed., *The Writings of Thomas Paine* (New York, 1894), II, 293.

49. Adams, "Dissertation," in C. F. Adams, ed., *Works,* III, 452 n.

50. A. A. Cooper, Third Earl of Shaftesbury, *Characteristicks,* 4th ed. (n.p., 1727), I, 53–54; Moore Booker, *Two Letters Concerning the Methodists* (Dublin, 1751), p. 16; Stanley Grean, *Shaftesbury's Philosophy of Religion and Ethics: A Study in Enthusiasm* (n.p., Ohio University Press, 1967), p. 31.

51. [John Shebbeare], *Letters on the English Nation: by Batista Angeloni, A Jesuit,* 2d ed. (London, 1756), II, 182.

52. John Adams to Mr. Niles, Quincy, Feb. 13, 1818, in Jedidiah Morse, *Annals of the American Revolution* (Hartford, Conn., 1824; reprinted 1968), p. 219.

53. [Shebbeare], *Letters,* II, 181.

54. Samuel Taylor Coleridge, *The Statesman's Manual: Or the Bible the Best Guide to Political Skill and Foresight* (London, 1816), pp. 27–28; Ralph Waldo Emerson, "Circles," in *The Portable Emerson,* ed. Carl Bode in collaboration with Malcolm Cowley (New York: Penguin Books, 1981), p. 240.

Index